Constance Briscoe practises as a barrister and in 1996 became a part-time judge – one of the first black women to sit as a judge in the UK. She lives in Clapham with her two children, Martin and Francesca. Her partner is Tony Arlidge QC.

Praise for *Ugly*:

'Horrific, but remarkable too. Let us hope that Constance's story will inspire young people everywhere to not only hold on to their dreams and make them happen, but also to be better parents themselves.'   Lesley Pearse

'This is a lawyer's memoir with a difference, an inspiring antidote to the usual catalogue of tedious milestones towards legal eminence . . . She's also managed – a rare feat for a lawyer – to write an absorbing book in language untainted by convoluted legal-speak.'

Marcel Berlins, *Guardian*

'Utterly extraordinary . . . harrowing, often deeply disturbing, but ultimately inspiring.'   *Daily Mail*

'Reading the book is like an exercise in bottling up your rage. Afterwards, you feel helpless and disturbed. Which is only right.'   *Evening Standard*

'An astonishing true story of hope over adversity.'

Mail on Sunday

'Remarkable.'   *Good Housekeeping*

Ugly

CONSTANCE BRISCOE

HODDER

First published in Great Britain in 2006 by Hodder and Stoughton
An Hachette Livre UK company

This revised paperback edition with details of the trial published in 2009

6

Copyright © Constance Briscoe 2006

A CIP catalogue record for this title
is available from the British Library

ISBN 978 0 340 99465 8

Typeset in Plantin Light by Hewer Text UK Ltd, Edinburgh
Printed and bound by Clays Ltd, St Ives plc

Hodder Headline's policy is to use papers that are natural, renewable
and recyclable products and made from wood grown in sustainable
forests. The logging and manufacturing processes are expected to
conform to the environmental regulations of the country of origin.

Hodder & Stoughton Ltd
A division of Hodder Headline
338 Euston Road
London NW1 3BH

www.hodder.co.uk

This book is dedicated to Miss K.

Contents

Acknowledgments

I met John Grisham on 25 February 2003 when he was in the UK for the launch of *The King of Torts* at Middle Temple. That same night I met his publisher Gail Rebuck. I had previously written a note to John Grisham about my life and was minded to hand it over to him but instead I handed it to Gail. She contacted me a few days later and invited me to Random House. I was put in touch with Sue Freestone, who eventually turned the book down. I am entirely grateful to her for had she not done so I would never have met my agent, Darley Anderson. As soon as I met him, I knew that he would become my agent. He created a buzz about the book – an agent provocateur.

He is exceptional. He told me what he would do for me and did it. Through Darley I met Sue Fletcher of Hodder and her team. I would like to thank Sue for the practical advice and commitment given to me and *Ugly* (her title). Now everybody knows that supporting me is an agent extraordinaire and a publisher whose professional judgement is beyond value.

I would also like to thank Tony Arlidge, my long-suffering partner. His suffering is now over. It was he who actually persuaded me to write the book, who told me to keep going when I had had enough. I am certain that he has gone over the manuscript more often than I have. His attention to detail, grammar and style is renowned. I am entirely indebted to him and his commitment to me overwhelms me. Finally, I would like to thank Mrs Chrissie Wadworth for reading and typing my old-fashioned handwritten manuscripts. Lucie Whitehouse, a heartfelt thank you – you are truly the Mistress of foreign rights. Joan Deitch, a special thank you for giving the manuscript the first professional edit. Darley's praise of you was entirely justified.

Prologue

'Do your parents know you're here?' asked the lady at Social Services.

'No,' I said, 'but I want to know about children's homes.' I had to stand on my toes to see over the reception desk.

'How old are you?' asked the lady.

'Eleven.'

'Things bad at home, are they?'

'Yes,' I said. 'What do I have to do to book myself in?'

'Let's have some details,' she said.

I gave her my name and address and said that I would like to move in today, if that was possible.

'You cannot refer yourself to a children's home, luvvie. You need to get your parents' consent first. Why don't you go home and think about it? You can always pop in again and see me.'

'But I don't want to go home.'

'Well, I can't book you in just because you feel like leaving home. Do you want us to contact your mother?'

'No, thanks,' I said. 'I'll handle it myself.'

If my mother found out what I was doing, I would only get a beating. I walked back up the Walworth Road towards our house in Sutherland Square, south London. It was a nice sunny day, but I felt very down. Nothing I ever did came right and now even the children's home did not want me. Life was not worth living at all.

That night I decided that no one would miss me if I just disappeared. Before I went to bed I wrote a letter to my mother. I put the letter in my school embroidery bag and went into the bathroom. I removed the top from the bottle of bleach, diluted it with tap water, drank it and went back to bed. I chose Domestos because Domestos kills all known germs and my mother had for so long told me that I was a germ. I felt very sick, happy and sad. I was happy because tonight, if the bleach worked, I would die. No more tomorrows. Hip, hip hooray. I was also very sad because I wouldn't see my sisters again, but maybe that was no bad thing. As for my mother, I swore to God I would come back and haunt her for the rest of her life. Slap her on the head, trip her up on the stairs and pull the covers off her as she slept. Yes!

The following morning I woke up and thought I had died. My bed-wet alarm was ringing in the far distance. The lights on the bed flashed on and off and I lay in a daze, unable to move my feet or my arms.

My mother was looking down at me. 'Get out of bed,' she ordered. I stayed still. I could not talk as my mouth was sore from the bleach. Blisters bubbled up around my lips like Rice Krispies. 'Come on – out of bed.' She pulled the blanket back. 'I'm not going to tell you again. *Out.*' She grabbed my arm and pulled me up. Then she let go and I flopped back, half on the bed. I began to vomit. That was when she realised something was wrong. 'Eastman!' she shouted. Eastman was her new man. He called for Pauline and she called for Patsy, my two older sisters. 'Lord God,' said my mother, 'she's going to get me into trouble.'

Eastman said my mother should phone for a doctor and get an ambulance for me, but my mother said that Pauline should fetch some fresh sheets, change the bed and put the old stained sheets in the wash. She then busied herself tidying up my room, opening the windows to get the stench out. Once all that was done, my mother said I should be moved to another bedroom. Any doctor entering this one might get the impression that I was neglected.

My sister Pauline was ordered to change my nightdress. My mother returned with a dry one, and together they struggled to get it on me. My mother must have sensed that her presence made me sick and she told Pauline to carry on. She left the room, taking with her my wet nightdress. It had been consistently wet for three days. The clean one came down to my ankles and covered an assortment of bruises, cuts and marks which might otherwise require an explanation.

'Come on, Clare,' said my sister. She fed me water with a spoon. 'Come on, open your mouth and drink up.' She kept spooning water down my throat. 'Come on, Clare, what have you done this time?'

I must have dozed off. When I came round it was dark and my younger sister, Christine, was by my bed.

'Mum said you're going to get her into trouble,' Christine told me. 'What have you done?'

A little later, Pauline came back and gave me some oxtail soup to drink. I drank it and then vomited all over the bed and carpet. Eastman and my mother kept away from the room. I heard my mother outside the door. She was talking to Eastman.

'She might recover,' she said. 'Wait and see. Keep Pauline with her and if anything happens, the doctor and ambulance will be called.' My mother started to rant outside my door. 'Sweet Jesus, meek and mild, what have I done to deserve this child?'

'Come on, Clare,' said my sister. 'Wake up.'

I fell asleep, and the next thing I remember was waking up in the dark. My sister was sleeping at the bottom of the bed and as I tried to raise my head she jumped up, ran to the door and shouted for my mother, who came running in with Eastman behind her. He was telling her to call the doctor.

'Carmen, call a doctor before it's too late.'

'No,' said my mother. 'Wait a little longer.'

'Carmen, you are go to end up in jail. You think me coming with you? No, sirree, not me. Call the doctor, Carmen, you don't know what's wrong with the child.'

'Eastman, if Clare is to dead, she would have dead by now. Jailhouse turn you stupid!'

When I woke up next it was daylight. My sister was still in my room and, oddly enough, I had not wet the bed. As I stirred,

Pauline rushed out of the room and returned with my mother and another bowl of oxtail soup.

'Come on, Clare, eat,' said my sister as she fed me the soup with a spoon.

'Oh, sweet Lord, You had a son,' said my mother. 'Tell me, where did I go wrong? Baby Jesus, above my head, get this child right out of bed. Oh, sweet Jesus, meek and mild, am I not Your obedient child?'

My mother stood at the bottom of the bed. 'Do you want a doctor?' she demanded.

'No, I don't.' Go away, I thought. Do I want a doctor? Of course not. I do not wish to be saved. I want to stop being a germ.

My mother left the room. 'Pauline,' she called back, 'if you need to, call me.'

My sister fed me the soup. 'What have you done, Clare? You can tell me,' she said.

'Four Eyes, are you spying for Mummy?'

'No,' she said. 'No. Why do you think that?'

'Well, don't ask questions.'

She fed me in silence and I eventually fell asleep again. I woke up with a burning sensation between my legs. Scabs had developed and had matted in my pubic hair. The urine scorched my minnie and a heat rash formed at the top of my legs and on my bottom. But I was grateful for several things. No alarm went off. No one dragged me out of bed by my minnie. No one twisted my nipples or punched me in the stomach. My sister simply reappeared with a fresh set of bedclothes and a clean nightdress.

I

My Family

I shall write my story down. So far I have always been a very private person, so this is the first time that my story is being told. It's difficult to remember the order of things. My father, George, and sister Pauline might help with that. It would be easier if I had my diaries. I kept a diary from as soon as I could write. My mother stole them all.

I will begin with my name. Constance. This is the name that is on my birth certificate. I only discovered that when I was eighteen. Before that, I thought my name was Clare. My mother called me Clear, because she said I was transparent and she could see Clearly through me. If I was in her good books (which wasn't often) it was Clearie. My sisters turned that to Clare. They still call me Clare. My school reports called me Clare. When I worked in hospices I was known as Nurse Clare. My driving licence says Clare. So that's how you'll know me in the story.

My mother, Carmen, came to England from Jamaica in the early 1950s, when she was a teenager. She was brought up a good Catholic girl. She knew my father from Portland and met him again over here. George was ten years older than her. When she was eighteen he got her pregnant. They got married. She had a boy, baptised Winston, but he died at four months. Mother kept a photograph taken of him in her arms when he was dead. I was their fourth child. I was born, brought up and educated in England. I am British Black full stop.

My family in the end consisted of:

George, my dad. He was quite short for a man. His grand-mother was white, so he was mixed race. He had very smooth skin – he wasn't even wrinkled when he was old. George was always a dapper dresser and had a neat moustache.

Carmen, my mother. George called her Carmel. She had a very slim figure and was stunningly beautiful. She looked more like a film star than a mother. Her skin was coffee-coloured.

Pauline, my eldest sister, born 6 October 1954. We called her Four Eyes because of her glasses – she was bottle rims on legs. Her squirrel features were almost covered by the large lenses. They were so large and dense you could not see through them. She was dark-skinned, thin and five feet seven tall when fully grown. Her hair was short. Sly and secretive, with her finger in every pie, Pauline always protected her own interests.

Patsy, my other elder sister, also known as Precious Puss, born 8 March 1956. Her skin colour was fair, more yellow than black. She was all of five feet, fully grown. Although of a very small frame, her bottom stuck out. She wore a size three and a half shoe. Her hair was short and thick, and she had a large bust and bulbous eyes.

Then there was me – Clear, Clearie, Clare, born 18 May 1957. About five feet three and a quarter fully grown, medium build, who never made it on the looks stakes until quite late in the day. Described as ugly, just ugly. Completely confident on the outside.

Next in line our brothers, Carlton (usually Carl) and Martin, known as 'my sons' when in my mother's good books. Mummy's boys, never introduced to cooking, cleaning or shopping. They had an easy ride until their bottoms were big enough to take a beating. They were born in 1959 and 1961.

Christine, called Button Nose, Buttons or Beauty, born 27 November 1962. She was the fairest of us all – a high yellow colour. Four feet six fully grown, always a little overweight, she was clever, but too ready to sit on the fence, even when she did not need to.

Denise – our adopted sister, born at the same time as Christine. Her nickname was Blackie because of her complexion. Her features were completely inconsistent with the Briscoe family.

She was slim with short legs and a bottom that followed her everywhere. Denise was different from us Briscoes, too. She was kind and always generous.

Eastman – my stepdad, he never married my mother. A Barbadian, he was big and stupid. He had four children by my mother:

Cynthia, my half-sister. Naturally plump, was put on a diet practically from the day she was born. She was never able to sit up when she was a baby. Her grown-up height was about five feet five, and she was large-framed. Cynthia had her father's broad flat nose.

Norma, another half-sister. The brightest of the Eastman children. Tall, with the ability to go far. Thin. I got on with her. I was friends with her.

Winston, my half-brother. Five feet eleven fully grown, and thickset. Large feet. Looked just like his father.

Georgina, my other half-sister, known as Gina. Clever girl, attractive, could have made it but success was too much effort.

Bem, our lodger. He was an old man whom my parents had known in Jamaica. He witnessed my mother's treatment of me and her fights with George. He was a good friend to me, which in the end proved his downfall.

I had another good friend called Mary, but she was made-up. She could be found between the pages of my five year diary. It was ivory with brown edges. Mary knew what I knew and only I knew Mary. In the end Mary disappeared. I think my mother stole her.

Money was a constant source of tension between my parents. My father became wealthy when he was young, because he won the Pools twice. On the second occasion, Littlewoods Pools presented him with a large copy of the original cheque. My mother kept it over the fireplace as a reminder of how much money he had won and what she was entitled to. George invested his money wisely in property. He bought about a dozen houses in all, in Camberwell. This is in south London near the Elephant and Castle district. George's houses were all off the

Walworth Road. His nickname was George Nuff-house. During my early life we moved around in and out of these houses, so they play an important part in my story. I can remember some of the addresses:

4 Councillor Street
5 Myatt Road
7 and 16 Patmos Road
41 Offley Road
215 Camberwell New Road
6 Burnett Street
19 Sutherland Square

George let out the houses and lived off the rent. He did not work after he had won the Pools. The first thing he did when he won was to buy a flash motor. It was a brand new silver-grey Ford Capri. He spent most of the time cruising round in it and chain-smoking. After that he changed it for a new one each year, though they were always silver-grey Ford Capris.

My father left my mother after Patsy was born, but from time to time he came back. I have no recollection of him sleeping the night in our house or even having breakfast with us. My mother was always after his money. She tried to convince him to buy a house in her name. He refused, but he did let her collect the rent from some of the houses as his contribution to the upkeep of the family. It was never enough for her. In the early days after he left, my mother would persuade him to go to bed with her when he came to see us and, if he fell asleep afterwards, she would remove large wads of notes from his pockets. It must have been on one of these occasions that she fell pregnant with me.

Her treatment of my sisters was certainly very different from her treatment of me. They did not get the unkind words I got, or have their nipples pinched, and they were not beaten or punched. They were bought new dresses, but I had only hand-me-downs, third-hand from Pauline and Patsy. My mother had piles and piles of hand-me-downs, in plastic bags, ready to pass on to me. I was never the first to open the bag and try on a dress. My mother would throw a dress at me and say, 'Here, Clear, try this on and see if it fits you.' It never did, but I would grow into it eventually.

My mother had a lot of pretty dresses for herself – they had bright patterns on them, particularly roses. She had exquisite dresses for every occasion. I remember hiding in her wardrobe and watching her change out of the cardigan she usually wore round the house into her dusty pink dress which was her favourite. I wanted pretty dresses too, but I was too ugly to wear anything but my sisters' cast-offs.

Over a period of time my mother's treatment of me made me very nervous. I was bed-wetting ever since I knew myself. This infuriated my mother and was the cause of most of the beatings I had. When I was about five I was referred by our family doctor to an expert on bed-wetting. I went to lots and lots of appointments with my mother to get to the cause of the problem. I remember I had a very nice brushed-cotton nightdress which came down to my ankles. When I went to bed I would curl up in a ball and pull my legs up to my chest. At the same time I would tug my nightdress down below my ankles. I always slept on my side. One night I woke up in the pitch dark and felt as though I was drowning. I was soaked from below my neck to my ankles. My pillow and my blanket were also sopping wet. I had had a massive double accident in the middle of the night. That was the start of it all.

Because of my bed-wetting I was sometimes punished and put to sleep in a bed with just a bare mattress – no sheet, just a plastic cover – because my mother said that I would wet the bed anyway so it did not matter. She was given lots of books on bed-wetting and bladder training. At the age of five I got my first alarm system. It was, apparently, an extremely successful form of treatment. It came with a child-friendly noise box, which was placed at the side of my bed, together with a sensor mat, which went beneath the lower of two bedsheets. The noise box rang when I had an accident; it was supposed to cause me to wake up or to 'hold on'. Gradually I was supposed to learn to wake up and/or 'hold on' to the sensation of a full bladder without the alarm.

The 'child-friendly' alarm sounded like a fire engine on its way to an emergency call out. The first time it went off, I jumped out of bed and crawled underneath it. I was terrified that there was a fire in my bed.

My mother came rushing into the room and noticed that I was missing. She thought I had run to the toilet. If only. She silenced the noise box, pulled the top sheet off the mesh undersheet and went back to her room. I crawled out from beneath the bed, hardly aware of where I was.

Even as a small child I was sure that my bed-wetting was not due to laziness. The doctor said that the cause could be because of anxieties in my life. He said that I would be cured within four to six months with my alarm.

But my bed-wetting got progressively worse and my mother took me to expert after expert. I was given a top-of-the-range bed-wetting device with an audible alarm with two tones and flashing lights, which were supposed to help me by alerting me before the bed became too wet. Most of the time I slept through it. Nothing my mother did helped. At the start I would sleep in bedclothes and a hand-me-down nightie from my sister Pauline, but as my bed-wetting became a real problem, my mother insisted on my sleeping without any clothes. So it was that most nights I slept with just my knickers on.

My bed-wetting continued, so eventually my mother adopted a new policy: she started to come into my room just before bedtime to give me a beating, to remind me of what would happen to me if I wet the bed. She would wait until I was in bed then come in, throw the blanket off and grab me by the edge of my knickers and lug me out of bed. Holding on to the neck of my nightie to prevent me from running away, she would take off a shoe and beat me with it.

'What are you going to do?' she would ask.

'Not wet the bed'

'Liar! What are you going to do?'

'I'm going to wet the bed,' I said.

'Yes, I thought so. You see? You *are* a liar.'

She slapped me across the head with the shoe and punched me in the chest, and when I said, 'No,' she accused me again of being a liar and slapped me once more on the side of my head. She kept repeating the question; I repeated the answer and she slapped me on my thigh, my calves or my hand. I always tried to protect myself by putting my hand out, but it was more painful being struck on the hand than on the thigh. My legs were partly protected by my nightdress and sometimes I drew up my knees so I was in a ball.

After some of these beatings, my mother would leave with my nightdress in her hand, having physically removed it from my body. On other occasions she would leave with my blanket. If she was in a really bad mood or I had upset her, she would take both. My sisters were told that if they helped me or lent me a nightie they would get a beating too, so more often than not they made themselves scarce.

By the time I was seven, my beatings were as regular as ever. The alarm failed to wake me, yet my mother always heard it. She would dash into my room when she heard it ring and drag me out of bed. Sometimes when she came into my room, she would remove the wet bedclothes and give me a mighty slap on the bare backside, then leave me naked and shivering. My humiliation was complete. Not only was I unable to prevent myself wetting the bed, the mere presence of my mother and/or a bedtime beating made me so nervous that I sometimes emptied my bladder in front of her, which was seen as an act of defiance. Other times I would force myself to stay awake, but then as soon as I fell asleep, out of sheer exhaustion, I would miss my bed-wet alarm, and so the cycle continued.

2

An Addition to the Family

1962

In 1962 we were living in 4 Councillor Street. My mother and father were still together – just about, although they did not get on and spent most of their time together shouting at each other, fighting and generally behaving badly. My mother was the worst. She always picked on my dad and she never lost a fight.

One Saturday morning in July my father came to the house. He had been to Petticoat Lane and had bought two large chickens. Their feathers had been plucked and singed and their insides gutted. He arrived in his white van and parked it outside the house. One chicken was thrown over his shoulder and the other was carried by its feet, which were tied together. He knocked and then used his key to open the front door. We children ran down to greet him and then followed him up the three flights of stairs. The first chicken fell off my father's shoulder onto a table on the top landing as he tilted his shoulder forward. The second was slapped down next to the first. As he made his way back downstairs he said, 'How's my favourite girls?' My mother was behind him and he shouted, 'Morning, Carmel.' There was no reply. He went down and opened the front door. As he stepped outside a chicken narrowly missed his head. My mother had thrown it out of the window. As I looked up, the second chicken came flying through the air. My father moved out of the way and the chicken fell splat on the pavement. This clearly annoyed my dad because instead of getting into the van, he pushed past me and stormed back into the house.

'Come, come,' said my mother. 'You want dead? If is dead

you want, you will get it. Come.'

George told her to stop being silly and to go and pick up the chickens – they had cost a lot of money – and to stop threatening him. She simply pulled a pair of scissors from her waistband and held them in her hand.

'You want dead?' she said. 'You bastard, you want dead?'

'What you going to do, old girl, stab me?'

'You come here and the best you can do is bring two dead chicken. What do you expect me to do with two dead chicken?'

'Behave, old girl,' my father said and he started to sing, as he always did: 'La de da, la de da, tee tee tee.'

He knew this would infuriate her. My mother asked my father again what she should do with two dead chickens and when he ignored her and continued singing, she ran at him.

'La de bloody da,' she said, and lunged at him. He fell backwards on top of me, and when I tried to help him up, his stomach was covered in blood and there was blood all over my pretty dress.

'You want dead? You want dead this day?' she said, and raised the pair of scissors above her head again.

'Get me an ambulance, Clearie,' my father said to me.

My mother was shouting and cussing at my dad. 'You bring two dead chicken and la de da in my house. You want dead?'

George kept his hand over his stomach while I crawled from underneath him and ran to get help. I ran round the block. I did not know what else to do. By the time I returned my sisters were there, together with an ambulance and the police. The ambulance took my father away and the police took my mother and the two chickens away. My mother was gone for a while and when she returned she got a bucket of warm water, mopped up the blood on the landing and told us to go to bed.

Later we found out that my father did not want the police involved and so he had refused to make a statement about what happened, even though he had to spend two weeks in St Giles's Hospital in intensive care. We were not allowed to visit him during this time. When he came out he was not very mobile, but on the following Sunday he sent a friend of his to deliver food to our house. Every week my father went shopping for food. My parents were supposed to be living together, but he spent more and more time away from the house and whenever he came to see us my mother was waiting for him.

George did not start visiting the house again until September. He was careful to keep his distance from my mother and stayed outside. On those occasions my mother would join us at the door and argue with him, or she would tell me and my sisters to go back inside and then the door was slammed shut in my father's face. He ignored her. At first he would not go into the house, but in November they were back to normal, arguing and fighting. My two sisters and I were always in the middle of the fighting room.

My mother's view must have been that our father did not give her enough money. One way of her saving money was by not giving us enough food. She used to keep the food cupboard locked, with the key in her bra. One day my sisters and I were hungry and I asked her if we could have some biscuits. She said I had a father and I should go and find him and ask him for a biscuit. She brushed past me and we never got our biscuit. Later that week we were having breakfast. I climbed onto my chair and poured some cornflakes into my bowl. There was warm milk and sweetened water to go with them. My sisters already had theirs and were eating. By accident I spilled some of the cornflakes on my nightdress. My mother snatched my bowl from me and poured the contents down the sink. 'Go find your father,' she said grimly. 'He'll give you cornflakes.' Pauline and Patsy held firmly on to their bowls. She did not take them away. I was very upset. She had no right to take my cornflakes and leave theirs. They ate them up quick as lightning.

Over time George and Carmen's fights got worse and he took to irritating her by not leaving his wallet where she could have ready access to it. She was always hunting around after his wallet, and when she found it, she would help herself to a large number of notes. George spent his time looking for new hiding places. I once saw him hiding his notes in the back of the transistor radio. I was lying flat on my stomach behind the settee and watching him in the bedroom. I saw him unscrew the back of the radio, put his money inside and then screw it back up again. He then took some more notes and put them in his shoes, covering them with his socks.

Just before the last time my father left, George and Carmen had a big argument about money. I was hiding behind the settee again – it was my favourite hiding place. I would crawl in and lie very still and no one would think of looking for me there. On this day my father had come home, removed his shoe, put his money inside it and lain down. My mother had stolen this money while he was asleep and when he woke up they had a fight. On this particular day my father had had enough. When they were arguing he slapped her and she slapped him back. He then cursed and smacked my mother in the back. She fell across the bed, but got up in a fighting hurry. He gave her another mighty shove that sent her flying across the bed, landing half on the floor, with her hand on top of a wire coat-hanger. She got up cussing and strutting towards my father. He foolishly turned his back to walk away and she caught him with a left hook. The coat-hanger pierced his face just below the jaw and came out the other side. As my mother pulled on it, my father's face stretched like a bubble-gum bubble. He grabbed her hand and the wire hanger, and told her that if she wanted to die that day she should continue to pull. The look in my father's eyes must have told her he was serious. She did pull a little, but thought the wiser of it when she saw the blood that bubbled out of his face. She pushed past him and ran out of the room and I retreated further into the cavity between the settee and the wall.

My father turned the coat-hanger and it plopped out of his face. Once it had finally been removed, the blood started to spurt out, rapidly covering his face and turning his moustache red. He took a large towel to the hole in his face and left the house, and we did not see him again for a very long time. Normally he would stay away for a few weeks or so, but this time it was longer. When he did come back into the house my mother would ignore him at first, but because we were always happy to see him she would go somewhere else. Eventually she would calm down, but then a week or two later she was back to her old self. It must have been during this period that she got pregnant with our youngest natural sister, Christine.

As my mother grew larger, she was still busy, aggressive, still fighting and taking on my father at every opportunity. My father scarcely came to the house any more. Weeks went past and we wouldn't see him. Our mother's behaviour became difficult. As the youngest girl I was always in the way of my mother and sisters. I was often in the way of myself. One of my earliest memories is of her deliberately bumping into me so that I spilled my drink and then smacking me for spilling it. Many of the things my mother did then held no particular significance for me. They were simply acts of a mummy not being nice.

In November 1962 my mother suddenly went into hospital. We were told that she was having a baby and would be away for a while. Just before she went in we had a lodger come to stay with us. His name was Bem. He, my father and mother came from the same district in Jamaica. Bem was old and had a problem with his balance. He shuffled around. He never walked. He sort of shuffled, paused and shuffled again. He would hold on to things like the banisters to keep upright. He also had the shakes – he would shake whenever he tried to lift anything. Poor Bem was effectively housebound. He looked after us when my mother was away. I liked Bem. He was a kind and friendly old man. He lived at the top of the house in the back bedroom and spent most of his time there. On occasion he would venture out and sit in our sitting room and talk to my mother about the good old days in the West Indies. I got to know Bem very well and I think it's fair to say we had a special relationship.

One day, my father came to the house and told us that we had a new sister called Christine; she weighed seven pounds. He also told us that our mother would be home within the next six days.

Pauline was eight by now and she was in charge. My mother had asked two of her friends, a couple called George and Rose, to keep an eye on us. George was known as Georgie Porgie and he lived with Rose, Scottish Rose. Both were friendly with my mother. Georgie Porgie and Rose came round the next day. He was very tall and bald. Rose was a platinum blonde with tight curls. The first day she came round she had pipe cleaners in her hair at the front. The back was held in place by a scarf, which was tied from the back forward, with a triangular piece of cloth in a bow at the front. They amused us for some time and Georgie Porgie asked me to sit with him, which I did. I sat by his side. He told us Georgie Porgie stories, which were very funny and made us laugh. He then asked me to sit on his lap. I had not, to my knowledge, sat on my mother's lap – ever. Georgie Porgie was such a nice man. I sat on his closed legs with my legs apart; he put his arm around my waist. Rose asked Georgie Porgie if he would like some tea. He said, 'Yes,' and she left the room.

Georgie Porgie said to me, 'Do you know what Georgie Porgie does?' and tickled me under my legs in the crease at the back of my knee.

'No,' I said.

'Georgie Porgie pudding and pie kissed the girls and made them cry.'

We all thought that this was very funny and started singing: 'Georgie Porgie pudding and pie kissed the girls and made them cry.'

He moved his hand across the front of my stomach in a sort of bear hug from the back and squeezed me into his groin.

'Do you like that?' he asked.

'Georgie Porgie pudding and pie kissed the girls and made them cry. When the girls went to bed, Georgie Porgie got a big head.'

Bem entered the room and Georgie Porgie told me to sit somewhere else.

'Go and play with your sisters,' he said. Bem shuffled over to a chair by the window and sat down. Rose came in with some tea and asked where the milk was. I went off to get the milk from my mother's room. When tea was finished we were told that they would both come again the next day and every day until my mother came out of hospital. Bem said it was not necessary. He could manage.

My father turned up that night and he was in a cross mood. He was smoking a cigarette and had another in his hand, which he tapped on the cigarette packet. He spoke to Bem at the top of the house, and then he paced up and down. It was decided that he would go back to the hospital and he would take me. So we went to Lambeth hospital and made our way up to the ward.

My mother was in a four-woman ward. She looked very well. Next to her bed was our sister. Baby Christine was wrapped in a blanket and was asleep. She had lots of straight black hair and her eyes were closed. She had a tiny button nose and looked very odd, as if she had been squashed. My mother told my dad she would be home in about four days and my father asked if she wanted anything to be brought in for her. I noticed there was lots of fruit on the side.

The lady in the next bed and to the left of my mother looked very distraught. She kept staring at my dad and then at me, and when I looked back at her and smiled, she pretended not to notice. This lady was much darker in complexion than my mother. I was black, but she was dark black and looked quite frightening under the white sheet; she could give me nightmares. My mother had a pretty brown complexion and was quite beautiful. I wondered why it was they had allowed this ugly woman to be in the same ward as my mother. The cot beside the lady's bed was empty and she had no fruit or flowers on her locker. There wasn't a single 'it's a boy/girl' card there either. She was a pretend mother. She was there because she wanted a baby and wanted us all to feel sorry for her. I noticed a small green suitcase by her bed, and a pair of new slippers placed side by side.

At one point my mother said, 'George, meet Mistress Williams.' My father said, 'Hello' and she said, 'Hello' back. My father said, 'Where is your baby?' She said she didn't have one. We left when Sister told us that 'the happy mothers need to sleep'. Mistress Williams did not look happy, but she did look like she needed some sleep.

When I got home I told my sisters about Baby Christine. My father promised to return the next day to take us to see her. The next morning, I felt very happy. It was so nice at home without my mother. At breakfast I had cornflakes and milk. I then went into my mother's room and sat on the sofa – no one told me off. I even ate some biscuits. Bem was kind to me. He didn't mind when I went into his room.

My father came to the house and asked us who wanted to go and see my mother. Bem suggested that I should go again, alone, and that was what happened. I got into the back of my father's Capri and he drove us to the hospital.

That day, my mother was sitting on a chair and her bed was made up. My dad gave her some milk and fruit which he had brought with him and my mother said she had something to tell him. She said that she had made a mistake and when he had visited her the day before she had forgotten to tell him that she had had twins and not just a baby girl. With that my mother went to a crib and pulled it over in my father's direction. In the crib were two babies. One was very black in complexion and the other I recognised from the day before. She had a button nose. It was my sister, but now I had two.

My father asked my mother to repeat what she had just said. Then he strolled over to the crib and looked inside. The difference between the two babies was obvious. One was pretty like my mother and the other one was ugly. My father said the child on the left was not his and, if she had had twins, why hadn't she said so? It wasn't possible to forget something like that! George and my mother then got into an argument, because my father told my mother to remove the black baby from the crib. She refused. At that point, Sister came and told my father not to upset the happy mother and that if he did not keep his voice down she would have to ask him to leave.

More quietly, but still angrily, my father refused to accept that the black child was his, and when my mother would not budge from her position that she had had twins, he left the ward. I followed. On the journey home my father did not speak to me. We got out of the car and while I dashed off to tell my sisters what had happened, my dad went to talk to Bem. There was a lot of excitement. We now had two sisters, not just one. My father left the house that evening, and did not return during the period that my mother was in hospital.

Georgie Porgie came round with Rose. Again he told us stories and asked me to sit on his lap. I sang Georgie Porgie songs and he bear hugged me and tickled me under my arms. When I got tired of the tickles, he asked one of my sisters to sit on his lap. They did not because Bem told us all to leave the room and play elsewhere. Georgie Porgie said Bem was spoiling his fun and Bem said until Carmen returned he was in charge. We all left the room and Rose and Georgie Porgie left the house.

A few days later we went back to the hospital and my mother had both the black and brown babies by the side of her bed. The black lady in the other bed still had no flowers or cards on her bedside table. My father wanted to get to the bottom of the mystery baby and told my mother the child was not his and would not be coming home with us. He pressed the call button and summoned the nurse. When she arrived he asked her how many babies my mother had given birth to. The nurse went off, came back and said, 'One.' She then went back to work.

My father asked my mother for an explanation. She started by telling him that the nurse didn't know what she was talking about. She wasn't there at the time; she hadn't seen the birth records. How could *she* know how many babies my mother had? Had my father not heard of non-identical twins? I thought it was exciting to have two new sisters – a real one and a giveaway one. Did it really matter if my mother had given birth to one or to both of them?

The black lady in the other bed was hiding behind the curtains. Now she said, 'It's mine. The baby, it's mine.'

'What does she mean, "mine"?' asked my father.

Mistress Williams pulled the curtains aside so that she was facing my mother. 'The baby is mine,' she said again.

My mother told my father that the lady did not want her baby and had given her to us. I could not believe my ears. How could anyone want to give her baby away? I was only a child myself and did not understand. More recently, George has explained to me that Mistress Williams was in a happy relationship with her husband, who was a soldier. He was away from home and did not know she was pregnant from a brief relationship with another man. The father of the baby had tried to persuade Mistress Williams to have the baby and live with him, but she refused because she wanted to live with her husband. She did not intend to tell her husband about the baby and thought that if she gave the little girl away, then no one need know that she had ever had such a child. My mother had offered to take the child off her hands and between the two of them they had agreed to persuade my father that he had had twins.

My father was furious that the happy mothers had tried to trap him into accepting twins. Besides, the Williams baby was not only black it was ugly. He told my mother that she could only bring one baby home – Christine. She would get into trouble if she took someone else's baby. He described the whole plan as madness.

My mother said that the baby *would* be going home with her, and since he did not live with us full-time it was none of his business.

My mother came home a few days later. She was in a taxi and was carrying two babies, one under the right arm and the other under the left. A lady from the hospital was with her. She carried her suitcase and helped my mother to the door. So it was that the twins came home to join our happy family. I was five at the time and now one of seven children: Pauline, Patsy, me, Carl, Martin and the 'twins'.

My mother called the twins Christine and Denise. They shared a cot, top and tail. Social Services came round to visit my mother and the midwife came for daily check-ups. They were very concerned about how she would manage, but by then she already had five children. Another two would not really make much odds.

My father refused to have anything to do with Denise. He told my mother to send her back where she belonged, but she never did. The twins got on very well together. My mother called Christine 'Beauty' and Denise 'Blackie'. Christine was also called 'Buttons', because of her nose.

About a week after the twins came home, Mistress Williams came to our house to see my mother. She never touched her child. She wanted my mother to adopt Denise as soon as possible and had only come round to sign all the relevant forms. My mother agreed to adopt Denise and Mistress Williams handed over to her twenty-five shillings and the Family Allowance Benefit book to which my mother was now entitled. I never saw Mistress Williams again until Denise was fifteen years old.

My mother now had twins and she directed her anger and frustration towards us. Whereas before she would shout and argue with my father, she now shouted at us, punching me in the back more often than usual, each time I went past. She slapped my face when I was naughty and pinched me in the chest when I was close enough to her. I never knew why my mother wanted children. Not once did I think that she liked me or my sisters and brothers. Why she had so many of us is a mystery. We must have served some purpose. She had agreed to take someone else's baby, when she had never shown any signs of wanting her own. It did not make sense to me. Her behaviour got worse.

At the age of six my beatings were as regular as ever. My alarm continued to fail to wake me in time, and my wet bed would earn me a beating with a shoe or a belt or a cane. Over a period of time I became very nervous and jumpy whenever my mother was within striking distance. My bed-wetting was out of control. I slept through the night, often waking up when I could feel a hand under the bedclothes patting the bed, feeling for a spot of wetness. If the bed was wet I was pulled out of it by the leg of my knickers. If the bed was dry I would be warned as to the consequences if I made it wet. One morning I was dreaming in bed and did not hear my mother enter the room. I was lying on my back thinking nice things, when I felt a punch to my stomach which took my breath away. She never said a word, just stood there looking at me and I looked back. She then left the room and I went back to daydreaming with my eyes open.

In 1963 we moved from 5 Myatt Road to 6 Burnett Street. The house belonged to my mother, so the move gave her more freedom: my dad could not simply turn up when he felt like it since it was not his house. I don't know how she managed to buy a house in her own name as the only money she had came from my father. We occupied the top floor, the top rear addition and one room on the middle floor. In the rest of the house were our tenants – our aunt Ina Buckley and her children, and the couple we knew as Georgie Porgie and Rose. My mother put me on my own up in the attic at the very top of the house. It was not the sort of room that anyone would want to stay in for very long. In really bad weather the rain would pour in; sometimes it would set my alarm off and it would wake me up. So it was not just me who wet the bed – the rain did as well. Burnett Street was okay.

There were lots of children around, and across the road from us was a council estate – a large block of flats, four storeys high. We were very rarely allowed to play out in the street. Nor did we play much at home – there was always too much to do. When we did play it was in the yard at the back of the house.

Georgie Porgie and Rose were always quite welcoming. Georgie Porgie was very funny and always had time to play with us as he passed us on the stairs or when he came into our part of the house to talk to my mother. He was especially nice to me. Our father visited us often but did not stay overnight. My mother spent a few evenings per week away from the house. We were told that she had a part-time job. On her return she had lots and lots of cakes which she handed out if we were good. When she was away from the house Georgie Porgie and Rose would keep an eye on us. They became our babysitters.

We had been living at the house for about six months when one day Georgie Porgie was looking after us with Rose. We were all out in the yard. Pauline and Patsy had found an injured butterfly and we were gathered round trying to make it better. Georgie Porgie came out and looked over our shoulders as we crouched around the creature.

'Have you hurt the butterfly?' he asked.

'Of course not,' we all said.

'We want to make it better, Georgie Porgie,' I said.

'Good girl,' said Georgie Porgie and he put his hand around my shoulder. Then he said, 'Good girl,' again, and patted my bottom twice with the cup of his right hand.

We continued to play and Georgie Porgie went into the far corner of the yard and came back with a large brown hairy caterpillar, which was on his outstretched index finger. The caterpillar moved slowly at first, elongating its body until it was almost the length of the finger. As it did this, the caterpillar lifted up its head as though to look around. We all crowded around, but at a safe distance. Then I backed away from Georgie Porgie.

He called me back again. 'Clearie, Clare, come back. Come and see the caterpillar. It will not hurt. Be a good girl and touch the caterpillar.'

I refused. 'It's a creepy-crawly,' I said. 'I don't like creepy-crawlies.'

'No, it isn't. It's a beautiful soon-to-be butterfly,' he said. 'Come and touch it.'

As he moved forward, Georgie Porgie told me not to worry and he promised that he would put the caterpillar down. Then he walked back to the far end of the yard. When he came back he opened his hands.

'See?' he said. 'No caterpillar.'

We continued to play and Georgie Porgie watched. After a few minutes he returned to the corner where he had put the caterpillar. He then came back to us.

'The caterpillar has gone,' he said.

'Where has it gone?' I asked.

'I think it got very lonely over there and it has come back to join us.'

'Where is it?' I said, staring around.

'I don't know. We'll have to look for it,' Georgie Porgie said.

'"You silly, Georgie Porgie,' I said. 'How can it come back? Caterpillars don't walk that fast. Look, Georgie Porgie, I am a caterpillar. I'm coming to get you.' I marched over to Georgie Porgie and banged into him. By now, my sisters were in stitches.

'Well,' he said, 'it must be here somewhere. I'll have to look for it.' He looked in my sister's hair. 'No, not there.' He turned her round and looked at her back. 'No, not there.' He half lifted her dress and looked at her legs. 'No, not there. Patsy, you're next. Have you got the caterpillar?'

'No,' said Patsy and ran inside the house. Precious Puss.

'Clare, you must have it.' He walked towards me. 'I think I can see something. Stay still, Clare.'

'Get it off me, Georgie Porgie, quick!'

He said, 'Hold your arms out slowly.'

I held my arms out and he patted them. 'No, not there.' Then he patted my hair. 'No, can't find it.'

'Have you got it, Georgie Porgie?' I asked anxiously.

'Shush, still looking,' he replied. 'It's not up there – so it must be down here.' He bent down and patted my shoes. He started with the outside of my leg and worked his way up to my bottom.

'Have you got it, Georgie Porgie?'

'No! Still looking.' He moved his hand across from the outside of my thigh to the inside of my leg and patted my minnie. 'No, I can't see it. It must be hiding. Let's start at the top. Turn around. Aha – there it is!'

The giant caterpillar was on the back of my neck, all stretched out.

'Get it off, get it off, get it off, Georgie Porgie!' I screamed. 'Quick, off, off, off, Georgie Porgie!'

'Calm down, Clearie Clare. Georgie Porgie will get it off for you.'

'Off, off, off, Georgie Porgie!'

'Oh, there you are, you naughty caterpillar. We were looking all over Clare for you. I knew we would find you. You naughty caterpillar. When I put you down, you must stay put. No climbing on Clare. Do you understand?'

I froze, terrified of the caterpillar. At that moment, Rose came out and asked us what all the noise was about; she told me to calm down. Georgie Porgie explained that a naughty caterpillar had crawled onto the back of my neck, but he had found it. He shoved his index finger in Rose's direction.

'See?' he said. 'Naughty caterpillar.'

'Come inside with me, pet,' Rose said to me. 'Let's have a wee cup of tea. It'll calm you down.'

I went inside with Rose.

3

A New 'Father'

1964

I didn't think much of Eastman when he first appeared. He was a big ugly smallie with broad shoulders and thick legs. West Indians from the big islands call those from the small islands 'smallies'. Jamaicans call everyone else 'smallies'. Eastman came from Barbados, but he was still a smallie to us. He worked in the laundry at the corner of Myatt Road, near our old house which was owned by my dad. He was always hanging about at my mother's house. In fact, at first he was my aunt's boyfriend. When Ina lived with us at 6 Burnett Street, Eastman visited her about once a week. Ina was really my mother's cousin. I became aware of Eastman when my mother joined them. At first it was a very casual thing, but soon whenever Eastman was with Ina my mother was there too.

After some time Eastman would just visit my mother. He would sit in our kitchen and their relationship was obvious. They got on well together. He always had a copy of the *Sun* newspaper with him, so you can imagine my surprise when I found out later that he could not read. He always came when we were about to go to bed and she would prepare him a nice meal and leave it in the oven on a low flame – huge portions in a Pyrex dish, lots and lots of meat, tomatoes, carrots. One portion could have fed our family twice over for a few days. He seemed to spend more and more time in the kitchen with her. My mother was always preoccupied just prior to his arrival. She waited on him and made sure that he had no complaints. I could not believe it after the way she had beaten up my dad. She stabbed him, shouted at him, abused him and now she was coming over all stupid with this giant.

Whenever Eastman was due we were told to keep out of the way. We had to be in bed early. The house had to be spotless. He came far too often for my liking. I didn't know what my father would say if he knew about it. In any case, Eastman never bothered with us. After a while, instead of coming once a week, he was in the house at least twice a week and then it got to a stage when he was always in the way. Bem was mostly in his room and when he was in the company of my mother he did not speak about Eastman. Very rarely was Bem downstairs when Eastman came around.

After about six months Eastman began to appear in the early hours of the morning. He was in the kitchen eating our breakfast when I got up. We were never allowed in the kitchen when he was there. We had to wait until he was done eating. When he was about, he was never really very nice to us children. On one occasion when he came round, my mother told us to go to bed. I was in bed when there was a knock at the door. I did not say anything. I was at the bottom of the bed and faced the door as it opened. My bed was a single small three-foot bed, positioned in the middle of the room. Eastman came in and asked me how I was. I stayed perfectly still under the covers. I heard him pull a chair up and then he sat on it.

'I know you're in there,' he said.

I quickly pulled the covers down off my face and started to laugh. He laughed too and then pulled the chair closer to my bed. He started to talk generally about being good and going to bed on time and not giving my mother any cause to hit me. I listened to him, but did not say anything. I was lying on my back. He was sitting on my left-hand side close to the middle of the bed. He said that I should try to be good to my mother. She did not mean it, but it was just that she got a bit carried away sometimes.

I listened and then decided that I really did not want to listen any more, so I stretched past him and reached for my black doll.

I caught Dollie with my right hand, but lost my balance as I tried to scoop her off the floor. The covers fell away from me, half-exposing my bottom – I did not have any clothes on. As I tried to regain my balance I was partly on the floor on my hands and knees, and partly on the bed, with my feet in it and my bottom halfway out. I crawled backwards on my hands and ended up on my back in the bed, revealing my minnie. As I reached to cover myself up, Eastman grabbed my minnie and said, 'What a nice little mitt.' I pulled the covers up over myself and tucked the blanket in under my chin. He started to talk and I stared at him, not saying a word. I looked right through him.

'You better not tell your mammy,' he warned, 'or you get a beating and everybody know you a damn liar.'

He went out of the door and I heard him go downstairs. When it was safe, I sneaked out of bed, folded my blanket in half and wrapped it around my body three times. I then got back on top of the bed and went to sleep.

The next morning, Eastman never said anything at breakfast. He didn't have cornflakes or eggs or toast like the rest of us; he had fried rice and eggs mixed together. I think he was getting very comfortable in our house, then one day, out of the blue, my father came to see us. The doorbell went and I thought no one else had heard it so I opened the door and let my dad in. 'How are you, Clearie?' he asked and walked in. I followed and he came across Eastman sitting in the kitchen having breakfast.

My father called my mother and started to cuss Eastman. He told him, not very nicely, to put his breakfast down and at the same time he started to punch Eastman. They were trading blows until my mother realised what was going on and then she got involved and tried to beat my dad.

Georgie Porgie and Rose rushed out of their room and joined us in the kitchen. We all told the two men to stop it, but they would not listen. In the end I think that they both got exhausted and gave up. My mother told my dad not to come back. He went and we never saw him again at 6 Burnett Street. After this incident Eastman did not visit our house for a long time.

Ina Buckley moved out shortly after the fight between George and Eastman. It was she who had invited Eastman to the house and introduced him to my mother. She had known about my mother's activities and my father was not very pleased with her, so she decided that it was in her best interest to live somewhere else.

Georgie Porgie and Rose also left for a break in Scotland. They agreed with my mother that they could have their room back on their return as long as they paid the rent while they were away. The rent was reasonable enough and my mother was pretty civilised to them. In fact, they were more than just tenants, they were friends, and she often invited them round for a cup of tea so that she could gather information on the other tenants at the house. Sometimes when they came round to pay the rent they would stay a little longer and have a Guinness or rum punch. Georgie Porgie was no problem, always offering to help my mother out with an errand here and an errand there. My mother thought this was kindness itself, after all, she wasn't paying for it. One Friday, Georgie Porgie came round to pay his rent and my mother made him some tea and then said she was not feeling very well. Georgie Porgie offered to go out into the garden and pick some peppermint leaves for her to make some peppermint tea, and I offered to pick some with him. We went out into the garden together where there were rows and rows of peppermint plants standing about three feet tall.

'You start up that end,' said Georgie Porgie, 'and I'll start here. Try to pick large leaves or, better still, get a stem with the leaves on.'

I set about my job, pulling the leaves off the peppermint plants. I took only the leaves at the front. The taller plants, towards the back of the garden wall, I kept well away from.

'Come on, Clare, get some of the tall plants,' Georgie Porgie called out.

'I don't want to.'

'Why not?'

'Because the creepy-crawlies will crawl up my legs.'

'Don't be silly, there are no creepy-crawlies in there.'

'Georgie Porgie, the caterpillar just magicked itself on my neck. It came from nowhere and it was on my neck. It's magic, Georgie Porgie.'

'Oh, yes, the caterpillar. Quite right, Clare, I'd quite forgotten all about that. My, my, you have a good memory. We had better watch out for creepy-crawlies, but I don't think we have to worry about the caterpillar.'

'Why not?'

'Because I know where it is.'

'Where is it?'

'It's asleep at the moment, but if you're very, very good I'll show him to you.'

'Can we wake him up, Georgie Porgie? Can we wake him up now?'

'Yes, but it's not that easy to wake the caterpillar up. He's very tired. If you want to wake him you can stroke him very gently and he'll wake up very slowly. Caterpillars don't like the light, remember, so he's been hiding and he has to be kept ever so warm.'

'Yes. Georgie Porgie, can I see the caterpillar now?'

Georgie Porgie removed the belt from his trousers, placed it on the grass and then undid the top button of his trousers.

'Georgie Porgie, what are you doing?'

'I'm getting the naughty caterpillar,' he said as he started to undo the rest of his trouser buttons. 'Come on, you sleepy caterpillar,' he said. 'Clare wants to see you.'

'Why is the caterpillar in your trousers, Georgie Porgie?'

'Because he fell asleep and he is nice and warm,' said Georgie Porgie as he fiddled with yet another button.

'Georgie Porgie, I don't think it's a good idea to wake the caterpillar.'

'Ah, but I think it *is* a good idea. Just put your hand in here, Clare, and feel the nice warm caterpillar.'

He pulled open a gap in his trousers and a mass of hair was

exposed just like the back of the hairy caterpillar that had climbed on my neck.

'I don't like caterpillars after all,' I said, and turned to collect my mother's peppermint leaves.

I ran inside the house. Georgie Porgie made his excuses and departed soon after that.

In November 1964 we moved into Sutherland Square. I often have flashbacks of this. My mother moved in stages. First she took Christine and Denise. Rose looked after us for a night in Burnett Street. Next day my mother moved the two boys. The third day, Pauline and Patsy joined them. That left me. I cannot remember Rose being there that night. My mother came back and picked up her coat and bag. When she got to the door she said she was leaving and not coming back again. She shut the door leaving me inside.

I sat with my back to the door for the whole night. I remember it getting darker and darker. The next thing I remember is the key turning in the lock the next morning. I did not have time to get out of the way. It was my mother. When she tried to push the door open, she felt resistance. She popped her head around and saw me sitting there. She pushed the door hard so that it opened, squashing me against the wall. Ignoring me, she marched upstairs. She never spoke to me all day. Later on she asked if I was ready. We both went outside and caught the bus to Sutherland Square.

She had bought it with my father's money that she had helped herself to. It was in her name and my father could not just turn up when he pleased. Bem was not invited to go with us at first because when my parents had a fight, each one asked Bem to be a witness for them. He had decided not to get involved, because he knew both of them and would not give evidence for one side or the other. After this my mother asked him to leave. She thought he was a traitor of immense proportion and had betrayed her. George collected him and he went to live in one of my dad's other houses, but moved into Sutherland Square later.

Georgie Porgie and Rose stayed in Burnett Street. Once we were not living with them and Bem, my mother was on her worst behaviour. She would shout at me all the time and punch and beat me for any no-good reason. Her temper got shorter and shorter. Nevertheless 19 Sutherland Square was a spacious house on three floors with a nice garden. There was lots of room to play. My room was on the second floor and faced the back of the house.

The best room was the sitting room at the front of the house on the ground floor, although we were only allowed in there by invitation – it was exclusively my mother's preserve. The sitting room was separated by a curtain from the ground-floor back room and bathroom.

When we moved in, Eastman came into his own. He truly believed he owned the house, whereas before he had been quite restrained and kept mostly out of our way. Now he acted as security guard, reporting all bad behaviour back to our mother. He thought the way to stay in her good books was to report us when we did something wrong. We all grew to dislike him and it became worse because he was not our dad and we told him so at every available opportunity.

Eastman worked at the Advance Laundry in Frederick's Crescent and would leave early in the morning and return late. My mother dealt with the situation by keeping us out of the kitchen when Eastman was eating, and making sure that he ate before we did. She always made him a massive breakfast and a huge flask of tea to take to work. When he returned, his dinner was ready – huge portions again in a white and orange Pyrex dish which was kept warm in the oven. His presence in the house meant we all had to prepare a lot more food, peel potatoes, pick the black eyes out of the rice and knead dumplings.

After a few months he started to complain openly to my mother about the cost of living with her and with us. He said that he was not our dad and he did not see why he should waste his hard-earned money feeding kids that were not his own. My mother was anxious to please him. She made sure that there was always food in the house for him. In the kitchen my mother divided the space in the wall cupboard. As you opened the door, the space on the left belonged to Eastman; his food would be kept there. No one was allowed to touch his food without his permission, which he never gave, not even if the rest of the household had run out. On the left were tins of Carnation Milk, large bags of sugar, sweet tea and loads of bread, jam, biscuits, tins of fruit, always available to Eastman. Sometimes when there was no food on our side of the cupboard and we knew he had biscuits, he would go to the cupboard, get them out and munch them in front of us. The right side of the cupboard was separated by an imaginary line. It contained rice and peas. There were no biscuits. Those were kept in my mother's bedroom so that she could control their supply. In fact, any treats like biscuits, crisps or sweets were kept in my mother's bedroom under lock and key. The key was tied to her bra strap.

My mother still worried that the arrangement upset Eastman, but he did not complain, because underneath I think he felt that my mother had taken proper steps to prevent our access to his food. He could go to work, having had his rice and eggs, in full knowledge that the dreadful little Briscoes were not munching their way through the fruits of his labours. The arrangement suited my mother, too; we were expensive to feed and the food needed to be rationed.

At mealtimes Eastman's food was served first in its own Pyrex dish. What was left was shared out between the rest of us. Mother and Eastman ate their food together. The Briscoe children had to wait and have theirs afterwards. Carmen knew how to work him. Eastman was happy as long as he had *all* Mother's attention. We were *not* happy and it did not help that even when he received preferential treatment he still complained about us.

When I was about seven, approaching eight, I used to think how nice it would be if, once in a while, someone bought me a new dress. Nothing fancy – just something that no one else had worn

– maybe a soft cotton dress with pretty buttons with little green flowers on a white background or maybe blue. Blue suited me, and it has always been my favourite colour. I had had so many blue hand-me-downs. A new pair of shoes would be lovely, too. If they had only been worn for a couple of weeks, I would not mind, but they had to be my size. Not tight. I fancied a small heel, not too high – I didn't want to fall and break my neck. Lace-ups were okay, but they had to be pretty with a black ribbon tied in a bow. To finish off, I pictured a hair clip, pink or silver, and a nice cardigan to protect my arms. Pink would be a good colour, but then again green, maybe blue.

I also longed to get my ears pierced, but that would enrage my mother. Maybe I could have my mouth done? I had read recently in some magazine that there were operations where the doctor gave you a new mouth and a new nose, ones that my mother might find acceptable. Maybe they could make me pretty at the same time and then I could run away and another family might want me. Families don't like ugly children – that's a fact of life. 'You are ugly.' That is what she said. Who would want *me*?

By the time I was seven and a half, things had taken a turn for the worse. My mother decided that her tried and tested abuse would not cure my bed-wetting and so she would try something new. The first of the new instalments came one Saturday. We were all sitting around the table waiting for dinner to be served, when my mother removed my plate and put it on the side. She then served up dinner to all the others. I was ignored. They had roast potatoes, chicken, carrots, sweet potatoes, onions and gravy. When I asked my mother where my dinner was, she said that if I were to eat it, it would go through too quickly and I would wet the bed. She then picked up my orange juice and drank it in one go. Then she put the empty glass back down on the table in front of me. 'You'll have a dry night tonight,' she said.

No one at the table said a word. I feared another beating so chose not to confront my mother.

'Peppermint,' she said. 'I need peppermint tea.' She put her hand on her chest near where she kept her key and burped loudly. Everyone at the dinner table remained silent. 'Go and pick some leaves,' she said to me. I went into the garden, pulled off a dozen leaves from her peppermint plants and returned. All at the dinner table ate their meal and one by one they got up and went. I stayed put, hoping my sisters would give me some of their food, but they did not because my mother was watching.

When I got up to leave, my mother told me to clear the table and wash the plates. I protested, after all I hadn't eaten, but she only punched me in the back and told me to shut up. The plates were all washed and dried and put away. Afterwards I went to my room. It was just before nine o'clock. I thought I was safe, but then my mother burst in, and said that I was not allowed to sleep with clothes on because I would only make them wet. She grabbed hold of me and removed my clothes. Then she shouted, 'Pauline, Patsy, Carl – come quick! Come, see your sister. See how she's naked – have a look.'

Pauline and Patsy came down and stood by my door and we made eye-contact. I was huddled by the wardrobe with my hands in front of my minnie as my mother tried to prise them away. My sisters did not stay long. Once they had obeyed my mother's command they disappeared. My mother then doubled her fist and punched me in the stomach and on my upper thigh.

'When are you going to stop? When are you going to stop?' Then she slapped me and punched me on the right shoulder. 'When? *When?*'

I moved away as far as I could get.

'I don't know when. Soon. Now. Now, I'm going to stop. Now.'

'Liar, you're a liar. Do you know how much water I've used, washing your bedclothes? Do you know how much soap powder I've bought, washing your stinking clothes?'

'No.'

'No, you wouldn't know, would you? All *you're* concerned about is wetting the bed. What are you concerned about? Go on

– tell me. What are you concerned about? *Wetting the bed. Wetting my bed.* Well, you're not going to wet my bed again.'

My mother pushed me back into the corner by punching me in the shoulder, and as I raised my hand to fend off the blow she grabbed my minnie and squeezed tightly.

'You're not going to wet my bed ever again. What did I say? Tell me!'

Still holding on to my minnie, my mother tugged me towards her. I went readily and tried not to make a sudden move because it hurt so much. I tiptoed towards her because she had grasped my minnie in an upwards motion and it was easier to tiptoe than to adopt a flat foot. She pulled me towards her and the bed, which was in the middle of the room but pushed back so that it formed an oblong shape along the back wall about three feet away from the wall. Suddenly, she dug her nails into my minnie. I seized her hands with mine to control the pressure. She let go abruptly and grabbed hold of my right breast. I had been hoping that she wouldn't do that. I was in sheer pain. As I moved my hands up to protect my buds, my mother grabbed hold of the other one and then she grabbed hold of both nipples and squeezed so that they were flattened between her fingers. By now I was standing on my toes, while my mother tweaked and twisted my buds. She continued to ask me: 'When are you going to stop pissing my bed? When? When?'

I didn't answer. Pain prevented me from speaking. My mother increased the pressure.

'When? When? Tell me, Clare.'

She let go of me, turned to my bed and tilted the whole thing over so that it lay on its side. With that she separated the mattress from the frame and the bed from the bed-wet alarm and struggled to get the mattress out through the door. Fool, I thought; stupid fool. What did I care for her mattress? I hated her. She finally managed to take my mattress with her when she left my room.

Peace at last. I found some clothes, covered myself up and started to make a bed on the floor, using a pile of old hand-me-

downs which had been in my wardrobe quite some time. Once
my bed was made, I got in it and turned the light off. My sister
Pauline put her head round the door.

'You all right, Clare?' she whispered.

'Yes, I'm fine.'

'You should not answer back, you know.'

My head was hurting, my nipples were on fire and the pain
between my legs was intense, but I had survived. Pauline went
back to her room and I pulled the blanket over my head and fell
asleep. Four Eyes was gathering information again.

The next day began badly. Despite not drinking before I went
to bed, I had wet the bed again during the night and the urine
had soaked into some of the carpet, which now made a squish-
squash sound when I walked on it. My mother was back in my
room bright and early.

'I smell piss,' she said. She came and lifted the blanket, sniffed
it. Picked up some of the clothes that I had used to make my bed
and sniffed them. 'You smell rank,' she said, and grabbed hold of
the edge of the blanket and pulled it. I rolled off the pile of clothes
and the blanket trailed along the floor as she left the room. I was
running out of blankets and old clothes but summer was
approaching and my father always bought us new clothes during
this time.

It was around then that Eastman started spying on us.

On one occasion I was in my room removing my sheet, which
I had wet the previous night, when I heard the stairs creaking and
then Eastman appeared at the door. 'Carmen, come quick.' In a
flash she appeared at the door and marched into my room.
'Look, Carmen, look how she piss the bed.' My mother grabbed
me in the chest, pulled me towards her and asked me why I wet
the bed. I said I did not know and she punched me in the head
and let me go. I continued to change my sheet and Eastman
observed through the crack in the door.

'What you looking at?' I said. 'Why don't you go and spy
somewhere else?'

'What you say? What you say, you black bitch? What you

say?' He came into the room and punched me in the back, forcing me forward onto the bed and then he left.

'Stupid,' I said.

He went on creeping around the house gathering information for my mother, complaining all the time about how much we were all eating, going out of his way to tell tales and get us into trouble. As Christmas approached he started talking to himself and to anyone who was within hearing distance about the expense. When we went past him he would say: 'Eastman, now you is a darn fool. How you going to spend your money on pickneys that are not your own? Not me! Look at how many mouths that me have to feed. Six mouths and not one mine. You better go and find you daddy and tell him no fool live at nineteen.' At other times he would say; 'No turkey going to pass your lips ah hoor.'

It was clear that we were expected to find our father and tell him that if he did not buy food for our Christmas, we would not eat.

4

Christmas Cheer

1965

Christmas Day finally arrived. Our mother woke us up quite early, as she wanted the house spotless before she got up. She went back to bed while I started on the cleaning. Today was a happy day because it was Christmas Day. Lots of food, lots of presents. I made a start on the stairs, landing, hall and my bedroom. Next I moved on to the sitting room and gave it a really good clean, pulling the settee away from the wall, hoovering behind it, then under the glass table and around my mother's china cabinet. All done. Next the kitchen. It was a mess but it wouldn't take very long to clean up. My sisters were doing their own bedrooms and then they cleaned out the bathroom. Once that was done, Pauline and Patsy joined me in the kitchen. All the dirty plates were washed, dried and put away and the floor was mopped. We placed all the food that would be cooked onto the sideboard, together with all the spices that we would need. Then it was time for breakfast: cornflakes, half milk, bit of sugar and a slice of toast.

I noticed that all the biscuits which we had put away when my father brought the food round had disappeared. The turkey was still there, so too were the potatoes, carrots and rice, but our biscuits, Jammy Dodgers and cream crackers had vanished. It didn't matter so much because it was Christmas and we would all have food. First we watched *Lassie* on telly. Liz Taylor was so wonderful. Then we watched *Whistle Down the Wind*. I wish I could find Jesus in my barn, I thought; maybe I could ask Him when I'm going to be happy.

Eventually my mother called Pauline, Patsy and me downstairs. It was time to start preparing Christmas dinner. Eastman's turkey was on the table. It was tiny, and mainly bald with a rash from a skin infection. We put our huge turkey on top of Eastman's, and it looked as if ours had just given birth to his little one. We set about plucking our bird, and as we did so I picked up a small wooden spoon. 'Who's been a naughty turkey?' I said. I whacked Eastman's turkey across the chest. 'You naughty, naughty turkey, you're on your own. Right, that's okay for your punishment, you're going to get eaten now.'

We had an enormous amount of food. I peeled the potatoes, while Patsy prepared the rice. She picked out all the off-colour grains, washed the starch out and put the rice on the side. The Brussels sprouts were peeled of their outer layer and crossed with a sharp knife at the stalk end. All the mince pies were ready to be warmed up and eaten. Eastman kept out of our way now that our father had come up trumps with our Christmas goodies; it took the wind out of his sails. His turkey remained unplucked. We just ignored it. If Eastman wanted turkey, he could do it himself. Once our big bird was in the oven I went upstairs to find out when we could open our presents.

On Christmas Day my father turned up at the front door with presents. We all had presents except for Denise; she did not exist as far as George was concerned. He knocked on the door, put the bag of presents on the step and waited. Eastman picked up a stick which was part of a broom handle and opened the door with it in his hand. My mother was at his shoulder. I was sitting at the top of the first flight of stairs with my sisters peering over my shoulder.

'What you want? Nobody lives here for you,' said Eastman aggressively.

'Why don't you do yourself a favour and go and sit down?' said George.

'Nobody lives here for you. Now move – move away from the door.'

'You've got too much mouth,' George said.

'Eastman,' interrupted my mother, 'don't waste your time with him. Eastman, come.'

'Move from my door, move – move!' Eastman raised his stick and my father grabbed him and stepped over the threshold. My mother tried to free Eastman and all three wrestled in the hall. In quick succession my father punched Eastman twice in the face and my mother kicked my father and tried to jump on his back. My father bent forward and my mother rolled over his head and landed partly on top of Eastman and partly on the floor.

My father stepped past both of them and went back to the front door. He turned again so that he was facing us and shouted, 'Come and get your presents!'

We rushed down the stairs, but stopped when our mother screamed, 'Stay where you are!' As she picked herself up, Eastman was still on the hall floor looking for his stick which had gone flying. 'Stay where you are!' she shouted once more.

My father called us again: 'Come and get your presents.'

Eastman shouted at my father, 'Wait, I'm coming for you. Wait, where's my stick? I had it here, who the body is take my stick? All right, good, you wait there. I soon come back.' He disappeared round the back of the house to find another weapon. My mother reappeared from the sitting room with a large nail; it must have been about nine inches long. Eastman returned with a plank of wood about three feet long.

My father was still at the door. 'Come for your presents,' he said.

'I've told you to stay where you are,' my mother screamed, raising the nail high above her head. The rust on it made it look like the stem of a flower, but she held it like a javelin. She and Eastman both slowly made their way towards my father.

George put his hand in the bag that was by his side, pulled out a large wrapped present and threw it into the hall. 'Pauline, this is for you, dearie. That's yours,' he said and threw at my mother's legs a large oblong gift. My father began to sing as he put his hand back into his bag. 'Patsy, you didn't think I'd forgotten you, did you? No, would I forget my little girl?' Into Eastman's chest went another present as he and my mother retreated towards the back of the house.

Seizing our opportunity, we rushed down the stairs, grabbed our presents and ran back upstairs again. My father was fiddling in his bag as Eastman approached him with his plank of wood.

'Don't be a fool,' said my dad. 'Go and have a Christmas drink with the old girl.'

Eastman raised the plank to hit my dad and my dad pushed the door into him, forcing him back into the hall. My brothers, Carl and Martin, were nowhere to be seen; they were probably hiding. Our dad threw the final presents into the hall. 'Merry Christmas, children,' he said as he turned to go back to his car. 'Eastman,' he added, 'you are a turkey. Carmel – see you soon.' Then he got into his car and we all ran to look out of the window and watch him drive away.

My mother and Eastman stayed downstairs. We opened our presents. Dad had bought shoes for all of us. New clothes. Some wooden toys, building bricks, a train set, a pencil case for each one of us and sweets.

For the rest of the morning we all kept out of Eastman and my mother's way, happily enjoying our gifts. So as not to be outdone, my mother popped her head around the door and looked in. We all froze – stopped what we were doing and stared in her direction. 'When you've finished, come downstairs,' she said. Then she closed the door and we heard her footsteps going back down.

About midday, I went downstairs, with Pauline, Patsy and Carl. In all my life I could never remember opening Christmas presents together, like other people did. It wasn't something that happened in our family. My mother sat on the armchair with her legs open. Between them she had a shopping trolley on wheels, a flat bag inside a steel case. She called Pauline to her. 'Come, P,' she said, and handed her a present. 'Thank you, Mummy.' 'Come, Patsy, here you are.' 'Thank you, Mummy,' said Patsy as she took her present. 'Come, Clare.' I got up and went over to my mother. 'Here you are – take it.' I took my present and went back to my place. 'Oh, Clare, here's another one.' She held out the wrapped present. I again got up and took the present. 'Thank you, Mummy,' I said and went back to my seat.

Once everybody had their presents we all sat around with them on our laps. Pauline was very pleased with hers. She had been given a new sewing machine. Patsy too had an identical new sewing machine. I opened my present. The first one was soft and squiggly. I peeled the paper off. 'Oh, thank you, Mummy,' I said. It was my black doll. I had last seen Dollie when I played with her at Burnett Street.

'What have you got?' Pauline wanted to know. 'Let's see.'

'It's Dollie,' I said.

'Didn't you get her last year?' said Pauline.

'And the year before that,' I said.

I opened the other present, which was my spinning top. I think I was five when I first got it as a present. 'Thanks, Mummy.' Everyone opened their presents. At least I'd got Dollie back. I was not too bothered about my spinning top, but Dollie had a nice dress – yellow gingham with wavy lace around the neck and white knickers. Her knickers were a bit grubby after all these years, but a good wash would sort her out.

After opening the presents we all stayed up watching telly. At dinner Eastman was silent because the food that we ate had been bought and paid for by my dad so he could hardly complain; in fact, he ate a great load of it. After kicking up such a fuss for so long he was now tucking into my dad's food. I had far too much to eat and drink and went to bed with Dollie, my spinning top and the presents my dad had given me. My bed-wet alarm was plugged in and I prayed to God to stop me wetting the bed. I crossed myself with the sign of the cross and went to sleep.

On Boxing Day I woke to the sound of my alarm. As I opened my eyes I saw my mother removing her shoe; with her other hand she was pulling at my nightdress. The nightdress was slipped over my head and she slapped me on my bare bottom with the shoe. It stung. 'You dirty bitch,' she said. 'It's about time you stopped wetting the bed.' She slapped me twice more on my right hand and my right upper arm. All of a sudden she stopped and pulled the wet sheet off the bed, which silenced the alarm. She removed my blanket and took it away with my sheet and nightdress. I found another nightdress in the wardrobe, put that on and made my bed up with some old clothes. Then I got back into bed and waited. I could hear my mother opening and closing the drawers in the kitchen. The best thing for me to do was stay where I was, and so I did.

Later that day I got up and went into my sisters' room. They no longer bothered to come and see me during the beatings because it just made my situation worse. Boxing Day was okay; we had a breakfast of porridge and toast, cleaned the house and later watched telly. My mother and Eastman spent most of the time in the sitting room. Twice I caught Eastman looking through the crack in the door while we played with the presents my father had given us. He was a spy and we nicknamed him 'the creep'. We ate more of the turkey and had potatoes, carrots, stuffing. My father had bought lots of fruit and nuts. It was okay.

At bedtime my mother came into my room carrying a black plastic bag. I tensed up as she approached me. 'You ready for bed?' she said. The bag was tied with two double knots. She undid those and peeled away the outer bag. She again undid a series of knots. In total she removed three bags. Inside the final bag were my sheet, blanket and nightdress – all wet and stinking of urine.

'You ready for bed?'

'Yes,' I said.

My mother pushed off the bed the clothes that I had used earlier that morning, picked up the sheet, opened it to display a large yellow wet patch and put it on the bed. The alarm automatically went off and my mother pulled the plug out of the socket. Carefully she made up my bed. She tucked the sheet under the mattress and put my pillow on top of it and then she draped the wet blanket on top.

'Put your nightdress on,' she said, and handed me the previous night's nightdress, which was soaked and smelled quite badly. I looked at it and then at her. 'Put it on,' she repeated and shoved me in the back.

I took my clothes off and put on the nightdress. I tried very hard not to let any of the wet patches touch my skin but it was impossible.

When the nightdress was on my mother pulled back the blanket and said, 'Get in.' Obediently I climbed into the bed and my mother pulled the blanket up to just under my chin.

'There we are! Good night, Clare. If you get out of bed and change your clothes you will live to regret it!'

When a reasonable amount of time had passed, I got out of bed. I pulled the sheet over towards the front of the bed and found a dry bit to sleep on. I then turned the blanket so that most of the wet bit was at the bottom. My nightdress was wet below my chest so I rolled it up and tied it in a knot. Then I lay down on my side in order to stay on the dry bit of the sheet. Twice my mother came in and twice I pretended to be asleep. After her last visit I got up and went off to the toilet. As I reached the first landing Eastman started to shout, 'Carmen, Carmen, come! Pissyarse out of her room.' My mother came running out and we met on the stairs. 'Go to your room,' she said. I went to my room and stayed there. The door was slightly open and I heard the creaking of the stairs. He was peeping into my room again. I spotted him from my bed so I got up and stood on top of it and deliberately pissed all over the blanket. He looked at me and I stared straight back at him, but he never called my mother. He just waited for me to finish and then he crept down the stairs like the spy that he was.

5

Ugly

1966

One evening, Eastman came home, went into the kitchen and then after a few minutes all hell broke loose. He started shouting: 'Carmen, Carmen, come quick! You does hear I call you?'

'Hold up, hold up, Eastman. I coming quick, wait.' I heard her go up the stairs and join him in the kitchen.

'Carmen, look.' The glass cover of the Pyrex dish clattered on the stove. 'Look, Carmen, you leave the dish so? Carmen, you could never have leave the dish so because I's a grown man. Look on me – you think I want picnic?'

'No,' said my mother. 'Give me the fork.'

After a short period of silence I heard her say that two potatoes, one dumpling and half a sweet potato were missing.

'It must be them blasted Briscoes that eat my food, Carmen.'

'Wait, Eastman. Let me find out.'

When my mother appeared in my doorway with a belt in her hand, I was lying on the floor with my homework spread out in front of me.

'Did you touch Eastman's dumplings?' she said.

'No.'

'Did you touch his potatoes?'

'No.'

'Did you touch his sweet potato?'

'I have no reason to touch his sweet potato.'

She departed from my room and closed the door. I heard her go upstairs. She'd be lucky if anyone admitted to eating his food. I knew where the dumplings had gone, because I had eaten them, but I could not remember having a go at the potatoes. Anyway there was more than enough left in the dish and he needed to lose weight.

'Come, stand in front of me and let me have a good look at you.'

I stood in front of my mother with my hands down by my side. Eastman, Pauline, Patsy and Carl were in the kitchen and I had just shown my mother my class photograph. The word *proof* was written all over it. If she wanted it, all she had to do was give me the money in the brown envelope provided and keep the big photograph and the five small copies that came with it. If she did not want them I was instructed to return the photographs within three days.

'Come, let me see you.' My mother took the main photograph out of its transparent sleeve and put it against the right side of my head. 'Stand still, let me see. Pauline, come here. Look good. What you see?'

Pauline came over and stood just behind my mother. 'I can see Clare, Mummy. What do you want me to look at?'

'Look good, P – look again.'

Pauline looked at me and then at the photograph that was now held up to the left side of my head.

'That's Clare, Mummy.'

'No, you can't see what I see. Eastman, come look good and tell me what you see.'

Eastman came over from the sink. He flicked his hands to get the water off and then dried them on a tea towel.

'My black arse, she's ugly, man.'

I stood with my face still, looking at my mother, arms motionless by my side, not wanting to move in case I set her off. Eastman rubbed his eyes and looked at the photograph. He then said, 'Gimme,' took the photograph out of my mother's hands and pushed it to within four inches of his face. 'I'll say one thing, you sure is fucking ugly. Is that you?' he said. 'Carmen, you ever see a child so ugly? Look good.' He handed the photograph back to my mother.

'Jesus Christ, me give birth to that?' She stared from the photograph to me. 'Lord, sweet Lord, how come she so ugly? Ugly. Ugly. If I hadn't given birth to her, sweet Lord, I would have sworn she was a fraud. Heavenly Jesus, sweet and kind, why have You given me a swine? Look at that nose, where did you get it from? Not from me,' said my mother answering her own question. 'If I had a nose like that I would cut off half and save the rest.'

'But, Carmen, you forget them rubber lips. Look, see, in the photograph? If I had rubber lips like that I wouldn't have my photograph taken – and she wants you to *buy* it! Clare, where you get them spots? You got potato skin.'

'Ah yes, Eastman, I see it now. Is not just too much mouth she have, she have too much nose. Where you get that nose?' My mother used her middle finger and pressed it on the edge of my nose so hard I stumbled. 'Don't walk away when I am talking to you. Come here.' She pulled me forward. 'Now, you want me to buy this photograph – that right, Clare?'

'You can return it, I can take it back to school tomorrow. You don't have to buy it.'

'But, Clare, you so ugly. Have you seen yourself lately? Look.'

With that my mother turned the photograph round in front of my face. I looked at it. I was actually very ugly. My head was too big, my lips were too large, I was covered in spots and my nose was too wide. I was not smiling.

'I've been telling you for such a long time now that you're ugly. How long has it been? Years. I been telling you for *years* that you're ugly. Have you paid any attention? Have you listened to me? No. Not one word have you listened to. Instead you bring your ugly pictures home and ask me to pay for them. Do you think I should buy them? Tell me, Clare, do you think I should put my money in this little brown envelope and buy them?' She picked up the envelope and counted out the smaller copies of the main one. 'One, two, three, four, five.' At five she started to laugh and threw the pictures on the table. 'Tell me true, Clare, do you think I should pay for *these*?'

The whole kitchen started to laugh. It was really funny. I wasn't being abused or anything.

'I don't think that you should pay for them.'

'Why not?' my mother asked.

'Because I don't want you to waste your money.'

'And?' she said.

'And because I'm ugly.'

My mother left the photographs on the kitchen table. I gathered them up, put them back in the envelope and returned them to school the next morning. It really was very silly of me to think that my mother might want a school photograph of me. She had never bought one before. I knew she would not buy them, but that was not something I could tell my teacher as an excuse for not taking the photographs home. When the register was called I handed them over to my teacher.

'Back so soon, Clare?'

'Yes, miss. Mum said the photos are too dark and they don't bring out my best features.'

Played netball that day. I got picked first. I played centre and we beat the other side. They were rubbish. Back home, I changed into my old clothes, did the washing and drying, swept the stairs and then did my homework. I kept out of my mother's way. It was okay.

Early that evening, I went down to the kitchen. It was my turn to cook. A chicken had to be prepared. My mother had bought it in East Street Market. Though it had been plucked, there were still feathers on it that needed to be burned off over the flame on the cooker. After that it had to be seasoned. I started by removing all the large feathers from the bird and then burning the fine feathers off. The potatoes were peeled and ready in a pan with water and salt; carrots were also ready to be cooked. All my preparations were going well until my mother came in, looked over my shoulder and asked if I had finished seasoning the chicken.

'Yes,' I said.

'Have you prepared the chicken?' she repeated.

'Yes.' I began to feel nervous.

'Look at the chicken – have you prepared it?'

I looked carefully at the chicken, but could see nothing wrong with it. It looked like a nice chicken to me.

'Look at it.' She pushed my head in the direction of the chicken. 'Tell me: what you can see?'

'I can't see anything,' I said.

'What?'

I checked again. Then I saw them. There were three white hairs visible on the skin on the back, and about another five lower down. Oh my God, I thought to myself, how did I manage to miss them?

I started to pluck at the hairs with my bare hands. 'I don't know how they got there,' I said nervously. 'The chicken must have been lying on them.'

The hairs did not want to come out. They kept slipping between my fingers. I tried the knife, but it too slipped and the hairs remained intact. I plucked again.

'You didn't see the hairs! You didn't see the hairs! Well, I can see them. Look, there is one. Can *you* see it?'

She picked one off and thrust it into my face. The hair was moist and stuck to the side of my cheek.

'Can you see it now?' she asked. She grabbed me by my right ear and pulled me away from the stove and work surface towards the kitchen table. 'Come, come with me. If you can't see the hairs, I have to show you.'

My mother pushed me down into the seat and sat opposite me at the table, which was covered in a plastic cloth. On it lay a small sharp knife with a burnt handle, which I had earlier been using to peel the potatoes.

'You can see that, can't you?' said my mother. 'I mean, that's not too difficult, is it?' She held the knife in her right hand. 'Can you see that? You're not blind, are you? Clare is blind, oh my God, sweet Jesus, Clare is blind. Can you see that? Tell me, Clare, what have I got in my hand?'

'It's a knife,' I said. 'You've got a knife.'

Ugly

'Yes, I know I've got a knife, but can you *see* a knife? Can you see the knife?' My mother's voice was raised.

'Yes, I can see the knife. You've got it in your hand.'

'Ah yes, so you *can* see the knife. Good. Can you *feel* it?' Quick as a flash she grabbed my hand and tried to bring it down across the table, but I would not let her. She then ordered me to put my hand down, but still I refused. Then she took my left hand in hers and forced it down across the table towards her. She put her elbow on my palm. I did not move. I felt trapped and was a little confused as to what was happening. Suddenly, she released my hand and, picking up an empty milk bottle, brought the edge of it down across the top of my knuckles. I flinched and moved my hand.

'Did you feel that? Ah good, yes, you did. Now put your hand back.' And she pointed at the table. The tears welled up in my eyes as I flexed my muscles.

'I'm not going to tell you again. Put your hand down flat.'

I did. Again she brought the edge of the bottle down across my knuckles. Tears trickled down my cheeks.

'Save your tears for when you grow up. You'll have something to cry about then,' she said.

Again my mother told me to put my hand down on the table. I asked her why and she said, 'Just do it.' In case I tried to move she dug her heels down on the toes of my shoes beneath the table. 'Down,' she ordered. 'Don't let me have to stand up.'

I placed both my hands on the table, palms up. She made no attempt to pick up the bottle.

'Now where were we?' she said. 'Oh yes.' She picked up the knife. 'You didn't see the chicken hair. Well, we'll just have to make sure that you don't miss it again.' My mother held the knife in her right hand and was playing with it, waving it around in small sweeping motions as she lowered the blade to a point which was about six inches from my hands. I thought nothing of it. My mother was just being my mother. I had my eye on the bottle and my mother's foot. Just then, she pressed the point of the knife into my wrist.

'The chicken!' she said. '*Now* do you think that you will forget to pull all the hairs out again?'

'No,' I said.

My mother pressed the knife harder into my wrist and drew blood. 'And why will you remember?' she said.

'I'll remember, because I'll remember.'

She pulled the knife across my arm. Beads of blood rose up from the track of the knife and a straight line of flesh opened up. Blood dripped down the side of my arm and all over the plastic table cover.

'Look what you have done,' she said in disgust. 'You have spilt your blood all over my tablecloth. You had better clean it up. Clean it up before you touch my chicken.'

And with that she was gone. The blood was forming congealed blobs between the stripes on the plastic tablecloth. My wrist stung and every time I opened and closed my fist the blood poured out. I got up and ran my arm under the cold tap. When the blood mixed with the water it made a very pretty pink colour in the sink, swilling around with the hairs pulled from the chicken. I went down and got some toilet roll, wrapped it around my arm and went back up to the kitchen. I burned the remaining hairs on the chicken and then pulled them out with a knife – the knife I had washed under a running tap. Dinner was hairless chicken, potatoes, carrots and peas.

Eastman and my mother sat up at the dinner table and the Briscoes waited for them to finish before we could go into the kitchen and have our own meal. We had to clean up after them and then set the table for ourselves. Pauline asked what was wrong with my arm and I told her, 'Nothing.'

'Why have you got toilet paper wrapped round your arm?'

'I cut my arm.'

'How did you do that?'

'I don't know. It just happened.'

'How did it happen?'

My mother walked by. 'You should be more careful,' she said. 'You might burn yourself the next time.'

I wet the bed that night and some of it soaked into the carpet. Because the carpet was multi-coloured it was not easy to see exactly where the watermark was, but the stench was quite strong. I got up early – it must have been about 6 a.m. – opened the window and shook the curtain back and forth in order to get the smell out of the room. I then put the wet clothes in the wardrobe, closed the door and made my bed again with a new pile of clothes, this time just under the window. My mother, if she came into the room, would walk towards me so she might not discover the wet carpet. The smell was the only giveaway.

My mother came in bright and early. She never questioned the open window. She just came up to me and, as she got pretty close, half bent down and grabbed hold of the edge of the blanket and pulled it. I got up and ran out of the way. The blanket trailed along the floor as she left the room, taking it with her.

The next day, I was still in a lot of pain from the cut she had given me. I got myself ready for school – a quick wash, bags packed. Breakfast I would do without. That way I would avoid my mother who was in the kitchen. My sisters and I walked to the bus stop. We did not talk about the events of the day before. We never did. At school I had a good day, sausage, pies, chips, spotty dog, pink custard and orange cake. The teachers said that I was not being stretched enough in class and I should move up a stream. Great. 'A' stream, here I come.

When I returned from school, I decided that I would like to leave home, get myself a job and a room somewhere. I was sick of the beatings, never having any decent clothes, and not being allowed enough food. That day, my mother and I had gone to see an expert about my bed-wetting. He said I was a nervous child and was there anything that made me nervous? My mother said, 'No.' The upshot of this meeting was that I had another new fancy alarm attached to my bed. I knew it wouldn't make any difference.

The next day at school we had Religious Instruction. Our teacher spoke to us about God, Baby Jesus and heaven. We were all Catholics, she told us – not just any old Catholics, but Roman Catholics, and there was a space waiting in heaven for all of us. All we had to do was to obey the Ten Commandments and lead a good *Catholic* life. Unlike other religions, ours was the only one that actually guaranteed us a place in heaven. If we were not quite up to going straight there, then we would have to spend time in the Garden of Peace, where small-time sinners waited until they had served their time before moving on to heaven. Purgatory was where you went after death to get rid of your sins – not big sins, because you were not expected to do those anyway, but little ones which we all do. The garden had a high brick wall to keep out others, those who were not Roman Catholic.

We then moved on to look at the life of God, and how He gave up everything. He sacrificed His only Son to make this world a better place for us.

Thou must honour thy mother and thy father.

Thou shall not kill.

Thou shall not take another life because you will *not get to heaven; not even the life of an ant are you entitled to take – they have the right to life too.*

'But, miss, what if it's your own life?' I asked. 'You can do what you want with your own life, can't you, without getting into trouble?'

Miss said only God could give life and only He could take it away. It was a mortal sin to take your own life or even the life of an ant. Think of that, an ant! How much more trouble would you be in if you dabbled in God's business? You would never get to heaven if you should ever interfere with God's little creatures. I was not too happy about that lesson. If God gave life, surely He would not mind if you gave it back to Him?

'No,' my teacher insisted, 'only God can decide what he wants; you'll never get to heaven if you allow yourself to get sidetracked.'

'What, miss, if life is so bad that you want to give God His gift back? Would He be upset? He is a kind God, miss. I know people in heaven, miss – my brother Winston is there. I think that it would be a better life than the one I have. If you decide that you no longer want to be on earth and would rather be in heaven, surely, miss, you would not be giving up your place in heaven just because you wanted to go sooner rather than later?'

'Clare Briscoe, hush your mouth, may God forgive you. You ungrateful child.'

'But, miss, what if life on earth is not what you expect and there is no fun in living on earth? You've said heaven is a joyous place. I could play in the garden and wait until I got into heaven. I could wear pretty dresses and nice new shoes and I could be so happy in heaven, miss. I—'

'Clare Briscoe, go right now to the Headmaster. Tell him I said you have no respect for the Lord. Out – now go.'

I stood outside the Headmaster's room, got bored after a while, and went to my next class. In heaven, everything is perfect and I would never wet the bed again. I would have a nice warm blanket. There would be no need for mummies in heaven. Most of the children there don't have mummies, because the children have gone on ahead. Winston didn't have his mummy. Anyway, I knew Winston was in heaven. I could get to know him. Maybe if I brought Dollie with me and my spinning top, Winston could play with my spinning top and I could play with Dollie. That sounded fair to me. But what if God was cross with me because I decided to go sooner rather than later? Surely God is a kind God? He would not shut the doors of heaven just because He was upset with me.

Was I prepared to take the risk? Yes. I did not want to be here. If I went now, quickly, no one would miss me. I'd be there before anyone knew I was gone. I don't want to be here, I thought. I don't like my home. I don't like my mother. I don't like my sisters or brothers and I would rather not be here. Maybe if I prayed hard enough and went to church, God would forgive me and let me in. I decided I had better start going to church more often.

Soon it was Friday again. I went to Sacred Heart Church and sat at the front. I wanted God to recognise me when I arrived early. Back at school after the service, my teacher said I was lazy and not putting enough effort into my work. She had no idea how much housework I had to do.

That afternoon we had Religious Instruction again. The teacher took me to one side and asked whether I had something to tell her. I said, 'No.'

'Why would you not want God's gift of life, Clare? Give me one good reason.'

'Miss,' I said, 'I might not want God's gift. In fact, I *don't* want it.'

'Oh,' she said, 'along with you, Clare Briscoe. You're always away with the fairies.'

I was *not* away with the fairies. I tried to explain that I was not with the fairies because I would be with the angels. Teacher said I should have my head examined.

That lunchtime Cook was pushing the boat out: we had soggy rice and chili con carne, lemon meringue pie and custard.

6

New Shoes

1967–8

One teatime, I was doing my homework in my bedroom when there was a knock on the front door. I ignored it, but then the doorbell rang. I picked myself up off the floor and pushed my homework to one side. As I made my way downstairs, my mother was already opening the door.

'Can Clare come out to play?' a girl's voice said.

'Oh Clearie, dearie,' said my mother. 'I think she is busy.'

No one had ever called for me before. I did not recognise the voice. From where I stood on the stairs, I could see that it was Mary – I could not remember her last name. We had had a fall-out in the school playground when she tried to push me out of her way. I pushed her back. She hit me and I hit her back. We had words and we were not speaking to each other. The truth was, we did not like each other at all.

'Can you come out to play?' she said.

Sure, I can come out to play, I thought to myself – but not with you. Of all the people in the world, she knew that I would not wish to play with her. Beat her up, yes. Play, no.

'No,' I said, 'I'm busy. Lots of homework.' I turned to go back upstairs.

'Why don't you come in?' my mother said. 'I didn't know Clearie had a friend, I don't remember anyone ever calling for her. You want to play with Clare?'

'Yes.'

'You are a friend of hers, are you?'

'Yes.'

'Come in, come in. I'm sure you're interested in seeing how and where your friend lives. Have you seen her bedroom?'

'No.'

I glared at Mary.

'It's okay,' she said. 'I'll see you at school tomorrow, Clare.' She made to move away from the door.

'Come in, my love,' said my mother. 'Come and see your friend; you can stay a few minutes.'

So Mary crossed the threshold into the house, with the assistance of my mother who had a firm grip on her arm.

'You want to know what your friend's bedroom looks like, don't you? Come up,' she said. Mary followed my mother. I was standing at the top of the stairs.

'I don't think Mary wants to stay,' I said.

'Come on up, dear,' she said. My mother ignored me.

They both started climbing the stairs, Mary right behind my mother. I ran off and started to tidy my bedroom. As I grabbed the clothes on the floor and threw them into the wardrobe, they entered.

'This is her room,' said my mother as she pushed Mary in before her. 'Now,' she said, 'is *your* room like this?'

Mary looked around and her eyes settled on my alarm. The large box was on the floor by my bed.

'What's that?' she asked. I stared at my mother.

'Oh, that's her alarm,' my mother said. 'Did she not tell you that she still wets the bed?' My mother kicked the box with her foot and the lights flashed. 'See? It is a bit like crossing the road,' she went on. 'Trouble is, you will not get run over, but you might be drowned.'

'You still wet the bed, Clare?' asked Mary, backing away.

'Only sometimes,' I said. 'Don't you?'

'Only all the time and twice at night,' my mother said.

'No, I don't.'

'You still wet the bed?' Mary looked at me as if an alien had landed on my face. Then she smacked her knees with an open palm and started laughing; she bent double with laughter and, when she straightened up, she started to choke with a succession of laughing splutters. My mother had to smack her back repeatedly. 'You still wet the bed?' Tears ran down her fat cheeks and her nose was running. She clapped her hands together and then slapped her cheeks, which went bright red. Then she stuck one finger in the air and said, 'Yes, swivel on it. You still wet the bed?'

'Swivel on what, my love?' said my mother. 'The trouble I've had with your friend. We've tried everything, everything, and she still wets the bed. Look at this, love.' She hurried out of the room. While we waited for my mother to return, Mary stared at me without blinking.

'Wait till I tell Ann.' Mary held her laugh in by covering her mouth.

The idea that the whole class would know that I wet the bed was too shameful for words.

'I don't wet the bed,' I said. 'I used to but I don't – not often, at any rate.'

My mother returned. In her hand, she had a jug with about 50mls of water.

'Watch this, dear.' She peeled back the covers and revealed my incontinence sheet, which covered the alarm. She poured the water over the sheet and the alarm system exploded into action. The lights flashed on and off. The noise was enough to stop Mary in her tracks. She looked on in horror as the lights flashed and the alarm bellowed out.

'Wait until I tell,' she said. 'Wait until I tell.'

'And don't think that that is all,' my mother said. 'Look at this.' She brushed me out of the way and fell to her knees. She forced her hand under the bed and scooped up all my clothes. 'Look at this,' she said. 'Oh my God, smell that.' She moved a nightshirt in the direction of Mary who, anticipating my mother's actions, backed away rapidly. She had been crouching down to look but, in her anxiety to get away, fell and tripped over. Supporting herself with her arms, which were behind her, she crawled backwards with her stomach facing the ceiling – a sort of press-up in reverse.

'It won't bite,' my mother said. 'It might knock you out, but the smell won't bite.'

Mary had had enough. She stood up and said, 'I've got to go, Mrs Briscoe, it's been lovely meeting you. Clare, I'll see you tomorrow.' She made her way downstairs and to the front door.

'I'll show you out, love,' called my mother. 'Come again if you are in the area.'

Mary got to the end of our front garden and then she started to run and she did not stop until she was a fair distance away from our house. Then she was gone. I put all the wet clothes back under my bed and got on with my homework, keeping out of my mother's way. Later I got myself organised. I put out my school uniform next to my schoolwork for the morning. Before I went to bed, I changed the sheets by turning them upside down.

The next day, I handed in my homework. When we had our early morning break, I looked for Mary but she was not about. I didn't know what I would say to her anyway. After break we had our English comprehension homework back. My mark said *Very good.* We had a great rounders match. We are the best. At lunchtime there was spaghetti bolognese – too much spaghetti and not enough bolognese – followed by jam tart and custard. I ate it all up and went out to play. In the playground I met Mary, who was with her friends.

'I know something you don't know, I know something you don't know,' she chanted as she pointed her finger at me.

'What? Tell us,' said her cronies.

'I know something you don't know, I know something you don't know,' sang Mary. She came up to me and rubbed her nose in my face. 'What's it worth not to tell?' she said.

I walked past her and her friends, and as I did so she punched me in the back. I turned to face her and all her friends were shouting, 'Go on, Mary, go on, hit her again.' She looked at me and said, 'If you hit me I'll tell.'

'Tell, tell,' said her friends. 'Tell, please tell.'

'What is there to tell, Mary?' I said.

'You know, your mum told me.'

'Well, you had better tell them, Mary,' I said.

'Go on, tell, Mary,' said the crowd.

I punched Mary in the back just as the teacher was approaching us. Mary cried out and held her head.

'She did it, miss,' they said, pointing at me.

'Yes, I saw with my own eyes,' said the teacher. 'Clare, go and report yourself to your class teacher now.'

I went to find my class teacher. By the time I found her, she had already received an account from the playground teacher. I had apparently punched Mary when Mary's back was turned. Mary had not offered any violence and was quite shaken by my unwarranted attack upon her. My form teacher felt that in those circumstances I should receive the ruler. She brought it down once across my open palm.

'Don't do it again, it's very unlike you, Clare. Now run along.'

I did.

My brother's birthday was 31 January and my mother bought him a toy plane which was remote controlled. They were playing with it in the front room as she showed him how to use the controls. As I entered the room, my mother turned the plane and deliberately flew it in my direction, it sliced my left cheek as it zoomed past. The plane turned, flying back towards my mother, then turned again in my direction. My mother lowered it as it approached me. Again it sliced my left cheek. Blood poured from the wounds. My brother laughed – he thought it was funny.

'Get out,' my mother said. 'You are not welcome in here.'

I turned and left as the plane buzzed around. In my room I examined my face. Two deep cuts had opened, exposing pink flesh. I squeezed the wounds together to stem the flow of blood and went downstairs for help. When my sister Pauline saw my injuries she ran upstairs, got the sticking plasters and she helped to patch me up.

Things settled down in our house. I kept out of Eastman's and my mother's way, although I continued to loathe Eastman. We often argued. On one occasion, when Eastman had threatened to do me serious bodily harm, Pauline contacted my father. George arrived at the house late one night and told me to pack a bag and get into the car. I did and he took me to a lady called Miss Lindsey. She had a flat at the Oval and I stayed with her for a week. She was very kind to me and I had my own bedroom. I was given a meal every day after I returned from school. She said it did not matter if I wet the bed and in fact I only wet it once while I was there. She dealt with it by simply changing the bedsheets. I said I was sorry, but she said I had no business apologising. I liked being at her flat. I missed my sisters sometimes but I was happier.

A week later I was taken home. My mother had insisted that I return because Miss Lindsey had asked her to hand over the child benefit that was due from my share of the family allowance. My mother said Miss Lindsey could keep me, but she was not getting any child benefit, and if she wanted to be 'funny' about it she only had to return me. My father took me home on a Sunday. He delivered me to the door, made sure I went inside and drove off.

In the summer of 1968 my final year at St Joseph primary school came to an end. It was a nice and friendly school and had served my sisters and me very well. Pauline and Patsy had long moved on and now it was my turn to do the same. Both my sisters before me had gone on to Sacred Heart School on Camberwell New Road. Amongst Catholics it had the best reputation in the locality, since the pupils went to church on Thursday, Friday and every Sunday. White gloves were worn at all times and a beret. The school had a fine reputation for turning out good wholesome Catholics, but not very bright Catholics.

I asked my teacher at St Joseph whether it would be possible for me to go to university from Sacred Heart. I am not at all sure where I got the idea from, but my teachers had told us that only very clever people went to university. 'My dear, a pre-condition

Ugly

to getting into the school is that you must have failed your eleven-plus exam.' I had never heard of the eleven-plus exam. I wanted to go to Notre Dame, a good Catholic grammar school. All my friends had applied to go there and so I thought that I would follow. I asked my mother where I would go to school after St Joseph.

'Sacred Heart,' she said. 'Like your sisters.'

'But I don't want to go to Sacred Heart School.'

'Oh?' said my mother. 'And where would you like to go?'

'I want to go to Notre Dame School with all my friends.'

'Why don't you want to go to Sacred Heart School?' my mother said. 'Both your sisters are there and you have in the past kicked up such a fuss about being separated from them. Why change your mind now?'

I explained that I was not changing my mind, but all my friends had applied to Notre Dame School and I was as bright as them and therefore I had a good chance of getting in.

'But, Clare,' said my mother, 'it is a grammar school for grammar-school girls. You are not a grammar-school girl. You see, you're not bright enough. If your sisters did not get in, there is no way that *you* will get in. You're stupid. Why do you think that Sacred Heart is good enough for your sisters, but not good enough for you? Why?'

But my sisters had not wanted to go to Notre Dame School, I objected. They had not considered it and this was the first time anyone had talked about it. My mother told me to get out of her sight and to stop being so awkward. I pleaded with her to consider Notre Dame School. At least if I did not get in I would still be able to go to Sacred Heart School.

'Oh,' said my mother. 'You think you're better than the rest of us, do you? Well, what are you going to tell them about the bed? How many grammar-school children do you think wet the bed? Do you think they will be able to cope with the smell? I mean, you do know that you smell, don't you? Not now and then but all the time. Come here.'

I moved towards my mother so that I was standing in front of her. She pinched my shirt between two fingers and pulled me close. She sniffed the air twice and let my shirt go.

'You see what I mean? You stink of piss! Have you smelled yourself recently? Go on – have a smell.'

She tried to bring the shirt up to my nose, but it was not possible so she put her hand behind my head and forced it towards the shirt.

'Smell,' she said. 'Tell me what you smell.' She paused. 'Piss – do you smell piss? Smell it again. We don't want to get it wrong, do we?'

I smelled my shirt; it wasn't that bad. A bit whiffy but nothing to write home about.

'Yes, it does smell,' I said, 'but I'll stop wetting the bed by then. I've got a while to go. I'm sure I can stop wetting the bed by September.'

'You're eleven, Clare, and you're *still* pissing my bed. If you didn't wake up you'd drown. You'd piss right up to your neck. I've never heard of a child to piss up to their neck. You've got a crack, not a dick. If you had a dick I could tie it down but you've got a crack. Well, if the worst comes to the worst I suppose I could always plug it.'

'Can we please try for Notre Dame?' I said. 'I would like to stay with my friends.'

'And I would like you to know that the world is not about you, Clare Briscoe. You will go to Sacred Heart like your sisters. It's good enough for them and it's good enough for you.'

That was it. We did not even try for Notre Dame. I certainly made no application to the school or sat any examination especially for it. I was offered a place at Sacred Heart to start the following term. All my friends, with the exception of Anne Cody, went to Notre Dame. My friends were school friends not home friends. Up until the end of my school days no one visited me at home. The only guest that ever turned up uninvited was Mary and she was not a friend.

When we broke up for our summer holiday, I was distraught, believing I would never see my friends again. My mother never mentioned Notre Dame again and I was too sad to bring the matter up. I was very lucky in getting a place at Sacred Heart.

When we broke up from St Joseph School, we were all happy and sad at the same time. Some of us were moving in the direction we wanted to go, others were moving in the direction they were made to follow. We promised each other to keep in touch and write during the summer holidays, but most of us knew that our good intentions would come to nothing.

The first weekend of the school holidays passed soon enough. On the following Monday my two sisters and I went off to find out where we could get our free school meals. Every summer holiday we were given special vouchers to use to get our dinner. Because we were entitled to free school dinners, a centre was open at a selected school all through the holidays. All we had to do was turn up at the agreed time, hand in our voucher and collect our school meal. We would eat it on site and then return home. It meant that children from our kind of background could be guaranteed at least one square meal every day during the holidays. Our mother was more than happy for someone else to provide us with meals.

We received another set of vouchers, for our school uniform. When they came through we had to go and select our uniform. My mother went with Pauline, Patsy and myself. This was a big day for me because I would be fitted out for the first time with the Sacred Heart uniform, which consisted of a black blazer, white shirt, grey pleated skirt, grey jumper, tie, white socks, Aertex shirt and grey knickers for PE. It sounded okay. I was excited. I cannot remember a single other occasion when I went shopping with my mother for new clothes for me.

The first thing my mother did when we got into the shop was to ask the assistant if Patsy could try on a new blazer. That was a waste of time, I thought, because Patsy had had a new one the year before. Her clothes, especially her blazer, were replaced, thanks to school vouchers, every *other* year. Because it was my first year I was entitled to new everything. It was also Pauline's turn to get a replacement jumper, skirt and blazer.

As my sisters tried on their new uniform my mother never invited me to try on my new clothes. When I asked her if I too was entitled to a new blazer, she said that I could wear Pauline's or Patsy's because both of them were a year or two old and had a few more good years' use. Since I was also entitled to a skirt and Pauline's and Patsy's did not fit me she agreed that I could try one on. I did. The white shirts that I was entitled to I got because, again, none of the old ones fitted me. I also got a new grey jumper and a beret. We all came away from the shop quite content. I had not got all my school uniform, but at least some of my clothes were new.

Two weeks before I started at Sacred Heart my mother told us to ring our father and tell him that we all needed new shoes to go back to school. He came round a few days later and gave us money to go and pick the shoes ourselves. Between us we had £60. When we informed our mother of this she suggested that she should look after the money until we were ready to shop for the shoes. The market was quite close to our house and there were a lot of shoe shops and stalls that sold trendy shoes. We could visit on Saturday or Sunday. The money was handed over and my mother quickly opened her blouse and pulled out her left bra strap. Attached to it was a bulging white handkerchief that had been secured in place by two double knots. She undid the knots, detached the handkerchief from the bra and opened it. Inside it were rolls of £20 notes, £10 notes, some jewellery and a key. She put the money we had given her into the handkerchief, tied it up and strapped it back in place against her bra.

I still needed some pens, a pencil case and school bag and a pair of white gloves. Pauline gave me her hand-me-down satchel which, although scuffed, would be fine once some polish and moisturiser had been applied. With less than a week to go I was ready to start my new school. There was one final thing to do – shop for shoes in the market. I quite liked the flat unisex shoes with the large buckle. They were a little expensive, but very popular. I asked my mother if we could have our money because we were planning on going shopping later that morning. She did not reply. I thought she had not heard me, so I asked her again. She said that I should discuss it with her in about half an hour when she had finished her tea. After about forty-five minutes I went back to the sitting room. My mother was sitting in the same place and I asked her if we could have our money as we were all waiting to go shopping.

My mother told me to follow her. She got up and went into the ante-room which was piled high with bags, clothes, old rubbish and things that did not have a home. She started to search through a number of bags, emptying the contents out onto the carpet. She did this with me tidying up as she went, until three matching pairs of shoes were standing in a row. 'Come.' She picked up the shoes and I followed her. As we walked up the stairs I heard the click of the door and knew immediately that my sisters were aware of what was happening and the fact that I had not got our money back. They had been hiding on the top landing, listening to the events unfold.

We went into the kitchen and my mother pulled out the shoebox from underneath the sink. Producing a tin of black polish and a cloth, she placed all three pairs of shoes on some newspaper on the floor and asked me which ones I preferred. I did not like any of them; they were not fashionable. If I had to choose then I supposed the middle ones. 'Those,' I said. My mother put the other two pairs to one side and set about polishing mine. I watched, unsure why she was bothering to clean up old shoes. To be fair they were nicely polished when she had finished spitting on them and rubbing them with her cloth. 'There,' she said. 'Try them on.' I pulled my sock off and slipped my right foot into the shoe. It was too small. My heel would not go in.

'Come on,' said my mother. 'Push.' I tried to do so, but it was difficult. She then removed the shoe from my foot, applied some cooking oil to the inside of the heel and asked me to try it on again. This time my foot went down.

'Now the next one,' she said. I steadied myself by holding on to the chair. She had the other shoe ready and oiled. My foot slipped in. 'That looks good,' said my mother. 'Wear them around the house, break them in slowly. Now go,' she said.

I had no opportunity to ask again for our money. Not to worry. I went upstairs to find my sisters. The shoes were a bit tight and pinched my feet. By the time I got to my sisters' room I needed to take them off. I told Four Eyes and Precious Puss that our mother had not given me the money, but I would try again later. Pauline was concerned. The shops and the market closed at one o'clock and if we wanted to have a good look around it was necessary to get the money sooner rather than later.

'Look what Mummy gave me,' I said as I went to the door and collected my newly acquired shoes.

'Where did you get those?' asked Patsy.

'Mummy gave them to me.'

'Oh,' she said, 'they are mine. I had those about six months ago – or was it a year? They are too small for me – do they fit you?'

'No,' I said. 'They are a bit tight but Mummy asked me to break them in.'

'Why did she ask you to do that?' said Pauline.

'I don't know, I didn't ask her,' I said.

We stayed upstairs for a while and then I went back down and found my mother in the bathroom. She was putting the wash on.

'Can we have our money, Mummy?' I said. 'We would like to go shopping.'

'What money?' she said.

'Our money that Dad gave us.'

'What money?'

'Our money to buy our shoes. We would like to go to the market.'

'What for?'

'We want to get our shoes for school.'

'What for?'

'What for what?' I said.

'Why do you need shoes?'

'I need shoes because I don't have any for school,' I said.

'Yes, you have,' said my mother. 'I've just given you a pair – what's wrong with them?' she said.

'When did you give me a new pair of shoes?' I said, looking around for a new box I might have missed.

'You had them on your feet a moment ago,' my mother said. 'You've got a new pair – why do you want another? Do you think that you're special? Why should you have two pairs of shoes and some pickney done have none?'

'I hadn't realised they were my *new* pair of shoes,' I said. 'And besides, it doesn't matter because we've got £60 from our dad and it belongs to us and we would like to buy ourselves some new shoes for school.'

My mother looked at me. 'Get out of my sight,' she said.

'Can I have my money?'

'I'm not going to tell you again. Get out of my sight.'

I stood my ground and put in yet another request for our money. My mother was standing by the washing machine. She put her hand in the twin tub, pulled out a wet shirt and, before I had time to move back, she slapped me across the face with it.

'You got shoes. What do you want more shoes for, you silly bitch? Get the fuck out of my sight and find something to do.'

She swung at me again but this time she missed. I darted out of the bathroom and went upstairs. After changing my wet dress I went up to my sisters' floor.

'What did she say?' Pauline asked.

'She said I've got shoes and I don't need any others.'

'Where are they?' they both said.

I pointed to the shoes on the floor. 'She's got two more pairs downstairs for you and Patsy,' I said. 'If they fit you, you'll have them.'

My sisters asked me to describe the shoes but I couldn't, except to say that they were black.

'You'll get a new pair of shoes, I think, if they don't fit you,' I said. I suggested to my sisters that they should pad their feet out with two pairs of ankle socks underneath their long socks so that their feet would be larger than normal. Once this was done they both went downstairs and asked my mother whether it was possible to go to the market. I listened on the stairs. My mother invited them both into her room and asked them to try on the shoes that she had waiting for them. Pauline started first.

'I don't think it fits,' I heard her say.

'Force your foot,' said our mother. 'Try and get your foot down.'

'No, it doesn't fit,' said Pauline. No cooking oil for Four Eyes, I thought. Patsy was next. It was hopeless – the shoes simply did not fit her feet. I heard my mother complain that she would have to fork out for new shoes.

'How much do you need for two pairs of shoes?' Pauline thought about it. 'I don't know, but I think between £13 and £15 each. If there is any change I'll bring it home.'

And so it was that my sisters were given £26 to buy two pairs of shoes to go back to school. I went with them to the market and they bought some patent-leather shoes and a very nice black pair of lace-ups with silver shoelaces. There was no point in me asking my mother for my share of the money.

The first day of school arrived and I woke up very early to the sound of my bed-wet alarm and flashing lights. There was no point in going back to bed. I was too excited. My alarm silenced, I gathered up my wet bedclothes, put them in the corner of the bathroom and had a wash. Back in my room I checked my school satchel and put my school clothes out. It was difficult unpacking all the pins that held my blouse in place and then the plastic spine had to be removed. I put my vest on, my blouse, skirt and socks. My jumper looked nice. Once I got my socks on I tried my shoes, but they still did not fit and I did not have any cooking oil. After putting on my tie I waited for everyone else to wake up. I opened my bedroom window as the smell was a bit much.

When the others woke up, it was complete disorder in our house. Pauline and Patsy had not put their school clothes out the night before and while they were hunting around getting themselves ready I waited by my bed alarm for my mother to take me to my new school. Once Pauline and Patsy were ready I got my satchel and went downstairs. My mother was in the kitchen.

'I'm ready, Mummy,' I said.

'Ready for what?'

'To go to school.'

'Well, what you waiting for? Go,' she said.

'But it is my first day at my new school.'

'And?' said my mother.

'Well, you always take us to school on our first day. You took Pauline and Patsy and Carl and Martin,' I said.

'Pickney,' she said, 'you have two sisters, they both go to the same school. They can show you the way.' She pushed past me and went upstairs, saying, 'Can you not see that I'm busy?'

'Come on, Clare,' said Pauline. 'We're ready now.'

We all left the house together and went to the bus stop. I was very conscious of the fact that I had an old school blazer on and my sisters were smart in new ones. My shoes were already hurting my feet. When we got on the bus I considered taking them off, but I wasn't sure that I would be able to get them back on. By the time we got off the bus and walked a short distance, my feet hurt so much that I was hobbling behind. We crossed the road into the school and were greeted by old friends of my sisters. I was directed into the main assembly hall while Pauline and Patsy lined up in the playground.

Mr Timmons, my new Headmaster, came into the hall and greeted all the new students and their parents. When he called out my name I stood up. 'Yes, sir,' I said.

'Who are you with?' he enquired.

'I'm on my own, sir.'

'Where are your parents?'

'My mother is at home, sir.'

'But who are you with, Clare?'

'My sisters are outside, sir, and my sister Pauline is in charge.'

He beckoned me forward and put his hand out. I moved towards him to shake his hand, but my shoes were hurting my feet so I shuffled.

'What's the matter with your feet, child?' he asked.

'Sir, I think my shoes are too small but I'm getting a new pair. My dad has given my mother some money to get me a new pair.' I shook his hand and then limped back to the rear end of the assembly room.

We were then all called again. This time we formed a line in front of the teacher who was our form teacher. I was in form 'Alpha'. My sisters were both in form Alpha so that was no surprise. My class teacher was very nice, she gave out general instructions and handed out lots of leaflets. We spent most of the first day getting to know our way around the building. At hometime my class teacher gave me a note to hand to my mother. It was in a sealed envelope and I was therefore prevented from reading it.

I waited at the school gate for my sisters and we all went home together. When we got there our mother was in the kitchen cooking. I changed my clothes and decided to make a start on my homework. As I emptied my satchel I came across the letter my form teacher had given me. I ran downstairs to the kitchen.

'This is for you,' I said.

She took it and opened it immediately. She read the contents and looked at me. 'Did you tell your teacher that I had not bought you new shoes and your father has given me money to spend on shoes for you?'

'No,' I said. 'I did not.'

'Did you tell your teacher that I had not spent the money on your shoes and I sent you to school with shoes that were too small for you?'

'No, I did not,' I said.

'Liar,' said my mother. 'You dirty little liar.' She picked up the wooden spoon and whacked it against the side of my head. I was dazed.

'First day at the new school and you bring shame on me,' she said. The following week I had some 'new shoes' that fitted perfectly. My mother had put some red kidney beans in a plastic bag and stuffed them into the old shoes and then she filled the bag with water. For a whole week she fed the beans water daily, so that the beans would swell, gradually stretching my shoes in the process. When I first put them on after the stretch, the leather was not smooth but bubbled in appearance, which looked a bit odd. It soon disappeared after a few weeks. The shoes that I had worn to school on my first day now fitted my feet just fine. They were my 'new shoes'.

7

Witchcraft

My mother was always going on about God. One day some
strange messengers arrived. There was a knock on the door and
no one moved to answer it. There was another knock, followed
by the bell which rang three times. I ran down the stairs and
opened the door, but only half-ajar at first. There were two huge
black women standing on the step. They were all done up in lots
of make-up and the most beautiful wigs I ever saw. The first lady
had a black Bette Davis wig combined with Barbie Doll curls.
These were gathered into one large curl at the back of her neck,
held in place by a big blue ribbon. On top of the wig was a black
hairnet, and on top of that was a large white Sunday hat with a
turned-up brim. The hat had been forced onto her head, and the
mass of the wig and hairnet were squeezed into the hat, which
caused the front of the wig to fall down to just above her
eyebrows. Her skirt was puke-green pleated crimplene and
she had a massive stomach. Her tights were white, which looked
beige on her black legs. She had butterfly-red lipstick, which
made her look as though she had been sucking a lollipop.

'Praise the Lord, sweet honey child,' she said. 'I call on the
mistress of the household.'

I stared at her; I had never seen anything like it. The other lady
was short and fat and also wore an ill-fitting wig. Although her
body was fat, her face was very thin with soft, caramel-colour
skin. She had pencilled in her eyebrows like Elizabeth Taylor's.
They were double thick and the pencil mark was smudged to
meet between the eyebrows; they tailed off into a sharp flick at

the ends. She was more smartly dressed than the big lady. She too had a pleated skirt but in black and white dogtooth, topped with a black jacket. The hat on her head was an altogether smaller affair. It was pulled tight over her wig and secured at the back of her head by a large hatpin. In her hand she held a magazine.

'Praise the Lord, sweet honey child. Is your mummy in?' said the tall lady.

'Who shall I say is calling?'

The smaller lady pushed her wig up with a large rubbery thumb and said, 'Tell the mistress of the household that we are messengers from God and we bring good news to this house today. Is that right, sister?'

She looked at the tall lady, who lowered her head and clasped her hands together. 'Praise the Lord, sister, praise the Lord. Yes, sweet Lord, that is right. Amen.' Both the ladies shook themselves. They looked like jellies on a plate. Then it was the tall lady's turn.

'Er, I can feel His presence – do you feel it, sister?' she said.

'I feel a presence, sister. God is with us today,' the other replied.

Then they put their hands up to shoulder height with the palms facing up. They shook like an earthquake.

'Er, honey child, go and get your mother.'

My mother was at the top of the stairs. She shouted down from the landing, asking who was at the door.

'God is at your door, mistress. Come – we have a message for you,' said the short lady.

I thought my mother would like that. She was always going on about sweet Jesus and the good Lord, but she obviously had not heard the lady because she called again: 'Who is at my door?'

I saw the magazine in the hand of the tall lady and tried to read what it said. 'Witchcraft,' I shouted. 'It's witchcraft at the door.'

The short lady blessed herself and the tall lady had a very pained expression.

'Witchcraft, honey child? No. Oh sweet Lord, bless us, bless us now, sweet Lord. Satan, get behind me. The Devil lurks behind us, honey child. Run, go get your mother.' They both started to shake again and say, 'Er.' All of a sudden they started dancing on the doorstep. They were turning in circles with their hands in fists held high above their heads, saying, 'Bless me, Lord, bless me.'

I took another opportunity to look at the magazine in the tall lady's hand. I'd read it wrong. It said *Watchtower.*

'I'm sorry,' I said to both ladies, and shouted up to my mother: 'It's *Watchtower,* not witchcraft. They've got God with them.'

'*Watchtower!* *Watchtower!*' said my mother. 'What the fuck are the Jehovah's Witnesses doing at my door? Shut the fucking door.'

Both the ladies stopped dead in their tracks. The dancing stopped immediately, and the short lady straightened her wig, pulled out a large white lipstick-stained handkerchief and patted dry her face and then smudged her lipstick. The tall lady was leaning up against the side of the door trying to catch her breath.

'Honey child,' said the short woman, 'is that the mistress of the household?'

'Yes,' I said.

'Honey child, what did she say?'

My mother shouted again and when I looked around she was standing on the top landing with her hands on her hips. From the front door we could only see her legs and her hands.

'Clare, tell them that no Christ lives in this house. I haven't got time for fucking Christ; you tell them I haven't got time for any fucking Christ. You see any vacancy on the door that says "Christ, come live here"? Now close the fucking door, you hear me? Close the fucking door!'

I turned again to face the women. The tall woman had fallen partly to her knees against the side of the door. She looked as though she was praying. She was certainly sweating profusely. The short woman had removed her hat. Her wig was well and truly down now, midline with her eyes. The hat was in her right hand and she was using it as if it was a tennis racket. Forehand and backhand. Lobbing invisible balls back into the house.

'Save me, Lord, save me. Bless this house, and contain the evil spirits that are within.' She looked a pretty sight, one hand on her wig, the other batting evil spirits back into our house. 'Sister,' she said to the tall lady, 'help me. Rise up, sister, like the Holy Spirit; rise.' She continued to bat with her hat as the tall lady started to pick herself up off the doorstep. 'Help me, sister, help. Are you filled with the presence of God?'

'Sister, I's a coming, I's a coming,' replied the tall woman.

'Close my fucking door! No Christ lives here.'

The short woman looked over at her friend and said, 'Sister Isis, don't pray – rise. Help me to do the Lord's work this day.'

The tall one got a handkerchief out from the waistband of her crimplene skirt and started to dab her brow, but as she did so she took a complete imprint of her black charcoal eyebrows. When she dabbed above the eyebrows it created another brow. She did this three times over the right eye and again with the left. To me, she resembled something out of a science-fiction movie. Her rows of eyebrows now went up to just beneath her wig.

Eventually, she put her handkerchief away and said, 'I's a coming, sister. I's a coming.' She looked up to the sky and said, 'Lord, I have today found my vocation. Give me strength to do your work.' She then put her hands on the pavement and pushed her bottom up into the air first. As she did this her wig and hat fell off and landed at my feet.

'I's a coming, sister. I's a coming,' she said as she got to her feet.

'Sister,' said the short woman, 'help me. God's work must be done.' She was still lobbing invisible balls back into our house.

My mother, having shouted out, decided I had not closed the door quickly enough and started hollering: 'I's a coming too. I's a fucking coming.' My mother's head appeared within view as she stormed down the stairs. The short lady looked up and took a few steps back towards the pavement and I opened the door to its full width.

'Step no more, Satan, unless you wish to approach a servant of God. Sister Isis, rise this day and help me to keep God's dignity,' she said.

My mother stood in the doorway and watched as Sister Isis put her wig back on and looked about herself for her hatpin. The short one had stopped playing tennis and was looking up to the sky with her eyes rolling in her head.

'Give me strength, sweet Jesus,' prayed Isis. 'Do not desert me now in my hour of need.' She embraced her hat and took it to her bosom. Her pretty ribbon had fallen from her hair. It was on the pavement, together with a handkerchief stained with red lips, lots and lots of them. My mother looked at both of them; the tall lady was unable to fit her wig back under her hat and the short lady looked like she was on a mission.

'Jesus fucking Christ,' said my mother. 'Two duppies doing the Lord's work.'

At the mention of the word 'duppies' Pauline bolted down the stairs and was by my mother's side in a flash.

'Where is the ghost, Mummy?' she asked.

'Look,' said my mother, 'duppie and duppie; I don't know who is frightening who.'

The tall lady touched the short lady on the arm. 'Sister,' she said, 'in the face of adversity persevere.'

The short one came out of her trance-like state and started fanning herself with her *Watchtower* magazine. She straightened herself, pulled her shoulders back, pushed her belly forward and approached my mother. She took two steps forward and then stopped suddenly as though there was an invisible wall between her and my mother.

'Mistress of the house, we can save you. Take God into your heart today. Do not be afraid just because you walk in the Valley of Darkness.'

My mother looked at them and then back at my sister and me. 'What time is it?' she asked.

'It's God's hour,' said the tall one.

'It's eight fifteen,' I said.

'Eight fifteen!' my mother repeated. 'That early! Did you want to save me at eight fifteen in the morning? Clare, shut the door.'

'Do not resist God,' said the short one. 'You will never walk in the Valley of Darkness.'

'Embrace God,' said the tall one.

My mother stomped back upstairs. 'Resist God!' she said over her shoulder. 'I tell you what – if I ever do walk in your valley, you will know all about it. You had better not bump into *me* in the dark. Close the door, Clare. I'm not going to tell you again.'

As I started to close the door, both the women were blessing themselves.

'Honey child,' said the short one. 'Have you found God?'

'I'm a Catholic,' I said. 'This has nothing to do with me.'

'Honey child, know your God.'

'I think I do,' I said firmly and closed the door. I made my way back upstairs. As I got to the first landing my mother had busied herself in the kitchen. Pauline was on the next landing up, just outside my bedroom. She had a pillow case over her head and was walking around with her arms outstretched.

'I'm a duppie,' she said. 'I'll find you in the Valley of Darkness.'

'I'm a duppie,' I said, 'and I walk in the Valley of Darkness.' I had my hands on my hips and I started to flick my hips from side to side. 'I is coming to get you, sister.' I heard her laugh and then I felt a blow to the back of my head that forced me forwards and I fell onto the stairs. I instinctively put my hands out as I turned to face my mother. She had the wooden spoon in her right hand.

'I am not a duppie so go and get ready for school.' Four Eyes had disappeared.

I was not happy with my mother. The blow stung my head and without thinking I said, 'When I have children I will never hit them.'

'What did you say? When you have what?'

'I will never hit my children.'

'What, you, you want pickney, you of all people want pickney, when you wet the fucking bed?' My mother started to laugh and then she clicked her fingers with one hand and slapped her thigh with the other using the wooden spoon. 'Well, bring them. Come. Bring them. You must have heard me say I want to be a fucking grandmother. Bring them, come. Before you turn me into a grandmother, I'll string up every single one of them from the nearest lamp post. It will save you the trouble of beating them, you fucking parasite. Now tell me, you going to get ready for school or you want to stay here and argue with me? Tell me quick because I have things to do.'

She was fidgeting around with the wooden spoon so I got up and backed away from her up the stairs and into my room. So much for messengers from God.

All my life I have been plagued by a recurring dream. I might be lying on the floor reading a book or just resting, when it comes. I'm about five or six, possibly seven, and I'm always doing the same thing – always standing in the same position. I must be about three feet tall and I am wearing a smock-type dress which is too big for me. The dress has my usual Peter Pan collar. The material is a plaid pattern and is casually gathered at the yoke to form a series of informal pleats which end just below my knee.

There are a number of buttons from the neck running the full length of the dress, which is a dull mustard yellow with vertical and horizontal stripes. The vertical stripes are about a quarter of an inch thick and the horizontal stripes are thinner still. The stripes are dark grey or green and they overlap at right angles to form a series of oblong boxes. In between every other stripe there is a faint line in off-white that gives the plaid or tartan-like appearance.

In the dream, I am always at the bottom of some stairs and facing them, with my back to the wall behind me. There are one, two, three, four, five, six, seven steps. At the top of them is a door and I can usually see a sliver of light beneath it. Sometimes, if the light outside is off, then it is not possible to see the sliver. I'm standing there, just waiting. Waiting in the cellar. I don't cry any more and then suddenly my feet rise and I'm about six inches off the floor with my arms away from my side. I don't know how long I stay in that position; after a while I return to the ground.

I am quite certain that when I was in the cellar in real life my feet remained on the floor, the sensation of being lifted from the ground is only in my dreams.

The first time I was locked in the cellar, my mother had asked me to go down and get some potatoes. She gave me a pot to put them in. We kept a sack of potatoes in the cellar because it was much cooler there than anywhere else in the house. Taking the pot, I approached the cellar door, pulled back the bolt, turned the light on and went carefully down the flight of stairs to the bottom, holding on to the side of the wall. The sack of potatoes was at the far end of the cellar, together with other household rubbish. I collected about ten potatoes in the pot and turned round to make my way back. When I was in the middle of the cellar I saw my mother's legs at the top of the stairs. She suddenly flicked the light switch off then moved backwards and the door to the cellar swung shut as I ran up the stairs. I heard the bolt slide home. I asked her to let me out, but she just walked away. I hadn't done anything wrong that I knew of. I started crying. In a panic I banged on the door and she shouted, 'If you know what's good for you, you will shut the fuck up.'

For a time I sat waiting with my back to the door. At least I could switch the light back on. After a while I heard the door being unbolted. I rushed out of the cellar only to see the back of my mother disappearing up the stairs. I went after her and asked whether she knew that she had locked me in the cellar. She told me to get out of her sight. It was the first of many occasions that I was trapped in the cellar by her. Eventually, whenever my mother asked me to go into the cellar I went with one of my sisters or brothers because she never locked them in there.

It was about three feet long and two to three inches wide. I had caught her with it one night when my bed-wet alarm went off; it was the night I saw my mother doing something strange on the stairs. This time I had managed to jump out of the bed to shush the alarm. It was silent in seconds. I pulled out the electric contact tab and waited. No one approached my room. Then I heard a yanking noise, as though someone was tugging at a resisting object. I remained rooted to the spot, listening. When I was sure my mother was not coming to my room to investigate, I tiptoed towards the door. It was just seven paces to the door. After the second pace, I waited. Another two paces. The noise was coming in my direction. I had to decide whether to go back four paces to bed and pretend to be asleep, or stay where I was. The noise stopped. I waited, ready to make my move. The footsteps turned left on the first half-landing and went into the kitchen. I stayed where I was. I could hear drawers sliding on their runners. After a while, the footsteps went back downstairs. There was a slight pause and the yanking noise continued. It was, I thought, a very odd noise, one that I could investigate from the safety of the banisters.

I opened my door just a little and then more. Getting down on my hands and knees, I crawled towards the banisters. When I was about three inches away, I peeped over the landing between the spindles. My mother seemed to be having trouble with the stair carpet. In her right hand was an instrument like a spatula, which she had inserted into the vertical fall of the step to help her prise away the carpet. She was yanking at the carpet on step three, which was resisting the spatula.

At this point my mother put the tool down on step four, rubbed her hands together and went back downstairs so she was now standing in the hall. She then took hold of the end of the stair carpet, held it firmly with both hands and with one sharp pull detached the carpet from steps four and five. She then retrieved the spatula tool and using the handle she inserted it into the plank of wood which formed step three and teased it out. The plank was about thirty inches by three to four inches wide. There was a natural crack in the wood and, with a modest amount of pressure, she used the spatula to split the plank in two. The largest part of the split plank was placed back into the step and the smallest plank was split again. After part of it was used to beat me, I called this the split-split plank. The smaller part of the split-split plank was reinserted into the stairs. The larger part of the split-split plank was put behind my mother's back as she worked. She leaned it against the wall. I had thought about going back to my room, but I was not in anyone's way and no one knew that I was there. Besides, I wanted to know what my mother was doing with the step. I watched as she moved gracefully and with one movement rolled the carpet back into position across steps four, three, two and one. It looked like a conveyor belt without steps. At this point she kicked the smaller split-split plank into the L bend where vertical meets horizontal. She then threw the carpet down and it immediately creased into place. With a few more kicks, some amounting to a light tap and some more intense, she put the carpet back exactly in place.

This exercise was repeated with each step and when my mother got to step four she jumped on it once and then again. She stretched up on her tiptoes and then back down again, securing the carpet. Why my adult mother would want to do tiptoes on step four was something which I found quite puzzling, even irritating. She was not a child; she was a grown-up and she never played tiptoes with me.

As I was thinking about this, my mother retrieved the larger part of the split-split plank, examined it and then quite suddenly brought it down across her hand. Then, as though not satisfied, she smacked her own bottom with it. I realised at once this was a bad omen for me.

8

A Good Catholic Girl

1968

One of the true delights of being a Catholic is not just that you are baptised and can go to a good Catholic school; it is the whole way of life. You have a sense of belonging. All children in Catholic school take their First Confession and then their First Holy Communion. First Confession is really preparation for your First Communion. At First Confession we confess our sins to a priest who is seated in a dark box, he on one side, the child on the other. He cannot see you and you cannot see him, but you can hear each other very well. It is always a good idea to confess sins, otherwise you get burdened down with them. My First Confession went very well. I entered our church, blessed myself and went into the confessional box. I leaned down and when I was sure that the priest was listening to me I started.

'Bless me, Father, for I have sinned.'

'Pray, child,' said the priest. 'What are your sins?'

'Well, Father, I wet the bed all the time. I told lies to my mother when I said I had not deliberately wet the bed. I punched my sister in the back and I called her names.'

'Such as what, child?' he asked.

'I called her Bottle Rim and Old Four Eyes.'

'Why bottle rim?' the priest wanted to know.

'Because she has eyes like a squirrel and her glasses look like the bottom of bottles.'

'Do you have any more sins to confess?'

'Yes. I don't like my mother and I would like to run away, Father.'

'You must honour your father and your mother, child.'

'It is not possible, Father, to honour my mother. I know that I have committed a sin and broken one of the Ten Commandments, but I don't want to honour my mother because she doesn't honour me.'

'You must try to be more forgiving, more charitable. That always brings rewards with it. Are there any other sins that you want to confess?'

'Yes, Father. I tried to commit suicide once but it didn't work.'

'You know that Catholics are forbidden from taking their own lives?'

'Yes, Father.'

'And you know that you will be denied everlasting happiness?'

'Yes, Father.'

'And you know that the Kingdom of Heaven will be denied to you?'

'Yes, Father.'

'Then I forgive you your sins. Your penance is four Hail Marys.'

'Thank you, Father.'

I got up and left the confessional box and went to the front of the church where I sat close to God and said four Hail Marys. I felt better, having confessed my sins.

It was only a matter of weeks before I made my First Holy Communion. I was looking forward to it so much. It was the only time that I would get to wear a white dress with a veil, white socks, white gloves and white shoes. The entire class of girls and boys were to take Holy Communion all dressed up in white. I had loved my sisters' Holy Communion. They both looked as though they were getting married, except that the dresses were knee-length rather than to the ground. We had practised time and time again and we had all prepared ourselves for a Catholic way of life. We had gone to Mass every Sunday for the past two months. We had all gone to church on Friday for ever and we had learned our words. We also attended special lessons at school to prepare ourselves.

My two sisters had worn the most beautiful dress. In fact, Patsy's dress was a hand-me-down from Four Eyes; my mother had kept the dress carefully in a huge plastic clothes bag. It had silk and lace on it. Beneath the dress were at least seven layers of taffeta and petticoats and then, to make sure the dress stuck out away from the body, more lace was attached to the underskirt from the waist to the hem. It was like Cinderella's ballgown. Tiny pale pink roses were sewn about six inches up from the hem and about twelve inches apart. The sleeves of the dress were short and puffed up, secured into place by white ribbon. Down the front of the dress were two double rows of buttons, which did not open and close, but were the most beautiful mother-of-pearl white buttons you ever did see. Either side of the buttons were two lines of stitched decorated gauze made of the finest silk thread in brilliant white.

The veil was another matter altogether. It covered the entire head and was held in place by a pretty silver headband full of whitish stones. Around the edge of the veil was a loose snake stitch, entwined in a very subtle figure of eight. The white ankle socks turned over to display a frill of lace about half an inch thick. The shoes were white strap-ups with a heel of not more than two inches. All the mothers cried when their daughters walked up the aisle. All the dads braced themselves and nodded in their daughters' direction.

Now it was my turn. In less than a week's time I would make my First Communion. My practice runs at school had gone well. All the girls in my class were happy and excited about the event. I asked my mother what I would be wearing for my First Communion. She ignored me. I asked her when it might be possible to buy my white shoes and socks. My sisters' shoes and socks might not fit me and, besides, I did not know whether she still had them. My mother told me to find something to do. About four days before my Holy Communion I found her in the sitting room, drinking peppermint tea.

'I'm making my First Communion this week,' I said.

'So?'

'I need a white dress.'

'And?'

'Well, I need a white dress and socks, shoes and a veil. I think I have got some white gloves.'

'And?'

'And I was just thinking that I need to sort my dress out and if I get ready now it will be easier nearer the time.'

'And?'

'Well, is it possible to try the dress on just to make sure it fits?'

'I have your dress,' she said.

'What if it does not fit?'

'It will fit.'

'Well, I don't have a veil.'

'I have a veil.'

'Is that the one Pauline and Patsy wore?'

'I have a veil.'

'Mummy, I don't have any shoes.'

'Really.'

'Well, I don't have any white shoes.'

'Really.'

'Yes, and I don't have any socks.'

'Really. There are quite a few white ones knocking around, I'm sure. You can find a white pair.'

'But I need a new white pair.'

'Really.'

'Mummy, can I try my dress on?'

'Go away, go on – out.'

'Well, I just want to try my dress on. What if it doesn't fit?'

'It will fit. I've told you.'

'But I won't know until I've tried it on.'

'It will fit. Now go away.'

'When can I buy my white shoes?'

'You're beginning to irritate me – *now go away*.'

'Will you be coming to my First Communion?'

'Don't be silly.'

'Well, what shall I do now?'

'There is a lot you can do. Go away for a start. Go and clean the house. You're carrying on as if God wants to commune with you – you of all people. You are so ugly. Have you looked in the mirror recently? You must have jumped out of your skin. Look at those lips. You didn't get them from my side of the family. Dunlop grip – made to stick to any surface. God, you're so ugly, with your shock-absorbent rubber lips. Well, you're not going to stick to me. Why don't you use them to clear the blocked sink? Plunger lips. The more rubber the merrier. Now get out of my sight and don't let me have to tell you again.'

I went to tell Pauline what had happened.

'Don't worry,' my sister said. 'She would not have gotten rid of the Holy Communion dress we used. There are too many of us. It would cost Mummy a fortune if she had to buy a new one every time one of us took Holy Communion.'

I left it at that. There was really nothing I could do. I had some dinner and decided not to drink anything before I went to bed but it did not do any good. I did wet the bed. I think I must have been a bit worried about my Holy Communion. My bed-wet alarm went off four times in the night and I swear to God I had not wet the bed four times. The first occasion I was awake. I had no idea I was wetting the bed until it suddenly occurred to me that the noise in the background was actually my alarm. I jumped out of bed, threw the covers on the floor and ripped the sheets off the bed-wet alarm. That failed to silence it so I ripped the undersheet off the bed and thumped the alarm hard, twice. Then I waited. No footsteps on the stairs. Not even my mother was prepared to believe that I would piss all over my bed when I was wide awake. What, just to get a beating? No, I would never do that. I was in the clear. Clearie was in the clear for a change. Well done me.

The house was actually very quiet. My sisters were upstairs somewhere. My mother was downstairs and I was stuck with a bed and an alarm that would get me into trouble at the drop of a hat. I turned my sheets upside down and folded the wet patch back on itself so that there was no contact with the steel gauze sheets. The undersheet I folded in half and put back onto the bed. It was not too bad. I just got into bed and fell asleep.

The next day was a school day. I got up early, had a wash, had some breakfast and followed my sisters out of the house. School was good. My teachers thought that I had untapped potential, but suspected I was lazy. I was full of excuses.

'Oh, miss, I didn't have time – sorry about the homework. Oh, miss, I was doing the washing-up, the drying-up, washing sheets, sweeping the stairs, cooking' – all sorts of excuses, every single one true, but Miss thought that they were the sort that a very imaginative and active mind could call upon when required to deal with the complete failure to return homework on time. Clare was certainly capable of spinning a yarn, involving all too often Fairy Liquid, yellow plastic gloves and a brush. What was needed was less housework and more homework.

Two days before my First Communion we all went to church to practise for the event. We were expected to walk in twos, in our dresses, from the assembly hall at school to the church next door and finally take our place in the pews at the front of the church. Parents and other family members would have a place reserved. However, I still had not seen my dress or any of the other necessary items. I went to my mother and again found her in the sitting room.

'Do you think I could have my dress tomorrow?' I said. 'It's just that we are running out of time and it would be nice to try on my clothes the day before.'

My mother pointed at the wardrobe and told me to take out the veil hanging up. I stepped past her and opened the wardrobe. Inside, squashed among all the other clothes, were the veil and a dress that had a plastic covering to protect it. In the bottom of the wardrobe was a pair of white shoes, flat with straps and buckles that went across the front of the feet, and tucked inside the shoes were a pair of white gloves and a pair of socks.

'I'll try them on,' I said.

'No,' said my mother. 'You can put them on when you need to.'

I put them back in the wardrobe, thanked my mother and went off to do my homework.

The next day I went into my mother's room to collect my clothes. I took them all up to my bedroom. The shoes fitted me, as did the white socks and the veil, which was the one my sisters had worn before me. Then I removed the plastic covering from the dress. Unlike the shoes and veil, the dress did not look familiar. It was not as I remembered it. I took the dress off the hanger, turned it over and undid the buttons at the back. The dress had scalloped sleeves. It was quite pretty, but it was the wrong colour. A very long time ago it had certainly been white, but the material was now a grubby off-white, as though the dress had been washed with the wrong colour garments. There were several greyish underskirts and the rose petals on the bodice were crushed and faded. At the back of the dress was a large circle, as though someone had sat in a puddle and stained the dress or as if someone had wet themselves. Some of the fabric around the sleeves and the hem was tatty and worn.

I tried the dress on. It only just fitted me across the chest and was far too long, coming to well below my knees. When I put the veil on my head, the dress looked even worse: it was obvious that the veil was white and the dress was not. Whereas the underbody of the skirt should have been a bit puffed out, it was completely flat. I went upstairs to see my sisters. When I entered the room, their mouths dropped.

'Where did you get that?' asked Pauline.

'It's my First Communion dress.'

'But where did you get it?'

'Out of Mummy's wardrobe.'

'Where did she get it?'

'She didn't say.'

'Looks like she got it at a jumble sale,' sniffed Pauline. 'You're not really going to wear that to your First Communion, are you? Go and ask her for our dress.'

I kept the dress and veil on and went downstairs to my mother's room. I knocked and when she answered I opened the door and went in. I spoke through the veil. 'Mummy, I think you've given me the wrong dress.' I turned round in front of her.

'I don't think so,' she said.

'This is not the dress Pauline and Patsy wore.'

'Who said it is? This isn't their dress; it is your dress.'

'But it's stained. It's not white. Look at it.'

My mother looked at the dress. 'It's not stained. It's a little off-colour, but it will do.'

'Why can't I wear the dress Pauline and Patsy wore?'

'Because it's not yours.'

'But this dress is not new. Where did you get it?'

'The second-hand shop.'

'Why?'

'Because you needed a dress.'

'Not this one. It has to be white. It's not white.'

'Well, I'm sure no one will notice.'

'I can't wear this.'

'It's the only dress you have so you have no choice.'

'Where's the other dress?'

'It's not for you.'

'This one has got a stain down the back as if someone has wet themselves in it. It has gone all yellow.'

'Well, maybe the previous owner had the same trouble that you have. Now if you have finished I have things to do.'

I returned upstairs where my sisters were waiting for me.

'Mummy bought it at a second-hand shop,' I told them. 'I have to wear it tomorrow.'

No one said anything. I took the dress and veil off and put them both under protective wrapping in my wardrobe. Then I went to bed. I do not know if it was excitement or fear that made me set off the alarm.

On the day of the service I got up bright and early, washed myself, brushed my teeth and combed my hair. I got dressed in my grey dress, white shoes, socks and veil, and put my gloves on.

My prayer book was in my white bag. My sisters and I made our way to school on the bus. When we arrived I went into the assembly hall and waited with the communicants. I sat by the window, conscious of the fact that my dress was not quite white. I had tried to wear my veil as long as possible so that it covered most of the dress.

'Hi, Clare,' said Anne.

'Hello, Anne,' I said, not looking up.

'That's an unusual dress, Clare.'

'Yes, it is.'

'What colour is it?'

'I don't know. I think it should be white.'

'Oh,' said Anne. 'Mine's white.'

I stayed put. There was no point in walking around and exposing my dress. I remained with my back to the wall and my veil spread out until we were called by the teacher to form a line to walk over to the church. We each paired up with our partner and off we went. I felt like the Emperor with no clothes – everyone was looking at me. In church we took our place at the front. All the mummies and daddies were there. My sisters were there, but Mummy was busy. During the service I wasn't thinking about God, only about my awful dress. We all went back to the school for a sandwich and some orange juice. Everyone else was happy and laughing and congratulating one another. I stood on my own in the corner.

When I got home I went up to my room, took my dress off and placed it back on the hanger and in the plastic cover. I took it downstairs to my mother.

'Mummy, what do you want me to do with this?'

'Just throw it down there,' she said, pointing at the floor by the side of the chair.

'Do you want me to hang it up?'

'No, just throw it down there,' she repeated. 'I'll tidy it up later.'

I thought possibly I had not heard my mother correctly, but as I was waiting she pulled the dress out of my hand and threw it on the floor.

'Now what's next?' she said.

'What about the veil?' I said.

'What about it?' she said.

'Where do you want it?'

She half turned in my direction. 'I just want it,' she said.

'I had a nice day today,' I said.

'Really,' said my mother. 'Close my door on the way out, will you?'

'I made my First Communion today,' I said.

'I would never have guessed,' my mother said sarcastically. 'Now – out.'

'It was a pity you were too busy to come.'

'Out.'

I went.

9

I Take the Law into My Own Hands

1969

By the time I was about twelve, my relationship with Eastman was at an all-time low. During one argument, he had punched me and I punched him back. He grabbed me and I hit him in the stomach and stamped on his giant feet. When he came after me, my mother was by his side. We met up in my room and started to struggle. He took his belt from around his waist and hit me twice in the face with it and then he punched me. The belt had a large bronze buckle.

As he raised it to hit me again my mother said, 'No, not her face, Eastman, not her face. You want police come take me? Lord God. Police are go come take me to jail. Jesus Christ, jailhouse for me tonight. Eastman, not her face – what wrong with you? You want jailhouse? You want jail? Well, me and you are not going to share a cell at no jailhouse.'

She grabbed the belt and Eastman took a swinging kick at my legs. Both of them left together.

School was good. Home was bad. One day I came back and did the cleaning, swept the stairs and had a fight with Eastman. He was in the kitchen and as he walked past me I muttered, 'Stupid fool.' He heard and thumped me. I turned round and hit him back. He shouted for my mother and when she came into the kitchen he told her his side of the fight. My mother did not ask me for my side. She boxed my ears and punched my upper arms.

'You little bitch, you've got too much mouth. Ignore her, Eastman. Clare will get you into trouble – leave her alone.'

'Yes,' I said. 'Why don't you leave me alone, you stupid man? You can't even read.'

He came over to me. 'Say what, say what? Go on – say it, you ugly black bitch. You think I'm your father, you fucking shithouse?'

'Don't call *me* a shithouse. If anyone's a shithouse, it's you! Look at you! Big man like you, so stupid you can't read. If I cooked your name in the frying pan you would eat it because you would not recognise it, you stupid fool.'

'You calling me a fool?' he said and removed the cigarette from his mouth. 'You calling me a fool?'

'No, Eastman, I'm not calling you a fool. I'm calling you a *stupid* fool.'

My back was against the work surface and my hands were both on the table in front of me. Eastman took the cigarette in his right hand and said, 'So I'm a fool, am I? All right, we'll see who the fool is,' and with that he stubbed the cigarette out on the back of my right hand. 'Who is the fool now?' he said. 'Er?'

I punched him and went to find my mother, who was in the sitting room. I knocked on the door and she said I could enter. 'Mummy, look what Eastman has done. He stamped out his cigarette on my hand.' I showed her where a circular area of flesh had been removed from my right hand. By now the wound was bleeding.

'Get your hand away from me, and clear off,' she said.

'But he stamped his cigarette out on me,' I said.

'Didn't you hear me? Get your hand out of my face. Go on, fuck off. Did you wet my bed last night, you fucking tramp? Look at you! Get out of my sight.' She turned away and then she shouted: 'P, P – quick, P.'

Pauline came running downstairs, passed me at the door and said, 'Yes, Mummy?'

'Make me some peppermint tea, dear, I've got a little heartburn.'

'Yes, Mummy.' She went away round the back to make some tea. I waited for some response from my mother.

'Well, what are you going to do about it? Look at my hand.'

My mother got up slowly, walked towards me, pushed me out of the door and closed it.

'Who the fool is now?' said Eastman. 'You think your mammy going to beat me, you black bitch?'

'Eastman, why don't you go and read a book?'

I reported the burn to my dad, George, and showed him my hand a few weeks later. He said he would deal with it, but I am not sure that he ever did. The burn scabbed over and then the scab fell off leaving a circular shiny scar patch. It was a constant reminder that Eastman could do no wrong in our house.

After that the atmosphere in the house was always hostile. Eastman and I continued to clash and my mother took his side. She was so sick of me that there was no point in reporting anything to her. She did not want to know.

My bed-wetting was by now beyond help and the beatings made things worst. My mother regularly stored my wet bed-clothes in plastic bags, double-knotted to keep the moisture contained. When she remembered, she would put them back on my bed. I now slept with the window open so if I wet the bed at least some of it might dry during the night. On other occasions I would sneak into her room and punch holes in the plastic bags in a vain attempt to assist the drying process. Life continued as normal.

One day, Eastman and I had a particularly bad fight. We were both close to the window on the ground floor and as we struggled he caught my chin, pushing my head through the glass.

My mother momentarily froze and then screamed: 'Lord God, Eastman, what you do?'

Eastman lowered his fist and took a step back away from me.

'Sweet Lord, what has Eastman done? Good God, Eastman, what you do?'

I was dazed and was busy brushing the glass out of my hair when specks of blood bubbled up on my hand. Eastman panicked and was removed from the room; my mother pulled him upstairs. I got my coat and left the house and went to find my dad. Both my eyes were badly swollen and a bead of blood had formed at the top of my forehead. I walked from Sutherland Square to 215 Camberwell New Road. My father was not there, but one of his tenants drove me to 41 Offley Road. Blood streamed down my face. Broken glass glistened in my hair. George took one look at me and went to the cellar to retrieve his axe. He put it in the car and asked me what had happened. I told him that Eastman had had a fight with me and pushed my head through a window. I then said that I was going to deal with it in the morning and it was not necessary for him to get involved. That night I stayed with George.

The next day, Monday, I asked Dad to drop me off at Camberwell Green Magistrates' Court. I entered the building and went to the first floor. The sign above the window said *Any Enquiries*. I pressed the bell and a lady appeared.

'Hello,' she said. 'What can I do for you?'

'My stepfather keeps abusing me and I was just wondering whether I could take out some action against him.'

'How long ago was the abuse?' she said.

'Yesterday – it was yesterday,' I said.

'Oh well, that's all right. We're in time. You can take out a private prosecution. I'll just get the forms.' She disappeared and returned with the forms that I needed and helped me to fill them in. I'm not sure whether I paid a fee, but I certainly signed a lot of documents. No one ever asked me where my stepdad was, or my mother.

'Okey dokey,' she said. 'He'll be notified within seven days and you will both have to return to court on the date on the summons and then you can tell the Magistrate what you want.'

I left court and returned home. I had seven days before Eastman would receive his summons. I decided not to tell my dad what I had done.

The seven days passed quickly and the letter arrived. But, because Eastman was unable to read, my mother opened it and read it to him.

'Oh my good Lord God, Jesus Christ, Eastman, Clare are go

take you to the courthouse. Jesus fucking Christ, what she do now? Lord God, where is the pussy? Jesus fucking Christ, Eastman are go jail,' said my mother.

'What me do? What me do? She are go take me to court for assault? Assault, what, who assault she? Carmen, you see me assault she? Is she assault me? Wait – she kick me on my big corn.'

They both came into my room, my mother waving the letter and Eastman pretending to read it over her shoulder.

'So you and Eastman in the courthouse,' said my mother.

'You know how long me live in this country and me never go to courthouse and now me go to courthouse because she bring me,' said Eastman. 'You are go take me to government court-house.'

'Lord God,' said my mother, 'Eastman are go jail.'

'Me not going to jail. You know me not going to government courthouse. Not me,' said Eastman, and he shivered.

'What you going to do, Eastman?' I said. 'Put my head through another window? Save your reasons until we go to court and if you touch me again I'm going back to tell them, so you can do what you want.'

'You cheeky bitch,' said Eastman. He took a step in my direction.

'Eastman, don't touch her,' my mother warned him. 'You will get yourself in trouble. Leave her.'

'Go on, Eastman, why *don't* you hit me?' I goaded him. 'I'm going back to court anyway so I can tell them while I'm there.'

My mother pulled Eastman out of my room. Neither of them bothered me at all during the period while we waited to go to court.

On the Wednesday I put on my school uniform and made my way to the court. My father was waiting outside. My sisters had told him what was going on.

'You all right, Clearie?' he said to me.

'Yes, I am and I don't want you to come in.' I was about to get into trouble and if my mother thought that I had hatched a plan with my dad, I would be in trouble big time. This was between me and Eastman.

The case was called on. 'Briscoe and Eastman,' said the usher. I walked into court. Eastman appeared from the side room to the left; he was with my mother. I stood in the well of the court. The Magistrate was a short fat man with a red face and a long parting in his hair that went from the front to the very back of his head. The Magistrate told me that it was my application and I should tell him something about the case. I explained to the Magistrate who I was and the fact that Eastman was my stepfather. I showed the burn on my hand and told him of the time when he beat me up and he put my head through the glass window.

'What do you want?' the Magistrate said.

'I want it to stop,' I said. 'I'm tired of it, sir. I just want it to stop.'

'Anything else?' he said.

'No, sir, but I would like to go into a home.'

'Let's deal with one matter at a time,' he said. 'Mr Garfield St Clements Eastman – what do you say about this application?'

Eastman said that it was an accident that my head went through the window.

'What do you say about the assaults?' said the Magistrate.

'Assault, what's that? Judge, me never assault she.'

'Mr Eastman,' said the Magistrate, 'I'll tell you what I'm going to do. I'm going to bind you over to be of good behaviour for the next twelve months. What that means is if you touch Miss Briscoe again within that period I'll send you to prison. Do I make myself clear?'

'Yes,' said Eastman.

'And do you agree to be bound over in the sum of £200 to be of good behaviour?'

'Yes,' said Eastman, 'but me no have no money.'

'Well,' said the Magistrate, 'don't worry about that. You only lose that sum if you commit an offence within that period. Now go home, Mr Garfield St Clements Eastman, and remember, do not touch her. You are both free to go after you have signed the register.'

We left court, my mother taking Eastman's arm. I met my dad outside; he was waiting for me in his Capri. I explained what the Magistrate had said.

No more beatings for the next twelve months! I was free at last! George drove me to school. I arrived late and made my apologies. For lunch we had fishcake, peas and chips. There was semolina and jam for afters. It had been a very good day. Eastman was terrified at the thought of the jailhouse that was waiting for him if he touched me. My mother was worried about what my aunts Ina and Josephine might think. It would bring shame on her if they thought that she had allowed her man to take liberties with me. Worse still if they read about it in the *South London Press*. Anyway, I told Mary all about it.

About a day or two later my aunts arrived with another message from God. I recognised Josephine's posh voice on the other side of the front door. I could hear them speaking as I stood in the hallway.

'Oh Lord,' sighed Josephine. 'I *do* hope the house is not in a mess.'

'You shouldn't say that,' said Ina. 'God gives everyone their circumstances to live. Carmen has not chosen her circumstances.'

'Oh Lord, Carmen really should do better,' said Josephine. 'I do hope we've not come all this way for nothing.'

I was about to open the door but decided not to, so I moved away and went quietly round to the back of the house. They knocked again and I ignored them. I did not like the pair of them. Ina was just too religious and Josephine thought that she owned the world.

'Who goes there?' said Eastman, finally coming to investigate. There was no answer. 'Who the body is? Speak now or you not coming in this house, that's for sure. Who the body is? Speak.'

'Oh, Eastman, sweetie, it's Jo and Ina.'

He opened the door; my mother was half peeping out of the sitting room.

'Is you?' said Eastman.

'Hello, Eastman,' said Josephine, 'and is you too.'

'Praise the Lord, Eastman,' said Ina.

He stepped aside to let them in, exposing Josephine and Ina to my mother's gaze.

'New wig,' said my mother, looking at Josephine.

Josephine thought she was real class. Her wig was always well pinned down onto her head. Today she was Greta Garbo.

'Oh, it's a little something I picked up.' She flicked a curl out of the way. Her false eyelashes had a touch of glitter about them. She wore a brightly coloured blouse, large plastic flower, earrings, a white pleated skirt and gold stiletto shoes. The cocktail was completed by a large straw hat and pink lipstick that matched her long pink false nails.

'Hello, Carmen, how are you?' she said, stepping over the threshold.

'Let me look good,' said my mother, marvelling at her appearance. 'Come in, too, Ina. How is God?'

'God's in His heaven,' Ina replied.

Ina really spent too much time at church, when she should have been at home with her children. She was never there, always preferring to be in God's house. Although she had four children despite the fact she had never been married, she did not allow her children to visit or play with us because we were sinners. My mother said *she* was the sinner.

'God be with you, Carmen,' said Ina.

'Is that right?' my mother laughed. 'I thought that He was always with you.'

Ina was a large woman with mustard-coloured skin and short Afro hair. She did not wear make-up. She did not pluck her eyebrows or use lipstick, saying that what the Lord gave her should not be tampered with. She was, as she often told us, one of God's naturals.

'Wait, Ina, what you got in that bag?' said Eastman. 'You got God with you? Take Him out.'

'I'm going to forgive you because I know you are a fool,' replied Ina.

'Oh, Carmen, I must sit down, these heels are killing me,' said Josephine. She bent down and started to undo the straps at the back of her shoes.

'Where you get time to paint your toenails?' said my mother.

'Oh, girl,' said Josephine, 'you know, Carmen, it is always important to look one's best.' She was fumbling about with the straps and after a few minutes, my mother asked what the matter was.

'I don't seem to be able to undo the straps,' Josephine told her.

'Why,' said my mother, 'just kick them off if you don't want to chip your nail paint.'

'No, old girl,' said Josephine. 'I glued these nails on last night and they are too long. Have you got a nail file? I don't want to lose one.' She stretched her hands out in the direction of my mother. The nails were pearl pink and stood about one inch beyond the top of her finger.

'Do you really mean to tell me that you stick those on? You mad?'

'Well, a girl's got to do her best.'

'Wait,' said Eastman, 'what about housework?'

'Beware of false gods,' said Ina.

'Well,' said my mother, 'if you can't take your shoes off you must keep them on.'

'God moves in mysterious ways,' Ina declared. 'Give your heart to the Lord; all are welcomed in His house, bare foot and unpainted toenails. Blessed are the plain for the Kingdom of Heaven.'

'Ina,' said my mother. 'Come and have a cup of tea.'

They all went into the sitting room. I waited until the door was shut then hurried upstairs. I was just thinking about my homework when my mother called me down to meet the visitors.

'Hello, Clare, how are you?' said Josephine.

'I'm fine, thank you.'

'How are you doing at school?'

'Good, thank you, Josephine.'

'My sweetness, how you've grown. Come – come let me see you.'

I moved into the middle of the room.

'Go and make a pot of tea,' said my mother.

'Come, let me see you – come.' Ina pulled me towards her and patted the back of my leg; she squeezed my elbow and felt my wrist. 'You know that God moves in many mysterious ways,' she said.

'We can see how He work on you,' said Eastman. 'There is no mystery. God turn you fool.'

'Clare take God to your bosom. Do you have God in your heart?'

'I don't know whether I've got God in my heart.'

'Leave the pickney, if you want tea,' said my mother.

She pointed at the fake orange mother-of-pearl tea set. I removed four cups, four saucers, the milk jug, sugar bowl and teapot. Then I slipped past my mother and pulled apart the curtains to the back room. I walked to the French windows and found the tin of Carnation milk and an open bag of sugar. I went to the kitchen and made the tea nice and strong, beating the tea bags against the side of the teapot. I arranged the tea set on the large tin tray we had for our posh guests and took it into the sitting room.

'Sweetness,' said Ina, 'do you go to church?'

'Of course she goes to church,' snapped my mother. 'What – you think is only you close to God?'

'She is a sinner, Carmen.'

'*You* a sinner, Ina. You have four pickney, every one born again and not a father in sight. Born again and again and again. We are all sinners, Ina,' said my mother. 'You think is only you know God?'

'Would you like to come to my church, Clare?' said Ina, ignoring her.

'Yeah, sure.'

Josephine applied some lipstick and then pushed her lips out.

She whipped a mirror from her bag, opened it and looked at herself. 'That's better,' she said. 'Oh, Carmen, girl, my feet are killing me.'

'Well, take your shoes off, Josephine. What's wrong with you?'

I poured four cups of tea. 'Tea, Ina?'

'Yes, child. Blessed are the thirsty for I shall quench their thirst.'

'Sugar, Ina?'

'Yes, please, child – three.'

I put three spoons of sugar in the cup, stirred it and gave it to Ina on a saucer.

'Thank you, child,' she said. 'God will reward you in heaven.'

'Sugar, Josephine?' I bent down to pick up the sugar bowl and something flew past my head. At the same time, Josephine started getting emotional.

'Oh no, oh no, what have I done, what have I done?' she cried. My mother jumped up and Ina blessed herself.

'What's the matter?' they both cried.

Josephine was bent double in her chair.

'Do you want a doctor?' my mother asked.

Ina got up and put her hand on the other woman's forehead.

'Did you want sugar, Josephine?' I said.

'Oh Christ!' was all she said.

'Never take the Lord's name in vain,' said Ina.

Josephine sat upright and pointed her finger in my direction. 'Oh no,' she said. 'I just cannot believe it.' Josephine's protruding finger had no nail polish and it was missing a nail. Her false pink nail had disappeared when she had tried to remove her shoe.

'Look!' she screamed, holding out her hand. 'For God's sake, everyone, don't move.'

'I think it just whizzed past my head,' I said.

My mother, realising that there was a problem, asked Josephine to put her fake orange mother-of-pearl cup down.

'Don't scratch my cup,' she said.

'Don't what?' said Josephine.

'Scratch my cup,' said my mother. 'Put it down.' She moved over and tried to take the cup and saucer.

'Don't move,' said Josephine. 'Mind my nail!'

'Beware of false gods,' said Ina.

'Do you want sugar?' I asked again.

'Don't move!' wailed Josephine. 'Everyone, stay still!'

I stood still. Josephine still had her cup.

'Put it down,' my mother shouted. 'Put it down.'

'Carmen, have you lost your marbles?'

'Don't scratch my cup with your false nails.'

'Everyone, don't move. Clare, dear,' said Josephine, pointing her finger in my direction for the second time. 'Do you think that you might be able to find my nail?'

'Sure,' I said. I went down on my knees by the door and patted the carpet. It wasn't there. 'It might have gone behind the settee,' I said and crawled behind the settee, patting the carpet as I went along. When I came out the other side, I had not discovered the false pink nail, so I decided to crawl round the glass table.

'Ladies,' said Josephine, 'please put your legs in the air.'

Ina looked at Eastman, who looked at my mother and said, 'The whole fucking world has gone mad.'

They all placed their cups on the table and leaned back in their seats, legs up in the air. I crawled round the table from east to west and then I patted under the table. No false pink nail. I crawled under their legs.

Ina started to pray. 'Beware of sinners, for many, I tell you, many will come in My Name. Blessed are the meek.' Her eyes were rolling in the back of her head and her feet were still up in the air.

'Ina,' said my mother.

'For they shall inherit the earth.'

'Be quiet,' said my mother.

'Blessed are those who come in My Name.'

'Oh Lord,' said Josephine. 'All this praying, just for a false nail.'

'Blessed are those who shut up because peace will be upon us and we can put our legs down.'

Ina came out of her trance-like state. I kept crawling around on the floor looking for the false nail.

'It's not here,' I said.

'Ladies,' said Josephine, 'it's no good. Please put your legs down.'

The women dropped their feet.

'This is a mad house,' said Eastman. 'One false nail and everyone have them leg in the air, me never see anything like it. Josephine, if I was you I would pull off all the others.'

I crawled around the front of the glass display cabinet. 'Got it!' I said. 'Here it is.' I held it up.

'Oh, thank you,' said Josephine.

Ina snatched it out of my hand. 'Beware of those who worship false gods,' she said, waving the nail at Josephine.

'Oh Lord, Ina, not again. Give me the nail.'

'There is still time for you to be saved,' said Ina. 'God welcomes all.'

'I do not wish to be saved,' said Josephine. 'Now give me the nail.'

'Sinner, repent,' said Ina.

'Dizzy and Dopey,' said my mother, 'how could you two share one God? Ina, give Josephine her nail so she can stick it back on. What's wrong with you?'

'Carmen, I am a messenger of God.'

'Yes,' said my mother, 'and I have a message from God – give Josephine back her nail.'

'My child,' said Ina, turning to me, 'you know you are welcome in God's House.'

'Yes, I know.'

'And you know that God is a very patient God.'

'Yes, I know.'

'He will wait for you every Saturday every week. We will go together and meet our Maker. Are you ready to meet your Maker?'

'I don't mind,' I said.

'You know that God works in mysterious ways.'

'Yes.'

'And he is there for you.'

'Yes.'

'Is there anything that you seek from your God?'

I thought about it. It would be good if he could help me to stop wetting the bed.

'Yes, I think so.'

'Well, next week, child, you and I have a date with God.'

'Okay,' I said.

Ina put the nail on the glass table and Josephine picked it up and put it down her bra.

'Hallelujah,' said Josephine, and tapped her bra twice. 'That will save me buying a new set.'

Now they had settled down, I left the room and went back upstairs. I was behind on my homework and really needed to get down to it. I got my books out, spread them on the floor and then stretched out in front of them. Peace at last and a date with God.

10

Jacksonmania

1969

Jacksonmania had hit London and everyone was growing their hair in huge Afros and using an Afro fork to keep it in shape. It got round school that the Jackson Five would be in the West End in the Hilton Hotel. My friend Shirley Williams and I decided that we would go to the hotel the following day on the way home from school. Before we did so, we needed to get a Jackson Five wig. We went to school in the morning, had our lessons, but at dinnertime Shirley said that she had some spare money and would let me have it to go and buy a Michael Jackson wig. I did not even have to contribute to the cost. All I had to do was watch her back and do all her detentions for the term if she got any. That sounded like a good deal to me so we agreed.

Because Shirley had an elder brother, we were able to persuade him to ask his girlfriend whether she could go and buy a wig that day. Shirley did not need a wig – she had a beautiful natural Afro that was styled to perfection and had a lot of body. I, on the other hand, had short hair, which was more straight than Afro. I had to look the business when I went to the hotel. School ended and I went home with my sisters. Shirley promised me the wig the following day.

At home, I had a regular weekly routine. I washed the kitchen floor, cleaned the gas stove, swept the stairs and tidied my bed. Every third day it was my turn to wash, dry and put away all the plates, pots, knives and forks. When I arrived home that day, my mother was not in so I put my wet sheets from the night before in the wash. If I was quick enough I could get them washed and spun-dried before my mother returned; if not, I would just have to hope that she did not notice what was being washed. In any event, I had had the same wet sheets now for two days and I did not think that I was hurting anyone or doing anything wrong by washing them. More recently, my alarm had been going off without me wetting the bed, because the sheets were already wet. Fortunately, the washing cycle ended before my mother returned, so I spun the sheets in the top-load spin-dryer and put them back on my bed. I opened the window in order to let the fresh air dry my sheets.

I did not mind too much sleeping on wet sheets as long as I did not smell. I did not mind anything as long as my alarm did not go off. I did not want to be pulled out of bed or beaten or pushed or pulled. It was all in my control. All I had to do was to stop wetting the bed and then things would get better. My mother was right; it *was* entirely within my control. No one could zip up my minnie, just me, so to some extent I suppose I got what I deserved. After all, Pauline did not wet the bed, Patsy did not wet the bed. Both of them had stopped when they were very little. It was just me. I had gone on and on and on, and, like my mother said, there really was no reason for it. I had put her to great expense, unnecessary expense was what she called it, quite deliberately.

Sometimes going to bed was a bit like having a cold bath; when you got in, it wasn't very nice and was a bit cold, but after a while you did not notice. I had not noticed for a very long time, years and years; all my beds were the same. It did not matter to me whether it was warm or cold, I had got used to getting into bed no matter what. Bed was bed. I was lucky I had a bed, *she* said.

Maybe one day when I was grown up I would have a nice bed, a four-poster with curtains, with a nice soft mattress that would never get wet no matter what. Abracadabra, the wet would be magicked away; just go straight through when I had an accident, or maybe I could find a mattress where the wet evaporated without an alarm. I would ban all bed alarms; no child should ever have an alarm. Then I would have a supersoft pillow, two pillows and a huge duvet to wrap round and round my body – a pink cotton duvet case and matching pillowcases with embroidery round the edges, possibly some bows, one in each corner, pretty bows. No leaks in the middle of the night. Dear God, I thought, if only I could stop wetting the bed just for a week. No beatings, no pain. My mother might even like me for a week. It wasn't too much to ask, was it – a wetfree bed for a week? It wasn't as if I was asking for a permanent cure. I would just like to be normal, normal for seven days.

The next day I got up, had my breakfast and went to school with my sisters. I did not see Shirley until early afternoon, when she pressed a plastic bag into my hand.

'Meet you at the gate at four,' she said and walked away from me.

I put the bag in my pocket, went into the girls' toilets and took it out. Inside was the most superb wig you ever did see. Watch out, Michael Jackson, because I am a serious contender. The wig was inside out in the plastic bag. I turned it the right way, gave it a bit of a shake and then pulled it onto my head. It was a perfect fit. I looked first division. I tugged the wig down just behind my ears and tweaked out the synthetic hairs. A bit of patting and pulling was required but my wig was glorious. It was a good fake.

At four o'clock, Shirley met me at the school gate. 'Clare, eh, eh,' she said. 'That's *cool.*' We made our way to the West End and when we got off the bus, someone pointed out the hotel where they thought Michael Jackson was staying. Shirley and I jumped up and down and screamed outside the hotel. There were a few of us there actually, but Michael Jackson never appeared. After maybe an hour and a half, we decided to go home. I loved my wig and decided I would wear it to school in future. I patted it down so that it looked like a small Afro.

When I arrived home, no one paid the slightest bit of attention to me. They didn't seem to notice any difference. The next day I went to school wearing my wig. Both Shirley and I were oozing about Michael Jackson, although to be fair we were not at all sure that he was actually in the country. A few girls commented that my hair had acquired a new texture and firmness but, beyond this, my new hairdo went relatively unnoticed.

That day, we had apricot crumble for lunch, together with ice cream. I loved it.

The next day we had shepherds pie, peas, carrots and sweet potato followed by jelly and ice cream.

School was cool. I got my homework back with two stars – A++ and *could do better*. I loved school and they thought I had potential. If I wanted to, I could make it. School was the only place I was guaranteed not to get a beating. I was very good at netball and athletics, which made me popular, though I was never one to mix readily. I had decided I wanted to be normal, whatever that meant; of course, the moment I went home, my happiness evaporated. Mum punched me in the head when I walked past her. I cannot remember the exact reason now. Probably it was just, as she once said, that I was alive and breathing.

My relationship with Eastman had never recovered from the low point in the Magistrates' Court. I disliked him and that was that. I refused to acknowledge him in the house, although I did keep out of his way. He continued to mumble under his breath whenever I went past, but he was no longer so keen to get into conflict with me. My mother was more open about her feelings and attitude towards me. Taking Eastman to court was something that she would never forgive, and she took it upon herself to settle Eastman's score.

As we approached the spring term my mother told me that she had found me a Saturday job and I would be required to work. When I asked her where the job was, she said that I would be working with Eastman from 7.30 in the morning to 3.30 in the afternoon. Eastman had left the laundry and was working on a building site, which had its own cafeteria for the workmen; I was to help out there.

That Saturday I got up early. My alarm had gone off so I changed the sheet by turning it upside down, and switched off the alarm. Then I went back to bed and waited for a little while. I was at the beginning of a new adventure – new people, new clothes, new money. Half an hour passed and I went and had a wash, brushed my teeth and combed my hair. I put on a long-sleeved T-shirt, jeans and plimsoles. When I was ready, I switched the light off in my bedroom and made my way down-stairs. It was now 5.15 a.m.

Eastman was already up. He was in the kitchen filling his Thermos with tea and condensed milk. He pulled his hat over his head and walked out of the front door in the direction of the Square, with me tagging along behind. We walked in silence for about forty-five minutes until we eventually came to Vassall Road. Most of the houses were in the process of being demol-ished. The whole neighbourhood appeared to be covered in corrugated-iron fencing and there were any number of signs that said it was a hard-hat area. We crossed the road at some traffic lights and walked on. The fencing was about six to seven feet high and went on for ever. Eastman turned right and then left and approached a sign that said *Knock Loudly*. He did so and a large man with a fat face and greasy beard came out and greeted him.

'How are you, Saint E?'

'Holding up,' said Eastman.

I was astonished. Eastman never seemed like a saint to me.

'And what's this you got here? What's your name?'

'Clare.'

'That's a pretty name,' said Greasy Beard. 'And what gets you up at this time of the morning?'

'I've got a job in the kitchens.'

'Really? Tell me more.'

'It's a Saturday job.'

'Really, I see. Saint E, what's this all about?'

'I don't know,' said Eastman. 'It's her mother's idea.'

'I'm to cook sausages,' I told Greasy Beard.

'Anything else?'

'Yes – I'm frying eggs and making tea.'

'Saint E, tell me what's going on.'

Eastman shook his head from side to side and then removed his hat and scratched his head with his giant hand. 'I don't know. Her mammy thinks it is a good idea for her to spend some time with me. I tell she is not a good idea. Don't blame me.'

'How old are you?' Greasy Beard asked me.

'Thirteen.'

'Saint E, come with me. You, sweetheart, go and wait over there in the kitchen.' He took the hard hat off his head and put it on mine as he assisted me to the kitchen. Then he was gone.

The cafeteria was vast. There was lots of brushed chrome and steel. The seating was a little primitive – rows and rows of tables with seats bolted to the floor. The sitting area was divided by a large serving counter behind which were at least three sinks, a huge fridge/freezer, which said *Vacuum shut* on the outside, and a walk-in storage space for food. On the counter was a till. The stove had at least eight burners. It was a bit grubby.

Greasy Beard returned on his own. 'Now,' he said, 'why do you think that you are here?'

'I've got a job,' I said. 'I'm going to get paid. I'm going to be working in the kitchen cooking sausages and making tea.'

'Do you know how to cook?'

'Yes,' I said. 'It's easy-peasy.'

'Right. Do you know that you don't really have a job? You are here because your mum and dad think that it is a good idea.'

'He is not my dad.'

'Whatever. They think that it is a good idea that you two spend some time together and while you're here you can mess in. And we are going to give you a bit of pocket money because your dad tells us it would make you happy.'

'He's not my dad.'

'How about nine quid – no, call it a tenner for helping us out.'

'I think that's fine. What do I have to do?'

Greasy Beard took my hard hat and disappeared, then returned with John, who described himself as 'the one and only, but you can call me John'. John flicked all the switches down and one by one rows and rows of lights flashed on. He then set about removing food from the fridge – eggs, bacon, sausages, mushrooms. John asked me to get him two tins of baked beans from the storage room at the back of the kitchen. In the store were huge tins of beans, they were about twelve inches high and eight inches wide. The bottles of ketchup were dazzling. The ketchup drum was about two feet high with a large nozzle. It was used to refill the ketchup bottles at the end of the day. The Old English Mustard had clearly not been very popular. There were perhaps twenty or thirty tins of mustard, isolated from the rest of the food. The tins of beans were heavy and I had to make two trips from the storeroom to the kitchen.

'Now,' said John, 'I hear you're good at sausages.'

'Yes, I am, but I can do other things. I can cook a chicken.'

'I'm sure you can!' he laughed.

Greasy Beard asked me to help him prepare the food for breakfast and make a menu. The workmen would be in at about eleven o'clock. Huge steel frying pans, coated in a layer of black, were kept to the right of the stove. The sausages were pulled out of the fridge and it was my job to separate them by cutting them with a sharp knife. Eighteen sausages were placed in a frying pan over a low flame. Greasy Beard broke the eggs without once splitting a yolk. They went in a separate frying pan a little before eleven o'clock. Together we prepared the mushrooms and put them in butter next to the sausages.

The tins of beans were placed on a rotating table. A fixed opener was clipped onto the edge and as the table spun round at a slow speed, the top of each can was screwed from the body. John showed me how to fill the urns with water ready for the men's tea. The teapot looked like a watering can and we had three of them. The bread was taken out of the bread bin so that it could breathe. The toaster was again on a massive scale – it could easily accommodate eight slices in one go.

In addition to the toaster, we had what John called the 'warm bed'. It looked like a conveyor belt, which simply went round and round slowly; a slice of bread was placed on one side of the belt, it went through a heated tunnel that toasted it and as the conveyor belt turned back on itself, the toast fell off onto the plate below.

We removed the bacon from the fridge and I put it under the grill. Greasy Beard supervised me. John said the men liked their bacon butties, so we had to prepare a dozen rolls filled with slabs of butter that were placed close to the stove. When John gave the word, I would slap three slices of bacon in the middle and shout, 'Bacon butty coming up!' All was done by about 10.30. The time had passed so quickly. John was very nice to me, helping me, explaining how the machinery worked and showing me where the fire extinguishers were kept and which one to use.

'Come on,' he said, 'let's put our feet up and have a cuppa before the lads turn up.'

I got some milk out of the fridge and John turned two cups the right way up.

'We don't need a saucer, do we? We're not posh,' he said. As we sat opposite each other he asked if I had had my breakfast.

'No, but I'm not hungry.'

'We'll have an eat-up after the boys have gone,' he said. 'You sure you don't want a sausage butty?'

'No, thank you,' I said.

I had forgotten all about Eastman. I hadn't seen him since we arrived. John asked if I would be coming next week.

'I would like to,' I answered, 'but I don't know.'

About 10.45 we checked the stove and all the food was cooking nicely. The sausages had to be pricked and the heat turned up. The boys came in at about 11.30.

'A breakfast special and a tea, love,' said the first. John picked up a warm plate, flicked two sausages onto it followed by eggs, two slices of bacon, mushrooms and a dollop of baked beans. Two thick slices of bread soaked in butter were placed on a separate plate. While John was taking the money, I asked the next lad what he wanted and he said the same. I very quickly got the hang of it. I took another two plates and served up two breakfast specials in one go. John was impressed. The bread soaked in butter was on the plate before he asked for it.

'Bacon butty,' John shouted.

'Bacon butty coming up,' I said.

'Sausage butty!'

'Sausage butty coming up.'

'Make that two, love.'

'Two sausage butties coming up.'

I put more sausages in the frying pan. John said it was a good idea not to go below eight. The warm bed was kept warm and the toast was consumed as quickly as it tumbled off.

'Tomato ketchup?' I enquired, giving the bottle a little squeeze so the nipple bled.

'Just a squidge.'

It was heaven running around. The lads took the tea and I turned another dozen cups the right way up and poured tea into five of them. I then topped the teapot up with boiling water from the urn. The lads came and went and then another lot came in and eventually John and I were left on our own in the kitchen. I had not seen Eastman all day and it was now one o'clock.

'Bacon butty?' suggested John. 'And a nice cuppa? You were good, kid, and you got the hang of things very quickly.'

I opened my bacon butty and peeled the fat off from around the edges. I then used the back of a knife and scraped the butter off the roll. I didn't want to put on weight. We washed our butties down with a large mug of tea. John put his feet on the table and pulled out a packet of cigarettes from his pocket. He tapped a cigarette out of the box, flicked it into his mouth when it was still half inside the packet and lit up.

'I enjoy this moment best and I damn well earn it,' he said.

While John was having a smoke I filled the dishwashers, put the food back where it belonged and started to disinfect the work surfaces. John lit up another cigarette and I checked the store and emptied the bins. He told me where to put them.

'Where's the mop, John?' I asked busily. 'I can do the floors for you.'

'Sit down, love, and have a rest. You work too hard.'

I obeyed him and poured myself another cup of tea. I did not want any complaints: Eastman would only tell tales about me. A few moments passed and then John suggested we make a start together. I followed him and we both tidied the kitchen, removed all the grease from the stove, cleaned the oven and swept and washed the floor. We were putting our mops away when the boss came in. He was wearing a hat with *Boss* written on it.

'How you doing?' he asked.

'Good, thank you.'

'Any complaints? John and the lads been okay to you?'

'Everything's fine.'

He came up to me, took hold of my hand and squeezed a brown envelope into my palm. 'Hope to see you soon,' he said, turned on his heel and went away. I put the envelope into my pocket and continued to help John. When we were finished I hung my overall up in the storeroom. While I was doing that I heard Eastman turn up.

'Where is she?'

'Oh, you mean Clare. She's in the store, she'll be here in a moment.'

'How she been?'

'She's fine, nice girl.'

'You think so? Well, is only you think so.'

I waited for a minute and returned to the kitchen.

'You ready to go home, Clare?' said Eastman.

'Thank you very much, John.'

'It's a pleasure, come again.'

Eastman walked ahead of me and I walked behind him, just a few paces. We did not speak to each other as we made our way through the back streets of Kennington. We walked past the library and crossed over into Lorrimore Road and then went underneath the house on stilts. We turned right at Sutherland Square and continued to number 19 where Eastman put his key in the door. For a moment my attention was diverted: I thought I saw my sister up under the bridge. I was looking to my left when

I heard the front door slam shut. Eastman was no longer in front of me and his key was missing. I knocked on the door and waited. After ten minutes I knocked again and waited. After twenty minutes I took my coat off, folded it up and put it on the ground. I sat on it with my back to the front door. Someone had to open it sooner or later, I thought, it was only a matter of time.

Three minutes or more passed and I saw my mother at the ground-floor front window. She was looking in my direction, but was unable to see me because I was sitting on the ground. She disappeared from the window and I heard her next at the front door. She opened it and stumbled over me.

'What do you want?' she said.

'Nothing,' I said. 'Can I come in?'

'Why do you want to come in?'

'Oh, for no particular reason.'

'Well, stay outside.'

She closed the door and I remained seated. A few moments later the door opened and no one came outside. When I was sure that the door would remain open I got up, collected my coat and went inside. I made my way up to my bedroom. Once inside I took out the envelope and lay down on the bed. I peeled the flap back carefully. When it was loose I peeled the whole flap backwards. Oh dear! My mother came in and I jumped off the bed. She grabbed me to her, so we were standing tit to tit.

'What have I done now?' I asked. My heart was beating fast with fear.

'Oh, so you are answering back. Can you smell yourself?'

'I had a wash this morning,' I said.

'And you think a wash can get rid of that smell? Have you got something wrong with your nose? Smell yourself.'

I took a deep breath in, at the same time making myself tall by stretching my neck. I held my breath in and then let it out.

'I can smell something,' I said.

'I can smell *you*,' said my mother. 'You stink like a sewer, but then you *are* a sewer. Go and have a wash.'

I half stepped backwards and when my mother loosened her grip, I went towards the door.

'I'm just going to have a wash,' I told her. 'No, sorry, I'm just going to have a bath.'

I took two steps down the stairs while my mother was putting her shoe on.

When she went downstairs to her room I sneaked back to mine and opened the envelope. It contained £5. So much for a tenner. Not bad. But it was not what I was promised. I put the money in my purse and the purse in the bottom of the wardrobe next to my packet of Jammy Dodgers.

After my bath I went to find something to do. The plates in the kitchen were piled high. The place was dirty and untidy and the floor needed to be washed. I cleared the sink of all the cutlery and put the plug in. Pauline came in.

'Why you working with Eastman?' she said. 'I thought you didn't like him.'

'I don't.'

'Then why you working with him?'

'I don't know.'

'What did you have to do?'

'Oh, just cook breakfast,' I said.

'Did you get paid?'

'Yes – five pounds.'

'Oh!' said Pauline. 'Are you going next week?'

'I don't know. It wasn't my idea to go in the first place.'

While I was washing up Pauline disappeared upstairs. My mother came into the kitchen, made a cup of tea, took the rice out of the cupboard and left it on the side. I continued with the washing up, not looking in her direction. Once everything was washed I pulled the plug out, gave the sink a clean and rinsed the plates under running water.

'You will have to pay your way now,' she said. 'No one gets anything for free and this is not a free house.'

'I don't know what you mean by pay my way. I can't pay my way if I've got no money.'

'You cheeky little bitch. You want to live in my house, eat my food, drink my drink and not ask where it's coming from? Where do you think it's coming from? You think it grows on trees? You think I'm your meal-ticket. If you work you must pay and, by the way, you owe me for the soap powder I bought to clean your bedclothes.'

I continued to rinse the items in the sink and place them on the draining board. 'How much do you want?' I asked.

'Half,' said my mother.

'Well, I did not get much money and if I give you half I'll not have enough to look after myself.'

'If you want to eat in this house you better hand over the money, I'm not going to tell you again. You want to eat my food, sleep in my bed, use my hot water and electricity and you don't want to pay for it?'

'I didn't say I didn't want to pay for it. I said I didn't have enough money.'

I finished the dishes, dried my hands and went to my bedroom where I removed the £5. My mother was in her sitting room having a cup of tea in her fake orange mother-of-pearl cup. Eastman was sitting opposite her. I handed her the £5.

'Have you got my change?' I said.

My mother took the note and continued talking to Eastman. She put her right hand in her top and pulled out the left bra strap. She untied the handkerchief that was double-knotted to it and removed a large roll of money that looked like a fat cigarette. She took the elastic band off and added my £5 note to the roll. Next she replaced the elastic band and then folded and double-knotted the handkerchief into place. She carried on talking to Eastman and drinking her tea. I waited by the door not wishing to interrupt my mother's conversation. After maybe ten minutes she looked in my direction.

'You still there?'

'I'm waiting for my change.'

'What change? Someone owe you?'

'I'm waiting for my change from the money that I gave you. You owe me two pounds and ten shillings.'

'Go on, get out.'

'I'm waiting for my money.'

'I said clear off out of my sight. You know how much it cost to feed you and you want change.'

I didn't know whether to ask for my money again or to leave it. While I was thinking about it my mother got up out of her chair, turned to face me and when she was up close she said, 'Go on, button it. If you buttoned it a bit more it would save you pissing my bed. You need your crack sewing up. Get out and close my door.'

I backed away, turned round and left my mother to my money. I went upstairs and lay on the bed.

After a short while my mother called up to me: 'Clare, get down here now. Don't let me have to call you again.'

I went back to the sitting room.

'You've forgotten something,' said my mother.

'Have I?'

'Yes.'

'Oh, my change.'

'Your what? Think again.'

'Just my money.'

'You forgot to close the door on your way out. Close the door, out, shoo.'

I shooed, this time closing the door behind me. Upstairs I lay on my bed. Pauline came in.

'What are you going to buy, then?' she asked. She sat down on the floor. 'What about some sherbet lemons and fruit salad? I'll go and get them if you like. Or how about some strawberry bonbons?'

'I don't think so.'

'Oh, well, maybe just some lime snakes and pear drops.'

'I've got no money.'

'Liar. You just don't want to spend it, meanie.'

'No, Mummy has taken my money.'

'Never. Why would she do that?'

'She thinks I owe her.'

'What for?'

'Washing my sheets, I think.'

'Well, you do piss the bed a lot, Clare, you got to admit it, but she could have left a bit for a fruit salad. Why don't you have a Jammy Dodger?'

We ate our Jammy Dodgers and when we were finished Pauline went off to get on with her affairs. I remained on the bed. I was so tired from getting up so early in the morning that I fell asleep. I don't know how long I was there for but I woke in a state of confusion; my alarm was ringing, the lights were flashing. I could hear the footsteps on the stairs – my mother was on her way up. I quickly put my hand between my legs. Dry knickers, nothing to worry about. I jumped off the bed and stood to attention as my mother entered the room.

'Lord my God, Jesus Christ, Clare, what you do?'

'I haven't done anything.'

'Jesus Christ, Clare now start to piss the bed in broad daylight. Jesus fucking Christ, she don't know the difference between day and night. Jesus, she piss round the clock.' My mother grabbed my clothes around my chest.

'I did not wet the bed,' I said.

'Did not wet the bed! Look.' She pointed at the alarm. 'Look, can you see it? That is a light and it is flashing on and off. Look, can you see it or are you blind, too? Oh no, don't tell me you deaf as well. You can't hear what we can hear. Can you hear that, listen.'

My mother and I stood perfectly still. Yes, the alarm was loud and it was true that it was still ringing, but it had nothing to do with me.

'I did not wet the bed.'

'Someone else piss on the bed when you were on it? Now let me see, Clare, who would do that? Who would do that? *Liar.*' My mother tightened her grip and pulled me towards her.

'Look,' I said, and stepping back I pulled my skirt up to my waist.

'Pauline, Patsy, come quick! Clare are show me her drawers.'

Pauline was the first in, Patsy just behind her by the door.

'What's the matter with your drawers, Clare?'

'Nothing, they are dry.'

My mother was removing her shoe from her foot.

'My drawers are dry,' I shouted over the alarm. 'My drawers are dry, I did not wet the bed.'

'What?' said my mother. 'You mean you take your drawers off and piss on my bed?'

She raised her hand with the shoe above her head and the alarm stopped.

We all looked in the direction of the alarm and it went off again.

'See? It wasn't me,' I said.

My mother let go of me and pulled the cover off the bed, exposing a large yellow area; the outer edges had three different tidemarks.

'See?' I said. 'I did not wet the bed. That was last night, the night before and the night before that.'

'You dirty bitch – how old are you? It is about time you stop wetting the bed.'

I slipped out of the room and away. As I got to the bottom of the stairs the alarm started up again. That must be my mother pissing on my bed, I thought. As she said herself, alarms don't just go off on their own.

The following day, Ina came and picked me up for my date with God. We travelled on the bus to the Pentecostal church. It had a scruffy little door, but once inside it was a different story. The entrance hall was marble, polished to a high degree, and the doors to the church itself were freshly painted. On the outside of each door was a sign that said *This way for Jesus* with an arrow pointing up. There was a similar sign stuck to the hall floor. We followed it to the main body of the church.

'Good morning,' a man said to me.

'Good morning,' I said back.

He turned to Ina. 'Good morning, Sister Buckley.'

'Good morning,' Ina said back.

'Now do introduce me to this fine specimen of a child,' said the man.

'This is my niece, Clare,' said Ina.

'And what brings Clare to God's house?'

'I've come to find Jesus,' I said.

'And you will find Him today, praise the Lord. All who seek will find.'

The man tapped me on the head before we moved off. Lots of people greeted Ina. They all called her Sister Buckley. I did not know that she had so many sisters. The entire church was related to her, and then there were all the brothers. Brother this, and Brother that. I was feeling a bit out of it really; no one knew me and although they all made me feel very welcome, there were only a handful of children my age. After all the greetings we were told to take our places. Ina and I sat next to her sister. We were in the front of the church, which was not at all like a Catholic church. There certainly was an altar of sorts; but there were no pews, only chairs which were divided equally either side of the centre aisle.

Suddenly there was an almighty roar from behind one of the doors that had said *This way for Jesus*. The noise was repeated and then seemed to move to the next door that had a similar sign. The whole congregation spoke as one: 'I am blind, sweet Lord, make me see.' The fat lady to my left and Ina were looking down at their feet and mumbling, 'Praise the Lord, sweet Jesus, praise the Lord.' The voice roared again and both women looked up, shook themselves, waved their arms in the air and shouted: 'I am blind, sweet Lord, make me see.'

I was staring in the direction of Ina. I wanted to look into her eyes, because I was sure she *could* see. I then heard the roar again and this time I was able to make out the words. 'Do you see Jesus?' Whereupon Ina and the fat lady did it again – they looked up to the ceiling, waved their arms above their heads and, shaking themselves, shouted: 'I am blind, sweet Lord, make me see.' The voice was a male voice and it appeared to go all the way round the outside of the hall. I was beginning to get a bit worried, when Ina nudged me and said, 'Clare, honey child, praise the Lord.' I did not hear her at first so I asked her to say it again. Between shaking herself and looking at her feet she said to me, with her eyes closed, 'Praise the Lord, honey child.'

'I don't know how to praise the Lord, Ina,' I said.

'Just follow me,' she said. 'Do as I do.'

So I started to look at my feet and when Ina shook herself I did too. When a few minutes later she threw her arms up in the air and said, 'Praise the Lord,' so did I, only I was a little out of time. When Ina and the fat lady and the rest of the congregation shouted, 'I am blind, sweet Lord, make me see,' I was slightly out of step again. Ina nudged me.

'Clare,' she hissed, 'keep up.'

'I'm trying, Ina, but I don't know what's coming next.'

Just then, the door burst open and in came the fattest man I've ever seen. All the ladies were looking at their feet, but he was a sight not to be missed. His head was tiny in comparison to his body and he had a very large Afro, almost as large as the wig I was wearing. He wore a purple shirt, trimmed in gold and black lace, and underneath that, another frilly white shirt. His shoes were similar to a pair I had seen in a shop and quite liked for myself. They were black patent and glossy with a large golden buckle on the side. His arms were outstretched as he walked into the room.

'Do you see God?' he said. He repeated his words as he walked into the middle of the congregation. 'Do you see God?'

I was still looking at his shoes. How I envied him them. They were too big for my feet but the style was perfect. The fat lady and Ina were in a trance. I looked around the room and it became obvious to me that I should be in a trance as well. Everyone had their elbows tucked in at the side with their head almost touching their knees. Others were too fat for that position, but had done the best they could. I was the only one sitting upright looking at his shoes.

'Do you see God?' he cried and started to shake. The women got off their elbows, straightened their backs and shouted, 'I was blind and now I see. I was blind and now I see.' I thought that it was only right to follow, so I did. When the ladies started to shake I did so too. Then Ina nudged me again and said, 'That's the Pastor, he is a messenger from God.' Now all the congregation had miraculously got their sight back and were able to see and praise the Lord.

'You see?' said the Pastor. 'Whatever door you choose in life they all lead to God.'

That simply was not true because he was the one outside all the doors – we had all heard him roar. The Pastor then asked us to join with him and thank the Lord for what we had. We all rose to our feet and started dancing with our hands held high above our head. One of the gentlemen kept shouting, 'Yes, yes, yes.' A young lady to his right kept shouting, 'No, no, no.' People began to dance in the aisle and the Pastor weaved in and out of the dancers and every now and then he roared out, 'Hallelujah.' I got up and danced too and shouted with the rest.

When we got tired we sat down and were given a lesson on greed. We should not prize our worldly possessions, he told us, because there were prizes awaiting us in heaven. I thought this was a bit rich coming from a man who was so fashion-conscious. A large pot was produced at the front and handed to the gentleman at the end of the row. The Pastor told us all to dig deep into our pockets and invited us to relieve ourselves of our worldly possessions. 'Remember,' he said, 'what awaits you in that other place.'

By the time the pot got to us it was full of money, loads of money. I looked behind me – there was still two-thirds of the gathering waiting to make a contribution.

'That's right,' said the Pastor, 'dig deep.'

The pot made its way beyond us and the Pastor told us all to get up and celebrate God. So we all got up and started dancing again. The pot was then brought to the Pastor who held it up high and thanked us for our donation. The pot disappeared. I asked Ina what happened to the money. She told me that the Pastor decided that. As I was thinking about the Pastor and how he would decide on spending the money, he shouted out, 'We have a visitor.'

'Praise the Lord,' came the mass reply.

'We have a visitor who wants to find Jesus,' he said.

'Praise the Lord.'

'Shall we help her find Jesus?'

'Help her to find Jesus.'

The Pastor was walking in my direction and when he was pretty close I knew that he was coming for me. I kept my head down. Ina and the fat lady started saying, 'Help her to find Jesus, help her to find Jesus. Oh Lord, help her on her way.' I started singing too. When Ina and the fat one fell to their knees, I did too. The Pastor was standing right in front of me. As I looked ahead I saw two legs covered in purple fabric. To the side of me, both the ladies were singing. As the ladies shook themselves, the entire congregation appeared to be looking in my direction.

The Pastor started to dance in front of me. He raised his hands and waved them around, shouting at the crowd, 'Shall we save her? I want to hear you say it loud. Shall we save her?'

The crowd were almost in a frenzy. 'Yes, yes!' they shouted.

The Pastor brought his right hand down on top of my head suddenly and unexpectedly. He dislodged my wig and tilted it slightly to the left. 'Do you feel God?' he asked, shaking my head with his hand and making my wig slide forwards and sideways.

The front of my wig now covered my left eye and just as the Pastor shook my head again I looked to my right. Ina had walked round to the front of me and stood behind the Pastor where she could see me. Her mouth was open and her head slightly back as though she was going to sneeze. I immediately sensed that I was going to cause her colossal embarrassment when my wig came off in the Pastor's hand in front of all her sisters and brothers.

'Can you feel God?' said the Pastor, as he shook my head again.

As my wig was on the move again, I brought my right hand down very firmly on top of the Pastor's and steadied his hand.

'I feel it,' I shouted. The quicker I felt it, the quicker I would get my wig straight.

'Praise God,' intoned the Pastor.

'I feel it,' I shouted, as I brought my left hand up and pulled the wig backwards. As I looked between the Pastor's legs Ina had disappeared. I saw her to my right; her mouth was closed.

'I can see,' I cried at the top of my voice. 'I can see, I can see!' I was really getting the hang of this now.

'Praise the Lord,' said the Pastor. 'The child can see.'

Still using my left hand I placed it on top of my right hand, which was on top of the Pastor's, which was still on top of my head. I then shook his hand, which shook my head and took the wig backwards and sideways. I did this a couple of times until the wig was back in place. As the congregation stared at us they were very surprised at the speed with which the Good Lord worked.

'She came here a sinner and now she can see,' said the Pastor. 'God is with us today. Do you feel a presence, child?'

'I feel a presence,' I said. That at least was true.

'Do you see, child?'

Keeping both hands tight on top of his hand, I looked to my right. I could see Ina. I looked to my left and the fat lady was still there.

'I can see!' I screamed. 'I can see!'

The crowd shook themselves and started dancing on the spot, giving thanks for the working of the Lord.

'She can see, sweet Jesus, she can see. She was blind and now she sees.'

I refused to let go of the Pastor's hand and Ina, realising that an embarrassing incident was about to unfold, kept her distance from me. As the Pastor tried to walk away he was jolted back in front of me.

'Let go of my hand, honey child,' he said.

'I can see, Pastor,' I said.

'Yes, honey child, but let go of my hand. I have God's work to do.'

I was terrified that the Pastor's sudden movement might cause my wig to fall off so while the congregation looked on I very slowly released the Pastor's hand. I raised my hands very, very gradually up in the air. The Pastor, aware that something was wrong, gently removed his hand. He did not disturb my wig.

'Let us praise the Lord,' he said as he walked away.

Ina came over closer to me. 'Can you see?' she said.

'Yes, I can see clearly.'

We started to sing again and shake. After the main ceremony lots of sisters and brothers came up to me and enquired if my sight had truly been restored. I was able to reassure them.

'The Lord sure works in mysterious ways,' said one sister as she walked off.

The Pastor approached me as I waited by the door. I quickly put my hand on my head. 'Honey child,' he said, 'you are a miracle. You were blind and now you see. You must return to God's house soon.'

Ina told the Pastor that she would give me lots of encourage-ment to return. I thanked him for an interesting day and we then made our way to the bus stop.

When I got home I changed my clothes and went to the kitchen to tidy up. As I washed the dishes I decided that I would not go back to the church. They were nice people, but it had been too embarrassing. My sisters were in the house – I could hear them. When I sat down to do some homework, Pauline and Patsy put their heads around the door.

'How goes it, Clare?' said Pauline.

'Fine,' I said.

'Where did you go?'

'Oh, to Ina's church. My wig nearly fell off.'

'I thought you always pinned your wig down,' said Patsy.

'The Pastor grabbed my wig and it nearly fell off. It did get embarrassing. Ina thought that my wig might come off, but it didn't.'

'Why did he grab your wig?' asked Pauline.

'Because he was not keen on worldly possessions and wanted me to find Jesus without my wig.'

'And are you going again?' asked Patsy.

'No, it's not for me.'

The Pentecostal church was certainly different from our Catholic church. Although my mother never went to church herself, she sent my sisters and me every Sunday to St Mary's on Lorrimore Road. We put on our Sunday best and walked there together. I had a large pink hat with a brim and plastic flowers on the side, white buckle-over shoes, white gloves from school, my brushed crushed velvet dress, and the coat that I wore was a brown mushroomy fake fur with different piles on it so it looked a bit like a tree trunk. Pauline had an identical hat, but hers was green. She had a Dalmatian coat with black and white patches in fake fur, and she wore her school gloves. Patsy had an identical pale blue hat and coat. The Father wore a black cassock with a sort of silk scarf over his shoulders. He did not look at all like the pastor at the Pentecostal church.

II

Cinderella Goes to the Ball

1969

'No, you cannot go out. There is work to be done. Have you cleaned the kitchen? Have you swept the stairs? Where is Pauline? Whose turn is it to cook? Get out of my way and go and find something useful to do.'

We had until Friday to work on her, if we wanted to go to the church disco, which was held in the church hall in Dulwich every Friday. If we all worked hard, she would have nothing to complain about. Pauline and Patsy, I was pretty sure, would have been hanging about on the third floor listening to the conversation I had just had with our mother. Pauline would have crept out of her bedroom onto the top landing with Patsy. They were always there, always listening in, always on the third floor. As my mother walked away, I waited a little while and then I heard the click of the door. I was right; they had retreated into their room.

As I made my way upstairs, it seemed like a good idea to tell my sisters what my mother had said – after all, it was their idea that I should make the approach. I was quite certain they would both like to know what was said even though she said it loud enough for the good Lord in heaven to hear, never mind my sisters on the third floor who I knew had heard anyway.

The house made me sick. My mother made me sick. My sisters just made me hate them. But they were young; maybe they could do more, say more and be around more, but they wanted to remain on good terms with my mother. Who could blame them?

My mother had disappeared into the bathroom area, which was situated in the ground-floor rear extension. The bathroom area also housed the washing machine. The room was permanently damp for two reasons: the floor was concrete and the walls were painted in a gloss white finish – as a result of this, whenever the bathroom was used the steam would rise up to the highest point and form droplets on the ceiling and steam drips along the wall. On most days it was possible to write on the wall with one finger. It wasn't pleasant working in this damp atmosphere, but today we would have to brave it and get all the washing done immaculately.

With a bit of luck it might be possible for me to get back to the third floor without my mother calling me. I knew now why she had been interfering with the stairs – she was not trying to make a death trap, but ensuring that the stairs creaked when you walked on them. That way she thought she would know whenever we went up or down the stairs.

I took the first step, one leg still on the hall carpet and one hand on the banister. I listened. There was no sound. My mother was preoccupied. I raised my left foot, placed it on the second step, paused and waited. Still no sound from the back. The door was slightly ajar but I was unable to see through the crack, since that would require me shifting my weight onto my right foot. Next it was important to swing over the third step, using both feet and both hands. I would need the assistance of the dado rail. I had been caught a few times on the third step recently and this time it was necessary to complete the task.

Over. Wait. No noise. Good. I crept up the stairs to the top of the first flight, waited on the half-landing. Still no noise. No one in the kitchen. I turned and crept up the second flight of stairs. On the landing there was no one in my room or the room next door. I thought they had taken cover when I was speaking to my mother. I turned and went up the final flight. Now it was easy-peasy. The two rooms at the top were unusually quiet and both doors were shut. Straight ahead of me was my sisters' room. They had a nice room

Ugly

away from it all, at the top of the house. My brothers shared the back room. My sister Christine and adopted sister, Denise, shared the middle-floor front bedroom and I shared the back bedroom with myself. Because I wet the bed and smelt of piss all the time, no one could or should be expected to put up with my dirty habits. It was also the first bedroom upstairs after my mother's room. I opened my sisters' door a fraction. I could feel the tension on the other side of the door and when I was quite certain that they did not know if it was me or my mother, I aggressively turned the handle and burst in.

'What do you want?' said Pauline Four Eyes, looking scared. Patsy did not say anything. Precious Puss.

'She said we had to do the housework. She said I should get out of her sight and if I asked her once more she would slap me. She said we should clean up the house, go and wash the plates and start cooking.'

'I told you we shouldn't have asked her,' said Four Eyes.

'You're lying, Four Eyes; it was you that sent me.'

We decided we would clean the house, do the cooking and I would ask her again. It was better for me to ask, because I was always in trouble with my mother anyway and things could not get worse for me; if my sisters fell out with my mother they had a lot to lose – there was always a chance that she might dish out similar treatment to them. Anyway we had a vote as usual as to who should ask my mother and I lost. I went downstairs making no attempt to remain quiet. When I got to the second floor, I opened my bedroom door and closed it loudly. I then went down to the next half-landing and looked into the kitchen. The place was in a mess, but we were so practised that it would not take very long to clean it all up. I then carried on down the stairs. I decided to step on the very step as there was no point in doing otherwise and besides I had not yet shared the secret of the step with the others and wasn't sure that I would. Step seven was okay, as was step six, and step five was fine – but step four squeaked a little, which was nothing in comparison to step three.

The entire staircase seemed to creak once I put both my feet on the step, so much so that oiling the step did not seem inappropriate. As I stood on step three thinking it was all very funny, my mother appeared. Step three had brought her out. She appeared from the back of the house like a drooping sunflower which had finally discovered the sun.

'Didn't I tell you to clean the house?' she said. 'Wait. You think you're a big woman, don't you?' With that, she produced the split-split stick, which I had seen before.

'You think – Jesus Christ – Clear thinks she's a big woman. Oh, I see. Well, there's only one fucking big woman in this house. If you're a fucking big woman wait, Jesus Christ. Lord my God. Clear thinks she's a big woman.' With that my mother grabbed me by the collar of my Peter Pan dress. She crushed the button and the pretty lace, which met in the middle section of the bodice, as she scooped the material to the left and right of my collar bones.

'Jesus Christ, Clear thinks she's a big woman.'

She dragged me over the banister as I was trying to slip out of my dress and run back upstairs.

'No, I don't,' I said. 'I never said I was a big woman. I never said that. Who said that? I said that? I never said that.'

My mother increased her grip and dragged me partially over the banister. She was standing on the step which led to the back of the house and I was standing on step three holding on to the spindles and the banister.

'I never said I was a big woman. Leave my dress alone! Get off!'

'Oh, so you're a big woman that answers back. Oh, I see.'

With that my mother moved around the step and into the hall, still holding on to my Peter Pan collar. As she got in front of me, she raised her left hand and brought down the split-split stick across my left arm with some force. I was trying to protect my arms and legs, but my dress had short sleeves with lace that was stitched into the lilac gingham. My legs were protected as long as I sat on the stairs, because my dress had lots of pleats, which fell below my ankle when I was huddled up. The next blow landed on the same arm above my elbow and I saw my skin rise almost in defiance of my mother.

'What have I done this time? What?' I moved to step four. The higher up the stairs I was, the less leverage my mother had.

'What have I done now? I was only coming downstairs to ask if you wanted a cup of tea and to hoover the stairs. I can go back to my room.'

'Do I look as if I want a cup of tea? Look at me good. Do I look like I want you, Miss Piss-the-bed, to make me a cup of tea? You smell like piss. Go and find something to do.' With that my mother let go of my Peter Pan collar and grabbed my hair in front. 'You've always given me trouble. Why can't you be like the rest? Abortions were not legal when I was carrying you otherwise I would have strung you up.' She pulled me towards her, which caused me to lose my grip on the banister and fall forward. The rest of my body was spread out over steps two, one and the hall. I grabbed the hand which held my hair to ease the pain. She brought the split-split stick down across my hand.

'Move your hand, bitch. Move your hand. Wait. Do you want to fight me? Move your hand, bitch.'

I held on to her hand. She brought the split-split stick down across my back.

'Yes, it's a good thing that abortions were illegal. I would have strung you up. Do you think I would have poisoned myself for you, Miss Piss-the-bed? Do you think you're worth a plastic stem? You've got no manners, always answering back, always causing me trouble and still pissing the bed. You pissed my mattress. Why did you do that?'

Several blows missed their target as my mother ranted on and on. As she brought the split-split stick up and over her head, it caught in the glass chandelier, which only infuriated my mother more. As the chandelier swung in a violent mood, the light see-sawed above my mother's head from light to dark and back again. My Peter Pan collar had lost a button. I thought quite clearly that I would find it later. My mother would not defeat me.

'All I said was would you like a cup of tea,' I said. 'Why don't you just kill me? Go on, kill me dead. They will all know what you have been up to. You know you want to. No use pretending. Go on – what is stopping you? You make me sick and I don't like you. I never did, ever since I knew you were my mother. So kill me now, because, if you don't, when I go to school on Monday I'm going to tell Miss Golding *everything* you've done.'

My mother stood with her split-split stick above her head with the chandelier swaying ever so gently. And then I heard it. The door clicked upstairs, clicked and then clicked again. Four Eyes and Precious Puss and my brothers had retreated into the bedroom.

'Go on,' I repeated. 'What are you waiting for? Might as well kill me, because I'm going to tell on Monday.'

With that my mother's right hand grabbed my Peter Pan collar, while with her left hand she gathered up the front of my dress and pulled me towards her, so that my nose was about twelve inches away from her. Her pink cardigan had become snagged in the split-split stick during the beating. I had always liked that cardigan. My mother often wore it. I called it my mother's beating cardigan. The buttons were oyster pink and they bulged with pink thread which held them to the wool.

'Tell what? What is there to tell?' She pulled me towards her again and moved her hand down towards my nipple as she scooped my left breast in her hand. 'What is there to tell?' She pinched the skin to the left of the breast and twisted it in her hand.

'Nothing,' I said. 'I'm not going to tell. Nothing.'

'And why are you going to tell nothing? Why? Why? Why?' She pinched my breast like a crab using a pincer movement.

'I'm not going to tell, because you don't want me to tell.'

My mother moved her hand to my left nipple and squeezed it between her fingers. 'No, wrong again. I want you to tell everything. But what is there to tell? Has something happened to you? Tell me. What?'

She dug her nails into my nipple and pulled me towards her.

The pain was such that I imagined my nipple coming off in my mother's hand. The tears welled up in my eyes. As they splashed onto my hand, it began to sting. There was already a criss-crossing of raised skin from contact with the split-split stick. I used my left hand to wipe my face with my Peter Pan collar. My collar had a speck of blood on the lace. I decided not to wipe the other side of my face. The pain was unbearable and I was sinking fast to the floor. I had to remain standing and I did not want her to think she had won. I had to talk to her face to face.

'Nothing has happened which the school need know about.'

'No,' said my mother. 'Wrong again.'

She let go of my nipple, doubled her fist and then she punched me in the left breast. The force caused me to fall backwards. The split-split stick fell to the floor. I turned and took to my heels back up the stairs to my room. My arms were stinging and my hands hurt. My dress had come apart from the bodice, but was reparable. My left breast felt like it had been stung by a bee. There were pinchmarks above the nipple and to the left, and a soft indentation separated by a ridge, which was about an inch long. My dress had little bits of carpet fluff on it from where I had been dragged along the hall and the hem was unstitched. My eyes were quite swollen from crying, but the swelling would soon disappear.

As I was looking at my face in the mirror, she came in. She stood in the door with the split-split stick in her hand. We stood in silence as we observed each other. She did not say a word and I chose to copy her. As we looked at each other she came into my room and raised her hand, bringing the split-split stick down across my back.

'I'm not going to tell you again. Go and find something to do.'

With that, she was gone. I closed my bedroom door and continued to look at my face in the mirror. I dabbed it with the hem of my dress, pressed my hair backwards with my hands, blew my nose and went downstairs. The hoover was kept in the ante-room along with all the rubbish. My mother was nowhere in sight and my sisters were hiding upstairs somewhere. I took the hoover up to the third floor, plugged it in, did the top landing and made my way down, hoovering each step. The bedroom door opened.

'You all right, Clear? You should shut up,' whispered Four Eyes.

I made no reply.

'Can we help?'

Just at that moment, we heard footsteps on the floor below. We knew it was my mother on the first half-landing. As I turned round to face my sister, her head disappeared and her bedroom door shut. My mother was now behind me and I could sense her watching me as I worked down each step. When I came to her I hoovered around her as though she wasn't there. I hoovered around her feet, in front of her feet, behind her feet and to the side. Not a word was spoken between us and when I was satisfied I had done a good job I moved down the stairs.

My mother remained motionless, arms crossed, but we both knew she was watching me. Job complete, I put the hoover away. She wasn't on my landing and she wasn't in my room. She had to be upstairs. In my room I soaked the hem of my skirt in spit and wiped my arms. I spat some more for my legs and the back of my hands. I didn't look good and I felt sad. My dress was unstitched. I tied the unstitched material in a small knot and tucked it up and underneath the bodice. I went downstairs to find my button and then went back upstairs.

'Chicken!' she shouted. 'Clare, how long do you think the chicken should wait for you? Do you want to come down or shall I come up for you?'

'It's not my turn to cook,' I said. 'It's Pauline's turn. It's my turn to wash up.'

'Come down now,' she said.

I made my way downstairs. Pauline had heard what was said, because she joined me on the landing and we went downstairs together while our mother stood in the hall, watching us. When we got to the bottom we had to walk around her. As I was ahead of my sister, I decided to stay in front. As I passed my mother on the bend in the hall, she raised her right hand and punched me in the back of the head. I continued to the kitchen. My sister followed. No words were exchanged.

I glanced round by the kitchen door to see if my sister too had received a punch; but no. My mother simply stood there with her fist clenched. We set to work and my mother disappeared downstairs to the back of the house. We worked in silence. Pauline cooked, I helped. She washed the rice; I prepared the chicken. As I cleaned up the feathers and washed up the dishes my sister asked what did I think about Friday. Should we not bother, or continue?

'Continue,' I said. 'Just make sure that all the clothes are washed, the sitting room is hoovered, the bedrooms are all tidy and I'll ask her again.'

Nothing more was said. Dinner was uneventful. We all sat and ate and my mother had her food served up on her special dinner service. I took her meal down to her and asked her if she would like a cup of tea. Tea was served in her special cup. I asked very politely if she would like me to get her some condensed milk. 'Yes,' she said.

The back bedroom was dark but I made my way towards the French doors which led to the garden. The food was piled high there because my mother thought it would stay fresh with all that cool air coming through. There were biscuits, lots of biscuits, Jammy Dodgers and custard creams, cream crackers; milk, fresh and condensed, and one tin of evaporated milk. I took a packet of Jammy Dodgers and put them in my knickers at the same time as I picked up the condensed milk. It was an open tin of Nestle's Carnation milk. My mother poured it into her cup and then I had to put back the tin to its rightful place in the back room. As I returned I paused and turned so I was half facing her.

'I think I'll do the laundry. Have you got any washing?' My mother remained silent. 'I'd like to hoover this room when you've finished eating.'

The washing was finished, bins emptied and the sitting room hoovered. All the laundry was spun in the spin-dryer and hung on the line. By about 7.30 the house was spotless. I knocked on the sitting-room door. My mother invited me in.

'Can we go to the disco?' I said.

Without looking at me my mother said, 'Go and find something to do.'

'There is nothing to do; can we go to the disco?'

'Go and clean the kitchen,' she said.

'It's done.'

'Go and hoover the stairs.'

'They're hoovered.'

'Well, there is washing – dirty clothes that need to be washed.'

'It's all done and the sitting room and the bathroom and the kitchen are all done. Can we go to the disco?'

For a while my mother was speechless. I stayed put and waited.

'You can go if you want to, but if you do don't expect to sleep here.'

When I went upstairs, my sisters were on the top landing; they were huddled together holding on to the spindles.

'What did she say?' asked Four Eyes.

I walked into their bedroom. Precious Puss was behind me. I took my time.

'She said that we can go, but we shouldn't expect to sleep here afterwards.'

We had a general discussion about what this could mean but we didn't really care – we were all going anyway.

That Friday I went to Mass at Sacred Heart. I wore my white gloves, pleated skirt and beret. Next I went off to school, which was next door, and assembly took place after Mass, the same as always. Miss Golding, my form mistress, took me to one side in assembly and asked if anything was wrong. I assured her that there wasn't.

'Are you sure, Clare?'

'Yes,' I said. 'Nothing is wrong, miss.'

'And you would say if there was, would you, Clare? Promise me,' she said.

'Yes, miss,' I said. 'Yes, miss.'

'You know you can always talk to me, don't you?'

'Yes, miss.'

'Is there anything you want to talk about?'

'No, miss.'

We looked at each other as she sat next to me and I knew that she knew that something was not quite right.

We had a wonderful lunch that day. I stood in the line for free dinners; we always seemed to be first, because we were more needy and hungry than those who paid for their school meals. Friday was a good day for Catholics – cod, chips, peas, two carrots, lumpy custard, apple crumble. Delicious.

Classes were soon over and we were able to make our way back home. We three girls had never been to a disco before. Well, it wasn't quite a disco, more a local gathering in the church hall in Dulwich where there were soft drinks, music and lots of new people to meet. They opened the hall in Cobblestone Place every Friday. It was miles from our house. I'm not sure how we first heard about it, but now we were definitely going.

Back home from school, we all decided that it was best to keep out of our mother's way, to stay in our rooms, and if at any time we came into contact with her we would pretend to be busy. We did not want to risk her changing her mind at the last minute. At last 6.45 arrived and we were all ready. We met on the top landing all dressed up – no make-up – and all we had to do now was get out of the door. We all went downstairs, checking as we went along that the stairs were hoovered, kitchen clean, plates washed up, all items dried and put away, the bathroom clean, ante-room full of rubbish but tidy. Finally, I knocked on my mother's room but she did not answer.

'We're all off now,' I called from outside the door. 'We'll be back at ten thirty.'

We ran out of the house as quickly as possible just in case my mother wanted us to do some more housework. When we were at a safe distance from home we started to slow down. Our first disco was less than an hour away.

The group of us travelled on the 184 bus to Dulwich and got off at Underhill Road. The church hall was a five-minute walk from the bus stop. My sister Pauline took charge once we got off the bus and she instructed us as to how we should behave when we were inside the hall. We should not drink any drink at all, unless she bought it or we bought it ourselves. We should ask for a bottle of Coke and make sure the bottle was opened in front of us. It was dangerous to have a sip of someone else's drink and no one was allowed to leave the hall. We were happy with those instructions as we all knew that tonight had to be a success if there was to be any possibility of going again. We needed to return home without incident.

We all paid a shilling and were given a raffle ticket. We could leave the hall and re-enter once; after that we would have to pay another entrance fee. There really was no reason to leave the hall once we had entered. We went down three steps into the main hall and turned left into a large room. In the far corner of the room were huge speakers which spat out Gregory Isaac and Stevie Wonder. Lovers' rock was simply for the lovers. There were about a hundred people packed in the room, some so close together that it was impossible to distinguish one from the other. Some of the men had lined up against the walls, while the girls seemed to be mainly in the centre of the room or outside in the hall. It seemed odd that the men were along the walls. Surely they would want to mingle, come over and talk to us, me especially.

During the evening we stayed quite close together; only Pauline went out of the hall and across the way to purchase soft drinks for all of us. The drinks were very expensive so she bought two bottles to share between us. As she was returning with our drinks a man grabbed her hand; it wasn't an aggressive grab, but it was firm. I saw it in the pool of light that shone into the room from the hall. He was short, a little taller than my sister, but short for a man. He was standing just in front of the door on the left as you went in. It was then that my sister, instead of bringing our drinks to us, decided to put them on the floor as she danced with the short man. He put his hand round her neck and my sister looked around the room quickly and then put her hand around his waist. As the music bellowed a slow meaningful tune the lovers rocked.

The short man arched his back away from the wall and thrust his groin into my sister's crotch. Connected, he began to rock with her by moving his left shoulder down the wall while his back remained arched and his right shoulder rose in a circular movement only to be drawn down. The purpose of this movement was plain to see. The short man was able to lovers' rock his groin against my sister's minnie, while pretending to dance. The wall behind prevented the short man falling backwards as he rocked and rocked. My sister was arched over him as was every other girl in the room – each arched over her dancing partner, having their lovers' rock. When the music stopped my sister picked up the drinks and made her way towards us. She handed over our drinks and told us how much we were allowed to have before it was her turn. Patsy and I said nothing, but I could not contain myself. I started to laugh.

'What were you doing with him?' I chuckled. 'Wait till I tell – you'll get a beating.'

'No,' said Pauline, '*you'll* get a beating. You asked to come here, not me. So if you tell, you'll get a beating.'

That was true; it was also true that old Four Eyes was at it again. It was never her fault even when it was. I had no intention of telling anyway. Once I'd finished my turn with the drink, I handed my bottle over and put my hands in my pockets. No one was going to grab my hand, let alone my minnie. I didn't mind dancing on my own and I didn't want a lovers' rock.

The evening was quickly exhausted. We had a good time, no cooking, no washing, no beating, no mother. The disco ended all too quickly. As the party poured out onto the street we all hung around with everyone else and then made our way slowly to the bus stop. Most of the crowd had dispersed but a fair number of people got on the bus with us. The short man was sitting next to my sister, but she was trying to ignore him – if he turned up at our house, my mother would kill him, her and me. Between now and home, she had to get rid of him. When we got to Peckham, a few more people got on the bus, but Short Man got off at Camberwell Green. My sister had said that she would be there next week and he was happy to believe her.

By the time we arrived back at Sutherland Square, we were within fifteen minutes of our expected time of return. It was late and dark. Our mother would be waiting for us. She would not have gone to bed without knowing what time we returned home. As we approached our front door, Pauline had her key in her hand to stop it making a noise and alerting our mother, who was probably in her bedroom. Pauline put the key in the door and told us to take our shoes off so we wouldn't make a noise on the stairs. I told my sisters not to walk on step three – I didn't give reasons and they didn't ask. They knew that I knew something they didn't and now was not the time to ask.

The key was eased into the door, and slowly Pauline turned it; it moved with ease anti-clockwise. As we lined up behind her to step into the house, she whispered, 'It won't turn.' She tried to force the key, but it would not move beyond three o'clock. It was removed from the lock and Patsy's key was tried. The key turned slowly to the left and then again to the right. At three o'clock the key would not budge and no amount of delicate persuasion would encourage it to do so. My key was also tried and it failed in the same way.

As we looked at each other and wondered what to do, it was clear to us that the latch was down on the lock, preventing us from entering. In hushed voices, we considered our options. It was now eleven o'clock; we were late and there were no lights on in the house. We could sleep outside, try to get inside, or ring the bell. The last option was quickly dismissed; we did not want to cause our mother any unnecessary emotional overspill, not on our evening out. We decided that the door had failed to open because we were not inserting our keys the right way, so one by one each key was retrieved and inserted into the lock once more, and one by one each key failed.

As we were putting our keys away, we heard what we thought was movement on the other side of the door. We froze like shadows on the pavement. We listened in silence . . . nothing . . . and then we heard it again. I pressed myself up against the door and I was certain there was something the other side, a presence, not a nice presence, but a familiar one. I put my finger to my lips and silenced my sisters with a glare. They pressed their ears to the side of the door. Very gently I opened the letter-box flap a fraction and then, satisfied that the movement would not cause any squeak, I applied more pressure to the flap. It opened just enough for me to see the floor on the other side of the door. My mother's shoes were visible. She was standing in the far corner of the hall. I paused for a moment, not knowing whether to point her out to my sisters, or just ask her to open the door. It was clear that she did not want to be detected, but it was silly. Maybe she did not know that the latch was on the lock, maybe it had fallen down by accident. Maybe not.

I lowered the flap and considered what to do next. Pauline and Patsy were inviting me to try the key again, but I shook my head. It was now really late and we were all getting anxious. Next option, ring the bell. As we were considering this, we heard the sound of the bolt slowly being pushed into position. Someone on the other side of the door had bolted us out. The latch was no mistake; whoever had put the latch on wanted us to remain outside. I opened the flap of the letter box again just a fraction and this time the shoes had gone. I turned to Pauline and Patsy. I didn't think there was any point in trying to get in. We decided to go around the corner and think about what to do.

As we got to Sutherland Square, I turned back and looked at the house and was sure that I saw my mother looking out of the twins' bedroom. We went to the grass area just before the square turned into Lorrimore Road. The houses across the square were built on stilts so it was possible to walk or play beneath them and they provided us with shelter.

'I've got an idea,' I said. 'Why don't we go around the back? We can get in that way.'

'Good idea,' said Pauline.

Each of the houses in our row had a small garden consisting of a narrow strip of concrete opening up into a decent-size London garden. It was about fifty feet from the French doors to the back garden wall. Beyond the row of gardens was an area of wasteland the size of a football pitch, full of rubble, weeds and wild flowers. It was surrounded by a corrugated-iron fence. The sharp edges at the top of this, together with the rust, were not ideal to climb in our church hall best. It proved difficult for all of us. Pauline suggested that we help Patsy over the wall first and then she could find some rubble and throw it over the wall and then we would use that to climb over.

Pauline and I crouched and locked our hands together to form a step upon which Patsy stood. She held on to our shoulders and we stood up slowly which allowed her to grab on to the edge of the corrugated-iron wall and get her leg over. Once that was achieved, the other leg was easy-peasy. Patsy ran off and found some old tyres. She threw them over the fence and Pauline and I piled them up into a pyramid. Then Pauline climbed up and pulled me up after her. Within no time we were all the right side of the iron wall.

Making our way across the wasteland was more difficult than we could possibly have imagined. It was dark. Piles of rubble blocked our path; giant weeds rubbed themselves against our hands and face and sometimes stung our bare legs. We followed in a line, up and down across the rubble, Pauline, Patsy, and me. Keeping close together was not difficult. We were all so terrified that the bats, ghosts, Dracula and Frankenstein would get us that we moved as a solid block. I was terrified of creepy-crawlies. As we bumped into each other in the dark our terror became all the more acute. We all wanted to be in the middle, no one wanted to be first or last. In the middle you were the filling in the sandwich and anything trying to get us would have to start on the outside and work its way in.

The back of our house was easily recognisable. It was the seventh house along from the railway and it had a ladder in the garden, which luckily was up against my bedroom window. Recently our neighbours on one side had had a problem with the pigeons which were in their lean-to. In order to get rid of them the workmen had to have access to our side of the lean-to. Although the work had been completed some weeks ago the ladder was still there.

Climbing over the back wall was easy and the drop into our garden was only a matter of feet. All we had to do now was to watch out for our mother's peppermint plants. We agreed that we would go up the ladder into my bedroom and then Pauline and Patsy would sneak up to their bedroom on the third floor. No lights would be turned on and there would be no noise. They would remove their shoes in my bedroom. My mother's bedroom was directly below mine and I was beginning to question whether I had really seen her in the hall. I mean, had I really, *really* seen her – or was it my imagination?

I went first, it was my room and I was familiar with it. I stood on the ladder and opened the window from above, conscious of the fact that my mother might decide at any time to look out of the French door and up the ladder. The windows to my bedroom had recently been replaced. The old ones had slid up and down on invisible cords. The new ones opened out; the plain glass filled about two-thirds of the windowspace. Above that were three louvred strips of glass, which opened inwards all at the same time. Unfortunately, the main window was shut. I had shut it the night before, after I had aired my room from the previous night's bed-wetting. However, we had not come all this way to be defeated. I twisted the slit windows and managed to open them to the maximum. Then I squeezed my hand through and flicked the lock on the main window. Next, with just a small amount of pressure on the frame, the main window opened. I jumped down inside my room, quickly followed by Pauline and Patsy. The windows were closed without noise or incident.

I drew the curtains and bent down in order to flick my shoes off. My sisters followed. I removed one shoe and then, just as I was about to remove the other, the bedroom light was switched on. It was our mother; she was wearing the same shoes that I had seen in the hall when I had opened the flap of the letter box. She looked at me and I looked right back. She did not move in our direction. She did not alter her position at all. She stood by the door and said, 'Go back the way you came.'

I did not need to be told twice. I was the first to move. I put my shoes on, opened the curtains and the window and climbed back down into the garden. Poor Patsy. Poor Precious Puss. When she came down the ladder she looked terrified. Pauline joined us in the garden and my mother shut the window, drew the curtains and switched off the light. By now Patsy was in tears and Pauline looked at me more inquisitively than anything else.

I walked back towards my mother's peppermint plants and trampled over them deliberately as I scaled the wall. Back we went over the rubble, through the bats to the iron wall. Patsy had a leg-over again and then threw the tyres for us to climb. Once over the wall we stood exhausted and in silence. We had nowhere to go and it was dark. We decided that we would go and wait under the flats in Lorrimore Road and just think about our options. I'm not sure who suggested that we go and try the front door again. We thought perhaps Denise and Christine had heard the commotion in my bedroom and had unlocked the door.

We walked back to our house and Pauline tried the front door. There was no need to be silent putting the key in the lock because our mother knew we were outside. It was not as if we were going to wake her up. Pauline inserted the key. She hesitated at three o'clock, but when she turned the key, it rotated to six o'clock and then nine o'clock. The door was open. We all rushed into the hall fearing that our mother might decide to ask us to leave the house. No one turned the light on. We simply went upstairs with our shoes on. I went into my room, Pauline and Patsy continued upstairs.

Once inside, I took my clothes off, put my nightdress on and turned to get into bed. It was gone. I turned the light on and looked again. My bed was not in the room. My sheets, blanket and pillow were on the floor, but the bedhead, springs and mattress had gone. It was now two o'clock in the morning. I was very tired and did not want to upset my mother by asking her about my bed. I cleared a space on the floor, folded a blanket longways, covered it with a sheet, put the pillow at one end and folded the remaining sheet and blanket and placed them on top. I then slid into the middle of the blankets. I thought about the short man and my sister, the music and the fun, the music and the peace. We would go again.

12

The Vanishing Bed

1969

The next morning was Saturday. I was startled and immediately felt the bedclothes. No, they were dry. I felt behind my
bottom. Dry. Lower down. Dry. Thank you, God. I got up
and went to the toilet just to make sure that there was no
accident. I did not want an accident – not today. Sometimes
when I was daydreaming in bed, I had such a wonderful
sensation of being warm and happy in my own world that I
would forget myself and wet the bed. I liked daydreaming
happy dreams.

I must have dozed off again, because when I opened my eyes,
my mother was standing next to my makeshift bed. She bent
down, took hold of the edge of the blanket beneath me and
pulled it, rolling me over into the wall. Then she was in front of
me with my blanket in her hand. She was working her way from
the top of the blanket to the bottom, checking it for wetness. It
was all very silly: all she had to do was ask me. I knew it was not
wet. She then threw the blanket in my direction, not at me, but
more in my face. It landed on my ear and I left it there until I
heard the door pull to. I stayed there for a while and when I was
sure that she was not going to return, I pulled the blanket over
my head. My back ached, my neck was stiff but I had had a good
night's sleep. No wet bed.

Pauline and Patsy were both upstairs. My mother did not
need to check on them. I waited in my room until it was
necessary to get up. I did not really want to leave my room.
It was *my* room. I was wrapped up in my own world, where

mummies were kind. I did not want to leave, but the life I had to live every day would begin soon enough.

Pauline came downstairs. I could hear her on the stairs outside my door. Christine was also up. They went downstairs. It was not my turn to make breakfast, was it? I turned over onto my stomach and rested my chin on my folded arms. Yesterday was so funny – my sister and that man.

When I finally got up and went downstairs, my mother was nowhere in sight. I slipped past the third step, had a quick wash in the bathroom and went back upstairs to choose a dress for the day. The good thing about hand-me-downs is that there is so much to choose from. My pink crushed velvet dress fitted me very well. Besides, it had been bought for *me*. My father bought three in a market in the East End for Four Eyes, Precious Puss and me. I had been the first to wear it. I thought that I'd wear it again. I always preferred to wear clothes that were bought especially for me, but there was an exception. It was another crushed velvet dress, but this one was green. Two years earlier it had belonged to Patsy and before that it was Pauline's. I had grown well into the dress, but it would take me a little while longer to grow into the sleeves. Meanwhile the sleeves were worn turned back and tucked in. I felt good today. I put on the green dress.

Then I set about my weekend work. I hoovered the stairs from top to bottom, cleaned the kitchen and the bathroom. Still no sign of my mother. The sitting room needed hoovering, but that could wait. The plates left over from the morning's breakfast were in the sink. They did not take long to wash, dry and replace in their rightful position. The toilet was a mess. The floor was made of concrete and painted dark red. The watermarks were obvious and someone had pissed partly on the floor. I hated cleaning the toilet. I squeezed the Ajax and shook it vigorously into the pan. Dust clouds slowly made their way to the side of the pan and settled. The other clouds reset on top of the water like a film. Next the clothes had to be washed for Monday. My bedclothes needed washing; although they were dry, the smell was not good. I had had a number of bed-wet incidents during the week. The ironing came next, after a spin in the twin-tub. Finished.

Homework should have been next, but I thought it wasn't worth taking the risk. Maybe breakfast? I nipped downstairs but heard my mother moving about in the kitchen. On second thoughts I'd have breakfast later. At the back of my wardrobe I had my emergency supply of Jammy Dodgers. I removed one from the packet and set about my homework. Stretched out on the floor, I did my English comprehension.

Pauline came into my room and I turned to face her.

'Where's your bed?' she asked.

'I don't know. It's vanished.'

'Beds don't just vanish. When did you last see it?'

'Yesterday, before we went out.' She didn't say anything after that. 'Have you got a bed?' I asked.

'Yes, it's upstairs.'

She left and I stayed in my room. Within a few minutes of Pauline disappearing, Patsy, Christine and Denise came into the room.

'Where is your bed?' asked Christine.

'I don't know. It was here when I left last night and it's not here now.'

'Do you want us to go look for it?' said Denise.

'No, I don't think so. It will turn up.'

They stood against the wall and watched me. There was no need to say anything else. We all knew that the disappearance of my bed had everything to do with my mother.

In the early afternoon, about one o'clock, my mother called me. 'Clear, come downstairs, now. Or do you want me to come up and get you?'

I put my homework away and went downstairs. She had been shopping in East Street Market and had bought the food. The huge shopping basket was in the hall. I emptied out the sweet biscuits, cream crackers and sugar first, took them into my mother's bedroom and piled them by the French doors. Next came the milk – condensed and evaporated – also put by the French doors. Potatoes, carrots, onions and meat went into the kitchen. The chicken had a purple neck and many of its feathers. Its beak was open, and there was dried blood down the side of its gullet. Crisps – into my mother's room. Black-eye peas, rice and porridge into the kitchen. The sarsaparilla was always kept in the front sitting room, next to her glass display unit, together with the orange juice.

As I put it down next to the unit I looked in the glass and saw my mattress in the reflection. I turned round and there was my bedhead. It was all stacked behind the settee. She must have worked very hard to dismantle my bed while we were out at the disco. It would have been easier if she had simply asked me to sleep on the floor, and then there would have been no need to take my bed away.

Once I had finished my task I went to find my mother. She was sitting in the kitchen with my sisters, Pauline and Patsy. They were her favourites. It just seemed to me that their life was so much easier than mine.

'Is there anything else to do?' I said.

'Go and clean the bathroom.'

'It's done, and the toilet is cleaned, all the hoovering is done and all the clothes are on the line.'

'Go and find something to do!' she bellowed.

'Do you mind if I make myself a cup of tea?' I asked.

She ignored me and continued talking to Pauline and Patsy. I stayed by the door, in sight but out of arm's reach. I stood there and waited. She had a large bag in front of her, crushed up. 'Try these on and let me see if they fit,' she said, and with that she handed Pauline and Patsy a sherbet-lemon and lime-green skirt and jacket, really fashionable. While they were holding the garments up to themselves, I went round the back of my mother and sisters, put the kettle on and made myself a cup of tea. I squeezed out the tea bag and disappeared downstairs and then, when I was sure that she was distracted with my sisters, I dashed into her room, quickly seized the milk, poured the sugar in the cup and rushed back to the door. I waited for a moment and when I heard the laughter from upstairs, I sneaked outside and pushed the door closed. I went to the ante-room, took a sip of tea and then hid my cup behind some old clothes. I walked back upstairs into the kitchen. Pauline had her new garments on – a very nice two-piece with a mid-length skirt and mid-length jacket.

'That's nice,' I said as Patsy stepped into her skirt.

'Go to your room, get out of my sight,' said my mother.

I hesitated and then went to my room. English composition next. Then I had some free time. Soon my mother would call me again, but in the meantime I had no more homework. I went back down into the ante-room, finished my tea and returned to my room with the cup. I hid it at the back of the wardrobe with my biscuits. It would be returned to the kitchen when it was safe.

A mood of depression settled on me. Life was unfair. I was tired of having to take biscuits from my mother's room, tired of the struggle to keep out of her way. I did not want any more hand-me-downs. It was then I took a decision to find myself a Saturday job, the kitchen job with Eastman had been a one-off. Any job that would help me pay for new clothes. But who would employ me? There might be a job where I did not have to use National Insurance cards. Then I would be able to afford my own dresses and underwear. No more baggy knickers.

I kept out of the way most of the day, only venturing out when the coast was clear. My sisters and brothers were upstairs. It was possible they were watching telly with my mother.

All my homework was done, packed into my satchel and placed by the door of my bedroom. My hand-me-down school blazer was still too big for me. It was worn away at the elbows and a dull shine was now a permanent feature. My skirt was still too long for me, but it would fit if the waistband was turned over four times. When I did that, the waist bulged from compressed pleats. My grey skirt and black blazer and blouse were laid out flat on the floor next to my satchel. My school shoes were beyond repair, but would have to last until my next hand-me-down. By about nine thirty everything was laid out ready for school. I hadn't had any dinner but that could wait. I wasn't hungry, just full of hunger. My sisters would probably bring me some food if they remembered that I was not at the table. There was no point in worrying about this now. One day I would be able to be me.

I drifted into sleep, then became conscious of someone in my room. Patsy was poking me.

'Clear, Clear – quick,' she whispered. I didn't feel like answering. She didn't think of me when she was eating, why come into my room now? There was a pat on the blanket and with that she left the room and shut the door. I popped my head out from under the blanket and saw on my pillow two dumplings wrapped in tissue. She had *not* forgotten about me. Mmm – *nice* brown dumplings. I sat up on the floor on my blankets and started to peel off the tissue from around one of the dumplings. The blanket was still wrapped around my shoulders. My back ached and there was a draught coming from the fireplace, but under the blanket I was quite comfortable. I had no idea how long I had been asleep, but it was now dark outside.

Just as I was tucking into my food, the first that had passed my lips that day, apart from one biscuit I had taken, I heard my mother coming up the stairs. By the time she got to the first landing I had swallowed the first dumpling and put the other one in my knickers. I covered my head and lay down facing away from the door. She came in. I stayed still, not breathing. She was standing over me now. She called me: 'Clear.' I said nothing. 'Clear!' I turned over onto my back, stretched my arms above my head and slowly pulled the blanket down from over my face. 'Hello, Mummy,' I said.

She stared down at me. 'Where is your bed?' she asked.

'I don't know. It was here the other day and now it's gone.'

She went as quickly as she came and I hid under the blanket.

I retrieved the dumpling from my knickers and under the cover I savoured it slowly.

13

A Saturday Job

1969

One Sunday I was sent to East Street Market to get some shopping. My mother gave me a shopping trolley with huge wheels that jammed every now and then. The shopping list went on and on and it was not as if I could get all the food in the same place. There were certain stalls which were prepared to break rank and underprice their competitors. I knew exactly where to go. The stalls were familiar to me after months and months of following my mother around. I left home with half of the money in my purse, which was pinned to the inside lining of my coat, and the other half in the bottom of the shopping trolley underneath the thick base lining. My route to the market took me past Carter Street Police Station. There was a sign up outside saying someone had gone missing; the police wanted anyone who might have information to come forward or ring a number, which was on the poster in red. I wished that I could go missing, but then again, everyone would be looking for me. My mother would have a fit. She would be frantic with worry that I might never return and frantic with worry that if I did return I might just say what had caused me to go missing in the first place. Thinking about it, running away might have its advantages.

At the traffic lights I crossed over to Dolcis, the shoe shop, and went down the middle of East Street Market. It was packed.

'Three for a shilling, love, feast your eyes on those. Come, on missus, best English. Take them away, or if you want more for your money you can have a dozen foreigners for the same price.

That'll surprise the old man! Get your purses out, ladies. Hello, miss! You look foreign! What do you want foreign – or English?'

'English, please,' I said.

'Three apples it is. Coxes or Smiths?'

'Six Coxes, please.'

'Ooh, you greedy little mare. Come on, ladies, take home a foreigner tonight, surprise the old man. Make him sit up.'

The stallholder put the apples in my bag and handed the lady next in the queue a melon.

'It's enough to make your eyes water,' he shouted at the women passing. 'Ladies, ladies, ladies, get a load of that. Have you ever seen such lovely round ones. Every one a winner. Drop that in the old man's hands tonight.'

'A bunch of bananas, please,' I said.

'Ladies, ladies, ladies, come and get your bananas here and now. We've got ripe ones, we've got soft ones, we've got green ones and, ladies, I mean *very* green. And the experienced ladies will know that the only banana worth having is a bunch of green bananas. Come on, ladies, grab a bunch from me. You'll not find a cheaper offer. Guaranteed to turn your green bananas yellow.' He put the bananas in a brown bag and put them in my trolley. 'Anything else, miss?' he said.

'Some plums, please.'

'Oh, ladies, ladies, ladies – what's red and juicy with a hard core and a thick skin? My plums, ladies. Get in the queue. They're falling over themselves to get at my plums. Six for half a crown. Every one a prize-winner. Anything else, love?'

'Yes. May I have three pounds of King Edwards, please?'

'Ladies, ladies, ladies, do you want my King Edwards or what? They are the best, they are the biggest, they are the cheapest. Get a load of my King Edwards. Anything else, love?'

'No, thank you. I think that's it.'

He totted it all up on a brown paper bag. I handed him a ten-shilling note and he gave me the change. I thanked him. As I walked away he shouted, 'Another satisfied customer! Can't get enough of me.' He turned to the next woman in the queue.

'Madam, how can I satisfy you? Does your husband know you're here?'

I jostled my trolley among the other ones being pushed round the market. I needed Carnation milk, condensed milk and sugar. There was a stall somewhere up to the right, my mother had said. It was cheaper than anywhere else. The milk was piled into the bottom of my trolley and next on the list was corned beef and cornflakes. How I hated shopping. What if Lizzie Lock saw me? She would tell the whole class. I avoided her parents' stall and found one that sold cornflakes at a competitive price.

'Three boxes, please,' I said, 'and four bags of sugar.'

'You not sweet enough, love?' said the trader.

'No, I'm not,' I replied.

'No need to get all huffy about it,' he said. 'Anything else?'

'Yes, three tins of corned beef.'

'Go on, love,' he said. 'It ain't all that serious – have a laugh.'

I fixed a smile on my face and grinned at him.

'Come on now,' he said. 'Talk to your uncle Pete. What's the matter?'

I was still grinning at him, but the look in his eyes told me he was serious. I kept on grinning with my fixed grin and then suddenly started to cry.

'I would like a Saturday job,' I said. 'Have you got a vacancy for a Saturday girl?'

'No, love,' he said. 'I don't think I have.'

As he spoke, the tears just seemed to well up in front of my eyes and before long large dollops had run down my cheeks and fallen onto my corned beef and my hands. Then suddenly I started to cry hysterically and as other shoppers gathered around, Pete took me to one side.

'What did you do to make her cry?' shouted one of the shoppers.

'Pervert!' shouted another. 'Call the police.'

Pete ignored them and pulled me between the sugar and the strawberry jam.

'Do you want to talk about it, love?'

'No, I don't,' I said.

'Is it home? Is it bad?'

'Yes.'

'What can I do?'

'You can give me a Saturday job.'

'Honest to God, love, I wish I could help you, but I don't need a Saturday girl.'

I continued crying. I just could not help myself. In the end he gave me a brown paper bag to dry my tears. I scrunched it up and blew my nose.

'Tell you what, miss, I was passing that shop on the Walworth Road . . . what's it called? . . . Just near the library – Roses, that's it, Roses – and there was a sign in the window for a Saturday girl. You know where I mean, by the lights, near the library? Why don't you pop along there and see if they can help you out?'

I continued to cry and he put an arm around me. 'Cheer up, lass,' he said. He took the crumpled brown paper bag from my hand, straightened it out and wrote *Roses, by the lights near library*. He crumpled it back up and pushed it into the palm of my hand.

'Dry up, love. You better go now or someone else will get the job.'

I put my corned beef into the trolley, dried my tears and tucked the wet paper bag into my pocket. I thanked him and turned my back.

'Let me know how you get on, love,' he called out. 'Good luck!'

I walked down to the start of East Street Market and turned right, pulling my trolley behind me as I went up Walworth Road towards the library. At the lights I crossed and Roses was on the corner. It was a ladies' dress shop with lots of pretty fashionable outfits in the window. I had a quick look in. They would never take me, I decided. I did not look at all fashionable and it was clear that I had been crying. I could not possibly go in there and ask for a job. They would laugh at me and then throw me out.

I walked up to J. Baldwin, looked in the front window at their sarsaparilla bottles and considered my options. I could go in now, later or not at all. If I went in now the chances were that I would not get the job. Not going in at all was not an option. The only sensible thing to do was to go in later. That was it. I would take the shopping home and then return to Roses and ask for the Saturday job.

I rushed home as fast as the trolley would let me. Once inside I put the food away, apart from those items which went automatically into my mother's bedroom. I found her sitting in the usual place.

'I've forgotten the butter and milk,' I said. 'I'll just go and get it now.'

'Be quick about it,' she snapped.

I went to the bathroom, splashed my face with cold water, cleaned my teeth with Colgate toothpaste and brushed my hair. Ready, steady, go.

I tried not to hurry back too quickly so I would not be sweaty. Once I got there, I paused outside the door not knowing what to say. There were two window displays, on the left and right of the entrance, which was set back about twenty feet from the pavement. They were full of skinny models wearing the latest fashions. Most of the women in the Walworth Road did not have that shape. I walked in.

The lady on the cash till was elderly, probably in her late forties. I took a deep breath and plucked up my courage.

'Excuse me,' I said, 'someone in the market sent me and told me that you wanted a Saturday girl. Is the vacancy still available?'

'Who sent you?' the woman enquired.

'I don't know. I think his name was Pete.'

'How old are you?'

'I'm fifteen,' I lied.

'Have you worked before?'

'Yes.'

'Where?'

'In a canteen as a cook.'

Perhaps the job with Eastman would prove useful after all. Sucks to my mother. After more questions the woman said her name was Eileen and she was happy to give me a trial period starting next week. She told me there were two other full-timers in the shop and one other Saturday person.

'You will have to be here by nine o'clock and we finish at six o'clock. You get one hour for lunch and sometimes only forty-five minutes if we are really busy. You are expected to dress smartly at all times and not cause any embarrassment to the store.'

'That's fine,' I said.

'Finally,' said Eileen, 'you get twenty-five per cent discount on anything you buy in the store.'

Brill! As I left the shop I felt altogether a different person. I had a job. The only problem was that I would have to tell my mother, otherwise she would wonder where I was.

I found her still in the sitting room.

'I've got a Saturday job, Mummy. I start next Saturday.'

'How much do they pay you?'

'I don't know, but they want me to start next week.'

'Why didn't you ask how much they pay?'

'I've got a job, Mummy.'

'What is the point in having a job if you don't know how much you're going to get paid? You will have to pay your keep. You cannot expect me to support you.'

'I never thought that you did support me,' I said.

'What do you mean by that?'

'Well, it never once dawned on me that you were paying my way. I thought my dad did.'

'Don't play silly games with me, you black bitch. If you work you'll pay your way and if you don't want to pay your way, don't work.'

I closed the door behind me and went up to find my sisters to tell them the good news. They were impressed all right. They fired dozens of questions at me, but most of all they wanted to know what the dresses were like. So there it was – me, Clare Briscoe, first Briscoe ever to pick herself up and go out and get a job. Things would change.

I was as excited as a Christmas tree with lights all weekend. I couldn't wait for next Saturday to come round. At school I was as good as gold. All the homework set was returned on time. I had a clear deck. No homework at the weekend. I could concentrate on selling the latest fashions. Saturday morning I got up early, had a shower to get rid of the stench of urine and chose an outfit to wear. I selected my blue crushed velvet dress, which fitted me. At 8.30 I had a cup of tea and at 8.35 I walked from Sutherland Square to start my first Saturday job.

I arrived at 8.45. The shop was not open, but I was happy to wait – at least I wasn't late. Eileen arrived shortly before nine o'clock and asked me how long I had been waiting.

'I've only just arrived,' I said.

I took her bags as she unlocked and when we went into Roses she dashed to the back of the store to deactivate the alarm. That done, she returned to the shop, switched all the lights on and sent me to buy her a cup of tea across the road. She gave me £1 and said I could have a cup myself if I wanted. I chose not to, since I had only just had one. The float had to be counted, the till opened and the shop sign switched to open. By 9.30 a.m. all the other staff were present – Mary, who was pretty and keen on Rod Stewart, Hanekia, who was Greek and getting married soon, and Linda, who was a bottle blonde, with beautiful straight hair, in a difficult relationship with a difficult boyfriend. They all made me feel very welcome. Each of them, quite separately, asked me how old I was. I stuck to the same answer of fifteen.

Working in Roses was glorious. The ladies would come in and look around. I helped them find the right size, showed them to a changing cubicle, drew the curtains and waited to make sure I got the garment back. Once they had the garment on I would say, 'Oh, that looks nice,' or 'The colour suits you,' or 'I think you should try a smaller size, would you like me to get that for you?' They always liked that one. If the customer was happy with the garment and wanted to buy it I would take them to Eileen at the cash machine. Her job was to take the money and to issue a receipt. My first day was very fancy, exciting, funny. So many customers. The girls all thought their tits were bigger than they actually were and the larger ladies would try something on that didn't fit and then comment that they had put on weight. It was extraordinary the number of ladies who did not know their size.

At lunchtime Eileen gave me a full hour for my break. I felt good, very good. I walked down the Walworth Road looking at clothes, shoes and even books that I might buy once I had saved up. I had money now. I stopped off at Dolcis. I just wanted to have a look at all the pretty shoes.

Down the market I went to try to find Pete. He was at the back of his stall.

'Hello, Pete.'

He turned in my direction and then his eyes focused on me. 'Now where do I remember you from? No, no, no, don't tell me. Let me guess.'

I stood still and waited.

'I know,' he said. 'You were here last week, weren't yer? You gimme the fright of me life, you did. How are you now – no weepies?'

'Pete, I got that Saturday job. Thank you very much, Pete. I'm sorry I frightened you.'

'No worries,' he said. 'How is it now – better? You know, that business that made you go all wet on me?'

'It is better, Pete, and thank you very much for telling me about the job, I started today.'

'Yer don't say, yer kidding me! Get away with yer.'

'No, Pete, it's true. I'm on my break. I've got to go. I don't want to be late.'

Pete put his hand in a high pile of apples, picked a green one and rubbed it on his apron. He selected an orange, gave it a squeeze and put them both in a brown paper bag. He handed them to me.

'Now don't you forget your old Pete,' he said. 'If you ever want an old brown bag to cry on, I've got loads.'

I got back to Roses within my hour and out the back I had my sandwiches and a cup of tea. I continued to work until 5.30 p.m. when Eileen asked me to start tidying while she cashed up the till. I cleared the changing rooms, put all the clothes back on the rails and made sure the hangers were all facing the same way. The mirrors in each changing room had to be cleaned and the rubbish put out at the front of the shop and then finally the carpet had to be hoovered. We finished just before six o'clock. Eileen was very happy with me. She handed me a brown envelope. I thanked her and put the envelope in my pocket. When I went to the loo, I opened the envelope. Inside was £8 and a payslip.

On the way home down the Walworth Road I stopped in the Wimpy Bar and bought a cheeseburger and chips. I paid for it with my own money – brill. By the time I put my key in the door, all that was left was a faint smell of chips. I spread the money out on my bed and counted it again. Pauline and Patsy came in and Carl popped in briefly to see if I had bought any sweets. I had no idea what I was going to do with the money. I would save some every week and the rest would be used to buy food. Both my sisters decided that they wanted to look for a Saturday job. At least it would get them both out of the house. When my mother shouted up to me I gathered up my money, put it in my purse and went downstairs.

'What about your keep now that you're working?'

'It's only a Saturday job, I don't get paid that much money.'

'Forget about only a Saturday job. You use more electricity than anyone else in this house. For a start your alarm is on all night every night, week in month out. You don't expect me to pay for that, do you? I mean, I did not tell you to piss the bed. Hand it over.'

'Well, how much do you want?'

'By rights you should give it all to me.'

'Then there would be no point in working. I might as well stop now.'

'That's your business, no one forced you to get a job.'

'It's my money and I worked for it.'

'Well, what do you say? You seem to think that you are the woman in this house, what do *you* think is the sum of your keep?'

'I think three pounds would be fair.'

'Well, that will pay for the electricity, but from now on you will buy your own food and clothes. If you are old enough to work you're old enough to look after yourself.'

And that was that. It wasn't fair. Mary agreed about that.

14

Hospital

A few days later I returned from school and went into the kitchen to find my dinner. It was all gone and no one had left any for me. There was no point in asking my mother where my food was because she didn't know. I organised my books and then went upstairs. My bed was back. It was just there as though it had been there all along. Dry sheets. The alarm had recently been checked and was in full working order. My bed-wetting had not diminished. I pressed a button on the top of the alarm and it flashed on and off. I got into my nightdress and once in bed I pulled the sheets up over my head. The smell of clean sheets is a truly glorious smell. I could not remember the last time I had had clean dry sheets. I had no idea who had left the sheets out for me. It was not important. It did not matter. There was a hint of Daz on the linen – my mother's preferred washing powder. I put my hand under the bed. My potty was there. My mother had been advised to get a potty to help train me to get up in the night before the alarm went off. It was early days for the potty. It looked like a large bucket with a handle. Well, it was there if I needed it.

By the time I was twelve, my boobs were not developing in the way I had expected. For a start I thought that they would grow together and be roughly equal in size and shape. In fact, they were of different sizes and shapes. It was only recently, when I examined them after one of my mother's nipple-squeezing sessions, that I realised that both were lumpy and deformed.

My left was constantly painful to touch, the nipple looked sore with a thick crust around the edge which peeled off when moist. The scabs were dark brown with shiny bits and flaky skin. Underneath that was pink flesh, which wept amongst the scabs.

At the top of the breast, especially at about nine o'clock, I could feel a large lump the size of half a boiled egg. It moved like a see-saw when touched, first to the right and then to the left. My right breast was so deformed that an examination was almost impossible. There was a huge raised area at the top, at about twelve o'clock, with stretched skin that was paper-thin. Quietly, at the back of this skin, I could see a ticking pulse. I was quite certain that the lumps had a life of their own and moved around without any assistance from me whenever they wanted to. To the right of this lump was another, slightly smaller in size but equally painful. I thought that all three had been caused by my mother's pinches and punches, forgetting about the twisting and pulling of my nipple. There was only so much a breast could take and both of them had had enough. I decided that when under attack from my mother, from now on I'd fight back.

I had heard and read about cancer and the deformity of my boobs warned me to see a doctor immediately. At school I had been paying attention to my friends' tits and none of them looked like mine. When we were in the changing rooms preparing for gym, I saw they all had nicely formed breasts. As soon as I could, I booked myself in to see Dr McManus. He was such a nice man. I sat in the waiting room with my sister, who had no idea what I wanted to see the doctor about. When my name was called I told her to wait and went in on my own.

'What can I do for you, my dear?' Dr McManus said, checking on my file. 'How's the bed-wetting? Well, never mind, it will come right soon. Now what can I do for you?' I sat in front of him and said nothing. 'You wouldn't have wasted your day, queued up to see me, if nothing was wrong.'

I explained to him that recently when I removed my clothes I had found three lumps in my breasts that should not be there. I did not know what they were.

'How old are you? Oh, I see, twelve. Well, my dear, I'm sure it's nothing to worry about. Just go behind the screen and take your top off.'

He pointed in the direction of the examination bed. I jumped up on it and he pulled the curtain shut. I took off my coat and jumper, undid my blouse and waited. He came in.

'Now, my dear, just tell me where you feel these lumps.' I pointed out the first on my left breast. 'Just breathe in for me. Good – and out. Once more. And again. Now, Clare, I'm just going to touch this breast around the edges. If you feel uncomfortable, please say.' He started at six o'clock, patting my breast with one hand and pushing with the other. Any fool could see the lump. The skin above it was paper-thin and it was lumpy.

'Now the next breast, same as before. Breathe in, and again, and again. That's good. My dear, how long have you had these?' I was trying to think what to say. 'Not that there's anything to worry about. Not anything to worry about.'

He measured the area, width and length of both boobs and asked why my mother was not with me. 'She is cooking,' I said. While the doctor was reassuring me that I had nothing to worry about, he was on the phone. I heard him say, 'Oncology emergency.' He explained into the phone that he had a delightful young girl, 1C3, aged twelve, who was presenting with three major traumas in her breast. On the left at nine o'clock and on the right at twelve noon and three o'clock. The traumas were flexible and moved freely, north and south. My presentation was rare given my age and there was no history. He wondered whether I might be seen soon as a matter of urgency. The traumas were painful and appeared to be growing at an alarming rate. The two on my right breast were separated by three inches and it was vital that I see someone immediately. There was no obvious reason why I should present in this way. An appointment was made for me for the next week. I thanked the doctor, and left the surgery on the understanding that if the lumps got bigger, I would return immediately. He followed me into the waiting area and called my sister over to him. 'Hello, Pauline.

How are you? Well, I hope. Now when you get home, do you think you could ask your mother to ring me at any time during surgery hours? She has got my number. Tonight is better for me, but tomorrow morning will do.' He held the door open and we both left.

On the way home my sister asked, 'What's wrong with you? Why does he want to talk to Mummy?'

'I don't know,' I said. 'Nothing to do with me. I don't want to talk to her.'

'What's wrong with you?'

'Nothing.'

'Well, there must be something wrong with you – tell me.'

'They have found a cure for bed-wetting,' I said. 'I think that he wants to be the first to tell her.'

We carried on walking in silence. What was a trauma? Could you die of it?

When we got home I went straight to my room. Pauline knocked on my mother's door and entered. I changed out of my school uniform and went downstairs to do the housework. The kitchen was clean; all the plates were dried and put away. The bathroom was clean and I poured bleach down the toilet. I got the hoover from the ante-room and went to the top-floor landing and started to hoover the stairs, ending in the hall. I put the hoover back, went to my room and started my homework. I enjoyed homework, but there was never enough time. My hours after school were never mine. My work at school was good: I had potential, my report said, but was not always consistent. A decision had been taken that I would be moved up a stream. Maybe one day I could get in the top stream.

Homework finished, I went into the kitchen to find out what we were having for dinner. All the food was gone. There was nothing left for me. I had to eat biscuits from the hiding place in my wardrobe. Thank goodness for school dinners. They were great. I adored them. There were lots of complaints from other girls, but I thought: 'God save school dinners.' I never left any food on my plate, but then again I never asked for seconds unless it was offered. No one could ever say that I was greedy.

That night my mother came into my room and told me that the doctor had spoken to her and that she would go with me to my hospital appointment. I told her it was not necessary. Anyway she didn't have to worry, I wasn't going to tell.

My appointment at the hospital was not what I expected at all. When I turned up I was told that I would have to have a number of X-rays and then once they were developed the doctor would see me. He might have to take another X-ray, but then he would report back to my doctor. I stood pressed to a machine with my clothes stripped to the waist while the radiologist ran behind a screen. 'Now, breathe in, Clare. Don't move – that's it. Breathe in and out. And again, in and out, hold it. Good.'

The red light above the screen flashed on and off and the radiologist returned to the front of the machine. She undid a clip and a large square film box was removed. I dressed and waited outside for the results. The nurse came and told me that it would be necessary to have an ultrasound; she gave me a document to take to the Ultrasound Department. When my turn came, a cold substance was applied over both breasts and a wand was waved over them. An image appeared on the screen which the radiologist was able to read.

No one spoke to me, not really. They didn't explain what they were doing. Everyone said, 'How are you, Clare?' and 'You're a bit young,' but no one told me why I was a bit young.

After my examination I got off the table, removed the gunk from my breasts and cleaned myself up with tissue. I put my clothes on and went home. A few days later, Dr McManus rang the house. He said he'd been sent a letter. He said it was important that I come back to the surgery as soon as possible. I did.

The doctor told me he wanted me to return to the hospital, as it was necessary for me to have more tests, although there really was nothing for me to worry about. The hospital was a teaching hospital and since I was a rare case, a number of surgeons would like to meet with me in the lecture room. To say that they were interested in meeting *me* was inaccurate – it was my tits that they were interested in. It was nothing to worry about. It was a teaching hospital and they had plenty of experience. As I left, he said, 'By the way, there will be plenty of students there. They will probably have a whip-round for you.' This was really to put me at my ease and I think to encourage me to take my clothes off for them. My medical presentation was rare.

When I returned to the hospital, I was booked in and taken to a lecture room. Just inside the lecture room there was a waiting and changing room to the right. I was ushered into the changing room and asked if I would like to remove my upper garment and slip into a nightdress which opened at the front. When I went into the main lecture hall there were about seventy people present. They all appeared to be dressed in white. The man at the front, the teacher, was not in a white jacket. I was his object.

I stood before the crowd as the man in black pointed out my lumps and explained that this was a rare case. He then referred the crowd to the blackboard behind him and there was a drawing of my tits with three arrows pointing to the three areas which were shaded by a criss-cross pattern. The man in black turned me to the side so that the students had a good view of me and then with a white stick which had a red nipple, he pointed out the areas of trauma on my body. He then thanked me for being so good and patient and invited the class to come forward if they wished to examine the patient. I stood there, arms down by my side, and tried not to look at them. Some of the students came forward. They made polite conversation with me, asked me what school I went to and what I did and what I wanted to be when I grew up. Others came up, looked, touched, felt my tits and went back to their seats.

The man in black asked me if I had suffered any trauma to my breasts. I said, 'No.' First, I did not know what he meant by trauma, and secondly, even if I did know, I was not about to tell him about my home life. He thanked me and told me I could get dressed and return to the reception, which I did. I was given an appointment to come back to the hospital to have the lumps removed and a small envelope with some loose change, as a thank you from the medical students. In the meantime I should make an appointment with my doctor and he would explain all.

That Friday, I went to church, wearing my white gloves, beret and tie. Why did church on a Friday have to be compulsory? I walked down to the front and sat three rows back. I wanted God to see and hear me. I had something to say to Him.

'Dear God, please, *please* help me to stop wetting the bed. Dear God, it's not like I'm always asking for a favour. This one is important to me. A lot turns on it, so if You could see Your way to granting my wish and curing me of wetting the bed I would be ever so grateful. Amen.'

Back at school, our Headmaster told us that God was everywhere if we had a problem. He knew about it before we did. If we were unable to manage, all we had to do was to tell Him. Well, I had done my best.

That evening I packed my bag ready to go to hospital. I took my toothbrush, comb, a pair of clean socks and a nightdress that did not smell. I made sure to stop eating at 6 p.m. I have no recollection of how I got to the hospital, or whether I was with anyone, but I do remember that I was shown to my bed. A nurse checked that I was the person they were expecting and then she clipped an identification band onto my wrist. For some silly reason she checked again that I was the person identified on the wristband. My temperature, pulse and weight were taken. After this general procedure was complete, the doctor arrived. My curtains were drawn and he sat on the side of my bed. He informed me that it was a routine operation and they would have me in and out in no time. There were three lesions that needed to be removed and once out they would be stitched up and would leave a tidy scar. I assumed a lesion was a lump. There was a small problem in that some black people were prone to keloid scarring. That was where the skin raised up to form a solid ridge at the site of a wound or stitch. If this happened in my case it would be unfortunate but quite normal in black people.

After that conversation the surgeon came in to see me. He told me he would take the lumps out and then he would see me the following morning on the ward round. I would be informed then whether they were malignant or benign – either way there was nothing to worry about.

The next morning the curtains remained drawn and two nurses arrived with an injection. One said that it would make me relax, but I was not too sure about that. I had never felt so unrelaxed. The injection was in my bottom and it stung just a little bit. The surgeon returned, checked the name on my wristband and asked me to remove my nightdress. I dropped it on the bed and he whipped out a red pen from his pocket then, looking at a document in his hand, drew on my left breast and wrote the word *enter* with an arrow pointing to the right. With my right breast he did the same, only there were two *enters* at three o'clock and twelve o'clock. He then drew a line about two inches long away from the entry point. He checked again that his drawing/sketch matched the document in his hand, thanked me, commented about his drawing skills and left.

The nurse asked me to hop over onto the trolley. I did so and was wheeled through the ward, into the lift and then on to the operating theatre. The nurse and surgeon were there. The surgeon inserted a butterfly needle into the back of my hand and asked me to count to ten. I don't remember counting to ten, but I do remember waking up in extreme pain. The ward lights were dimmed and there were lots of monitors and a drip in my arm. My breasts were heavily bandaged, the dressing extending over the entire front of my chest, with lots of adhesive tape along the edges. As I looked down, I threw the blanket off. I spotted three areas of red spots on the bandage where the blood had seeped through. I felt the bandage. There was a lump underneath. I felt the other one. Another lump. I still had my tits.

The doctor turned up the next morning together with three

others in white coats. I assured them that I was fine. He said that I would be sent home as soon as I was ready, but because of all the monitors and drips I should stay in hospital for another five days. I agreed. I was happy to remain in hospital for ever. If only I never had to return home! He said I had not got cancer. Still, the operation had been quite complicated. All the lumps had now been removed and hopefully I would make a full recovery. I drifted back to sleep.

No one visited me in hospital. During the time that I was there I remained on my back. Any other position was just too painful. After two days the drainage tubes were removed from my breasts. After three days my wound was inspected and my bandages changed. Seven days later I was allowed home.

It was advisable to wear a bandage at all times, I was told. Not only did it give support, but it would prevent infection while my body was going through the healing process. I agreed to keep the bandage on and went home. I was off school for three weeks and sports were banned for the whole term. My wounds did not heal according to plan. The fact that I still continued to wet the bed was an additional complication. The bandages became con-taminated and needed frequent changing. My mother did not trouble me at all during this time. In many ways I suspect that she prayed for me to recover. Both she and I knew why the lumps had appeared in my tits and she would not have been too keen for me to tell.

There were certain advantages to having an operation. East-man kept his hands off me and my mother never again pinched and twisted my nipples. When I went back to school I wore my sister's bra, which was two sizes too big for me, but the padding and swelling filled the bra to its maximum. My form teacher was pleased to see me. I was standing in a line outside the classroom and she came up and hugged me. It made me cry. She was very surprised to see me. She knew that I had been in hospital and that it had something to do with cancer. I assured her that I did not have cancer, but that I was not allowed to do PE. She said that she would tell Miss Gillespie. A few days later I picked up a very serious infection on my face that would not respond to treatment. I was sent home and did not go back to school for a very long time. The days rolled into weeks and the weeks into months.

15

A School Trip

1970

While I was away from school I had begun to watch television out of sheer boredom. There was a courtroom drama in the middle of the day called *Crown Court at One*. The actors were dressed up in black gowns and wigs; the heroine defending, the hero prosecuting. The judge was fantastically old and played little part in the trial. The programme was about an hour long. I decided that I wanted to be a barrister in court in a wig and gown. Every day a new incident, a new defendant to represent, a new trial. It was so exciting. I wanted to dress up there and then. Both the men and the women wore white tabs round their necks. The women wore them over a beautiful white collarette with lace over the high neckband; the men wore them over high wing collars as if they were in a period drama. It was clear I would become a barrister just like the characters. I'd find out all about it when I went back to school.

After my operation, food in our house was still under lock and key. My mother, post-op, kept away from my breasts but she punched me in the head or in the back or in my stomach instead. I never did see the split-split stick again, but in its place she had obtained a leather belt, about a yard long from tip to buckle, and the buckle was a large circular bronze disc through which the leather strap was fed. Sometimes I got belted with that.

When I finally went back to school, I made an appointment to see the Careers Advice tutor. It was for Thursday, in the Careers Office at the end of the school main corridor. I turned up at the appointed time and the tutor asked me what I had in mind. I told her I wanted some advice about my career and what I could do when I left school. She went to a metal cabinet, pulled out a file from the top drawer and read out a list of vacancies. Boots the Chemists were looking for five bright ambitious young girls – must be well motivated and manicured, excellent chance of promotion. Woolworth's in the Walworth Road were looking for a sales rep with five O-levels.

'No,' I said. 'Miss, I want to be a barrister.'

'A barrister? Now who put that idea into your head?'

'I've seen it on TV, miss. That's what I want to be.'

'Well, it's good to aim high, I'll give you that. But this is Sacred Heart, pet. You failed the eleven-plus, that's why you are here. You have to go to university to become a barrister, and we don't turn out university material here.'

'I didn't fail the eleven-plus, miss,' I said. 'I'm here because my sisters were here before me. I wanted to go to Notre Dame.'

'Yes, of course you did, pet, of course you did. We all want to go to heaven, pet, but we're not all suitable. Now run along, dear, and think about what I have said. If you ever need more advice, my door is always open.'

I had no idea how to be a barrister, but on the way home from school I stopped off at the library. I told the librarian I wanted to be a barrister when I grew up. 'Congratulations,' she said. 'Don't we all?' I said that I would like to know what qualifications I would need. She went off and returned with a book and a leaflet. The book could not be borrowed, but the leaflet I could keep. She had marked a particular paragraph in the book.

Good O-levels, minimum 5. Three A-levels – good grades. University degree. A year's training at the Inns of Court School of Law to take the Bar examinations and finally pupillage with a pupil-master. At this point it is possible to specialise in a particular area such as aviation, building, crime, family, general common law or commercial.

I thanked her and left.

It seemed to me that I needed to find a pupil-master as soon as possible. Fortunately we were due to go on a school visit to Knightsbridge Crown Court. I would try to find one there. We travelled by bus from Camberwell Green and made our way along Hans Crescent, at the back of Harrods, to a red-brick building that stood back from the road. We were not really supposed to go into the courts because of our age, but the teacher had made an agreement with the judge prior to our arrival that we could go into one court for about half an hour before lunch. The court was down some stairs, in the basement. The case was about boys stealing purses from handbags. They were black boys. I liked one of their barristers. He was called Mr Mansfield. He was good-looking. He had a nice smile and stood out from the others in the way he asked questions.

During the lunch break we went into the canteen to get some sandwiches. In the queue ahead of us were some of the barristers who had earlier been in our court. Two of them still had their wigs on in the queue. The teacher ordered on our behalf and we then sat at a table with chairs bolted to the floor – four or five at a squeeze. When we sat down, Mr Mansfield came and sat alongside of us. 'What did you think of the case?' he said, throwing the question open to all of us. Before we could speak the teacher answered for us. She was, of course, very grateful to be here, and the children were behaving themselves and oh, what a delight to meet a real barrister who had given up his time to talk to us. We all crowded round him.

'Can I feel your wig?'

'What's it made of?'

'Sure,' said the barrister. 'These wigs are dreadful. It's about time we did away with them.' He took his wig off by tilting his head forward. It fell off and he caught it in his hands and passed it around our crowd. 'It's bad for your hair,' he said.

The children were busy touching the wig. There were two curls that hung down at the back, a bit like pony tails, the curl being at the bottom. The inside of the wig was a stiff net of very tiny squares on to which the curls were sewn.

'They are made of horse hair,' the barrister explained.

He was now joined by three more barristers. He stood up, took off his black gown, folded it, folded it again and put it on the floor beside his chair.

'What are you all doing here?' he enquired.

The teacher told him that this was a school visit. Hopefully there may be many more to follow.

'I want to be a barrister,' I piped up. 'I am going to university and I will study Law and then I am going to the School of Law, and when I have done that I am going to find a pupil-master in London.'

'Good, good,' said the barrister. 'Now just tell me how old you are?'

'Nearly thirteen,' I said.

'Good, good,' he repeated.

'What's your name?' I asked.

'My name is Mike, Mike Mansfield.'

'My name is Clare, Clare Briscoe. Mr Mansfield, when I qualify as a barrister, do you think that you can be my pupil-master?'

'Sure, but you've got a long way to go. Stay in touch and when you qualify I'll give you pupillage.'

'I'll hold you to that, Mr Mansfield. A promise is a promise.'

'Sure,' he said and laughed. 'Call me Mike. You'll need to get in touch with me to arrange your pupillage. Here are my details.'

He gave me a card and I put it in the top pocket of my blazer. My teacher had wanted us to talk generally about the case and she was not happy about my forwardness.

'As for being a barrister,' she said as we left, 'it is good to have dreams, but they have to be realistic. Dream about something that you can achieve. That way you can never be disappointed. Dreams and hopes must have boundaries.'

I did not understand that, but then again it was not really necessary to as it sounded like a load of rubbish. I would qualify as a barrister. Mary and I knew that I would keep in touch with Mike Mansfield and he had promised to be my pupil-master. All I needed now were my O-levels, A-levels and a degree. Easy-peasy.

16

Good Morning Heartache

1971

'Feel that, what is that?' asked my mother.

'It's a tit, Mum.'

'And what's that?' she asked, moving my hand across to her other breast.

'It's another tit, Mum.'

'And who do they belong to?'

'They are yours.'

'And?'

'And what?'

'And what does that tell you?'

'Well, it tells me you've got tits.'

'Good. Now what else?'

'I don't think there is any more what else.' I moved my hand from my mother's chest.

'You obviously don't understand,' she said. 'Let me try again. What's that?' My mother used the flat of her right hand with an open palm and her fingers pointing up to shove me backwards by my left tit.

'You just shoved me backwards.'

'And?' said my mother.

'And you shoved me backwards by my tit.'

'Really?' she said. 'And what's this?' My mother used her open left palm with her fingers in the same upward position to shove me back again. She flattened my right tit and pushed me one step backwards.

'You shoved me again,' I said.

'And?' prompted my mother.

'You shoved me by my tit.'

'Wrong,' said my mother. 'Try again.'

'You did push me,' I said.

'And?' said my mother.

'And you pushed me by my tits.'

'Wrong,' said my mother. She came forward and using both her hands she shoved me backwards again. 'And why are you wrong?' she said.

'I'm not wrong. You did.'

'Try again,' said my mother, shoving me back again. My tits were beginning to hurt and, if I kept getting the wrong answer, I'd be out of the window in three more moves.

'I don't know,' I said. 'I thought you had pushed me backwards by my tits but I could be wrong.'

'Well, you are wrong – and do you know why you are wrong?'

'No, but I expect you are going to tell me anyway,' I said.

'You're wrong because you don't *have* any tits. Have you forgotten you had them removed?'

'I did not have them removed. I had lumps removed and whose fault was that?'

'Now,' said my mother, 'there is only one person in this house with tits – do you agree with that?'

I decided it was easier to agree with her than get into some futile argument, even if what she was saying was not strictly true. I was sure that Pauline and Patsy had tits. I had tits as well. If I was wrong, then my operation must have been something I imagined, although the scars were real enough.

'Yes, I agree,' I said.

'Good,' said my mother. 'So it follows, do you not agree, that since I'm the one with the tits, I must be the woman in the house?'

'Well, I'm not the woman in the house. I never once said I was.'

'I am glad that we can agree on that. And in future you will do what I say, because this is my house and if you don't like it you know what to do. You've got a father with lots of houses. Why don't you just fuck off with him? The sooner I see the back of you, the sooner we will get on.'

'I don't want to live with you either and I'm more than capable of looking after myself, so if you want to throw me out, that's up to you, really,' I said.

'You would like that, wouldn't you? You could call Social Services. I'd get into trouble and you would get a new home. That would make you happy.'

'I'm just saying if you want to get rid of me you can always throw me out.'

My mother moved towards me, punched me in the left shoulder and took a step back. Then she grabbed my hair, forced my head down to about waist height and marched me towards the door.

'You are a dirty whore. A dirty, dirty whore,' she said, as she banged my head into the door. 'Repeat after me: "I'm a dirty little whore." Go on – say it. "I'm a dirty little whore." '

'I'm a dirty little whore,' I said.

'That's right,' said my mother. 'As long as you've got a split up your crack, you can sell it.'

She grabbed me in the middle of my head, and pulled me backwards, which caused me to fall over. Then she opened the door and walked out. I felt dazed for a few moments and remained on the floor until the feeling passed. It would be good not to live with that woman. She made me dislike her and I no longer considered her as my mother.

I got up off the floor and made my way to bed. I lay on top of the bedspread, and fell asleep. Just as my alarm was about to go off, I silenced it, got up and went to the toilet. It must have been in the early hours of the morning as it was still dark outside. I did not turn the light on while I was in the toilet. I was sure, well almost sure, that I heard the stairs creak. I listened again, but it was silent. I flushed the chain and made my way back upstairs in the dark, taking care not to stand on the third step. As I approached my mother's door I paused and listened. She was asleep. I could hear Eastman snoring. Huh! I hoped he choked. At the top of the first landing I stopped. I had an odd feeling that all was not right. I looked left into the kitchen. All was still. I carried on up the second flight of stairs. Outside my bedroom door I paused. Was it just my imagination? I went into my bedroom; the light was still off. By the side of my bed I took off my shoes and pulled the covers back, and nearly screamed in fright. My mother was in my bed.

'Shoo!' she said.

'What are you doing in my bed?'

'Shoo!' she said again, pulling the covers up under her chin.

'Where am I going to sleep?'

'Fucking shoo!' she said.

For a few moments I did not know what to do, but then I gathered up some old clothes from the floor and made a pile in the corner. An old coat would do as my top blanket. I lay down and covered myself up.

'Out!' she said.

At first I thought she wasn't talking to me, so I remained still.

'Out!' she said again.

I sat up, brushed the coat to one side and waited for my mother to explain what she meant by 'out'.

'Get the fuck out,' she said. 'I don't want you in this room.'

'Where shall I go?' I said.

'Anywhere you like, but fuck off now, otherwise you'll disturb my sleep.'

I got up and gathered together a few dresses and a pair of old curtains and went outside. I closed the door behind me. Next door my little sisters Christine and Denise were fast asleep. There was no space for me in their beds and the floor was no better than the one in my bedroom. I closed the door behind me, tiptoed upstairs and opened my other sisters' bedroom door. Pauline was spread out all over her bed and Patsy was much the same. I went back downstairs with my old clothes and curtains. As I stood outside my bedroom door I heard my mother singing. I did not catch the first line but it was definitely a Billie Holiday song called 'Good Morning Heartache'. She repeated the words as I made my bed outside my bedroom. I spread my clothes on the landing, lay down, curled up and covered my upper half with my old curtains. As I tried to make myself comfortable I listened to my mother. Was my life a heartache? Would heartache be there to greet me every morning? No, I decided. Soon, very soon, my heartache would end.

In the morning, I got up and went into my room. My mother was gone.

Despite my recent illness, the women at Roses had kept my Saturday job open for me. I was so happy to be working with them again I felt like crying. You had to have tits to wear the latest fashion. I still had tits but the plunging necklines on some of the garments were out of the question. I was too conscious of the revolting scars. There was an offer of occasional summer holiday work too, if I wanted it. I now owned two new dresses, bought and paid for by me. Clare Briscoe was the first to wear them.

That Sunday, I went to church as usual. I thanked God for all that I had, including my tits, and I cursed Him for all that I didn't have. I prayed especially to stop bed-wetting – I could not afford to get an infection in my tits – and I prayed for my mother to stop beating me. 'If I could have a wish, just one wish,' I told Him, 'it would be to leave home immediately and never return, not even when I'm a grown-up. If I had a second wish it would be to be happy. Not all the time, just now and then, maybe like on my birthday, Christmas and summer holidays. But then all things come to those who wait.'

After church we all walked back home. Pauline and Patsy were dressed in their Sunday best, as was I. My prayers might be answered, I thought hopefully, and I felt within me that things would change. We got out of our best clothes and I set about preparing dinner. We were having roast chicken and potatoes and it was my turn to cook. Eastman came into the kitchen, sneaking around like the spy he always was. He hung about just a little longer than was expected behind my back. I turned to him with the knife raised in my right hand. Both he and I knew what I had in mind, if only I had the courage.

'Why don't you go and spy somewhere else?' I said.

'Who you talking to?'

I turned to face him full on and tightened my grip on the knife. 'Who is an idiot?' I said.

'Who you calling a fool?'

My mother appeared at the kitchen door. 'Eastman, leave her. Remember your discharge. If you go back before the Judge he will send you to prison.'

'She wants me to go prison for her.'

My mother pulled Eastman backwards out of the kitchen and then stepped in front of him with her hands on her hips. 'What!' she said. 'You want to fight me?' She lunged at me and grabbed my hair, she brought my head down level with her knee and then she punched me on the back of my head just above the nape of my neck. I fell forwards with the knife still in my hand. Once I had steadied myself, she kneed me virtually in the face.

'Eastman might have a discharge, but I don't have one, you piece of shit.'

The impact of her knee had sent me flying backwards as she took aim again and her foot made contact with my stomach. My fall was broken only by the table behind my head. I was knocked out as my scalp came into contact with the sharp edge of the corner. When I came to I was sitting at the table and my mother and Eastman were bending over me. My mother kept telling me to hold my head up and open my eyes. Eastman was saying in the background, 'I never touched her. Carmen, did you hear that? Not me, I never touch she.'

'Put the kettle on, Eastman. Make her a cup of tea; put four spoons of sugar in, quick.'

Eastman disappeared from my vision at about the same time as my sisters and brothers appeared at the kitchen door.

'What's wrong with Clare, Mummy?' asked Carlton, who was the first at the door.

'Nothing. She fell,' my mother said. 'She banged her head on the side of the table, didn't you, Clare?'

I could not think straight. My head hurt and the sugary tea she was trying to get down my throat made me feel ill.

'Go on, all of you, go and find something to do,' said my mother.

All the children ran from the door; they did not need telling twice. At the back of my head a large lump had formed and in the middle of the lump was a puncture wound. A speck of blood was on my hand when I rubbed my head.

'Carmen, this have nothing to do with me,' said Eastman. 'Carmen, I tell you before, you are go kill the pickney. You don't want to listen to me, you just want to knock she out. Not me. You on your own. When police come you tell them you on your own.'

My mother, who was busy looking at my head, told Eastman to shut the fuck up and hold my head so she could see how deep the wounds were.

'Drink up,' said my mother, lifting the cup and placing it back in my hands. 'Drink.'

I had never before had a cup of tea from my mother, never mind with four spoons of sugar. Normally four spoons of sugar in one cup of tea would secure a thorough beating. I bent my head forward and my mother parted my hair. She said the cut was not deep. She picked up a kitchen towel, rinsed it out in the sink and applied it in dabs to the back of my head. After a while she said it had stopped bleeding. I sipped my tea. Eastman's nerves could not hold out and he had disappeared. When my mother called him he refused to come.

'You stay there and finish your tea,' she said, as she washed the blood off the tea towel. Then she went downstairs.

I did not feel too good. My head hurt, my knees hurt and my face and neck were sore. I stood up but felt giddy. My head must still have been bleeding because there was blood on the end of my fingertips. The knife that I had had in my hand before all this happened still lay on the floor. I went up to my bedroom and got on my bed. Sitting there I started to cry – not a loud hysterical cry, but crying to myself. With my legs on the bed and a pillow behind my head I must have dozed for a while because I heard Pauline saying, 'Clare, it's your turn to cook. Mummy says you need some help. Do you?'

'No, I don't,' I said, with my eyes still closed. 'I'll do it in a minute.'

'Well, if you want I can help you, as long as you help me when it's my turn.'

'No,' I said. 'It's okay.'

Old Four Eyes was ever the bargainer. Nothing for nothing. There was a great deal of friction between Pauline, Patsy and me. Pauline, as the eldest by several years, had always kept out of my mother's way. She was happy to receive Carmen's attention and gifts and new clothes, and avoid beatings in return for not speaking out and defending me when I was given a beating. She and Patsy were my mother's favourites. Well, that was until the Eastmans came along. And here she was now, old Four Eyes, asking if she could help. Patsy, Precious Puss, was not much better. She kept right out of the way. As for Buttons and Denise, they were still very young.

I got up, went to the kitchen and washed my hands, picked the knife up off the floor, washed that too and continued with the chicken. All the time I was conscious of the fact that Eastman was on the top landing. I recognised his footsteps as he crept down the stairs. Spying again. When he got to my bedroom he stopped and I heard him open the twins' door. I had my back to him, facing out over the gardens. I knew he was looking in their bedroom. He was trying to work out whether he or my mother had anything to worry about.

'Beauty, Blackie,' he shouted. 'Where the body is?' No answer. He closed the door and walked slowly down the stairs. He was staring at the back of my head, I could tell. 'Beauty, Blackie, where the body is?' He was facing directly into the kitchen and it was obvious to any idiot that I was alone in there. As he stared at my head I refused to acknowledge his presence but I knew and he knew what he was looking at.

The wound at the top of my head was not serious but it was deep and had continued to bleed. The blood had formed a scab at the entrance to the wound but the scab had lifted itself off and a trickle of blood had made its way down the back of my head and formed a large red patch at the back of my pretty lime-green and yellow dress. The blood stood out like a tomato on a white sheet and I had made no attempt to stem the flow. How Eastman must have shit himself.

Staring at my head he called again in a softer, more stupid voice, 'Beauty, Blackie.' The voice of an idiot. Still he did not move. He knew perfectly well that I would refuse to acknowledge him, never mind talk to him. Then he started to talk to himself. 'Not me,' he said. 'Not me. I never touched you. Did you see me touch you? No. Not me. Did you see me raise my foot to you? No. Not me. I never touched you. No police going to take me away. The Judge not waiting for me. Did you see my foot move? No. Not me. Carmen, come see what you do. And you know what? You do it on your own. You never get any help from me.'

My mother made her way up the stairs and found Eastman on the half-landing. I had moved on to the potatoes and carrots. My mother looked at my head from where she stood and realised why Eastman was getting excited.

'Clare, what's wrong with your head?' she said.

'I don't know. It's bleeding.'

'Why is it bleeding?'

'I think someone beat me up and kicked me in the face.'

'Not me,' said Eastman. 'I never touched you. Carmen, move. I'm going downstairs.' He moved my mother to one side. 'This got nothing to do with me. I never trouble she, she pull a knife on me.'

My mother stood looking at my head. 'Well, are you going to clean yourself up?'

'No,' I said. 'It is not necessary.'

'Why don't you clean it up?'

'It's not necessary. It's my head and I like it like that.' I turned to face her; the left side of my lip was badly swollen and my right eye had closed. 'I think I'll go to the doctor later,' I said.

Then I turned and continued with the carrots.

My mother did not know what to do. Well, she did in a way. She knew when I was in one of my moods and she should leave well alone. She stayed on the stairs a few minutes more and then went all the way upstairs to my sisters' room. Pauline's door opened and closed. A few more minutes passed and the door opened again. She went straight down to her room and Pauline appeared a few minutes after that.

'Can I give you a hand, Clare?' she said.

'No.'

'Well, at least let me help you with the potatoes. You don't have to pay me back.'

'No, I can manage.'

'Oh, Clare, your head's bleeding.'

'Yes, I know. You know what happened, Four Eyes. I got beaten up.'

'Who beat you up, Clare? I never saw a thing.'

'How come you got Four Eyes and you can never see? You're blind most of the time. Can you see my head? What a surprise. I got beaten up and I don't want to talk about it.'

'Why don't you put a plaster on it?'

'I haven't got one.'

'We'll soak a bit of toilet paper and put it on your head. You will spoil your dress if you don't.'

'I'll think about it.'

'Well, don't think about it too long, because if we wash the dress now the chances are the blood will come out, but if you let it dry you might ruin it for good. I thought you liked that dress, Clare.'

The thought of losing my dress spurred me into action. I put the knife down, went to my room, removed my dress and put it on my wet pile. I found an old dress to put on and buttoned it up the front on my way back to the kitchen. Pauline was busy hacking at the carrots.

'Tell you what, Clare, I'll go and fetch the dress and see if I can get the blood out. I'll also sneak the wet pile in the wash if I can.'

She dropped the carrots in the sink and went to my room, emerging shortly afterwards with a large pile of wet and some dried urine-stained sheets. As she passed the kitchen she said, 'Clare, shush – look.' I turned to look at her and she dropped the pile of sheets and put her finger on her lips. Then she dived into the middle of the pile and produced my dress which had stained the wet bedsheets pink. She then put the dress back in the middle of the pile and took it downstairs to the bathroom. The blood continued to ooze from my head onto the collar of the dress I had changed into. The pace had slowed down. I felt that nothing really mattered. My mother's door opened and I heard her go round to the bathroom. Pauline was still round the back – I had not heard her go upstairs. She and my mother would make sure that my dress was clean. Every bit of blood would be washed away. As for my sheets, they too would be nice and clean and fresh-smelling. My mother knew that in my current mood I was unpredictable. I could very easily make my way to Dr McManus's surgery and she would have to explain my injuries. Better to wash my dress and give me clean sheets. Pauline returned from the back of the house.

'It's done, Clare,' she said.

I gathered up the potato skins and the carrot peel and put them in the bin. I spotted my mother at the bottom of the stairs near the back-room door, eavesdropping on us.

'Why don't you go and have a rest?' Pauline said. 'I'm sure your head must be hurting.'

'I think I'll do that,' I said. I stepped out of the kitchen onto the half-landing as my mother moved. She backed away into the corner. I could see her all the same.

'Pauline, can you find out when Dr McManus's surgery is open?' I said. 'I think I'll go and see him about my head.'

'Why don't you go to your room, Clare?' she said. 'I don't

know the times of the surgery, but I think they're closed on a Sunday. I'll go and check. Then I'll bring you a cup of tea.'

I went to my room. My stomach was hurting from my mother's kick. I lay on the floor with my hands under my chin. Pauline entered my room with a cup of tea sweetened with about half a bag of sugar.

'Disgusting,' I said, as I rubbed my lips on my sleeve.

'Drink it,' she said. 'It is good for you.'

As she left the room I pushed the cup away from me and fell asleep. The smell of roast chicken woke me up and I turned my head so that I was facing the bedroom door. My eyes slowly focused on the red trackmarks down my right arm. There was a blob of blood about a penny in size which had a skin on top. From there the blood had dripped along my arm and down onto the carpet. There were fine trackmarks leading away from the blood. It looked like a red spider. As I looked up away from my arm I could see steam rising from a plate of chicken and potatoes. It was between Pauline's feet.

'Clare,' she said, 'I thought you might like to eat in here – save you moving around. By the way, the doctor's surgery is closed on a Sunday. Let me have a look.' She came round the back of me and parted my hair a little. 'It's stopped. Ugh, what's that?'

She pointed at the carpet. As I moved my right hand I exposed fine clots of blood, all standing proud. 'How did that get there?' she said. 'Don't tell me, it's from your head. Let's have another look.'

I felt a slight pressure at the back of my head. 'See?' she said, showing me her fingers. 'It's stopped.' I twisted my head towards her as she stood behind me. 'I'll help clean that up if you like,' she said, pointing at my right arm and the blood. 'Anyway, look what I've got.'

On my bed were two piles. The first pile was on my pillow close to my alarm. There were a number of sheets, clean, folded but not ironed. The second pile consisted of just my dress. She picked it up, gave it a shake and turned the back of it around to face me.

'Gone,' she said. 'See. See? I thought you would be pleased.' She folded up the dress and put it back on the bed. 'How is your head now?' she said.

'Fine,' I said.

'Good. What about your eye? It's gone down a bit and if you can eat with that lip then you've got no problem.' She picked the food up off the floor. 'Where do you want this?' I tried to get up by pressing my hands, palms down, on the carpet, but my stomach was not having any of it. I fell back down on the floor.

'What's the matter now?'

'I've just got cramp,' I gasped. 'I'll stay here for a while.'

The food was then placed back down on the floor in front of me and Pauline left the room. I managed to turn on my side to eat. The potatoes were hot and the chicken did not taste too bad. I picked up a spoonful of gravy and poured it over my arm; the bloody blob melted and started to make its way down my arm. I poured another spoonful of gravy over it and then used the little finger of my left hand to make a bloody puddle on my arm. When all the blood was moist, I cut open a potato and used half to clean my arm. Then I put the bloody potato on the carpet and ate my dinner.

I did not feel like doing my homework or organising my school bag for the following day. I remained on the floor and at some point fell asleep again. Someone covered me with a blanket in the middle of the night. Someone also woke me up and reminded me to go to school. As I came through the school gate I was feeling quite ill. My head still hurt, although it had stopped bleeding long ago. My lip was still swollen and my eye partially closed. The pain was in my stomach and neck. My school bag was hanging off my right shoulder as I walked slowly up the path to the playground. There I would wait for the bell, which came at nine o'clock precisely, and then we would all make our way into assembly. I turned right off the path into the playground with my sisters and Mr Timmons called me.

'Clare Briscoe,' he said. 'Clare Briscoe, come here immediately.'

As I walked over to our Headmaster I tried to open my eye and suck my fat lip in so it didn't look so big.

'Yes, sir?' I said.

'What is the matter with your face, child?'

'Nothing, sir.'

'I said, what has happened to your face?'

'Nothing, sir.'

'Go to my room immediately and stay there.'

I went into the school, up the steps and stopped outside the Headmaster's room. I missed assembly and my first class and I did not even know what I had done wrong. Shortly after eleven o'clock, Mr Timmons appeared. Without saying a word to me he stopped, used his little finger to point at me and then his room. I went in and waited by the wastepaper bin. He entered after me and sat at his magnificent desk. It was all dark brownie-black wood, spit-polished to a high shine.

'What's the matter with your face, Clare?'

'Nothing, sir.'

'You can tell me – what happened?'

'Don't know, sir.'

'You must know what happened.'

'I got beaten up, sir.'

'Who by?'

'I don't know, sir.'

'Well, was it someone at home?'

'Yes, sir.'

'Your brothers and sisters?'

'Oh no, sir.'

'Well, how are you feeling today, Clare?'

'Not well, sir. I don't feel very well.'

'Would you like to lie down for a while?'

'I'll get behind with my work, sir.'

'Leave that to me,' he said. 'Come on, Clare, follow me.'

Mr Timmons took me to the Cookery Department, which was at the end of the corridor. He went in and spoke to the cookery teacher and she came out with a bunch of keys and opened up the first aid room. This had another room off it, which was painted in orange and blue and had a little glass table and a few soft chairs. A huge rug was in the middle of the room.

'You stay here and when you feel better, go to your class,' he said.

'Thank you, sir.'

The cookery teacher returned to her class and Mr Timmons pulled the door closed and disappeared. It was a very odd room which I did not know existed until then. I took my blazer off and put it on top of my bag which was on a chair. I loosened the waistband of my skirt and my tie and I lay down. The rug was very soft and welcoming. My stomach was not too good so I turned over onto my back and fell asleep.

At lunchtime my class teacher came to see me. My sisters were getting worried. Normally I would have lined up with them or my mates in the free school dinners queue, but they were unable to find me. By one o'clock my stomach pains had got a lot worse and I could hear the teachers standing above me wondering out loud what to do. It was agreed that my mother would be called to the school and she could then take the responsibility.

Shortly after two o'clock I was woken up again, this time by the sound of my mother's voice. Someone had put a pillow under my head when I was asleep. The teachers were explaining that I was unwell and had slept the whole morning and they thought that I should see a doctor or go along to hospital and have a check-up.

'Clearie dearie, what's the matter?' said my mother, ever so kindly.

I ignored her and pretended to be asleep.

'Clearie dearie,' said my mother, as the teachers looked on.

I opened my eyes and looked at her.

'You're not well, Clearie dearie, what's wrong?' she said.

'I got beaten up.'

'Well, why don't you get your things and we'll go home.'

At first I didn't think that I had heard my mother correctly.

Before my very eyes the teacher started to help me up to a sitting position. My mother put her hand on my blazer and school bag and asked if they were mine.

'I'm not going home,' was all I could say.

My mother turned round to face me. 'What did you say, Clearie dearie?'

'I'm not going home.'

'No, we're not going home. We'll go to the doctor's first and then we'll go home.'

'I'm not going with you. I'm not going home, Mummy, I'm just not going home.'

'Oh, Clearie dearie,' she said, 'you've had a bump on your head. The sooner we get you home the better. Where are your shoes?' My mother glanced about herself as the teachers looked on. I sat up straight and a shooting pain went straight through my stomach.

'I'm not going home with you, not now, not ever – and you know why I'm not going home.'

My mother looked at me. Her silly 'Clearie dearies' were getting her nowhere. She glanced quickly at the teachers and then back at me.

'If you don't want to come home, you don't have to,' she said.

'I don't and I'm not going with you. I would rather go into a children's home.'

'Well,' said my mother, 'if Clare does not want to come home I cannot make her.'

She then turned and walked out of the room, and was gone before the teachers could ask her what she wanted them to do with me. I lay back down and closed my eyes. It was well past lunchtime and I had missed my free school dinner. At about three o'clock the teachers came back to see me. I was feeling much better. Again they tried to persuade me to go home.

'Give me one good reason why you don't want to go home, just one,' said Mr Timmons.

'I'm just not going home, sir.'

A little later in the day Miss Korchinskye came in to see me.

She was from Poland or Russia and had that voice and that look that told us she was from one or the other.

'Clare, why are you not well?' she asked.

I had always got on well with Miss K as I would call her from now on. I had never played up in her class and my work was good. Office Practice, Typing, Accounts and Economics were her subjects.

'I don't want to go home, miss.'

'Why, Clare? Something you don't want to tell me?'

'Yes, miss.'

'Your face – is that something you don't want to tell me?'

'Yes, miss.'

'Anywhere else, Clare?'

I pointed to my stomach.

'Right – you come and stay with me for as long as you like. I have no children and a big flat.'

Some of the other teachers crept in behind her. I knew what they were thinking. This was the Sacred Heart Catholic School. Children applied years in advance to get into this school and still we turned them away. Amongst the pupils we had two nuns and three priests in the making. What more could be asked of one of the finest Catholic schools around? Everyone knew that it was a good school and turned out good Catholics. Luckily, touch wood, there had been no disasters, no silly girls getting pregnant before marriage. Imagine the shame of that. To see them walk up the drive with their bellies hanging out for all the good Catholics to see. The shame of it. God, no, let it never happen in our lifetime. Now we have a scandal of the same magnitude on our hands. Imagine, a young Catholic girl wants to go into a home, a children's home. She didn't even ask for it to be a Catholic children's home. What are we to say? Jesus Christ, what if Social Services sniff around and find out more than is good for the school? What of our reputation? Sacred Heart, blessed is the most Holy Virgin, Mary Mother of God. Holy Mary, what are we to do?

Mr Hughes, the Deputy Head, wiped his head and then patted his hair down. 'Are you sure she will not go home?'

'Yes,' said Miss K. 'She is still refusing.'

'Where are her sisters? Maybe they can talk some sense into her.'

'I don't think that would be a good idea,' said Miss K.

'Why ever not? She gets on with them, or is she refusing to play with them?'

'She wants to be on her own at present.'

Mr Hughes wiped his brow again. 'Holy Mary, Mother of God, Jesus Christ, where are You when we need divine intervention?'

'I think we should leave her for the time being,' said Miss K. 'It may be that if we accommodate Clare, she will agree to return home later. The last thing we want is to be involved in a scandal.'

'Just tell me, for the Mother of God, how we accommodate Clare?' said Mr Hughes. 'That is just the point. We *cannot* accommodate her even if we wanted to.'

I turned over on my side away from them and opened my eyes. I was not going home, of that I was certain.

'There is a way out of this. It is a temporary measure, but in a few days she might change her mind.'

'For the love of God, what is that?' said Mr Hughes.

'Well, we could allow Clare to come home with me while tempers calm down. All we need do is ask her mother whether she gives her permission. If she agrees I'll take her home.'

17

A Taste of Paradise

1971

There was a stunned silence for a few minutes as Mr Hughes took in what Miss K was saying.

'What if her mother refuses?' he said.

'She will not.'

'What if Clare decides she wants to go to a children's home?'

'She will trust me, Mr Hughes. It is the only way out of this mess and you know as well as I do that we do not want to do anything that will blacken the school's name.'

'Well, if you think you can get the mother's permission and you really don't mind having her for a few days, we would be indebted to you.'

'I'll get on the phone to Mrs Briscoe and we'll take it from there.'

Miss K disappeared and I closed my eyes. Mr Hughes came round and looked down into my face.

'You okay, lass?' I stayed perfectly still. 'We'll soon have this sorted out one way or another. Are you awake, lass?'

'Yes, sir,' I said.

Mr Hughes took a step backwards and lowered his voice. 'Clare, why don't you want to go home? It would be easier all round if you did. Surely to God things cannot be that bad.'

'I don't want to go home, sir.'

'Well, you might change your mind, say in a day or so.'

'Yes, sir, I might, but I don't know.'

Miss K came back. She had spoken to my mother and it was okay for me to go with her for a few days until I came to my

senses. Mr Hughes was now not totally against the idea if my
mother was agreeing to it. It was more a private arrangement
between Miss K and my mother. It had nothing at all to do with
the school. Except, of course, that I had refused to go home
when I was on the school premises and the school therefore had a
duty, as a Catholic school, to find me somewhere else overnight
rather than see me out on the streets. What happened after that
had nothing to do with the school. Miss K put forward that if my
mother was in agreement and she herself was willing, it was very
difficult to see what that had to do with the school.

At four o'clock I was asked to wait behind and when Miss K
came for me at 4.25 I went with her to her home. We drove in her
car with my school satchel on the back seat and my blazer across
my knee. She lived in a very nice spacious flat in Streatham. The
flat, on the second floor, was painted white. In the sitting room
she had a gas heater set in a white fireplace with a huge white
goatskin rug on the floor. Everything was in order. There were
no clothes lying around. No plates in the sink, no rubbish on the
floor. The bedroom was blue and pink with a small wicker basket
at the bottom of the bed and lace curtains looking out onto a
paved area. She showed me my room and told me to treat the flat
as I would do my home. In the sitting room she turned the gas
fire on and pressed a button to ignite it. The whole thing clicked
into action on the third go. There was a loud whooshing sound
and then the flames raced up in twelve-inch-high rods of fire. It
was glorious. Miss K told me to lie on the goatskin rug and to
make myself comfortable. She said I could ring my mother if I
wanted to. I didn't.

As I lay on the rug I thought over the day's events. I would
have to make sure that Miss K did not tire of me. She had no
children, dead or alive. She had told me so in the car. She was
from Poland – that explained her accent – and she lived alone.
She had no husband.

The first night at Miss K's I was terrified that I would wet the
bed. I stayed awake for most of the night, running to and from
the toilet, willing my bladder to empty. When I fell asleep I tried

to wake up at about the same time that my alarm usually went off, only it did not. I rushed to the toilet to do a wee. If Miss K knew that I was capable of wetting her bed she would ask me to leave immediately. Somehow I got through the night. No wet bed. Miss K had washed my whites overnight and the following morning I went into school with her. Pauline and Patsy were waiting for me by the school gate.

'You coming home, Clare?' they said together.

'No.'

'Well, here are your schoolbooks and your clean knickers.'

I took them and put them in my school bag. 'Thanks,' I said.

We all walked through the school gate together and got into our lines in order for assembly.

Later that week my sisters handed over some general clothes and more of my schoolbooks which I took to Miss K. I did not have a problem with my sisters. I got on with them the same as I ever did, but I was free now. Not literally free but freer. I told Miss K about my Saturday job and we worked out the bus route from Streatham to the Elephant and Castle, and then from the Elephant and Castle I would take a number 12, 35 or 171 bus to Walworth Road.

Life was getting better and during my time with Miss K not once did I wet the bed. She was very kind to me. My mother was happy for me to stay there as long as the embarrassment was kept away from the school and from her. Miss K had not asked for a contribution for my keep although my mother was still getting child benefit for me. I suppose in a way my mother was quids in.

I travelled into school and was dropped off round the back of Sacred Heart Church. I made my way to the front entrance and Miss K went into the school car park and entered via the teachers' door. At home time I would wait in the assembly hall until a quarter past four and then meet Miss K at the church. It worked very well. After a couple of weeks there was no more mention of my going home. I got news from my sisters in the playground and at the end of the school day as I waited for Miss

K. My schoolwork picked up, my marks improved and my artwork was pretty impressive. I had more time to be creative. I never discussed my new home with my mates. It was my business, and any gossip might result in me having to go home again, and that was the last thing I wanted.

Once on the way home I mentioned to Miss K that I wanted to be a barrister and she burst out laughing, rolled her head back and slapped the steering wheel twice.

'That's right, my girl, aim high,' she said. 'There's only one person who can stop you, Clare, you remember that. Anya Korchinskye says there is only one person in the whole world who can stop you.'

'Who is that, miss?' I said.

'You, Clare. Only you can stop yourself. You have the ability to go far. So just go.'

We drove to her flat in silence. I had never considered that I might want to stop myself. Why should I do a thing like that? My exams came and went and my results across the board were excellent. All my teachers were pleased.

> *Clare no longer makes excuses. Work is now on time and a great deal of thought goes into it. A truly excellent round of results – well done.*
> *A very able girl – will go far.*
> *Clare has been making steady progress. If it continues she should do well in the next set of results.*
> *A truly delightful and intelligent young lady with remarkable recall. Should do well in life.*

My school report was given to my sister to give to my mother. It was returned the next day and handed back to me. The envelope was unopened.

Maybe it was time to write to Mr Mansfield.

Dear Mr Mansfield,

 I hope you don't mind me writing to you but I wanted you to know that I recently passed my exams and I am on my way to becoming a barrister. I will contact you again when I have more news.

Clare Briscoe

The half-term holiday arrived and I asked Miss K if it was okay to stay with her. She agreed, but said I could go home any time I liked, and if I chose to do so we would always be friends and I could always stay with her whenever I wanted. No matter what, she would always be there for me. I would be the daughter she had never had.

Miss K never asked for any money for my keep so after the third month I offered her £8, which I had saved up from my Saturday job. She told me not to be silly and to put the money in my purse. I secretly bought her a box of Cadbury's Milk Tray and put it on her pillow in her bedroom. When she went to bed she started to cry. She cried and cried and I got frightened. I did not know whether to go in or call out. In the end I remained in my room. The following morning, it was as if it had never happened. She told me not to waste my money on such rubbish in future. Then she thanked me and told me it was the kindest gesture she had ever known since she came to England. She and her parents had escaped the concentration camps in Poland and she had ended up as a teacher in economics, commerce, office practice and typing. She loved her job. Her biggest regret in life was that she had no children.

'How could we in those days?' she said, in her strong Polish accent. 'It was not possible, just not possible.' She shook her head from side to side as she drove and her eyes became moist and red. I was dropped off in the usual place.

It was a Wednesday, a happy day. The lessons were interesting, and we had my favourite school dinner – chocolate cake with pink custard, and for first course a steak and kidney pie with a thick savoury crust, Birds Eye peas, mashed potato, carrots and gravy. After school dinner I met up with my sisters. Not much had changed at home according to them.

'How long you going to stay there for?' they asked.

'I don't know, but I'm not coming home.'

'Mummy says Miss K will tire of you wetting her bed.'

'Well, that's funny,' I said. 'Since I've been with Miss K I've not wet the bed once.'

'Liar.'

'Swear to God, hope to die.'

'Well, Mummy says you'll come home sooner or later with your tail between your legs.'

'I haven't got a tail.'

The bell went and we all lined up and returned in an orderly fashion into the main building. The afternoon session had begun.

I now owned a number of pretty dresses, all thanks to Roses of the Walworth Road. I was a dab hand at serving the customers. No matter how fat or ridiculous they looked in their chosen outfit, I could always find something nice to say – some remark that would swing the sale. I was very good, and Eileen knew it. I got a pay rise. We were all pleased with the progress of Clare Briscoe.

On 18 May I was fourteen years old. Miss K knew it was my birthday. She bought me a book, *The Little Princess* by Frances Hodgson-Burnett. It was beautifully wrapped – a first edition copy in excellent condition. The pages were thick, slightly brown in colour and the print was easy on the eyes. I loved Miss K – she was the mother I had never had. As I looked at the book the tears welled up in my eyes and a large tear blobbed onto the page.

'Miss K, this is the best present I've ever had.' I put my arms around her and kissed her. She kissed me on the cheek and hugged me and then she pushed me away.

'Get away from me, Clare; all this childish nonsense. It's only a book – and not even a new one.'

We looked at each other and she started to laugh. She tapped me on the nose. 'Homework,' she said. I tapped her on the nose. 'Homework,' I said.

At school my sisters had clubbed together and bought me

some bath salts from Woolworth's and lavender cubes with a hint of honeysuckle. There was no present from my mother. I had never received one in the past, so I could hardly expect one now. No birthday card, nothing. Not even 'Fuck off, Clearie dearie.' *The Little Princess* made me cry. That poor girl lost her father. He died. She had dreadful people looking after her and she slept in the most awful conditions. She was very badly treated, but she never gave up, not once, and in the end it all came right. I cried and cried and cried when I read the book and then I cried again when it all came right. *The Little Princess* instantly became my best ever book. Miss K and I were talking about the story some weeks after my birthday.

'The book has a message, Clare – never give up, never. Whatever you want, you can do it if you want to.'

My schoolwork was improving all the time. Mr Timmons called me into his office in early June and told me that I would be moving up to the next stream the following September. My progress in class was an example to everyone else. He also said that he wanted to see a string of excellent results in the forthcoming exams. I was pleased. Schoolwork was easy-peasy now that I had more time to do my homework. I was on a high. I told Miss K and she said it was very good news. I just needed to apply myself and concentrate. I worked very hard in my spare time, revised, did model questions and answers and model essay plans. When the exams came along I was ready. Just before the results were published Mr Timmons called me into his room again and extended his hand.

'Well done,' he said. 'Next September you will start in the A stream. I understand that you will be made Class Prefect and Games Captain. Congratulations.'

He shook my hand and showed me out of his room. It was very good news, but I did not know what my results were. On the other hand it did not matter.

Then the devastating news arrived. Miss K picked me up after school.

'Clare,' she said, 'you will have to go back to your mother. I'm sorry, but I cannot look after you during the summer holidays. You can come and stay again after the holidays.'

I was stunned. 'Why don't you want me?'

Miss K patted my knee. 'It is not a question of want,' she said. 'I have to go back to Poland in August and it would not be right to leave you on your own, so you must go back to your mother. I cannot take you to Poland with me.'

'Oh, Miss K, you mean it's only for the summer holidays?'

'If you want,' said Miss K.

'Yes, I want. When do I come back?'

Miss K was going to return at the end of August and I could join her any time after that. It was not as bad as I thought.

On the last day of school we got up early in the morning. Miss K had put most of my belongings in a large case which had a lock. It would be kept in her car until the end of the school day and she would be waiting for me at the normal time.

The last day of term was the usual chaos. I collected and returned all my old reference books and generally said my goodbyes to my class. Next term I would have a new set of classmates. My sisters were pleased that I was returning home. Since I had left they had borne the brunt of cleaning, cooking and hoovering. At least when I was there it was shared on a rota of one in three. The boys in our family were never expected to do any housework. After the last class I made my way down the path to the front gate and turned right.

'Clare, shall we wait for you?' Pauline and Patsy shouted. 'Clare, we'll wait here.'

I shouted back that I didn't want them to wait for me. Round the back, Miss K was in her car and when she saw me approaching in her rear-view mirror she got out and went to the boot of her car.

'Hello, miss,' I said.

'Call me Anya.'

'Thanks, miss,' I said.

I looked at her: she did not look as though she had been crying but she did look as though she was upset. It was not necessary to take me all the way to my house, although she insisted on it. She eventually agreed with me that it was not a good idea. I had left the house myself. I had refused to go back. Now I *was* going back and I had to go back on my own. Me, Clare, going back. Whatever happened it would happen and, besides, it was only for six weeks. Miss would be back and I would leave home again.

'I will not send you a card, Clare. I will be travelling and it will be difficult.'

'That's okay, miss.'

Miss K said I should keep up with my schoolwork while she was away and she would see how much I had learned when she came back. I gave her a hug, told her I would miss her and then turned my back and walked off. I did not hear Miss K's car go. As I crossed the Camberwell New Road I still did not hear it go. I walked up past the alley and turned left at the second-hand car showroom and waited for a bus. Six weeks with my mother.

18

Paradise Lost

1971

My old bedroom looked the same. My bed was made up, the alarm had been switched off and there was a film of dust on the top of the box. I had forgotten all about the alarm. Since leaving the house there had never been any cause for one. I could not remember the last time I had wet the bed, certainly not at Miss K's. The wet piles in the corner had gone and the room had a certain freshness to it. In my wardrobe was a packet of Jammy Dodgers. My clothes were still hanging up, but all my cheap perfume had gone. While I was unpacking my bag Pauline put her head round the door and as she was talking to me she was pushed into the room by Patsy, who in turn was pushed into the room by Beauty and Denise. They waited as I unpacked my books and clothes.

'Mummy wants a word,' said Pauline.

'Don't hurry,' said Carl. 'Only in your own time or would you like her to come to you?'

'No, I'll come now.'

I put my books down on the bed and walked past my sisters and brothers who had formed a line along the wall leading to the door. As I walked past they all literally fell out of the room and queued up along the banister to get the best position. Downstairs I knocked on the door and waited. I knocked again and went in.

'Get out unless you're invited in,' said my mother.

I stepped backwards out of the door, closed it, knocked and waited. She did not answer. There was no point in knocking again. She had seen and heard me. It was she who wanted to see me. I was in no hurry to see her.

'Come in,' she said eventually. I waited. 'Come in,' she said again. I waited. There was no point in hurrying. I did have six weeks. I heard her move the chair and put her cup down. In I went.

'Hello, Mummy.'

'Oh, is you. The prodigal daughter has finally been slung out.'

'Carl said you wanted me.'

'What you doing here?'

'Carl said you wanted me.'

'What are you doing back in my house?'

'What do you mean?'

'Well, I didn't give you permission to come back, did I? You ask me if you could come back? No. So what the fuck are you doing here?'

'I can go if you like.'

'You would like that, wouldn't you, and then you can walk and tell people that I've thrown you out.'

'I did not come back to argue with you,' I said.

'Well, what did you come back for? No one wants you here, so why don't you fuck off back where you came?'

'Yes, all right, I can do that. I can go now or later – it's up to you. I've got somewhere to go. Anyway, George said I can always go to his house, so if you don't want me I'll go and pack.'

My mother sat back in her chair and I think that in many ways she feared me as much as I feared her. Cynthia and Norma were sitting at her feet. Eastman was in the chair opposite.

'Is there anything else?' I said.

'Yes, you can pack your bags and fuck off. This is not a doss house.'

I closed the door behind me and my sisters and brothers scattered. As I walked back upstairs Carl asked if I was off again. I nodded. My schoolbooks were piled in the bottom of my wardrobe and my nice dresses were packed in a bag and then placed in the case that Miss K had given me. I stuffed some old

clothes in bags and picked up *The Little Princess*. I walked down
the steps, out of the front door and closed it behind me.

My father had given me an address in case of emergencies –
52 Ethnard Road, Peckham SE15. I had been there once or
twice, but was not sure how to get there. I caught a number 12
bus to Camberwell Green and then a 36 to Peckham. At
Peckham High Street, just before the road that leads to Sumner
Road, I got off the bus. I asked at the police station for directions
to Ethnard Road. The officer had a huge map behind him and
pointed out for me where I was and where I wanted to be. His
directions led to the back of a large council estate, where there
was a quiet private residential street. I knocked on the door of
number 52 and a large fat lady answered. This lady identified
herself as my father's girlfriend, Dolores.

'He's not in,' she said. 'You can wait or go to 215 Camberwell
New Road.'

The 36 bus took me all the way to Camberwell New Road,
virtually to George's front door. When I rang the bell he was not
in and the tenants said he was probably at 41 Offley Road by the
Oval cricket ground. It was within walking distance, so I carried
my bag round there. He wasn't there either and they had no idea
when he would be. I remembered that round the back of the Oval
was a block of flats where another friend of his, Miss Lindsey,
had put me up on a number of occasions in the past. It was on
the third floor. After walking around for a while I found what I
thought was the right block of flats. My memory told me it was
the third flat on the left after the stairs. Outside the door it did not
look familiar but I knocked anyway. The door was opened by a
man in a string vest, who called his wife immediately and then
went back inside. His wife, a huge lady with red lipstick and fat
feet in slip-ons came out and asked me who I was looking for. I
explained that it was Miss Lindsey. She did not know the name,
but when I described her, the fat lady with the slip-ons immediately recognised her.

'Upstairs, love, left at the stairs and second on the right.'

I thanked her and made my way upstairs. Miss Lindsey was

in, thank heavens. She asked if my mother knew I was there. Did George know? And finally who else knew? After I explained my journey she told me to get inside while she put the kettle on. I was shown to my old bedroom. It had not changed much, although it looked as though a lodger had occupied it recently.

'I have a lot of people staying with me, love. Just get yourself in and make yourself comfy.'

Miss Lindsey went off to put the kettle on and I was left to my thoughts. No one knew that I was here. My mother did not give a fig and my father was God knows where. Miss K was probably on her way back to Poland.

Miss Lindsey was very kind to me and tried daily to contact my dad, but it was three days before he finally came to see me. He had not realised that I had been thrown out of the house. It was only when he went to visit his children at Sutherland Square that he realised I was missing. Pauline told him I was with him and he said he had not seen me. When he rang his girlfriend she told him that I had visited three days earlier and she had sent me to Camberwell New Road. From there he followed my track and eventually decided that I had to be at Miss Lindsey's. My father said I couldn't stay with him. He was just too busy, never in the same place, always on the move. He told Miss Lindsey that as Carmen had made it clear that she didn't want me, he would apply to the courts for custody of me and my sisters. I was no trouble, Miss Lindsey said. I could stay as long as I wanted to, especially since I didn't have a home to go to. My father agreed that it was the best place for me for the time being and as he left he gave Miss Lindsey some money to look after me until he could sort out something more regular.

It was four days before I next saw my father and when I did he only stayed for about ten minutes. He brought some food for Miss Lindsey and a bottle of Guinness Stout. For me he brought some biscuits and a packet of sweets. A week later he told Miss Lindsey that he had been to see his solicitors and the matter would be sorted out soon. It was not that I was unhappy at Miss Lindsey's. She was very kind to me and some of the clothes she had knocking around in her flat fitted me. I was still able to go to Roses on a Saturday. The 159 went from almost outside the block of flats down to the Oval where I could walk or catch another bus if I was feeling lazy. Eileen had asked me to work a few weeks during the holidays to cover the full-timers who were away. The money came in useful and it occurred to me to buy food for the flat on my way back from work. Miss Lindsey was glad of the company; it allowed her to fuss about the flat, cleaning, hoovering and generally being busy fetching and carrying.

Early one Sunday morning my father turned up with a large chicken and some fruit and vegetables. He slapped the chicken down in the kitchen and told Miss Lindsey that Carmen was causing trouble. He had been to see his solicitor about getting control of all his children – apart from Denise; he excluded Denise because he did not adopt her. The solicitor had contacted my mother and she refused point-blank to allow George to have custody of us. In fact, she said that I had to be returned immediately, because I was unlawfully in my father's custody and if he did not return me to the house by the end of the week she would report him to the police for child abduction.

I refused to go. My father thought that it was really all to do with the child benefit my mother was getting. With six Briscoes she was raking in a fair sum every week. She would lose all that if George had custody of us. Never mind about that, where was he going to put us all if he got custody? Surely not at 215 Camberwell New Road; it was full of tenants. What about Ethnard Road? Not on your nelly. His girlfriend would never allow it. Offley Road was a no-go zone, so my father had a bit of thinking to do. He thought that maybe I should go home and we could sort it all out from there. I decided that I would rather stay put. My father did not try to force me to go home. He made it clear that while he thought we were all better off with him, he did not know how he was going to manage.

I stayed with Miss Lindsey and at the start of the autumn term I decided that I could do without a new blazer. The one I had would do me fine. My skirt was okay, too. There was, in my view, no need to go home to get any items for school. I had but a few days left before I could go back to Miss K. If I had my way I would never speak to my mother again. I ignored her messages via my father to return home.

The school playground on the first day back was busy. The new students milled around like tadpoles without their tails. All of them looked as though they had lost their other half. My classmates were equally unfamiliar. Some of them I had not previously met, others I had a nodding 'hello' with. It pleased me greatly that the rest of my class did not feel the need to purchase a new blazer, skirt or shirt – come to think of it, they all looked pretty scruffy. It might, of course, have had something to do with the fact that they were regarded as clever and therefore there was no need to shine in a new blazer. Simple intellect was enough. Unlike my former class there was no messing about. No throwing chalk or trying to disrupt the class. The students were there to learn. All of them had done their summer homework.

In the break I was dead keen to find Miss K. Up in her block she had not registered and it was not clear where she might be. There was no message or note for the students. The Department of Economics, Commerce and Typewriting was simply closed. I was sure that if Miss K was around she would have got in touch by now. She was that kind of person. Good manners were important to her. I stood outside Mr Timmons's room until he noticed I was there. In his office the smell of polished floors and oak tables overwhelmed me and I sat down dizzy from my last intake of breath. I explained that I just wanted to know when Miss K was coming back to school. Mr Timmons sent me out of his room with a flea in my ear and effectively told me to mind my own business. It was dreadful.

After the third week I had heard nothing, not a word about Miss K and I had no means of finding out. I did not know my way to her flat and the school were pretty tight-lipped about it. At the beginning of the fourth week I asked the cookery teacher if there was any news about Miss K. She had been present when I had refused to go home last year. Maybe she might tell me if Miss K was coming back to school. She would not have just abandoned me, I knew that. Never.

I was taken to one side and Miss explained that Miss K was not very well and it was not clear whether she would ever be coming back to school. Miss K had gone to Poland and had been there for a few weeks driving around and visiting familiar spots. She had apparently called to see some relatives and was driving back when her car was stuck between the tracks on a level crossing. A train was coming: it did not have enough time to brake and crashed straight into her car. Poor old Miss K was trapped, and the impact of the accident was such that she had severe damage to her legs. The surgeons had done all they could, but eventually she had to have one leg amputated. The other leg was in such a bad state that it had been touch and go whether they would have to amputate that one too. It was no good to anyone, not even her, but the psychological damage was such that they had feared that she might not survive if they amputated the second leg. Miss K, had written that she would like to return to the school as soon as she was able to, but was in no fit state at the moment to look after anyone, never mind a child. All this was between us, Miss said. Miss K was still in Poland but would be flown back at the weekend. She was now just about well enough to travel.

The tears had welled up at the back of my eyes and had run down my cheeks without me noticing. They just refused to stop. Poor old Anya. Poor old Miss K. She had lost a leg and it was possible she would lose the other. How she must have felt, I don't know. There was me, whingeing on and complaining about my lot when she had lost her leg. The tears had dripped off the back of my hand onto my knee as I sat with the cookery teacher on one of her high stools.

'Is Poland far away?' I asked.

'Yes, it's a fair distance,' said Miss.

'How much will it cost to go there?'

'I fear rather a lot of money. Why don't you just pray for Miss K and wish her a safe journey? If you like, you could always pray for her left foot. I'm sure that will be a relief to her when she knows that she can keep it. If I were you I would concentrate all my efforts on praying. Miss K will need all the prayers she can get.'

'Thank you, Miss,' I said.

I went to needlework in a daze. Miss K had lost her leg and now she might die. I could look after her. If she returned to London, I could look after her. We could look after each other, much the same as it had been before. Miss Jones thought that my cross-stitching was not up to scratch and she got me to repeat the stitch four times until she was satisfied.

At Mass on Friday we all prayed for Miss K to make a good recovery, but as the priest pointed out, we all have a mission on earth and we should not question the workings of God. Whatever happened, Miss K was still my best ever friend and my favourite teacher. How the autumn term dragged without her clever cheerful presence. I missed our life together.

It started getting dark early and light late, and as we all made preparations for Christmas I could not get Miss K out of my head. What was she doing? Did she still have one leg? Did she remember me and the days we spent together at her flat? I wanted to tell her that I had re-read *The Little Princess*, but I had a sad feeling deep in my heart that I would never get the opportunity.

At school I had become more withdrawn. The combination of the loss of Miss K and my horrible home life caused my hair to start falling out. At first it was gradual. I combed my hair and some of it came out in the comb. I cleared the teeth, combed it again and an enormous chunk of hair became trapped. When I tried to free the comb, the hair all fell away from my scalp. There were two bald patches at the top of my head. I tried a brush and the same thing happened, and when I pulled a bit of hair between my fingers it remained between my fingers long after they were down by my side. I pulled the hair out of the comb and brush, put it in my pocket and pulled my Michael Jackson wig over my bald patches. Maybe my hair needed a wash? I would do it tonight. But the wash made no difference. My hair still fell out. I tried to escape from the present. On top of that, my father met me at the school gate and told me I had to go home. He made it clear that my best chances of leaving home permanently were to go there in the short term. I didn't really understand that, but my dad knew best.

With a very heavy heart I decided to go home. My mother was ecstatic to see me. There was all the dusting and cleaning and the cooking and washing and hoovering to do. No, she had not forgotten that for the best part of seven months I had been swanning around, refusing to come home, being cared for from pillar to post by those who should know better.

'Don't take any fucking liberties in this house,' she said. 'You've got no fucking fairy godmother in this house – never forget that.'

On my first night at home I woke in the middle of the night to a racket. The alarm flashed on and off and the noise pierced my bones. My bed-wetting had begun again. There was another blow. My father had been advised that he had no chance of getting custody of us – not even a one per cent chance. Mrs Carmen Briscoe was well known to Social Services. When my father had left her with six mouths to feed, to spend his Pools win as he wished, she worked hard to provide a roof over our heads and to put food on the table. She had an excellent record with Social Services. She had adopted a child straight out of hospital, and taken it home when it was only a few days old. She had treated it like her own and adopted the child against stiff opposition from her husband. There had never been any problems with Denise. Not a whiff of abuse in the family. Carmen Briscoe was a model mother. As for my father? Well, said the solicitor, where exactly did he live? How would he manage six children on his own? He had never held down a job since his Pools win and he was not a very good provider. Take, for example, the time when Clare had tried to book herself into a children's home. He rang up to say it was the best thing for her. How could a father, a rich father at that, agree that his own child should go into a home? What judge would be willing to give him custody of all the children? I told Mary I almost felt like giving up myself.

19

Another Christmas

1971

Christmas dinner in the free dinner queue was worth having. Just before we collected our raffle ticket for dinner we were given a paper hat to put on. The hall was decorated with a Christmas tree and paper chains. We had to get in the dinner queue early just in case they ran out of food. I had not eaten all day. I wanted plenty of room for my Christmas dinner. I picked up my plate and, using my sleeve, I wiped the edge clean. I was not satisfied so I spat on it and then polished it again with my sleeve. That was better. If I had my way, the food would be piled high on my plate and would fall off the edges if I were not careful.

'Yes please, Cook. Yes please, yes please, yes please.'

'Half a mo,' said Cook.

From where I was standing in the queue the line-up of food was roast potatoes, roast turkey, carrots, stuffing, Brussels sprouts, cranberry sauce, gravy.

'Yes please, Cook. Yes please. Yes please.'

My plate was piled high. I had to walk very slowly back to my table; twice I had to stop just in case my food went over the edge. I steadied my hand and got to my table without spilling a drop. I worked my way through it in silence. Then I went back for my afters – mince pies, Christmas pudding, yellow custard, ice cream and a cherry.

'Yes please, yes please, yes please, yes please, but no cherry.'

'You sure?' said Cook. 'It's not like you to refuse a cherry.'

'No, thank you, Cook.'

'What about some more custard?'

'Oh, yes please.'

I ate so much I missed the bell to get out of the dinner hall and when I did get up I had stomach cramp. Not much happened in the afternoon. At some point I packed up and went home. I had eaten enough to last me several days.

Mummy was getting ready for Christmas. She had been to the market to buy her Christmas presents and food and she had woken me up early one Sunday morning to go to find my dad. Patsy and Pauline were also awake.

'Tell him Christmas is coming and you cannot eat fresh air on Christmas Day. If he wants food in your belly tell him to bring it here.'

We all went to the bus stop and caught a bus to Ethnard Road. It was before 7 a.m. when we arrived and my dad was still in bed. We were not allowed into his bedroom. We sat and waited in the sitting room until my father got up. He was not happy to see us but on the other hand he knew that there were certain fatherly duties he had yet to carry out. Pauline gave him the message from my mother and my father started to sing.

'Tell the old girl she can count on me,' he intoned. 'Have I ever let you down? Have I?'

We did not answer that. My father drove to Petticoat Lane Market. When he parked he told us to stay in the car. We waited for his return, watching the Christmas shoppers rushing round for bargains. He eventually arrived with a chicken over his shoulder and a bag full of food in his right hand. He slung the chicken by its neck into the boot and set the food bag beside it. On the way home he stopped off at another food shop and the shopkeeper came out and handed my father another bag of food, which he also stuffed into the boot. We arrived home before ten o'clock and as my father unpacked the car, Christine, Carl and Martin surrounded him. My mother stood by the front door with her hands on her hips.

'Hello, old girl,' said my father.

'Have you done the Christmas shopping or are you saving up?'

'Are you still with that idiot?' my father said.

My mother ignored him.

'You're a silly girl, Carmen, but you don't need me to tell you that.'

My father put the last of the bags on the pavement at about the same time as my mother moved her hands from her hips. She stalked towards him as he was getting back into the car. As he attended to his seatbelt, my mother arrived by the driver's door and, turning her back on him, she took a flying backwards kick at his car and caused an indentation as large as the heel on her shoe. By that time George had wound his window up but he wound it down again just low enough to shout to my mother.

'You a silly old girl, Carmen. You and that fool of yours should live happy ever after.' Then he wound the window back up and drove away.

'Take it inside,' she said, as I grabbed the chicken by the neck.

On Christmas Day we had an enormous amount to eat. The Eastmans and the Briscoes ate together, at the same time. It was better that way because the Eastmans were able to share the food that my father had bought without any question. For once, there was no question about how much we were allowed to eat because we Briscoes all knew where the food had come from.

We finished eating in the late afternoon and all the girls, the Briscoe girls, helped with the washing-up. The Eastman side all sat and watched TV. Once I had finished washing up I went to change my dress. It was time to open my presents. My head was almost bald and, although I had been seeing a trichologist once a fortnight for special treatment, it had not worked. Underneath my Michael Jackson wig it did not matter so much, but sooner or later I would have to deal with my baldness.

Downstairs in the sitting room, the Briscoes and Eastmans were crowded in. Baby Winston Eastman slept on. Cynthia and Norma opened their presents. They always had more than us because that fool of a father of theirs always bought them extras – bigger and better extras than the Briscoes. Come to think of it, I don't remember a single occasion when he ever bought us a

Christmas present. He would never bother with me and it was understandable. I was a lost cause; nothing he did would ever make me like him.

The Eastmans opened their presents in the first round while the Briscoes waited for them. Round two, all were given presents, both the Eastmans and the Briscoes. Lots of new clothes and lots of toys. I unwrapped my present. It was Dollie. Good old Dollie. I honestly had not noticed that she had gone missing again. Still, I was happy to have her back. The second present took a bit of unwrapping. It was an awkward size that was well padded. As the wrapping papers peeled away it was obvious that the present was my spinning-top. I thanked my mother for my presents and made a mental note to hide Dollie. I did not want her as a present next year.

As Eastman opened his present I looked the other way. The idea that someone had taken time to choose a present for him was something I simply could not understand. Surely he would be better off with a Peter and Mary book. He gave my mother a beautiful hand-knitted cardigan, pale pink with rose buttons interlaced down the front with ribbon. Around the neck there were six tiny rosebuds sewn into the cardigan which gave the impression of there being just one rose. She was also given bath salts, a china tea set, a hot-water bottle, a new apron, perfume, talcum powder, intensive body moisturiser and a new pair of slippers. The boys were given train sets and a gun with caps.

Christmas was over. I went to my room and put Dollie in the bottom of my wardrobe. The spinning top I left on the floor. I had played with it years before and it had lost its magical attraction. Someone else would be grateful to play with it now.

20

Bye Bye Bem

1972

The first day back at school I was asked to report after 'register' to the Economics, Commerce and Typewriting Department. I went up the stairs not knowing quite what to expect. I didn't think my homework was late from last term. All my textbooks had been handed in and I had not done anything bad as far as I could remember. I knocked on the door and went in – and there was Miss K, sitting at her desk!

'Miss K!' I exclaimed.

'Come in, Clare, come in and sit down. Now tell me, how are you?'

But I was looking under the table. Miss K was wearing trousers – something she had never done in all the time she had been at Sacred Heart. She was a tweed skirt and twinset teacher. The trousers were very elegant and tailored. Looking at her legs close up, I noticed that one was much fatter than the other under the trousers, and that she wore odd shoes. One was familiar – I had seen it before at the flat and when she had worn it to school – but the other was more of a boot.

'How are you, Clare?' she repeated.

'How are *you*, Miss?' I said. 'I'm sorry to hear about your legs.'

Miss K stared at me for a long time and then she asked again how I was.

'Fine,' I said. 'I'm very well, miss. Can we go home now, Miss K?'

Miss started to laugh and then she started to cry. 'No,' she said.

I was shattered. I asked to be excused. She did not reply and so I slipped out of the room. I thought how, if I could wave a magic wand, I would make all the unhappy children in the world happy. All my life I had wanted someone to care for me. Children have the right to be happy, otherwise why bring them into the world? What is the point? If I died tomorrow, I thought, I would like there to be someone on this planet who would miss me. Children should have presents twice a year and new clothes once a month, I decided. An absolute necessity is that every child should have a dry bed, and parents who beat their children should get what's coming to them. No parent has the right to abuse their children. I had always wanted to experience happiness. Not day-in-and-day-out happiness, but just every-now-and-then happiness. When happiness arrived I would know. The first thing I would do would be to turn my bed-wet alarm off. Next I'd put all the food in the fridge or the cupboards, never in my bedroom. Finally, when happiness came knocking on my door, I'd be waiting. I'd open the door and say, 'Where have you been? What took you so long? And if you just give me a moment I'll pack and go with you.'

It had never once occurred to me that Miss K would not want me to move back in. After I left her I went into the toilets and sat in a cubicle with my legs off the ground just in case someone looked under the door. Bunking off classes was a crime. I stayed there for a while, deep in thought, and then I went to my next lesson. Miss K was quite unable to catch me. I had left in a hurry and her good leg was not capable of moving spontaneously.

When I eventually went back to my classroom, she was waiting outside. She looked tired. She told me to follow her and I did. She pushed and pulled her good leg down the corridor and when we turned right to make our way up the stairs it became obvious why she did not want me. She lifted her boot on to the stairs and then she hit it with the back of her hand and let out an expletive. Miss dragged her good leg up and did a little hop with the other. Then the boot foot swung into action and landed in front of her. Using her stick she put her weight on the boot and then swung the good leg in front of her. As she moved she scrunched up her eyes – the pain must have been excruciating. Eventually we got back to her room.

She invited me in. She pressed herself up against the wall and swung her boot out in front of her. Poor old Miss K. She was not at all well.

'Clare,' she said, in the strongest Polish accent that I ever heard her use, 'it would give me the greatest pleasure if you and I could be as before, but I am not capable of looking after you. Look at me, child – see.' She bent down and lifted her trousers up. The bottom half of her leg looked like one of the mannequin's legs in Roses.

'See?' she said. 'It is hollow. A useless leg. Good for nothing.' She bent down, unstrapped her leg and held it up as she balanced herself against the wall. 'How can I look after you? I have failed you, Clare, and I have failed myself.'

As Miss K struggled to get her leg back on I went over to her and helped her to put her stump back into the false leg. I held her trousers up and between the two of us we strapped it in. Miss threw her head back against the wall and she started to cry.

'Yes, I have failed you, Clare. How will you manage now? Don't think that I have not prayed every day. Yes, I wish it had not happened and of course I would turn the clock back if I could, but having escaped with my life from the concentration camp, maybe this was meant to be.' Miss continued to cry and I pulled her trousers down to cover her boot.

'Why don't you sit down, Miss?' I said gently.

I put a chair next to her and she swung her bottom onto it.

'I don't even know where I am going to live,' she told me tearfully. 'I cannot manage the stairs and I have to find a ground-floor apartment.'

'I can help you, Miss,' I said. 'You have been so kind to me. I can help you. Miss – I've got it! We can help each other. I can be your helper and you can be my teacher and we can manage.'

Miss started to laugh and then she started to cry again. 'You are so full of life, Clare. I would very much like you to live with me, but I am a cripple and your life has just begun. You must go ahead, Clare, and forget about me.'

Miss cried and I did too, and between the two of us it was obvious why we could not continue as before, but I still wanted to try.

'But, Miss, I *can* care for you,' I said as the tears ran down my cheeks. 'I can cook chicken and potatoes, rice, peas and carrots. I'm good at cleaning, Miss, and I know how to wash and shop. We will be okay, Miss. I'll be quiet and you won't even know I'm there. All you have to do is shout, Miss, and I'll be there.'

Snot from her nose had now joined forces with her tears and she blew a bubble large enough to make her stab it with a fingernail. It popped and fragments of snot settled down the front of her twinset. Using the back of her hand she wiped it away and then wiped her hand on her navy-blue tailored trousers.

'I know, Clare,' she said, 'but why swap one abuser for another when you can be free?'

Back home after school, Eastman was getting on my nerves. Cynthia had been very naughty and got into trouble with my mother. To diffuse the situation and to distract attention away from Cynthia, Eastman picked a fight with me. He deliberately bumped into me when I was on the landing outside my bedroom and twice when I closed the door he opened it and called me a black bitch. When I went to the toilet and returned he was waiting on the landing and asked me why I went to the toilet when I could just as easily piss on the bed. It was too much: finally, I lost my temper with him. It had been a hellish day and I was still reeling from my encounter with Miss K. Eastman stood in my way and I barged into him, on purpose. I was on the stairs leading up from my landing towards the top floor. Using his elbow, Eastman knocked me to the stairs. I turned round and punched him and he grabbed me round the neck. I had seen Big Daddy and Giant Haystacks wrestle the week before on TV, in *World of Sport* with Dickie Davies (Dickie had a quiff hairstyle with highlights), and I had learned how to perform a foul.

All of a sudden I grabbed Eastman between the legs with both my hands and pulled hard. I wasn't sure what I had grabbed because he wore Oxford bags, but he knocked me to the stairs again and still I did not let go. With my back against the stairs I held on and put both my feet up against his knees and pulled hard, straightening my knees to give me extra leverage. Eastman screamed and both my mother and Bem arrived at about the same time to witness what was going on. There was no way that Eastman could get at me, since every time he tried, I straightened my legs and pulled hard with both my hands – which caused him to reel back in pain.

'Jesus Christ, Carmen, stop she. Look, she having my dick in her hand. Where is my bollocks? Jesus Christ, Carmen, they gone. Clare tear my bollocks off.'

My mother tried to chop me behind my knees in order to get me to bend them, but I held firm and pulled on the body part in my hand.

'Jesus Christ, Carmen, you see my dick? Where it gone? Clare rip it off.'

Bem was now standing at the top of the stairs, shaking. He was just a jelly, but he managed to find his voice. 'Eastman started it, Carmen. He hit Clare first, I see him do it.'

My mother was still trying to chop me under my knees. It failed and Eastman was in serious agony.

'Let go,' she ordered.

'Why should I? He started it.'

My mother put her hand on top of mine and dug her nails in. Eastman shouted in agony. She had dug straight into his body part which was in my hand. A circle of blood began to appear at the crotch of his Oxford bags. Bem started to shout and shake at the same time.

'Both of you will kill the pickney. Leave her alone, Carmen. Eastman started it – I saw him.'

My mother was still trying to chop my knees while Eastman was holding on to the banister. At one point my foot slipped and I thought I had pulled off his body part. My mother took the opportunity to get between the two of us and I retreated upstairs.

Bem was calling me. 'Clare, come. Clare, come with me.'

At the top of the landing Bem pushed me up the stairs and told me to go into his room. I went in and he locked his door. We remained there for the rest of the night. He absolutely refused to open the door when my mother came after me. Eastman banged on the door on several occasions, but Bem told him that I was asleep and he should return in the morning. Later, when my mother knocked on the door she was met by silence because we pretended that we were asleep. If he had known the trouble he had got himself into by protecting me, Bem would not have bothered. The unfolding events proved disastrous to him.

For several days, Eastman kept out of my way. My mother did not speak to me and even though we lived in the same house it was not difficult to avoid each other. Bem, because of his shakes, kept himself to himself, but one Sunday morning he decided to come downstairs to ask me to help him shave. It took him a while to get down the first flight of stairs. By the time he was making his way down the second flight Eastman was coming up from the kitchen.

'You,' he pointed to Bem with his crooked finger, 'you arsehole, you said I was a liar.'

Bem continued down the stairs and I opened my bedroom door to listen to the conversation.

'Eastman,' said Bem, 'what's the matter with you?'

'You arsehole,' Eastman repeated. 'You said I attacked Clare. Did you see me attack her? Did you see me lay a finger on her? You got the fucking shakes. Has it affected your fucking brain?'

There was no answer, but Bem continued down the stairs.

'Oi, you – I'm talking to you.'

Eastman was facing Bem who had about another five steps to go. Bem had his left hand on the banister and his right hand on the wall to keep his balance.

'Did you hear me?' said Eastman as he grabbed Bem's foot and pulled him so that he lost his balance. Bem tried to hold on, but landed flat on his backside as Eastman pulled at his foot. I went onto the landing and saw Eastman was attempting to pull Bem down the stairs. Bem looked as if he was having a fit. His shaking was out of control.

'You, you fucking parasite,' said Eastman. 'You live here free of rent and you call me a liar.'

Bem was having a fit on his bottom and Eastman, stupid Eastman, could not have cared less. I took a running jump and landed on Eastman's back and started to punch him in the head and pull his eyelashes out as he tugged at Bem's leg.

'Quick, Bem,' I said. 'Go back upstairs.'

'Wait,' said Eastman. 'Who the body on my back?'

'Quick, Bem,' I said. 'Go.'

Eastman refused to release Bem's leg and had managed to pull him down the stairs. I stuck my fingers in Eastmans' eyes and pulled his ears in order to get him to let Bem go. I pressed my knees into his back then I grabbed him and punched him twice in the neck. It was a move I had seen when Giant Haystack wrestled with an unknown contender. Then I used my other elbow to jab him in the neck. Giant Haystacks had knocked his opponent out with one poke of the elbow. Eastman surely refused to be knocked out.

'Quick, Bem – move,' I hollered.

Bem stayed where he was, on his bottom. Pauline and Patsy came rushing downstairs and seeing me on Eastman's back, punching him in the side of the head, they called for Mummy. She arrived with a belt, but did not get involved with me and Eastman.

'Get off his back,' she said.

I ignored her. I held on tight, and landed a few more blows to his head. Then he bent forward and I slipped over his head onto the floor, after which he brought his massive feet up and stood on my stomach.

'It's always you,' he said. 'You, you, you. You're always

getting on my nerves, always causing me trouble. It could not have been anyone else but you.'

He kicked me in the stomach. My mother pulled Eastman away and reminded him that he had Previous for assaulting me. Bem was helped up by all the children. Once he was on his feet he complained to my mother and said that Eastman was out of control and had attacked him for no good reason. My mother listened and asked Eastman what he had to say. He denied assaulting Bem so I started shouting that he had and I had seen him.

Bem was crying and shaking as he confronted Eastman. He told Eastman that he was not my father and had no right to attack me and that as far as Bem was concerned, he had attacked me on more than one occasion over the years. He accused my mother of assaulting me and not doing enough to protect me. Neither Eastman nor my mother could believe their ears. Bem, quiet Bem, had finally decided to speak out against what he saw as unacceptable behaviour.

When Bem had finished my mother looked at Eastman, who was still on the landing. They both looked at me and then at each other. My mother was the first to speak.

'If you feel like that you had better pack your bags and fuck off.'

'You better go quick before I lose my temper with you,' Eastman said.

Bem was still shaking and I helped him walk step by step up to his bedroom. I told him to take no notice of them and that she had not meant what she had said. Bem was so shaken that he had to take a pill as he sat in his bedroom. My mother called me and told me to go to my room. I protested: I was helping Bem. She told me in no uncertain terms to go to my bedroom. I passed her on the landing as I went, then she and her idiot man went downstairs. Eastman did not attempt to get at me nor did my mother. When I heard their door close I went back upstairs to see Bem. He was still sitting on the bed crying. I put my arms around him. His left trouser leg was pulled up to his knee and the blood trickled down his shin. I helped to clean his leg and Bem lay down on his bed. He had stopped crying and I was sitting on the floor. Bem was such a gentleman. He had never had a bad word to say against my mother or my father. He had been through and witnessed whole events which he had never spoken about, and now Eastman of all people had pulled him down the stairs and hurt him. Eastman would pay for it – I was quite certain of that.

The following morning I got up and I heard my mother shouting at Bem. She said that she would be going out soon and when she came back he should be gone out of her house. She did not want to put him on the streets, but if necessary she would. I told Bem not to worry, but he had had enough. The final humiliation had arrived. Eastman had attacked him and he was not able to defend himself.

Bem packed and put on his tweed suit and his bowler hat. He sat on his bed and waited. He asked me to go and find my dad and tell him what had happened. When I did, George drove me straight back to 19 Sutherland Square. Bem was still sitting on his bed in his bowler hat. I went up the stairs and told him that George was outside. He picked up his suitcase and asked me if he had left his shaver behind. He had not. He made his way downstairs with his suitcase in his hand. When he got to the ground floor he knocked on my mother's sitting-room door and went in. I stood in the doorway, shaking. He removed his key from the key ring which was attached to a loop on the waistband of his trousers. He handed it to her, but she ignored him and looked the other way. He dropped it in her lap. He thanked her for his care over the years and his room. He tipped his bowler hat to her and then he shuffled out of the house and into my dad's car. I did not help him with his suitcase. He had moist eyes, but his dignity held up. He wanted to be independent. My father got out of the driver's seat, walked round the back of the car and closed the passenger door. They drove off. That was the last time I saw Bem. He never got over the shock of his expulsion and he died not long afterwards in the Maudsley Hospital.

★   ★   ★

We had come to an understanding, Miss K and I. She was always giving me advice, telling me that I should spend more time on my classwork. I would on the other hand go into school early and see her in the Economics, Commerce and Typewriting Department. I also called on her at the end of each day to make sure that she was managing and to help whenever she required it.

Early one Monday morning I arrived at school and went to see her. She was not at her desk. The department was closed and another teacher had been put in charge of arranging substitute classes. Miss K did not return that week and the following week we were informed at Friday Mass that she had developed complications in her remaining leg and needed our prayers. I prayed so hard for her and her leg. I knew that she was very proud and did not need or require us to pray for her, but I prayed all the same.

The week after that, Father informed us that Miss K had had her leg amputated and would require constant prayers for her recovery. No one ever spoke about her again, except at Friday prayers. I never saw Miss K again.

Towards the middle of term we were told in assembly that Miss K would not be returning to the school, but that our thoughts and prayers would always be with her. She never got in touch with me. I never expected her to. She had her own demons that she would have to fight in her own way and in her own time. The last thing I wanted was for her to feel that she had let me down, when she had given me such hope. Miss K made me feel that everything was possible: all I had to do was decide what it was that I wanted and go for it. I fully intended to do just that. In the end Father stopped mentioning her in prayers.

One Saturday in early summer my mother asked me to go with her to the shopping centre at the Elephant and Castle. This was unusual. She really wanted an extra pair of hands; because of my job at Roses I was never available on a Saturday. Today I would have to go. Apparently there was a new stall that sold food at a very low price and it was worth paying them a visit. She got

herself ready and emptied the trolley which was kept at the back
of the house between shopping expeditions. It still contained a
collection of old brown paper bags and newspapers. On the way
there I walked behind her; I didn't want to upset my mother in
any way. There was always the remote possibility that she might
buy me some new clothes as an act of overwhelming generosity.
At East Street Market we took the number 40 bus; it was only
four stops to the roundabout at the Elephant and Castle. The
Shopping Centre was on the central island. Following the signs,
we went through the pedestrian underpass. The new shop was
on the first floor. Sitting on a chair outside was a short white
man. He was very thin and the skin that was on his bones hung
like layers of honey when it is dripped from a spoon. His large
bulbous nose had lots of open pores and his skin had a gritty
texture similar to that of coarse sandpaper. A brown felt hat was
perched on his ears; it had a wide brim and a feather sticking out
of the hatband on the left. A huge black, badly worn belt held up
his baggy trousers, giving the impression that he had no chest –
which made him look even shorter. Although he was small, he
had massive hands with which he counted out the change for his
customers.

The shop was crowded with people. Sugar, baked beans,
pilchards and cornflakes were piled high on the floor. The
sardine tins were thrown higgledy-piggledy into a huge metal
bath. The rice was in huge canvas bags. You could have any
amount as long as you paid for it. The small man was not
assisted by anyone. He was very quick. As soon as he was
cashing up for one customer he was busy asking the next one in
the queue what she wanted.

When it was my mother's turn, she reeled off the items she
wanted and he piled them into her trolley at lightning speed. By
the time it was full we still had a few more items to buy. They
would have to go in the large toughened bag which my mother
had given me earlier. The small man took the bag from me and
packed the food in it. When he gave it back, it was so full the
handles did not meet in the middle. My mother paid him and we

left the shop. She was pleased because she had saved money – quite a lot, by the look of her purse.

Back in the underpass, on our way to the bus stop, my bag seemed to get heavier and heavier as I struggled with it. My mother became more and more impatient. She said I was forever a disappointment. She stopped pulling her trolley and started shouting at me. Then she became very personal. She mentioned my bed-wetting in the middle of the underpass. By that stage I had put my bag down: it was a good opportunity to give my hands a break. As the ladies and men passed us, going about their business, my mother carried on and on. The only reason she had asked me to go with her, she shouted, was not because she liked me – oh no, I shouldn't get the wrong idea – the only reason was because she needed someone to help carry the shopping. And look what happened! I couldn't even do that! I was completely hopeless. Worse than useless, she said, as she moved off quickly with her trolley. I picked up the shopping bag again and tried to follow. I was doing quite well, I thought, until the exit ramp. I tripped over. Some of the shopping fell out and three tins rolled ahead of me, in the direction of my mother. She realised what had happened and stood still on the pavement. I brushed myself off and started picking up the tins one by one. The final one lay right by my mother's feet. As I bent down to pick it up, her hand swooped down and in broad daylight she removed my Michael Jackson wig from my head. I stood up bald. 'Look at your nose, you bitch,' she said, 'you fucking useless good-for-nothing bitch. That nose of yours, you certainly did not get it from my side of the family.' She turned the wig inside out, so that the inner netting was exposed. She then folded it up small and when it was a tiny ball she put it in her pocket.

People had begun to look at me. My bald head was certainly different and I would be the first to agree that I looked better with my wig on, but that was no excuse – it was rude to stare. Had they never seen a bald child before? Anyway I was not quite bald. There were a few strands of hair on my scalp, but not enough to write home about. Lifting up my tin of baked beans, I spontaneously covered my head with my lower arm so that the beans which were in my right hand were now down over my left ear. It wasn't enough to stop people looking, though. My mother, who had a full set of hair and was still very attractive, was with a child monster, a bald one at that. It must have made them feel sorry for her. How could such a beautiful woman give birth to a freak like me? You could see it on their faces as they walked past me, covered their mouths with their hands and then looked back from a safe distance. Still clutching the tin of baked beans, I walked back to my shopping bag at the top of the ramp. I placed it with the rest of my load and returned to my mother.

'What number bus?' I asked her.

For a moment my mother did not answer. She thought that I was going to ask for my wig back, but I did not. She ignored me and stalked off to the bus stop while I struggled with the bag. At the bus stop people continued to stare at me, but I could tell they now felt sorry for me. I clearly had some sort of problem otherwise I would not be bald, and the bag was obviously far too heavy for me. The lady I was with was pulling a trolley and seemed unconcerned.

Aware of the sympathetic looks that I was getting, my mother told me to stand next to her rather than behind her. I did, but the looks continued. It was too late for my mother to remove the wig from her pocket and return it to my head, so she asked me if I was cold and patted me on the head twice to show she understood.

When the bus arrived the queue of people made way for us, either out of sympathy or because they did not want to catch my baldness. On the journey, although the bus was full, no one sat in the two unoccupied seats next to me. My mother looked steadfastly out of the window, wearing a quizzical look on her face as though she was trying hard to make sure that the bus was going in the right direction.

When we eventually reached Sutherland Square, she went to her room to change and left me to unpack the food. I called Pauline and Patsy down to give me a hand. Pauline never said a word about my bald head, but Patsy laughed. Much later that day my mother gave my wig to Eastman and told him to get rid of it. He chucked it in the rubbish bin. When he had gone I quickly retrieved it and washed it. After that day I used large hat pins to secure the wig on my head.

Some weeks later, Eastman moved out. He just disappeared in the middle of the night. Not a word was said about his disappearance. I did not ask after him just in case it encouraged him to come back. During that time the Eastmans and the Briscoes got on a little better. There were more of us than them and once you took Eastman out of the equation, we could beat them hands down. One afternoon I returned from school to find he had returned. He was in my mother's room – I heard his voice. He was there for a few hours and when he decided to go he took with him three large bags. I was happy that he had gone and I hoped we had seen the back of him, but most afternoons he would turn up, stay until quite late and then go.

Two or three weeks after he moved out I sneaked into my mother's front room. It was almost empty. Many of her personal possessions were missing and there were a large number of cardboard boxes on top of the glass table and in front of the display cabinet. My mother was on the move and she had not mentioned anything to me. When I told Pauline of my discovery she said I was imagining things. However it was two days later, during our half-term holiday, that a van pulled up outside our house.

A man got out and knocked on the door and my mother showed him into the room. Eastman was in the back of the van and stepped onto the pavement when the rear doors were opened. Together with the driver, he helped my mother load her boxes in the van. The driver drove off and returned at least twice. It was on the third occasion, when my mother had emptied her front room, that she called the Eastmans to her.

Cynthia and Norma ran down the stairs to her and she put them in the front of the van. Gina and Winston had gone on an earlier trip with Eastman. As she strapped herself in the van, she shouted at Carl, Martin, Beauty and Denise to get ready to go with her. She said she would be back in about an hour.

In fact, it was over two hours before my mother returned and then she went into the kitchen where she sat down and made a cup of tea. The house was much quieter since the Eastmans' removal. I sat on the top step facing her. She looked tired. When she had finished her tea she called all the Briscoes except me to her. They rushed down the stairs like thunder. I remained where I was. She hadn't called me – but then there was no need: I was sitting in front of her and she could easily see me.

As they gathered around her she told them to go and get their coats and schoolbooks. When they ran off she told Pauline and Patsy not to bother packing just yet. Carlton and Martin were the first to return to the kitchen, Beauty and Denise next. She asked them to follow her as she went down the stairs to the front door. The van was parked outside. The driver opened the door and they all got in the front. I had followed them downstairs and was standing on the pavement with Pauline and Patsy.

'P,' she said, 'you know we are moving to the other house. I told you earlier. You can come and see it today with Patsy, but there is not enough room for you to live there at the moment.'

She handed my sister a note with an address on it at the same time as giving Pauline some money.

'Catch a number forty-five bus,' she said, 'and ask to be put off at Vaughan Road. The bus stops just outside number five. I'll meet you there in three-quarters of an hour.'

Above the noise of the engine I shouted at my mother, 'What about me?'

'What about you?' she said. 'I don't remember inviting *you* to go anywhere. You're a big woman. If you can take Eastman to court you can look after yourself. What about you?' she repeated. 'There has been too much about you.'

The driver did a U-turn outside the house, drove straight to the bottom of the road, turned right and disappeared out of my vision.

Pauline and Patsy ran into the house, collected their coats and ran back out to go to the bus stop. I did not see my sisters again for two days.

21

Home Alone

1972

When they returned to 19 Sutherland Square I was informed that my mother, Eastman and the rest of the family had moved to 5 Vaughan Road. They had the top floor and part of the middle floor. It was a huge house, apparently, with sitting tenants on the ground floor. There was not enough room for everyone so Pauline, Patsy and I were to carry on living at Sutherland Square and we would each occupy a floor. Pauline and Patsy had a standing invitation to go to 5 Vaughan Road for dinner on a Saturday and Sunday but there was no invitation for me.

When we looked in the kitchen we found that our mother had cleared out all the plates and most of the pots and pans. The only items that remained were the beds that Pauline, Patsy and I had slept in and the cooker, fridge-freezer and the table in the kitchen. Up until the moment when she actually drove away it had not crossed my mind that our mother was serious about leaving us to fend for ourselves. There was no food in the cupboards, no milk in the fridge. The provisions that were usually piled up by the French doors had disappeared. We were on our own.

The first few days we continued as normal, expecting our mother to turn up at any moment and tell us that we were her children and we would all live together. It was not until the following Friday that she reappeared. We had all gone out to try and buy some food. Mummy told Pauline and Patsy to follow her downstairs. She went into what was her old sitting room. They followed and I sat on the stairs. The door remained open.

She told Pauline that from now on she could occupy the whole of the ground-floor front and back rooms. Patsy could have the top floor to herself. I would remain on the middle floor because no one in their right mind would want to be in a room that had been pissed in as much as mine. The idea that our mother would no longer be around made me feel very happy. No more Mummy – hip, hip hooray! She once more extended the invitation for dinner on a Saturday and Sunday at the new house to my sisters, but made no mention of me. They could both also go round after school any time, she said. The house was within walking distance of Sacred Heart.

For the first few weeks, this new life was very happy. The house was very quiet and peaceful. I had even unplugged my alarm and put the machines away. After the excitement wore off, I settled down into a routine. I always did my homework as soon as I got home. That way it was done, and after that I would prepare myself something to eat. The gas meter took half crowns, and several had to be inserted at a time to guarantee a constant supply of gas. The electricity meter was housed above the front door on the left as you entered; above that, the fuse-board was secured to the wall in a large plastic case. My mother, having departed from Sutherland Square, regarded it as our responsibility to pay for the gas. Since I was the only one with money, that responsibility fell to me. When Pauline asked my mother about the gas she simply said, 'If you want to eat and if you want hot water you will find the money.' Between the three of us we decided that we would try to save energy. We wouldn't use the gas cooker unless we absolutely had to, and we would try not to use too much water.

We reorganised the rooms. I moved a chair from the kitchen into the front sitting room, what was originally the twins' room. There I would sit day after day doing my homework. My bedroom remained more or less as it had been before. The only items of furniture were my bed, the wardrobe and the dressing table. Pauline moved down to my mother's floor while Patsy moved her bedroom into the boys' old room and used the bedroom she had earlier shared with Pauline as her sitting room.

The three of us adjusted quickly. There were no real squabbles between us. We hardly saw each other, in fact, unless we were in the kitchen or in the bathroom. I was in no hurry to share their company. I soon found, however, that my money from Roses was not enough to pay for essential items. I had to cut back on quick meals like Wimpy burgers and fish and chips, but whenever I bought food, my sisters raided the fridge and ate a lot of it. They said they were looking for Saturday jobs, but there was no real pressure on them to find one, as they often ate at 5 Vaughan Road.

One of my grown-up friends was Angela Fuentes. Her relationship with my mother had long since taken a downward turn and they did not visit each other as they had done in the past. Angela did not like my mother. She thought that she was a very difficult woman. Once when Angela had been present in our house she had seen my mother grab me in the chest and push me backwards, banging my head against the wall. She had also popped in for a cup of tea the day after my mother had removed my bed. Angela could not get to grips with the idea that any woman could be capable of removing the bed on which her own child slept. Since then she had kept her distance. Her four boys spoke better English now than before and I had helped them to improve. I would go to Angela's flat one or two days a week for an hour and teach her eldest boy. Angela and I had become very close. She did not care for Pauline and Patsy because she thought that they were Mummy's girls, not willing to put a foot wrong just in case they fell out with their mother.

Angela was a cleaning supervisor and she held the contract for a block of office buildings in the West End. About three weeks after Mummy left home I asked her whether it might be possible to get a job with her. Initially, she said no. I was too young to work and, besides, I needed a National Insurance card and number – neither of which I possessed. At that time Angela was unaware that I was living on my own. It wasn't something that I spoke about, because I did not want to live with my mother and was quite happy with the current situation.

My schoolwork was fine since I now had more time for private study. My hair had started to grow back, but the process was slow and I wasn't sure it would ever be completely restored. One Sunday after Mass I decided to pay Angela a visit. At about ten o'clock I knocked on her door. Angela opened it and ushered me into her flat, where she sat me down on a high stool and made me a strong cup of coffee without me asking for it. She made herself one and stood with her back resting against the work surface.

'Tell me, Klare,' she said in her strong Spanish accent, 'what's happening with you?' She always accentuated the first letter of my name.

'Not much,' I said.

'Come on,' she said, 'you kidding me. With that mother of yours something always happening.'

Angela had dark olive skin with jet-black hair, which she wore short with a parting on the left side. The curls clung gently to her face like Greta Garbo. She was truly beautiful in a very Spanish way. She stood five feet eight off the floor and was slim. Just-right slim. She wore trousers, never dresses or skirts, and was always in the process of putting a cigarette in her mouth and lighting up. When she smoked, she tossed her head backwards and to the side, and blew the smoke out of her mouth in one go. Angela's four boys were running around her as she picked up her coffee cup.

'What that woman up to now, Klare? Tell me. Very bad woman. Very bad. Not like a mother. You know the problem with your mother? She greedy. She is gimme gimme gimme. Very bad.'

Angela sipped her coffee and I told her that I had not seen my mother now for over three months.

'What you mean – three months?' Angela exclaimed. 'You livvie in same houssie as your mother.'

I explained to Angela the circumstances in which my mother had left us in the house and she started to shake her head.

'She very bad woman. You tellie me morie, Klare.'

I started with Eastman moving out and as I paused for a sip of coffee, Angela said, 'I never likkie that man. Eastman, he makkie my skin crawlie. Aaah very bad man.'

I told Angela how my mother had moved out the Eastmans and left behind Pauline, Patsy and me; and finally I once more asked her for a job. I explained that while I had no complaint about being independent I had to find a way of supporting myself. She asked me to leave it with her for a few days and then to call her if she had not by then contacted me. I was really interested in a job I could do before school. I had no experience of office cleaning, but I could be shown. I had lots and lots of experience of housework. The only difference was the scale of it.

'I talkie with someone first then I talkie you. I see what I can do. Maybe – just maybe I can help.'

After that we chatted about Pauline and Patsy and my brother Carlton, who was good friends with her son Louis. As we drank our coffee, Angela's husband walked into the kitchen and said, 'Hello, Clare,' and walked back out again. Angela pulled a face. Her husband worked nights as a chef somewhere in the West End. She did not like him very much. He was always shouting at 'her boys'. They had to be quiet during the day when their father was asleep. This was something that was very difficult for four boisterous lads living in a three-bedroom council flat. Angela adored 'her boys' and they adored her.

Mr Fuentes was a rather interesting man. He was bald on the top of his head with a thin stripe of hair which went from his left ear round the back of his head and ended just in front of his right ear. It was all right for a man. He was of the same complexion as Angela but he was under five feet tall. He walked with a stoop and he muttered to himself when he was not telling off Angela's boys. He was a little on the plump side with a pot belly. He had very short legs and a long body. When he walked his hands were motionless by his side; his hands came to well below his knees and he looked odd. Angela never spoke to him but rather at him, and she was always glad when he was asleep or out of the house. Angela's children, Louis, Richard and the twins Ivan and Terry, treated their father with a similar disrespect. We drank up our coffee and said our goodbyes. We promised to be in touch soon.

22

Playground Bullies

1972

Super Monday at school. Roast potatoes on a Monday were unheard of. Yorkshire pudding and two veg with thick gravy. Extraordinary. Peas for those who wanted. There were always too few takers and the following day we all knew that mushy peas were guaranteed. Roly-poly jam pudding with lumpy custard or bread and butter pudding with lumpy custard. We all skinned the lumpy custard and left the lumps on the side of the plate. My group of friends were in the habit of falling out with each other quite often. There was always someone not talking to someone else which resulted in the rest of the group taking sides. It was all very silly. Both sides thought that they held the power in the group and it was therefore important for them not to be seen to be giving way. I could not understand what the dispute was all about. It had something to do with Lizzie Lock and Brenda, Irish Brenda. Both of them were now leaders of opposing groups. Each of them had convincingly persuaded four other girls to join their side, making five a side. The two girl gangs were sitting opposite each other not talking. I asked Liz if I could swap my roast potatoes for some of her roly-poly and she agreed. I asked Brenda if she wanted my Yorkshire pudding. She only wanted half so I cut it and put it on her plate. As I ate up my half, one of the girls in Lizzie's group shouted out that I was a two-faced cow. Before I could answer, a girl from Brenda's gang said I was a grass. Both girl gangs gradually became more vocal, accusing me of being a cow, a slag, a ponce and a toerag. The reason for their outburst was because I had refused to take sides; the gangs were evenly balanced and so it was important for me to join one or the other.

I felt intimidated as threats were issued as to what might happen to me if I refused to join the gang. The bigger girls were in Brenda's group and they threatened me the most. I told Brenda's group to shut up and continued to eat my dinner. Then Lizzie's group started and I decided I had had enough. I got up and moved to another table, taking my roly-poly with me. When I had finished I got up and went towards the exit with my plate in my hand. 'Bitch!' – that's what I heard, followed by: 'We are going to get you later.' As I was walking out of the dining room one of the girls crept up behind me and punched me in the head. My plate dropped out of my hand and smashed. My attacker ran away before I could see who it was. As I turned round, both the girl gangs were laughing at me.

In the school playground I went to our corner and waited. None of my group came over and both the girl gangs remained apart in different corners of the playground. They now had a new object of hatred – me.

I met up with my sisters and spoke to them about nothing very much. At the end of the dinner hour I got into the class line and we walked back into the main building in an orderly fashion. I thought over what had happened. Liz was quite a good friend of mine. I had always played fair with her when she had her troubles. There was never one occasion when I took against her, so I was surprised that she was able to see me as a grass and a traitor. Lizzie caught me up. She said that she was sorry about it all, but did not know what to do. I told her that I did not blame her. We were heading for our class when someone from one of the girl gangs punched me in the head from behind – the second such blow in an hour. It really hurt. The impact made me lose my balance and I almost fell flat on my face. My fall was broken by a wall, which I banged my forehead against.

As I turned round, a member of Brenda's gang was

standing in front of me. She snarled at me and her fist was tight and pulled back away from her plump body in a threatening mode. Brenda had never in the past fallen out with me. I was simply not that sort of girl. I was quite slim for my age and was about four feet ten inches, quite short in my group, with the exception of Lizzie Lock and Brenda who were shorter than me. As we made our way into the main entrance hall Lizzie walked alongside me. Brenda's girl looked in my direction. 'Oi, shitface,' she said. 'I'll see you outside the gate after school.' Then she punched me again in the shoulder and walked away with her cohorts before I could reply. She was quickly establishing herself as a leader.

Lizzie held my arm and asked if I was okay. I was a little dazed, but that was all. That was the least of my problems. Here was a direct invitation to fight after school. I was not naturally a fighter but to back out when the challenge was so public would be a huge humiliation. Lizzie said she had to go and walked off in the direction of the Art Department. I was due at an English lesson. To my dismay, the fat one was waiting for me again with her friends from the girl gang.

'Oi, you, shitface.' I continued to walk on. 'Oi, I'm talking to *you*, shitface. Don't walk away when I'm talking to you.'

She strutted towards me. Her gang members, who had all previously been my friends, were encouraging her to go all the way. The fat one prodded me in the chest.

'You heard what I said.'

'I don't remember,' I said. 'What did you say?'

'After school – me and you.' She walked away and shouted as she did that she would be waiting for me.

English was interesting. We looked at Oscar Wilde and his relationship with Lord Bosie. After English we had a maths lesson. During the entire afternoon I felt quite unwell from the blows on my head, and when the class ended ten minutes early I did not wait at the gate for my sisters but went straight home. The matter of the fight had slipped my mind entirely.

At home I had a very uncomfortable time. My neck was stiff,

my back was sore and I felt rotten. My homework suffered and I went to bed early. The next morning my sisters and I all went to school. As we crossed over Camberwell New Road the fat one and her girl gang were waiting for me. When they saw my sisters they ran from the pavement outside the school and into the school, and lined up by the fence on the left as we approached. No one spoke as we walked past, but as I looked back the fat one ran her hand across her throat and then pointed at me.

I somehow managed to avoid them until lunchtime. When I was having my semolina pudding, someone flicked some mushy peas at me and when I looked up the fat one was laughing. I ignored her, but bits of cabbage, carrots and plum stones rained down on me. Lizzie was in the hall and some of the others in her group. She kept quiet.

After dinner I avoided the playground because I knew they would be waiting for me and made my way to the girls' toilets where I locked myself inside the cubicle. I sat on the toilet seat with my legs off the ground just in case someone looked under the door. When the bell went I waited for a few moments, then quickly flushed the toilet and opened the door At about three o'clock it was the final lesson of the day. I was a bit worried about what would happen so I wrote our teacher a note, saying I was going to be beaten up after school. I put my hand up and asked for permission to approach the front. I then handed sir the note and he asked me to step outside the classroom where I told him that the fat one would be waiting for me at the end of the day. He asked why and I told him. Sir told me to forget it, because he would deal with it.

At four o'clock I walked down the path to go home. The girl gangs were there. I slowed down my pace as I walked past them. The fat one was missing, I noticed, and none of the others was prepared to be her substitute. With a light heart I walked to the bus stop and caught a bus home. The fat one had been given detention, I discovered. It wasn't clear what she had done wrong, but her detention had lasted only half an hour, which had given me enough time to get home.

The following day the fat one made it clear that the only reason she had not fought with me was because, as she was about to leave school, one of the teachers had called her and asked her to wait outside his classroom. She went, but the teacher did not arrive for half an hour and when he did turn up he had forgotten what it was he wanted to have a word about. By this time I had left the school instead of waiting to fight, like the scaredy cat that I was. All day I ignored her threats, the intimidating looks that she gave me, and even when she came right up close to my face and said, 'Tonight,' I ignored the urge to push her away.

At four o'clock I was held back by the teacher, who asked me if I had resolved my differences with the other girls. I said I had. I packed my bags and left the school. The fat one was nowhere to be seen, and all her mates appeared to have gone home. Breathing a sigh of relief, I crossed over the road and went off towards the bus stop. About halfway there, when I got quite close to an alleyway, the fat one popped out from behind a lorry and one by one the others also appeared and surrounded her. The fat one was very vocal, shouting at me and threatening me and pushing me backwards, as she was encouraged to do by the group of girls. There were in total about twenty to thirty girls and a few boys. Fights were always well attended and the word usually spread like an Australian bushfire.

During the pushing and pulling by the fat one and others I said that I would fight. Everyone stopped and listened as I struggled to make myself heard.

'I'll fight!' I shouted.

'Too bloody right you will,' said the fat one.

'I have to get ready,' I said.

'Excuses, excuses,' said the fat one as she punched me.

I took my school blazer off, folded it up and put it on the ground and then I took my tie off and put that on top of my blazer, which was underneath my school bag. I then took my jumper off and asked one of the girls to hold it for me.

After that I started to do stretches, limbering up and

jumping up and down on my toes. The crowd was silent. From watching wrestling on a Saturday, I knew that I had to come out of my corner fighting, and I had to surprise my opponent. The fat one was looking at me, not knowing quite what to do. I raised both my fists in front of me, a move I had seen many times when Cassius Clay fought his opponents, and then, holding both my fists close to my face I started jabbing out with my right hand, always ahead of me. My eyes were firmly fixed on the fat one. Then I decided on my surprise tactic. I opened my legs by about twenty inches and brought the left leg back and bent my legs at the knees. The fat one was looking at me in astonishment. She was speechless, as were her girl-gang members. I kept jabbing away with my right hand and then the left and then both in succession, which was called a quick one two. Then the surprise, as Giant Haystacks would say. I jumped forward, feet together like a frog, jabbing away with my right hand still held close to my face. Then I jumped again and again in the direction of the fat one. By now, her toadies had moved away: some of them had their mouths open. As I jumped towards her, knees bent, I could see Lizzie from the corner of my eyes. She was sitting on the bonnet of a car holding a book which covered the lower half of her face. She was pissing herself laughing. I knew that because the tears were rolling down her cheeks and she used her hand to wipe her tears away.

The fat one was pale as I approached her with a series of frog hops and ballet moves which I had seen so many times before. When I was eight feet from her I decided to keep up the attack and surprise her again, so I used my right hand to perform an almighty right hook on a mysterious target ahead of me. I swung my right arm so viciously that it caused me to swing round on one foot in a complete circle, a bit like a pirouette. Then I jumped forward again, this time using smaller, more sophisticated steps. The fat one was completely isolated and Lizzie Lock had fallen off the bonnet of the car.

'What's the matter, gob?' I said. Fatso turned to look for her gang, who had long deserted her, and I punched her hard in the back of the head, as she had done to me.

'Come on, scaredy cat,' I said, and punched her in the shoulder as she had done to me. 'That's for the cabbage and the carrots.'

She stood motionless and I told her to raise her fists and fight. She raised her hands, but a swift punch to the stomach left her winded.

'This wasn't my idea,' she whined. 'I didn't want to fight.'

Lizzie was standing there, but said nothing. Everyone knew the fat one was lying and Lizzie knew as well as I did that if the fat one lost, she could no longer claim to be the leader of their gang – if she did, she would be shot down in flames.

'Say sorry,' I said.

'Sorry,' said the fat one.

'Well,' I demanded. 'Do you want to fight, or do you give up like the scaredy cat you are?'

She agreed not to continue and I lowered my fists. Lizzie was quick to pick up my blazer, tie and bag. My jumper had been dumped when the girl holding it ran off. Lizzie handed it to me. The fat one walked off with a few of her gang who were not at all anxious to be seen with her.

After that I went to the bus stop and arrived home a little later than usual. The following day, when I arrived at school, the fat one and her group were nowhere to be seen. At lunchtime I got my free school dinner and went and sat down in the dining hall. I sat on my own, but by the time I had started on my afters Lizzie had walked over and asked if anyone was sitting on the spare seats. I said no, then she and some of her mates joined me. A few minutes later, some girls from the fat one's gang came over and asked the same question. I gave the same answer and they sat down and ate in silence. The fat one was sitting on her own. She stabbed at her mince and steak pie with no real enthusiasm. I shouted at her and when she looked up I asked if she would like to join us. There was a slight hesitation and then she said, 'If you don't mind,' and came over and sat next to me. No one spoke about the fight. It was over and we had all moved on.

Over the next few days we all became friends. Lizzie was reluctant to assume overall leadership. It never occurred to me that it was a role that I might want or enjoy. After that incident, the fat one never again tried to assert her authority with me or anyone else for that matter. We became friends.

23

Money of My Own

1972

My baldness was still a real problem. One of the things I had
feared most when I had to fight was the possibility that my wig
would fall off as we exchanged blows. I had spotted a hair
specialist clinic opposite the Brixton Police Station, quite close to
the market. At my first consultation the trichologist who saw me
made no promises, but when I asked whether it was possible to
have hair like Michael Jackson, he smiled at me and I took that as
a yes. However, after several treatments he agreed with me that
there had been no significant growth and he encouraged me to
break off from the treatment and give my scalp a rest. He
suggested that I should consider going without my wig and
sitting in the sun. I was reluctant to do this. Normally, if I had a
session after school, I would disappear into the ladies' and
remove my wig just before my appointment. Then I would wait
in the reception for my name to be called.

On this particular day, the trichologist told me to sit outside in
the sun for twenty minutes before having the second half of my
scalp treatment. While I was unhappy to do so, I did not refuse. I
walked down the stairs and sat outside on the brick wall. The
Hair Centre is approached through a metal gate. There is a small
garden to the left of the path. Straight ahead and up about seven
steps is the entrance to the Centre. Directly outside the Centre is
a bus stop which has a lot of people milling around, especially
drunks with cans of beer. As I waited for my twenty minutes to
pass I was approached by a man who had a beer can in his hand.
He asked me where my hair had gone.

It was difficult coming to terms with the fact that someone had drawn attention to my bald head even though it was obvious for all to see. I ignored him. No point in talking to strange men and he seemed drunk anyway.

'What's the matter with your head?' he insisted. 'Have you had lice?'

I certainly had not and I told him so, but he would not leave it alone. It was not that he mocked me or was sympathetic; he wanted to know as a matter of fact. I said I did not know what had happened to my hair – it had just fallen out. He got up, bent over and peered at my head. His nose was possibly three inches away from the nearest strand of hair.

'Not bad,' he said as he took another swig from his tin. 'Not bad, but not good.'

With his large grubby fingers he pulled a few strands out of my head. I told him to get off, but he said he meant well. I did not know what to do, but I stayed rooted to my seat.

'You want to stop wasting your bleeding time with them,' he said as he jabbed his finger in the direction of the clinic. 'Take a tip from a gypsy. You're better off pissing on your head for all the good that lot will do.'

His teeth were chipped and stained and the two at the side of his mouth were missing. He had no fillings to speak of but when he spoke, especially when he laughed, there were huge cavities that just cried out for the dentist's drill.

'My sister was as bald as a badger,' he went on. 'Not a hair in sight for miles. Twelve months later, you could weave a blanket with it. She had the finest hair in the land and, by crime, once it started to grow there was no stopping it.'

'What was the matter with her head?' I asked.

'Nothing much,' he said. 'Just a slapping from her old man. You'd think she'd have the strength for it, but she went all nervous on him and her hair fell out. Yes, as bald as a badger, she was.'

'How did she get her hair back?' I said.

'It was the ma,' he said, 'and her ma's ma before her. It was

them onions and vinegar that done it. Stunk like a gypsy's
armpit, but by crime it was well worth taking the risk – especially
if there was a chance that it might succeed.'

He did not look like the sort of man who would know a thing
or two about ladies' hair but, then again, why waste his time with
me? He did not have to tell me the secrets of his great-grand-
mother's armpits.

'Are you kidding me?' I asked.

'Why kid a kid?' he said. 'You need a head of hair, by gum you
do. Take a tip from a wise fool. Ah, go on, give it a try – you'll be
thanking me.'

He staggered away from me using sidesteps and ended up by a
bus stop. As he reached the bus shelter, he toppled forward and
banged his head on a metal pole. He dropped almost to his
knees, but saved himself at the last moment by grabbing at it and
levering himself upright again. Then he took another swig from
his drink. When a bus came, he fell onto it. The bus conductor
pressed the bell twice and my expert in hair growth disappeared,
still clinging to his beer can.

I fished my wig out of my pocket, slipped it very discreetly
onto my head and went home. On the way I stopped to purchase
four onions and a large bottle of malt vinegar. After my homework I set about my onions, chopped them into segments, added
vinegar and put them into an airtight dish, which went under my
bed. I would give it three days to work.

By midweek I had run out of money. My next pay from Roses
was three days away. It was becoming urgent to find another job.
I decided to pop in and see Angela again, just in case things had
changed and she was able to help me out. Angela was at home
with Louis and Richard; the twins were out playing. She put the
kettle on immediately.

I reminded Angela that Mummy had moved out and since that
time I had not seen her. There was no food in the house and I was
having to rely on school dinners. Angela pushed her lip out.

'That mother of yours, she is a wicked woman. Klare how
soon you wanttie jobbies?'

'As soon as possible.'

'You come with me, I give you job. Monday you come with me, but you must get up early. I come for you at 5.15 on Monday morning.'

I agreed. Angela said that we would work from 6 a.m. to 8 a.m. when I would be free to have a quick wash in the toilets before going to school. We agreed that we would work together for a few days until she had shown me the ropes and after that it would be down to me. She suggested that I wear my school uniform underneath a large overall and that way I could go straight to school if I was running late. I promised Angela that I would do a good job and I would never breathe a word about my age or the fact that I was still at school. As the cleaning supervisor, Angela had put herself on the line to help me out. I was not about to let her down.

On the Saturday I was run off my feet at Roses. Eileen was very happy – the tills rang all day and had to be cleared of money before lunchtime. The afternoon was busier than the morning and as closing time approached, we were glad to see the back of the last customer. That night, I had a terrible nightmare. I dreamed that my mother was in the room with me, using her mummy hands to have a go at my nipples in the way that only she knew how. My nightdress was soaked with sweat but when I opened my eyes my mother was not in my room. I felt my nipples. They were still there. I turned over and went back to sleep.

When my alarm went off early on Monday morning, I jumped out of bed, had a quick wash, brushed my teeth, combed my bits of hair and put on my wig and my school uniform. My tie and blazer went in my holdall. I decided against wearing socks and instead put on some thick black knitted tights, a black bobble hat and a scarf tied tightly round my neck. It was freezing cold this early in the day. Next, I pulled on my knitted gloves and then I sat on the bed and waited for Angela to arrive. At about 5.20 a.m. she had still not arrived so I went into the front room and looked out of the window. She was late. I was still looking out of the window at 5.25 a.m. when I saw the elegant Angela coming down the road. She had a bobble hat on too. I picked up my holdall and went out of the front door. It was still dark and I had never been up this early before, apart from when my mother had locked me and my sisters out after our night at the church disco.

'You thinkie I no commie for you, Klare?' Angela said. 'I sorry, is that bloody husband of mine. He bloody stupid man. I sorry, Klare.' I linked arms with her and we walked in the dark to the bus stop, which was packed with women all looking ever so grubby in their overalls and head scarves. I'd never seen so many Fag-end Lils. After a short wait in the queue the bus came and we caught it to Trafalgar Square. Most of the women seemed to get off at our stop. We crossed over and made our way down the back streets to Northumberland Avenue. It was still dark and cold and I clung on to Angela's arm. We were apparently in the West End.

Once inside a large ugly building Angela collected some keys, changed into her overalls and between us we took two mops, two buckets, a broom, dusters and hoover up in the lift to the fourth floor. We came out and turned right. The corridor went on for ever. There were rooms off both sides. When Angela said that I was expected to clean it, I almost fainted. I would never finish all this before school, I protested. Angela said that she would work with me and show me what to do, and that two hours was more than enough time to get the job done. What was more, I was only expected to clean half the corridor – another cleaner was responsible for all the rooms on the other side of the kitchen.

We put our mops and dusters down in the men's toilet and I changed into my cleaning clothes. Angela gave me a large black plastic bin liner and told me to run around from office to office and empty all the bins and ashtrays as quickly as possible and then take the bin liner and leave it by the lift. She started in the opposite direction to me and we met more or less in the middle with our bin bags. The next job was to empty the wastepaper basket and sanitary bins in the ladies' and gentlemen's toilets and then replace the toilet paper and hand towels. Angela and I collected our mops and buckets and Vim and started in the toilets. We gave them a good scrub and put Domestos down the pans. Finally, we cleaned the floor, walking backwards to the door so as not to leave footprints. The offices had to be dusted, the desks polished, the carpets hoovered and the chairs put back in their rightful place. We worked together, office after office, and as we went along, we hoovered the corridor behind us. Angela gave instructions and checked my work. It was quite surprising really how much you could get done in two hours.

At about 7.40, Angela and I went back over the offices and checked to make sure that the work was up to the right standard. My work passed the test but Angela said it could only improve. At 7.50 a.m. we took the rubbish bins down to the waste room on the ground floor. In the ladies' toilets I washed my face and picked the dust off my tights. We were now ready to go.

'You see?' said Angela. 'It is easy, no?' She told me she would work with me for another two or three days until I became a proper cleaner. I was really relieved to hear that. At the bus stop I still had my overalls on as Angela did not think it was a good idea to be seen in my school uniform so close to the office building – just in case. We rode together and when we got to the Walworth Road she said, 'You wantee the good news or the bad news, Klare?' I said the good news. 'You have only four more days to pay day,' she said.

'And what's the bad news?' I asked.

'I pickee you up tomorrow same time.'

We both laughed and she got off the bus. I went all the way to Camberwell Gate. It was a little early for me to enter school, so I found myself a quiet alley and changed out of my cleaning clothes. I looked okay apart from the fuzz on my tights. I took my Michael Jackson wig off and gave it a good shake. Then I turned it the right way, put it on my head and pulled it over my ears. Not only did the wig keep my head warm, it kept the stench of vinegar and onions from rising beyond the wig netting. Although my hair appeared to have stopped falling out, the stench was dreadful. In my school bag, I had some cheap perfume from when the Avon lady had called on my mother. It wasn't perfect, but it smelled a whole lot better than vinegar and onions. I sprayed my wig and then had a coughing fit when the mist got up my nose. I was now ready for school and I was smelling of roses – well, lavender, but you would never be able to tell the difference.

School was good. I had three jumbo sausages, mashed potatoes, peas and gravy. I saw my sisters; they had spent the previous night at our mother's house. They seemed very well. I had very little to say to them. I suppose I could have asked about our mother but I wasn't interested. After school, I went straight home, made myself something to eat and set about my homework. Once that was finished, I went to bed, exhausted. Next morning I was up at the same time.

The work seemed easier today. I instinctively started on the bins and, between the two of us, we were again finished at about 7.40 a.m. Angela was quite confident that I could clean the office corridor on my own. She decided that the following day I would do half the corridor and she would help me if I needed it. As I took the bin bags down to the ground floor, I began to resent having to get up early. It would be really nice if I could stay in bed like normal children, I thought, and just go straight to school. I didn't even know exactly how much I was to be paid. However, Angela was the supervisor. She, I knew, would never cheat on me. She would make sure that I was paid whatever I was due.

My schoolwork started to suffer; my marks dropped and the teachers were a little concerned about my lack of attention to detail. It was only a temporary thing while I made certain adjustments in my home life. None of my teachers were aware of my mother's absence from the family home and they did not have to know I looked after myself.

Thursday was a complete disaster. I tried very hard to empty the bins and clean, dust and hoover as quickly as possible, but at 7.40 I still had the polishing and hoovering to do. When Angela arrived to see how I was coping, she almost fell over my duster. I wasn't sure what had gone wrong. I had thought it was all under control. Angela grabbed the hoover and started to do the offices while I cleaned up and took the bin bags to the ground floor. By the time I returned, she had done about a dozen offices, which was unbelievable. Between the two of us, we finished at about 8.30 when the first of the office employees were turning up for work. Angela was very sympathetic. She told me not to worry about it and said it was only a matter of time and practice before I became an experienced cleaner. I just about got to school on time. Lessons were dull and I fell asleep twice in class.

When Angela called for me on Friday, I had made up my mind to try and work quicker to get through all the jobs. I felt bad about not being as efficient as the other, older cleaners. When I asked Angela if I could clean the offices on my own she said I shouldn't worry, it was very early days. Between us, we worked well, and again with Angela's help I finished in good time. While I took the bin bags down she went to the main office to collect the wages. When she returned, she handed me a small brown envelope. Inside was £14! As we travelled to the bus stop, Angela asked me when I had last seen my mother. I had no idea. She then shook her head and asked when I had last seen Pauline and Patsy. I explained that I saw both of them at school, but they were not often in the house. I had a good idea what Angela was thinking, but it really did not matter. I had not been abandoned. I was quite capable of looking after myself.

School dinner on Fridays was always fish and chips followed by custard (pink or yellow) and a jam tart. Brilliant. No early morning cleaning on Saturday – what more could I ask for? On the way home, I bought myself some jellybeans as a treat, and then I decided to completely spoil myself with a bag of apple drops. How I loved my new-found independence.

At home I decided to have a long soak in the bath. I put half a crown in the gas meter and ran the hot water. I was so happy I could have stayed in the bath for ever. Every time the water got cold I pulled the plug out, and topped up with hot water. Since I was paying for it, I could not be told off for wasting my own money. My sisters did not return on Friday and when I got up to go to my Saturday job at Roses they were still not home. Thank heaven for Roses. I had settled in there well and they all liked me. I could be relied on to do all the little jobs that needed doing, like making the staff tea, going off to buy Eileen a sandwich or a pair of tights when the girls caught theirs on a hanger or something else. My work took me out of the house. I knew what was the latest fashion. I got my clothes at a discount. Roses was wonderful and I got paid to spend the day with beautiful dresses.

My sisters turned up home late on Saturday night. I did not ask them where they had been – I think I ignored them. I stayed in my room all evening, and did not offer to share my apple drops or jellybeans. After three months, I had still not seen my mother and she had not invited me to her new home. It was not that I wanted to go, but it would have been nice to be invited, that was all.

By the time a week or two had passed, my early morning cleaning job was a well established part of my life. I could now be left on my own. Angela often knocked for me, but because she was the supervisor there were times when she was working at a different location or was required to go to work earlier than me. When Angela was elsewhere, I travelled to work by myself with all the old Lils. They were very nice to me. No one ever told me to go to the back of the queue. With my bobble hat and my scarf, I looked young but not that young. I had got into a routine with my jobs, cleaning during the week, selling clothes at the weekend and doing my own housework on a Sunday after church. My homework was always completed in good time. No piece of work was handed in late. In fact, there were a number of occasions when I finished off my homework after I cleaned the offices, sitting at a nice large polished desk until it was time to set off for school.

One evening I was at home revising for my exams when I thought I heard someone come in. Odd. There were only the three of us in the house and we never brought guests back, not ever. It must have been my imagination. I continued with my revision. My exams were about six weeks away and it was necessary for me to put up a good show.

I had finished my revision for English language, English literature and finally Religion, when I decided to take a short rest. I was thinking about making myself something to eat. Time had just flown by. It was now 8.30ish and I had spent the best part of the afternoon and evening revising. I was packing my books away when I heard the noise again. Maybe it was a burglar. My heart missed a beat. There was definitely someone in the house, moving the furniture about very carefully so as not to make too much noise. Then suddenly I heard the front door open and close.

I was terrified. I did not know whether to wait, shout out or cry. I decided to lock myself in my room. I was safe in here and no one actually knew that I was in the house. I pulled up a chair and forced it underneath the door handle and then pressed it against the door and sat on it. As I was wondering what I should do, I heard the front door open again and close. The person had come back in. Now there were footsteps on the stairs. I waited and, as the footsteps approached my bedroom, it occurred to me that my light was on. In a flash I flicked it off. The footsteps stopped outside my door. I held my breath, but then I remembered that I was sitting directly opposite the keyhole and whoever was outside only had to bend down and look through it to see me. Ever so silently, I pulled the dressing-gown that was hanging on the back of the door across the keyhole. As I did so I sensed the person on the other side bending down and peering through it. I nearly wet myself. I held my breath for an eternity while I could feel the eye peering through the keyhole. The door handle turned suddenly and I almost passed out. I thought that God had sent the Duppies to sort me out after all the trouble I had caused wetting the bed year in and year out. Once the door handle was turned to its maximum west it was then turned to its maximum east. Pressure was applied to the door and I started to pray.

'Dear God, I will never wet the bed again. I will never interfere with Your little creatures. I will never attempt to take Your name in vain. Dear God, oh dear God.'

Suddenly, the pressure on the door eased and the footsteps moved away. There was a pause and then they went downstairs. They seemed to get almost to the front door and then I could hear movement of the furniture again. Nothing was said. No 'Hello, anyone in? Are you up there?' Nothing. Rooted to the spot, I waited and waited and eventually the noise stopped. There was silence again and then the front door opened and closed. I had come out in a sweat. I remained seated on the chair behind the door in the dark, willing the footsteps not to return. They did not, but I could not bring myself to go to bed. 'What if' forced me to remain sitting behind the door.

All through the evening I nodded off, only to wake up from my uncomfortable position. Should I go to bed? Should I stay awake? Eventually I must have fallen asleep. When I woke up, the clock said 10.30. It was still dark so it must have been in the evening. I got up from the chair, changed into my nightclothes and then pulled and pushed my bed so that it lay across the door. Then I got into it, leaving the light on just in case it was necessary to make good my escape.

The following day I got up early as usual, ready for my cleaning job. Over my school uniform I wore a large pink smock-type dress with large spots. It was still dark as I walked to the number 12 bus stop. The usual crowd were there – the apron-wearers with their pipe-cleaner curlers. It was always a happy atmosphere at the bus stop. I got into the queue and when our bus arrived the women ushered me to the front as they always did. 'Youth before beauty,' one of them cackled. I was in Trafalgar Square by seven minutes to six and back at school by a quarter to nine. Excellent! I had a whole day at school ahead of me.

It was during the morning break that I felt a little tired. I found a chair in the hall and I must have dozed off as soon as I sat down. The next thing I remember is a teacher asking me if I needed to go and see Nurse. It wasn't necessary, but they decided that I should go to Sick Bay anyway and take a nap.

Once there, I immediately fell asleep again. When I woke up it was lunchtime and a decision had been taken for me to have my lunch and then go back to bed. Nurse came in while I was there and wanted to know if I had had any upset. I had not. I told her that I felt slightly unwell, but I would be fine in the morning.

I was allowed after dinner to go back to my class. I returned in time for geography and a French detention. My arms were tired, my legs heavy. It was unlike me to fall asleep in class, but the strange comings and goings of last night had worn me out and I was no closer to finding out what was going on. After detention I went straight home and was so tired that the moment I took my school uniform off I went to lie down, just for a few minutes, to catch up on my sleep.

As I started to doze off, I was almost certain that I was not alone in the house. It was a very odd sensation. My sisters were not around. I would have heard them. My door was slightly ajar and I saw what I thought was a shadow lurking outside. I opened my eyes wide and stayed perfectly still. It was my mother.

'Hello, Mummy,' I said.

She did not respond, she just came into my room and looked around. She did not say anything. I was wondering how she got in. I had not heard her enter, but then again it was her house.

'Please don't think you're going to live in my house for free,' she said. 'There is a gas bill here and an electric bill. You must pay for your keep.'

I did not respond. It was best not to say anything.

'How is this gas bill going to be paid?' she demanded. 'You cannot expect me to pay it, I don't live here.'

'I don't know how it's going to be paid,' I said. 'I haven't got any money.'

'Well, you work, don't you? How is this electric bill going to be paid? You need light to see – unless you're blind.'

'I don't know how it's going to be paid,' I said. 'What do you want me to do?'

'Well,' said my mother, 'I'm not going to pay the bill. You had better give me one-third of the bill.'

'How much is it for?' I asked.

My mother did not answer. She said that she wanted £14 from me, 'otherwise . . .'

'Otherwise what?' I said.

'Just otherwise,' said my mother. 'Please make sure you have got it when I return.'

I had no idea where to get that sort of money from. I did have a cleaning job and I did have a Saturday job, but they were for essentials. I couldn't pay the electricity bill as well. I decided that I would ignore my mother for now and adopt a wait-and-see strategy.

Although I loved my independence, getting up out of a warm bed to go to my cleaning job was not nice at all. But the money helped me to manage. I did not really have any friends – I was too busy for that. I suppose from that point of view I was regarded as a very private person, but on the other hand I liked being private. I liked being me. It was my mother who did not like me being me.

A week or so after she had first asked me to pay the electricity bill my mother turned up again. I was sitting on my bed when she entered my room.

'Where is the money to pay the electric bill?' she demanded.

I said I did not have any spare money and, besides, it was not my job to pay the bills. I had no choice whether to live there or not.

'If you want to live under my roof you obey my rules,' my mother said. 'Otherwise you know where the door is.'

I asked how I could be expected to pay the bills and she told me to get off her bed.

'What do you mean, get off *your* bed?' I repeated.

'The bed you are lying on is mine,' she said. 'Get off it.'

I got up off the bed.

'This blanket, that's mine,' she said as she pulled the blanket off the bed. 'See that pillow there?'

'Yes,' I said.

'Pass it to me, please. It's mine.'

'But what am I going to do if you take my pillow?'

'Don't ask questions,' she said. 'Just give it to me.'

I picked up the pillow and handed it to her. She took it from me and pulled out a plastic carrier bag from her pocket. She folded the pillow in half and then in half again, squeezed all the air out of it and stuffed it into the plastic bag. She folded my blanket in half lengthways and then in quarters and put it over her shoulder.

'You are sleeping in *my* bed, covering yourself with *my* blanket, lying on *my* pillow and keeping warm with *my* gas and electricity and you don't want to pay for it. We'll see about that,' she said.

She stomped downstairs, let herself out of the front door and slammed it shut. I ran into the sitting room and looked out of the window. My mother was striding down the road with my blanket over her shoulder and my pillow in her bag.

I went to school as normal and continued with my daytime cleaning job. The money that came in just about covered my fares and necessities. It wasn't possible to use my school pass when I went to the cleaning job.

My meals were taken care of at school. If I ate absolutely everything on my plate, I would have at least one square meal a day. The secret of course was to ask for the food that was unpopular with the other girls. If I stayed in the free school dinners queue and waited until about 1.45, Cook would be desperate to get rid of the unpopular food and she would pile it on my plate. Carrots, cabbage, Brussels sprouts, broccoli, cauliflower. Any number of meat balls in gunge. One meal like that was more than enough for me. My breakfast consisted of four cups of tea. An evening meal was not necessary.

Work continued as normal. I was doing well at school. My mother, never having met a teacher of mine during my entire school life, was quite unaware of my progress. Stupid Clearie was left far behind. As my exams approached I thought it was a good idea to put in a special effort just to see what I was capable of, so I devised a plan. Every day when I returned home from school I would spend at least four hours revising. It made me very tired during the week, but at weekends after my Saturday job I was more than happy to concentrate on my revision.

About two weeks after my last contact with my mother she turned up again. It was in the evening and I was in my bedroom revising. She did not call up, but I knew it was her. My sisters were in their part of the house and no one else except my mother had a key. She came straight up to my room.

'Well?' she said.

'Well, what?' I asked.

'Where is the bill money?'

I explained again that I did not have any money to pay bills and that I could not foresee any circumstances in which I would be in possession of the money.

'Oh,' she said, 'so you're not going to pay your share?' Then she doubled her fist and punched me on the side of the temple. I rocked on the chair and then steadied myself. The second blow knocked me off the chair. I fell sideways and put my hand out to steady the fall. I sat on the floor not quite dazed but not quite lucid.

'Well?' she said.

'I haven't got any money,' I whispered.

'Oh,' she said, and nodded. 'Well, I suppose I can't force you.' Then she walked round my bed and pulled the remaining covers off. 'How is your bed-wetting?'

'I've stopped,' I said.

'Really?' said my mother. There was certainly no wet blanket and the air in the room was altogether fresher. 'You think that you are so clever, don't you?' she goaded me. 'You think that you are better than anyone else.'

'No, I don't think that I am better, but I would really like a rest. I'm tired and I got up early to go to work.'

My mother turned her back on me and started pulling at the sheet on the bed. 'You want to sleep in my bed, and not pay rent. There is no such thing as a free bed.'

She ripped the sheet from the bed in one movement, folded it up in a ball and put it in her pocket. She looked very silly with the sheet draped over the side of her pocket. Even she realised the foolishness of the situation because she started asking me whether it was my intention to buy sheets, pillows and a blanket with the money I was earning. I was speechless. She disappeared and I heard the front door slam. I wanted to get out of this house as soon as I could.

My mother's late-night visits to the house were increasing. The next time she came, I heard her moving the furniture in the hall. I waited on my chair thinking she might pay me a visit but she never did. She had another trick up her sleeve. I was reading a textbook when the lights went out and the entire house fell dark. My mother had removed the fuses from the fuseboard and taken them away with her. The electric clock in my bedroom flashed on and off at zero. How would I get up in the morning? How would I revise? There were only three weeks to go before the exams. I called out, but no one answered and I went to what was left of my bed. At least she hadn't taken that.

Next morning when I woke my watch said five o'clock. It was difficult, feeling my way around in the dark. Well, not to worry. I packed my school bag as usual and went cautiously downstairs. At the bottom I tried the light switch again. No luck.

Back at school, the notes on my last batch of homework said that I gave the impression of completing it hurriedly. That of course was true! When I got home there was still no electricity so I went out to Woolworth's and bought a box of candles. I lit three, then I spread my homework out on the floor and got on with doing it. I had no idea when my mother would consider returning the fuse. I could ring her, but then she would have been abusive. There was no point in contacting her. Sooner or later she would have to return it.

In the meanwhile, I finished my homework and started to prepare my school bag for Monday. We had PE and I had no idea where my gym skirt or T-shirt were.

24

Hard Times

I had not seen my father for a while. Maybe George could find me somewhere to live, I thought. He had enough houses and all I really needed was a room. There was still no way of getting in touch with Miss K. I didn't even know where she was and I had promised myself that I would not contact her unless she contacted me first. Miss Lindsey would have me, but that would cause problems for my dad. My mother did not want me, but she obviously did not want anyone else to look after me either. At least we could agree on one thing: my mother and I knew that I was capable of looking after myself. After her last visit, I got it into my head that I was better off owning my own sheets, blankets and pillows, if only to stop her taking them away. I also thought I might as well pay her for the services she had provided me with; after all, gas and electricity did not come cheap. There were lots of spare old clothes around the place and with them and some old towels I could make a bed. I wasn't cold – in fact, I was too warm – but I was always uncomfortable. Lying on buttons, bulged fabric and old cardigans is really no fun at all.

I still had the problem with my hair; when I looked carefully at my head I could see thousands and thousands of baby hairs sprouting up all over my scalp. I had invested heavily in onions and vinegar and, had it not been for the smell, I would have been quite pleased with the results. Every night when I had my wash I removed my Michael Jackson wig and dabbed on my head the concoction which I now kept, appropriately, in a large pickledonion jar. It wasn't just my clothes that stank: my bedding did, too, my head – everywhere I went I left a vinegary smell. Once I had a bit more hair, I would cut down my applications to the weekends only.

During this period I was not getting on at all well with Pauline and Patsy. We were like ghosts in a house that was already haunted. We had nothing in common at all. School, too, was hard work; there was simply not enough time to get everything done, no matter how hard I tried. I was ready for a change in my circumstances. On the way back from school one afternoon I stopped off at 215 Camberwell New Road just on the off-chance that I might see my dad. He wasn't there so I walked from Camberwell New Road to Wyndham Road and I took the bus three stops to Woolworth's, to look at pillows. The last two in the store were reduced because they were grubby. The price did not seem unreasonable so I bought one. My intention was also to buy a blanket but they were too expensive. If I was really lucky my dad would find an old blanket for me. Back home, I unwrapped my pillow, puffed it up and put it on my bed. For much of the early evening I lay with my head on it, reading on my back, and then I turned on my front, put my elbows on my pillow and did my homework in that position. There was something quite grown-up about owning your own pillow. I was fairly certain that none of my friends did.

On the following Sunday my mother popped in again. It must have been before eight o'clock when she turned up. I was in bed but I heard her in the hall. She remained there for around five minutes, then marched up the stairs and went into the kitchen. Heaven knows what she was doing in there. I could hear her opening drawers and doors and slamming them shut. By the time she came into my room, I was dressed and sitting on my bed. We looked at each other and I then broke the silence: 'Hello, Mummy,' I said. She did not reply. She looked around my room and then she looked at my bed. It was covered in old clothes. I kept my eyes on her, not because I wanted to look at her, but because she was unpredictable.

'Where is my money?' she demanded.

'I don't have any money,' I said. 'I have only enough to look after me.'

'When are you going?' she said.

I had nowhere to go, I told her. It wasn't that I was unwilling to move out. I assured her that I would continue to look for somewhere to 'fuck off to', as she put it. She then gave me an ultimatum: I could pay my share of the bills and stay, or go now – right now. I decided that I would pay something towards the bills, but I needed to think about it. It was at this point that my mother spotted my purse on the dressing table. She walked over, picked it up and emptied the contents into her hand.

'This will do while you're thinking about it,' she said as she returned the purse to the dresser.

'If you take all my money I won't have enough to go to my cleaning job,' I said, 'and I won't be able to go to school.'

My mother put her hand in her pocket, fiddled around and put some coins on the dressing table. 'That should be enough to get you to work,' she said, 'and if it's not you can always walk.'

I looked over at the loose coins. Two shillings and sixpence. My mother had taken all my money and left me with just half a crown. I did not respond – I just ignored her. It was my fault entirely, because I should not have left my purse out in full view. The next time I would be more careful. My mother left my room and went back into the kitchen. After a few moments she returned.

'When are you going to start paying rent?' she said.

'I'm not paying rent,' I said, 'I'm not old enough. You have to provide me with a home.'

My mother was clearly not interested in knowing any more about me other than the fact that I was in a job and getting paid weekly.

'Let's say £3 per week,' she said. 'It's a bit on the low side, but we will see how we go. I'll get you a rentbook.'

She turned and went down the stairs, out of the front door and slammed it shut, leaving me at a complete loss. How could I possibly pay rent?

I had knocked at 215 Camberwell New Road after school but my dad wasn't there so I went to Offley Road where he had another house. After a while he turned up. He had a huge cigar in the corner of his mouth and when he saw me he said, 'How are you, Clearie?' I said I was fine. I was always fine. I told him that Mummy was expecting to collect rent from the end of the month and that I could not afford to pay her. George said my mother was mad and that I should not pay the rent because I was a child, for God's sake. I asked him if he had somewhere for me to live and he said no, but if I was desperate, he could always find somewhere for me to lay my head. When I told him that Mummy had removed the fuse and we had no electricity he laughed and said that Carmel was mad, mad, mad. Beyond that he was not able to offer any practical advice. He gave me £1 to buy some sweets.

The weeks passed into months and life was the same as ever. I resented getting up to go to my cleaning job, but once I was at the bus queue I somehow got on with it. According to Angela, reports were good about my work, which was considered satisfactory. My Saturday job with Roses continued to be stimulating and enjoyable.

My mother rarely visited the house; whenever she did come it was because of a bill that needed paying or to collect my rent. She had given me the rentbook and somehow I managed to pay £3 a week. One afternoon she was waiting for me when I returned from school, sitting on the bed. My bed. As I put my bag down on the floor, she immediately said that I could not continue to live at 19 Sutherland Square for £3 per week. My rent would be increased by £3 and backdated to the beginning of the month; she would return to collect £24 at the end of the month. If I did not wish to pay the new amount I had plenty of time to find somewhere else to live. I simply did not have any spare money to pay more rent and told her so, but she just got up off the bed and punched me in the head. 'You'll find it,' she said. When I repeated what my father had said – that I shouldn't have to pay rent to her because I was still at school, she punched me again – this time in the stomach. As she did so she said I could always go and live with him, that way I would not have to pay any rent at all. As my mother was squaring up to me she noticed my tampons which were on the mantelpiece.

'So you're a big woman,' she said, 'not a child now – and big women pay their own way.' She picked up my tampons and read the side. 'You should be careful,' she said, 'that you don't get toxic shock syndrome.' Instead of placing the tampons back where she found them, she put them in her pocket and then moved to my dressing table. As she opened the top drawer her eyes rested on my sanitary towels. 'Got these for a rainy day? Well, it's not raining – outside it's bright and breezy.' My mother produced a plastic bag from her pocket and put my sanitary towels inside it. 'Now that you are working I'm sure you can buy some more,' she said. She pulled open the next drawer down and took out my clothes, examining each garment then throwing it on the floor. At the bottom of the drawer was a very nice cashmere jumper which I had saved up to buy. It had taken me ages. She held the jumper up against her chest and looked at herself in the mirror. The colour suited her. It was a pale swimming-pool blue. My mother put the jumper in the plastic bag with my sanitary towels and pulled open the bottom drawer.

'You know, Clare, my biggest regret in life is that I gave birth to you, and you and I both know that it is not possible to turn the clock back. I'll regret that for the rest of my life. You can understand that, can't you, Scarface? How is the bed-wetting? Most normal people would have stopped wetting the bed years ago, but not you.'

I did not respond to my mother so she pulled my wig off and threw it on the bed. When I tried to retrieve it my mother snatched it and held it on her lap.

'Not only are you ugly and wet the bed, you're bald as well. Just how much can a mother take?'

I did not respond but turned my back on her and went to sit down.

'Can you please tell me, Mummy, when we can have the light on again?'

My mother ignored my question, but told me to stand up when I spoke to her. So I did. She reached for my candle and whacked me on the head with it.

'The trouble with you, Clare, is you never know when to shut up. That's your trouble. If you want the electric back on, you have to pay for it.'

I reminded my mother that she had removed the money from my purse earlier and if there was no electricity I would have to tell the teachers. At this she flew into a rage and stamped on my wig. She then slapped me around the face with it and, picking up the matches I had used to light the candles, she set fire to it and stuffed it in the fireplace. The flames shot up the chimney as my wig disintegrated in the heat. It crackled and spat out charred hair at my mother's feet. The room was overwhelmed by the glow from the fire.

'Have you got enough light now?' my mother said. 'Can you see?'

As I stared at my wig, which was a ball of black charred soot, my mother pushed past me, ran down the stairs and slammed the front door.

There was no point trying to save my wig – it was gone and I did not have a spare one. Although my hair had grown back, it had not done so sufficiently for me to make an appearance in public without my wig. The following morning I went to my cleaning job with my head tied in a scarf like all the other ladies. After my job, instead of going to school, I got off the bus at Camberwell Green and caught a 45 to Brixton Market where I found a shop that sold Michael Jackson wigs. I tried on several and when I found one that fitted me, I asked if I could keep it on. The lady in the shop cut the tag and label off and I paid for it and then went off to school as quickly as possible. I made my excuses to the form teacher and joined the rest of the class.

In my exams I did quite well. Not as well as my teachers thought I could have done, but well enough not to cause them any concern. I had got myself into a routine of work, school and homework, and it was not a bad life. I was free to go out if I wanted to, but I never did, and there was no one keeping an eye on me. At the end of the month my mother returned. I'm quite certain it was her because when I got home after school the lights were on in the house and she was the only person who had the fuses for the fuseboard. I was half-expecting her to be hiding in my room or behind the door. She did not pounce on me but it was clear that she had been in my room. The drawers to my dresser were open, my clothes were on the floor and some of my candles were missing. My mother had left a plastic bag on my bed. I settled down to do my homework. There was no point in checking to see what was missing this time because I would never be able to get it back. My windows were wide open and my room was cold. My mother never could stomach the smell of my room, or me for that matter, and would always open the windows upon entering. It was halfway into the following month when my mother turned up again. I was already in bed and asleep. It really was like waking up to a very bad dream. I opened my eyes and there she was.

'I've come for the rent and the bill money,' she said.

I tried to focus on my Mickey Mouse watch, but before I could check on the time my mother brought her foot down on my head – twice. This was followed by another request for money. I tried to tell her that I was having problems making ends meet, but she grabbed the edge of the sheet underneath me and snatched it off the bed. I rolled away from her, but she pulled me off the bed, shouting at me not to take the piss and to hand over the money. Pauline and Patsy arrived at the door. They thought we had a burglar, but when they saw our mother, of course they simply turned and vanished back to their own rooms.

We had a war of words, me and my mother. In the end she

punched me in the forehead and said I was a bastard and that she would be back the following day. She scooped up the sheet and took it with her. I put an old dress on just in case she came back, got into bed, made myself comfortable and went to sleep.

The next day when I flicked my bedroom light switch on, nothing happened. I tried the switch in the hall. Nothing. The light in the back room did not work. We were once again in darkness.

The weather had turned and there was a definite chill in the air. Getting up to go to my cleaning job was hard. It was getting dark sooner and when I woke up at 4.45 it was still dark. Groping around and trying to get organised in the dark was a pain.

I did not see my mother again for ten days. Then I arrived home from school and she was sitting on a chair in the sitting room. As I entered the bedroom she called me. I really did not have the stomach for another fight with her so I took £20 out of my purse and put the purse back at the very bottom of my bag. Then I entered the sitting room and handed her the money.

'And the rest,' she said as she took the cash out of my hand. 'You owe me another £17. When am I going to get it?'

'Next week,' I said. I collected my school bag and walked out of the room, down the stairs and out of the front door. I sat on a bench by the house on stilts until it was quite late. I could not bear the sound of my mother's voice and just seeing her was beginning to make me feel physically sick.

Thank God she wasn't there when I returned. I asked Pauline and Patsy whether she had demanded money off them. Both said she had asked for it, but had not insisted on it. They had had no scary visits late at night or punches to the head. Pauline was sensible – she had put a lock on her door.

On average I was expected to pay about £15 per week for my living expenses, never mind about rent. Although it was a lot of money it was better to pay it and avoid those dreadful early evening and late-night visits. Thereafter I did not refuse to pay rent, I just said I did not have it. She came at the end of every month and I had an envelope waiting for her. Sometimes I handed it over without even looking at her. Sometimes she would ask for more but I would ignore her. She knew I had two jobs but I was still at school and my earning ability was limited. Fortunately I was a member of the free school dinner queue and I always ate well there.

25

A Ray of Hope

1972–5

As I approached my fifteenth birthday I didn't feel there was much to celebrate. I was tired. My bones ached in the morning when I got out of bed. They ached in the evening when I went to bed. I was tired all day, every day, night and day. If this was what it was like being an adult, I wasn't at all sure that I could cope with it. I had one ray of hope. But it was my ray of hope. I decided to write to Mike Mansfield again, just to let him know that I was well on my way to becoming a barrister.

His reply came on 8 November: 'Good to hear from you. Just call round to Chambers when you feel like it. Yours, Michael M.'

For some reason, I decided that it might be a good idea to have a back-up position, just in case Michael Mansfield was not able to be my pupil-master. So the following day I went to the library and got hold of a book known as the *Bar Directory*, which gives details of all the barristers. I went through the bar directory and settled on the name of Henry Pownall. It was a nice name and I liked the sound of his Chambers at 2 Harcourt Buildings, Temple, London EC4Y 9DS. I wrote to him and explained my situation and the fact that Michael Mansfield had promised me pupillage. I wanted to know if he would be able to assist me, should the arrangement with Michael Mansfield fall through. Henry Pownall wrote to me in January.

Dear Miss Briscoe,

I have been able to have a word with Michael Mansfield. He would be delighted to see you. He is rather booked up,

but I do feel that if you were to see him, something might
come of it. His word is his word. Would you therefore
telephone his Clerk and make a mutually convenient
appointment.

With my best wishes.

Yours sincerely.

Henry Pownall

PS Let me know how you get on and what happens!

I did not make an appointment, because I was sure Michael M
would never go back on his word. I just needed to do my part, get
the right results and go on to university. Life was difficult
enough without trying to qualify as a barrister.

Christmas had come and gone and I hardly noticed it. I spent
the big day in my room on my bed, reading books and cooking a
modest meal of scrambled eggs and baked beans. I was not
invited to Christmas dinner with the rest of the family and Father
Christmas did not knock on my door. No matter – since what I
really needed was peace and quiet. It was my GCE year and I
needed to be able to study free of interruptions. My teachers had
wanted to discuss my GCEs with my parents, but since neither
George nor Carmen had ever attended a Parent Teacher meeting, it was unlikely that they would attend now. My schoolwork
could always be better, but it was okay and I was, according to
my teachers, 'a delightful young lady with huge potential'.

My timetable for revision and homework was all mapped out,
but I had the worry of not knowing what to expect when I got
home. I was always anxious in case my mother was waiting for
me. Sometimes I would walk home from school instead of taking
the bus; not only did I save money that way, but if my mother
was hanging around waiting for me she would get fed up and
leave. On other occasions I would stop off at 215 Camberwell
New Road and see my dad. I felt as if I was under siege, and the
thought had crossed my mind that my mother was stalking me.

Soon I was finding it harder and harder to concentrate. I never
felt quite relaxed when I was at home because I was always on

the alert – listening out for the front door. Every time someone opened it, I froze – and if I heard my mother's footsteps on the stairs I would dive under the bed. By the time she got to my door the room was in darkness and there was no one to be seen.

Life was getting me down. It was a constant battle to keep afloat financially. I started to economise even more on food, making do with a cup of tea in the morning, another cup when I finished my cleaning job and my free school dinner. The trouble was, once I put the ploy into practice it was pretty obvious to me that I did not really have to eat at all. If I just kept busy I could live off my energy.

When I confided in her about my money problems, Angela found me another cleaning job. It was two hours per day from 6 p.m. to 8 p.m., Monday to Friday, in Trafalgar Square. I was paid less than my wages for my morning cleaning job. The first week, it took me an hour to get to Trafalgar Square, so I had to leave school by 5 p.m. My strategy was to stay at school until 4.45 and do some work in the library or the fourth-floor common room. On my way to the bus stop I would change into my cleaning clothes. The money came in very useful when I was paid on Friday, but I was exhausted. I felt like staying in bed all of Friday night and Saturday but I had to be up to go to Roses. I spent the whole of Sunday tidying up and doing my homework.

The second week was more traumatic than the first. I was out of the house by 5.20 a.m. at the latest, but not returning until 8.30–8.45 p.m. There was very little time to do my homework and on one or two occasions I actually dozed off again in school. However, I looked forward to the money. At least I could eat, at least I could pay my way and not worry about being turned out of the house suddenly because I was not able to come up with the rent.

My work was comprehensively criticised in the third week of my evening job and while financially I had never been better off I was falling behind in my studies. One of my teachers was so appalled by the last homework I had handed in that I was required to do it again. She had refused to mark it and I got detention.

Angela was not at all surprised when I decided to give up the second cleaning job as soon as she had a replacement. She thought that I should not be working at all. Angela was like a mother to me at times. She was the mother I never had and I was the daughter that she always wanted. Her kindness made me cry.

Six weeks before the start of my exams my mother returned for her rent. I explained to her that I had given up my third job and therefore had no money. She said that there would be no argument this time, that she was sick and tired of arguing with me. When she left the house she simply pulled out the entire fuseboard and took it away with her. Although this behaviour was typical, panic set in and the next day I had to go off to Woolworth's again and buy as many candles as I could afford. Pauline and Patsy were also in darkness. Pauline put in a request to have the lighting back but our mother ignored her.

I did not see my mother again until after my exams. When they were over I celebrated by going round to Angela's and having a large cup of tea and a bowl of pasta. My exams had gone well although I was anxious all the same. What if I did not get into the sixth form? What could I say to Michael M and Henry P? Many of the girls in my class would not return the following year and quite a few of the boys had decided to take their chances on the employment market. Over the summer holidays I worked at Roses when they required me and covered for other cleaners when they failed to make an appearance.

On the day the results came out I walked very slowly to school, putting off the moment of discovery. I was given a slip of paper. Hooray! I had managed to pass all my GCEs! Now I had ten O-levels under my belt, the next stage was A-levels, which were two years away. There was a pat on the back for all of us from our teachers. I did not feel it was appropriate to contact my mother. There was no point really. I did contact Michael M.

Dear Michael Mansfield,

I would just like you to know that I have passed my GCEs and I hope to get my A-Levels in two years' time, so I'll start my pupillage in five years' time.

Clare

I could not wait for the sixth form! I would buy myself a new pencil case, some stationery, three new pairs of white socks and a matching pair of gloves. Over the past weeks I had fallen into the habit of missing my weekly Sunday meeting with God. The priest had noticed my absence at Mass. It wasn't a case of me wanting to avoid God, but I was usually so tired on Sunday mornings that I had to have a lie-in. Father asked me to come and see him and when we were on our own he wanted to know if I had anything to confess. I did not but said I was sorry and would try to attend on a more regular basis in the future.

That Sunday God decreed there should be light. I walked back home and when I entered the door I instinctively flicked the light switch and the lights came on. There was no movement upstairs, just complete silence as I waited for my mother to appear. She never did. I waited with my finger on the light switch ready to make her disappear at the flick of the switch, but nothing happened. I stepped into the house and waited again, no sound. As I made my way upstairs I was acutely conscious of the fact that my heart was racing and I was quite terrified, but my mother was nowhere to be seen. I counted my candles, all eight were still there. Either she had finally decided that she could not keep us in darkness for ever, or she thought that if we did not have electricity she would not be able to collect the rent and bill money. I put my candles away in the bottom of my wardrobe.

The summer holidays came and went in a flash. I spent a great deal of time in bed when I should have been reading. I was bone weary, but at least now I had time to catch up with my sleep. In September when we all went back to school I felt relieved and determined to be a good student. All I needed was a settled existence and at first I achieved that.

There was no sign of my mother until one day, after I had been back at school for about four weeks, she suddenly appeared from nowhere as I entered the house. I ignored her, but I was careful to remove the key from the lock and leave the door open as I went upstairs to my room. She followed about ten minutes later, by which time my bag, purse and schoolwork were stowed well out of sight. I sat on the bed and waited for her. When the woman came into my room she did not ask me how I was. She simply wanted to know why I was still living in her house. I said that I had not found anywhere else yet. How much more time did I need, she asked. Then she said that she wanted me out in two weeks and if I was not *out* there would be trouble. She went downstairs and slammed out of the front door before I could ask what sort of trouble. I had been in quite a lot of trouble over the years. That sort of trouble I could cope with, but I had a feeling that this time, my mother had something special in mind.

Two weeks later, I knew that something was wrong as soon as I got home from school and opened the door. I went up to my room and my mother was sitting on a chair inside my bedroom, facing the door.

'Hello, Mummy,' I said. I glanced to my left. My bed was not there, it had vanished. 'What's happened to my bed?'

'It is not your bed,' my mother said. 'It belongs to me and I've taken it back.'

'Oh,' I said. 'But what will I sleep on?'

'You can sleep on fresh air as far as I am concerned.'

'What have I done this time?' I asked.

'Oh, just the fact that you breathe,' my mother said. 'You breathe, nothing more than that really. You don't want to pay rent, you don't want to pay bills, you want to eat, sleep and breathe at my expense.'

I thought better of arguing with her. When she pulled the door shut behind her I went looking for my bed. I thought at first that she might have hidden it somewhere in the house, as she had done before, but it was nowhere to be found.

A fortnight later, on the Sunday, my mother arrived and informed me that if I wanted my bed back I would have to pay a total of £20 per week. Not only did I not have that kind of money, I was quite comfortable sleeping on the floor. When it became clear to my mother that I would not budge she threatened to throw me out unless I handed over £100 immediately. I refused so the debt was reduced to £50. We did not really argue over it, I just refused to pay. I reminded my mother that there wasn't much more she could do to hurt me. I didn't have a bed, she didn't cook for me, I had been without electricity for months and still I had managed. I invited her to do whatever she liked. It was only when she told me to pack up and go that I realised I might have gone too far and goaded her into throwing me out.

I remained seated on the floor and refused to move. Seizing my hair, my mother tried to get me to stand. When that failed, she kneed me in the spine, calling me a little whore and a piece of shit. Still I refused to move. Out of complete exasperation she then started kicking the clothes on the floor up into the air. 'There goes my bed,' I said calmly.

My mother punched me in the back of the head. 'There goes my fist,' she said, 'and there goes my foot,' as she kicked me hard in the side of the legs.

As she stomped her way to the door, she kicked a path through my bed. 'I'll be back,' she said.

A moment later I heard the front door click. Thank God. My mother was gone. It would be some time before I saw her again.

One day, returning from my early-morning job, I must have dozed off on the bus because I woke up past my stop, at Loughborough Road. I jumped up, pressed the bell and got off outside the Odeon Cinema, intending to cross the road and walk back to school. However, on the corner of Camberwell Green and Loughborough Junction was a furniture shop called

Thoroughgoods, and in the window was the most beautiful bed I had ever seen. It was a four-poster with brown curtains tied back in large bows and lots of frilly brown lace. It was a bed to die for.

I went into the shop and as I stood on the carpet just inside the door an alarm sounded towards the rear. A funny little man with a bald head, glasses, a V-neck sleeveless pullover, a starched white shirt and a black tie appeared from nowhere. 'Can I help you?' he said.

I asked him how much the bed was and he told me that it had only just arrived a few days earlier. He encouraged me to take my shoes off and lie on the bed, which I did. It was so comfortable. As I lay there I once again asked the price. The man said he would have to go and look it up, and disappeared towards the back of the shop.

The bed was delightful, the mattress cottonwool soft. I just sank into it. It was so welcoming. Eventually, I became conscious of a gentle tug on my arm, which was repeated several times. When I came round, the salesman was standing there and a small crowd had gathered. They were staring at me because I had fallen asleep. I rubbed my eyes and jumped off. Thank God I no longer wet the bed.

'It's a hundred and twenty pounds,' the man told me.

I said I did not have that sort of money and would never be able to afford to buy it. He said that it was a bargain. I did not wish to disappoint him so I asked if it was possible to pay for the bed over a period of time. He agreed and I put down a deposit of £5. He promised not to sell the bed. I put my shoes back on, and shook his hand and went to school.

All day I dreamed about my bed and falling asleep on it. When I was in the free school dinner queue I daydreamed. And when I went to bed that night on my pile of clothes on the floor, in my head I was sleeping in my four-poster bed. In order to pay for the bed and give her rent when my mother called for it I decided that I simply had to get another job. The evening cleaning job had proved a disaster; I needed something to do at the weekend, if possible. King's College Hospital was advertising for nursing auxiliaries on a full- or part-time basis for night duty or day duty. I applied immediately and left my details over the phone. The application form was filled in and returned on the same day. My interview took place four weeks later and the following Monday I agreed to go into the hospital and sign my contract. I got the job: Friday, Saturday and Sunday night duty from 9 p.m. to 8 a.m. At first it sounded exciting. We all had to attend the hospital a few days in advance of our start date to be shown how to carry out a bedbath, give a bedpan and change a bed. It really was easy-peasy but then I was not dealing with real patients, only make-believe. It was very important to remember the patients' privacy. To always ensure that curtains were closed, bedpans covered and inappropriate comments silenced.

On my first night I was so busy I forgot to get tired. The evening staff and Sister gave us a hand with the report which explained each patient's diagnosis and how their day had been, what to watch out for, any visits the patients may have had, any little accidents. Reactions to medication were always reported twice so the night shift had no excuse. I made a note in the little notebook I was given. Although I was an auxiliary nurse it was very important to be professional.

My ward was the female orthopaedic ward. Many of the women were in traction of one sort or other and many of them were in a great deal of pain. My job was to collect all the cups or give out more tea as appropriate, then place the cups in the kitchen and leave it in good order. All the women had to be provided with a bedpan, but this was a very difficult task because many of the ladies had enormously large bottoms that required gathering up. Once all the folds of skin were held in my hand and over the crook of my elbow, I would slide a bedpan in and then gently let the folds of skin hang down. This, of course, was accomplished while the patient held on to a vertical swing and pulled herself up in order for the bedpan to slide under. Once it was firmly in place I would start on the next patient and, while she was on the throne, I would go back to the previous patient, remove the bedpan, wipe the patient's bottom if necessary, change the sheet and then take the bedpan to the sluice for cleaning. The whole process would take anything up to two hours.

After that job was complete, I would then settle each patient. This involved tidying or replacing sheets, pillowcases and blankets, putting dentures in a liquid cleaner and generally making the patient comfortable for the night ahead. After that there were other errands that the qualified staff would require of me, fetching and carrying. It was great fun. I loved every minute. Once the patients were settled I would clean their side table, replace their water jug, get rid of half-eaten food and generally tidy up. Next the kitchen would need cleaning, followed by the sluice and it was always a dead certainty that some of the patients would have little accidents in bed. I felt so sorry for them, it all seemed so embarrassing and such a palaver. The entire bed had to be changed, which was quite a performance given that most of the patients were in traction. Most difficult were the patients with hip replacements which meant that they could not roll over on the left or right for the insertion of a bedpan.

It did not occur to me until I was two and a half months into my job that some patients deliberately messed the bed as an attention-seeking ploy. How I hated dealing with them: 'Come quick, Nurse, it's all coming out!' I also despised those patients who would try to pull rank for no other reason than class: 'A lady should *never* have to wait for a bedpan!' But I called them all ladies.

I was always sympathetic to the patients in pain, even those who insisted I warmed up the bedpan in advance. Soon I became known as Nurse Clare. I was by far the youngest and most energetic auxiliary there. Some nurses and doctors commented that I even appeared to have a brain.

On a Friday I would go home from school and try to get a couple of hours' sleep before I set out for King's Hospital. Lights went off in the ward at 11 p.m. and after that only the nursing station was illuminated. That was my opportunity to get some homework done. I always slept between two o'clock and three o'clock. At about 5.30 a.m. we, the night nursing staff, would all spring into action. We had a great deal of work to cover before we handed over to the day staff. The nurses had to do DDAs (Dangerous Drug Administration). I had to give out bedpans. All patients required a cup of tea. The beds had to be changed and made again. The curtains round the beds had to be tied and clipped back and the patients cleaned. Those who required a bedbath would hopefully have their toiletries ready. Those who simply wanted to sleep through would ask if they could have their curtains pulled to enclose them within their space. I was always ready to assist the ladies with anything that made them more comfortable. We would hand over to the day staff at 8 a.m., which gave me just enough time to run to the bus stop and catch a bus home. It did not take long – twenty minutes maximum.

At home I had a quick wash and a cup of tea, changed into my fashionable clothes and walked to Roses. I was usually exhausted on a Saturday morning, but it wore off pretty quickly once the customers started arriving. I loved Roses. Most of the time when I was there I was on automatic pilot. I hated being tired. Usually at about four o'clock I would so desperately need my bed that I feared sitting down in case I fell asleep. I was just as sympathetic a shop assistant as I was a nurse. I could make any fat lady slim with a few kind words. I could shave inches off the hips, thighs and stomach with flattering noises. The customers loved me. No one was too fat or too thin in my eyes. Everyone was just right. And everyone bought their desired outfit. The pay was good and the discount still worth having. By the time 5.30 p.m. arrived I was so tired I was capable only of collecting my wage packet. I would rush home and by 6.30 p.m. I was in bed. I fell asleep in seconds.

My alarm was set for 8.20 p.m. Wearily I would get up, brush my teeth, wash my face and put my nursing clothes on for duty at 9 p.m. The next time I would get to sleep would be on my break, and I always had a natural fear that one day I would simply nod off and not wake up for hours and hours. My patients enjoyed having a young auxiliary nurse looking after them. Most important for me, I was able to pay towards my four-poster bed every week. I was anxious to pay it off, because it was uncomfortable sleeping on the floor. It made my back ache. I longed for the time when I could sleep in my own bed and not be disturbed until I was ready.

After our Saturday-night shift I was desperate for my bed. On the bus home I always asked the conductor to put me off at East Street Market just in case I fell asleep. Once back in the house, I collapsed into bed, sometimes with my nursing uniform still on. Other times I would simply crash out, only to find that I was actually sleeping on the floorboards. Sunday was the only day when I could theoretically sleep straight through, from the moment I arrived home to the moment I had to be back at work. So much sleep was an attractive option, but I had to get up at some stage and cover my homework.

Although my shift started at 9 p.m. on Sunday and finished at 8 a.m. on Monday, if I refused to take a break during the night I could leave at 7 a.m., sometimes slightly earlier. On Monday mornings I would take the bus to Camberwell Green and then a bus from there to my cleaning job in Whitehall. Once that was finished, I caught a bus back to Camberwell Gate where I swapped my work clothes for my school clothes and went to school.

Monday was always a difficult day for me, simply because I was totally exhausted. It was a routine that was to repeat itself, year in and year out. I never complained, just got on with it. I had six months of sleeping on the floor like the Little Princess, but I did not want a ballgown or Prince Charming, simply a bed of my own. I became such a poor sleeper that I would thrash around at night, always restless, never completely at peace even when I was asleep. I think if I had had a wish at that time, it would have been to sleep and sleep and sleep – just to be normal and not to be tired all the time.

When my mind was completely worn out I sometimes thought about my old friend Miss K. Was she alive – and if so, what was she doing? Did she ever think about me? Did she care? Would she be proud of me? My dear friend Miss K. It would be so good if she got in touch with me. I would never know her pain but then again she would never know mine. In my heart I think that we could have made it. Looking after each other. I had all my ladies at the hospital to look after and I managed.

The two years in sixth form raced past. Precious Puss had left school the year before and was now training as a nursery nurse. Four Eyes was doing teacher's training. I saw very little of either of them. As my A-levels approached, Angela said I could take two weeks or more off the cleaning job and I could also book all my holidays in one go so I would have plenty of time to revise.

Eventually the day arrived for the first exam. I got up early and found to my surprise that I did not feel at all nervous. I worked my way steadily through the papers. Some were easier than others. Inside I felt like a zombie. I still wanted to go to university and be a barrister, but I had grown so chronically tired that I almost did not care. The last exam came and went. I did not go out celebrating, just went home, put my school bag down and caught the bus to work. The women on the orthopaedic ward were expecting me on night duty.

I had applied to a number of universities. Newcastle-upon-Tyne was my first choice. I had been for an interview there and found it an impressive place. The Law Department was isolated from the rest of the buildings. I had been shown into a conference room and introduced to Professor Elliott, Professor Clark and Mr Stevenson. The interview had gone very well and they were impressed when I mentioned that I had a pupillage lined up with Michael Mansfield. They offered me a place if I passed my A-levels with good grades. I had a decent report from my teachers, although some thought it was a bit adventurous to apply to a university. I also needed a grant from my Local Authority. My mother was required to provide details of her income and expenses so that the right level of award could be allocated. The form was large and complex and, while I provided as much detail as possible, she needed to fill in the rest.

I took the form to the local library and copied it and then took the original to my mother. I was let in by Cynthia, who was so surprised to see me that she stepped back from the door. I walked straight in and up the stairs where I could see all the other Eastman children hovering about. My mother was sitting in front of the ironing board, ironing. She did not look up when I entered the room.

'Mummy,' I said, 'I would like to go to university when I leave school. I've applied for a grant but you have to provide some details on the form. Can we fill it in today if possible?'

My mother asked me why I had applied to go to university and I told her that I wanted to read Law. 'But only clever people go to university, Clare – why do *you* want to go there?' she said.

'I want to be a barrister.'

'An embarrasser more like,' she said as she stretched her arm out in my direction. 'Give me the forms.'

I handed them to her. She looked at the front sheet, turned it over and looked at the following sheet, then repeated this action until there were no more pages to turn, and finally she started to tear it up into small pieces.

'Only clever people go to university,' she said, then she threw the small pieces of paper up into the air. 'Now fuck off out of my sight, if you know what's good for you.'

The pieces of paper fell like a snowstorm all over my mother, all over the furniture.

'Shut the door on your way out,' she said.

I waited for a little while, watching the tiny pieces of paper settle, and then I turned and walked down the stairs and out of the door. I sat on the wall outside just considering what to do next and then I went home.

My mother *had* to fill in the forms: without them I would not be able to go to university. The following Monday I telephoned ILEA (Inner London Education Authority) and they confirmed my suspicions. I could always apply for a grant on an independent basis, but I would need to establish that I had been self-sufficient for five years.

When my A-level results came through, my grades were good enough to get me the place at Newcastle and I expected them to contact me within a day or so but I heard nothing. In the end I contacted them myself, on the telephone, and they instructed me to send them a copy of my birth certificate as a matter of urgency. There was some sort of problem, it appeared, but they were sure it could be resolved. I sent a copy of my birth certificate by recorded delivery the next day. Three days later I was astonished when the Admissions Department telephoned me and asked me my full name. I told them. Clare Briscoe. Was I sure? they asked. Of course I was sure of my name. The following week, Professor Clark wrote to me and informed me that there was a discrepancy with my name and my qualifications. The birth certificate I had provided identified me as Constance Beverley Briscoe, yet all my qualifications were in the name of Clare Briscoe, and the university was not prepared to accept my qualifications in the name of another person. This came as an almighty shock. It had never occurred to me that my name was not Clare Briscoe. I had no idea that I was really Constance Beverley Briscoe. When I contacted the Admissions Department and spoke to Professor Clark and explained my situation to him he was as surprised as I was. We both agreed that the school class teacher and Headmaster should provide evidence to the university and confirm that Constance and Clare were one and the same. Until my identity was confirmed the university was, for understandable reasons, unable to offer me a place on the Law course. Within a week my identity was confirmed and I was invited by the university to use my proper name. I gave an undertaking that I would from now on be identified as Constance Beverley Briscoe.

So far so good, but I still needed a grant. I discussed the problem with the Sister on the orthopaedic ward and she suggested that since I had worked for four years I should defer for one year, by which time I would be eligible for independent status if I continued to work. I agreed to this plan since in many ways I had no choice. Fortunately the university agreed to delay my course by one year. I would start in October 1979. The Inner London Education Authority promised to grant me independent status for the year of admission to university and I would continue to work until then.

Lyndhurst Gardens Hospice in Hampstead were looking for staff on night duty and I applied. Because of my experience I was able to work for them whenever they were short of staff. I joined a local nursing agency which provided me with lots of work at the hospice.

Leaving school was a big day for me. In my year only three of us were off to university. Armed with my A-level results and my offer of an unconditional place at Newcastle University I applied for a full-time job at Guy's Hospital in the X-ray Department. The post was for one year only, and I would assist the radiologist with research as and when I was required to do so. The interview was very low-key and friendly. I was getting quite good at interviews. My offer of a job was notified to me first by telephone and a few days later by letter. My cleaning job had to go, but I kept my jobs at King's College Hospital and Lyndhurst Gardens. It was always possible to get two or three hours' sleep during the night when things were very quiet. My Saturday job at Roses also had to go. Although I loved it there and would have liked to stay, there was simply not enough time. I told Eileen that I would leave as soon as she had a replacement. Three weeks later I walked out of the doors to Roses for the last time. I went off to East Street Market and looked for Pete. He wasn't there. I would find him another time. I went home, lay on the floor and fell asleep.

Three weeks later I took delivery of the finest bed in the whole of south London. It was brown in colour with four claw feet covered in plastic gold. The posts were hollow metal poles covered in chocolate-brown plastic and at the top of each pole a gold plastic onion-shaped structure stood proud. The mattress was orange, beige and brown, sprinkled with tiny white dots and splash marks. The curtains were to die for; they were primarily brown with specks of white and they were hung up on a lateral pole from the hooks on the gold plastic onions. At the base of the bed, about eighteen inches from the floor, a pleated valance was attached to the plastic pole just below the mattress. Once the bed was dressed I pulled the curtains and went to sleep. During the following days I spent most of my days and nights in my bed. I ate, slept and got dressed in my bed. When I returned home after a long day I went to bed; even when I was not tired I could be found in bed. It was heaven reading a book in bed with my curtains closed.

After I had had my bed for a few days I went to Woolworth's and I bought a blue polyester duvet and a chocolate-brown duvet cover and matching pillow case. They had been significantly reduced because the customers did not want to buy them for love nor money, the shop assistant told me. They were not to everyone's liking. I was persuaded to buy two on the basis that there would never be anything like them ever again.

Epilogue

After I had made plans to put all my belongings in long-term storage, there was a little unfinished business that I had to take care of before the start of my new life. The final entry in my diary read: Dear Diary, I'm off to university soon but must see my mother today.

I took the bus to her house and knocked on the door. As always I waited for someone to open it. Not much had changed. The house was noisy. Untidy even. The Briscoes and the Eastmans were well represented. As for me, I had long since become an orphan. I had already made up my mind that this would be my last visit to the house. I walked up the stairs and went into the room facing me.

'Hello, Mummy,' I said.

She was sitting at the ironing board, and I saw that she looked relaxed and almost carefree. The room was a mess. Beyond my mother, in the small kitchenette, my sister Pauline was cleaning up imaginary spills, looking to see my mother's reaction to my appearance. I stayed just inside the door out of harm's reach of the hot iron that was firmly in my mother's control.

'Hello, Mummy,' I repeated.

She never once looked at me, but that did not matter very much. I stood balanced on one foot with my right leg stretched out in front of me, as I leaned on the wall. After some time she stopped ironing, looked up at me and said, 'What do you want?'

'I want you to know that I'm off to university in two weeks' time.'

My mother continued to iron. 'Really,' she said without looking at me.

'Yes,' I said. 'I'm off to university and I just wanted to tell you.'

My mother did not respond. She seemed preoccupied with the ironing. 'Well, you have told me,' she said. 'I thought it was only clever people who went to university.'

'Yes,' I said. 'I suppose I must be clever, but that's not the reason I'm here. I want you to know that I have arranged to have all my property stored while I'm away because I have no intention of ever returning to nineteen Sutherland Square.'

My mother looked up and then looked down and continued ironing.

'I also want you to know that I will never speak to you again – ever – as long as I live.'

She stopped ironing, put the iron on its heel and stared at me. Her hand remained firmly attached to the iron.

'What did you say?' she said.

'I want you to know that I will never *ever* speak to you again for the rest of my life. I have nothing to thank you for, Mummy.'

My mother looked up at me and steadied her glasses on her nose.

'I've never liked you, Mummy, never, ever. Oh, I tell a lie – I did once, but that was a long time ago.'

'Really,' said my mother.

'Yes. A long time ago when I was a child, you probably don't remember, but you left me in the house at Burnett Street. I liked you then but not since. I loved you then. You bought me nice cream cakes. You were my mummy and I was your child. What did I ever do to you, Mummy? Answer me that?'

My mother remained silent, but I was aware of my sisters and brothers and the Eastmans hanging about outside the door behind me.

'You made me hate you, and I do. You know what? I don't think that you should ever have had children. And you know what else? I think that one day you will realise that good old Constance was not that bad after all.'

My mother chuckled and told me to fuck off to university

sooner rather than later, as she picked up the garment next in line to be ironed.

'All I have ever wanted was a mum who loved me, not hated me, *loved* me.'

My mother continued to iron.

'Good old Constance is off to university,' I said. 'Me, Constance Briscoe, is off to university.'

'What did you say?' said my mother.

'I said good old Constance Briscoe is off to university and yes, Mother, I know my name is Constance, not Clare or Clearie but Constance. Constance Beverley Briscoe – that's me. By the way, just when were you going to get round to telling me what my real name was?'

My mother remained silent, but I began to cry.

'I came here to tell you that I was off and I've done it, so I'll be on my way now. Mummy, I will never speak to you as long as I live and I think you know why.'

Eastman was hovering about in the back kitchen and the word 'university' must have frightened him off because I never heard a peep out of him. As I turned to leave the room the Eastmans were on the stairs.

'You said you were Constance. Where did you get that from?'

'That's my name,' I said.

'You've gone all posh – your name is Clare.'

'What's your name?' said Pauline.

'Constance,' I said.

'Don't be ridiculous,' she said. 'It's Clare.'

'No, it's not, it's on my birth certificate. My name is Constance. Anyway, it does not matter what my name is.'

I went downstairs and out of the door.

The storage company arrived on the Monday of the following week and removed most of my possessions from the house. I kept my rocking chair, my TV, my diaries and my clothes. My four-poster bed was dismantled and the curtains placed in a large box. I would miss my bed, but we would be reunited.

Pauline and my mother were hanging about at the bottom of the stairs.

'So you're really going, Clare?' said Pauline.

'Yes, I'm going to be a barrister.'

'When will we see you again?'

'I'm not planning on coming back. I'll stay in Newcastle.'

'What about Christmas?'

'I'm not coming back. Not ever.'

I left my diaries on my rocking chair and went out to buy a warm cardigan. When I returned, my mother had taken my diaries and put them in her bag. I asked for them but she refused. She barged past me and walked out of the door. I ran down the street after her, pleading with her to return them but she ignored me. I never got them back. They had my life in them. The life of Clearie. Back at Sutherland Square, I cleared my room of my few remaining possessions and took a cab to King's Cross. I travelled on the afternoon train and arrived in Newcastle shortly after 7 p.m. I took a taxi to Jesmond Dene where I booked myself into the student house and waited for term to start. The first thing I did was write to Michael Mansfield.

October 1979

Dear Mr Mansfield,

Just a short note to let you know that I have now started university and I hope to start my pupillage in three years' time.

Regards,

Constance Briscoe

Between 1979 and 1982 I remained in Newcastle-upon-Tyne, returning only to work at Lyndhurst Gardens Hospice or to work in some other capacity. I never returned home to live again.

In 1982 I graduated with Honours as a Bachelor of Law and I informed Mr Mansfield of my good news. I asked to meet with him. He replied:

8 November 1982

Dear Constance,

Good to hear from you. Just call round to Chambers when you feel like it. If I'm not in court I am usually around between five and six thirty.

Yours,
Michael Mansfield

In 1983 I qualified as a barrister, having completed one year at the Inns of Court School of Law.

I wrote to Michael Mansfield again to tell him my news and to ask when I could start my pupillage. He replied:

September 1983

Dear Constance,

Come as soon as you like,
Michael

Editor's Note

After the publication of *Ugly*, which went straight to Number One in the bestseller list, and attracted massive publicity, the publishers received a solicitor's letter on behalf of Constance's mother, Carmen Briscoe, claiming that the book was defamatory.

It seemed inconceivable that she would pursue this claim all the way to the High Court, but she did:

This is an account of the trial.

Prologue

Saturday 16 September 2006

'Do you have any comment?' said the lady waiting on my doorstep.

I was on my way to the supermarket to get my weekly shopping. It was not even nine o'clock. I was certain that she had got the wrong person; maybe she had got the wrong house.

'Excuse me,' I said, trying to get past.

'Any comment about the fact that your mother has issued proceedings in the High Court yesterday? She says that your account in your book *Ugly*, that she abused you as a child, is pure fiction.'

'Well,' I said, rather taken aback. 'I don't know about that. I am sure if my mother had issued proceedings against me my solicitor would tell me.'

'Well,' said the reporter. 'I can assure you that the proceedings have been issued because I was there.'

'What do you mean?'

'I was present at the High Court when the proceedings were issued.'

I was very confused by what I had heard and concerned that the reporter appeared to know something about my case that I did not.

'Well, I don't just accept your word. I would like to call my lawyer.'

'Sure,' said the reporter. 'I'll wait here.'

I closed the door and made my way back upstairs. My phone

was on the glass coffee table. Tapping in Sarah's number I waited for her to pick up.

'Hello, Sarah.'

'Hello, Constance, how can I help you?'

'Well, I have got a reporter on my doorstep and she says that my mother issued proceedings against me in the High Court yesterday. Do you know anything about that?'

'Oh yes, Constance, that is right. They issued late on Friday and I decided not to tell you until Monday. I did not want to spoil your weekend.'

'Well, the reporter is asking if I have any comment.'

'How did she get on to you so quickly?'

'She said that she was there when the proceedings were issued.'

'Really.'

'Yes.'

'Well, make no comment and direct her to me if you like and I will deal with it.'

'And meanwhile?'

'Well, if she was present and found you so quickly that will probably mean the press will cover the story in the papers tomorrow.'

When I opened the front door the reporter was still waiting for me.

'Well, I can confirm that the proceedings were issued yesterday. I am a little confused. How did you get my address?'

'I cannot quite remember now whether it was provided to me or whether I got it from a document. It really does not matter. Do you have any comment?'

'I have no comment to make. I am sorry she has done this, but it is hardly surprising that she would want to pursue me.'

As I started to close the door the reporter scribbled on her notepad and walked off towards the road.

'By the way,' I shouted, 'what I have said is off the record.'

I closed the door. My mother was suing me for defamation!

What was the bet that it would be reported in the newspapers the next day? I did not have long to wait. The following morning, I got the papers early from the newsagent's round the corner. The *Sunday Times* covered the story:

One of Britain's most high-profile black women judges is facing a writ for libel damages from her mother over allegations that she was abused as a child. Constance Briscoe, who 10 years ago was one of the first black women to be made a judge, is being sued by Carmen, her 73-year-old mother, over the claims made in Briscoe's autobiography.

In the book, entitled *Ugly*, Briscoe claimed that her Jamaican mother not only beat and kicked her but spat on her and deprived her of food.

It was published earlier this year to critical acclaim and became a bestseller. However, it provoked an outburst of fury from Carmen Briscoe, who objected to her portrayal as a vile, abusive parent, which she says is untrue.

On Friday lawyers acting for Carmen issued proceedings in the High Court in London. The writ alleges 'libel and aggravated damages' in the High Court against Briscoe and publishers Hodder & Stoughton.

The article concluded by describing me as a QC and a part-time judge. The Press always liked to elevate my status. I was appointed a Recorder of the Crown Court in 1996. It is a part-time appointment, which involves sitting as a judge at least six weeks a year. Otherwise I practise at the Bar, but I am not Queen's Counsel. They would discover that sooner or later.

So a defamation trial beckoned. I had always made my position clear. What I had written in my book was true. If I was a liar then my mother should sue me. I could hardly complain about the fact that she had taken my advice. I soon learnt my mother had lined up my brothers Carlton and Martin and my sister Patsy, who I called Precious Puss, to give evidence against me. As if that was not bad enough, my stepsisters the Eastmans were out in force. Cynthia, Norma and Gina had all provided witness statements supporting my mother. According to them my mother was not the violent, aggressive woman that I had described. Precious Puss was on record in the papers saying that my book was pure fiction and my brother Martin described my mother as brilliant. Patsy had provided three statements, Norma eight and Martin four. My mother had made three statements which ran to fifty-four pages each. She said she was mortified by the publication of the book. Her distress had been acute. She had never laid a hand on any of her children and would never tolerate it. If Eastman had laid a hand on me, my mother would have thrown him out of the house. Eastman was a good and decent man and the allegations in the book of sexual and physical abuse were pure fiction. None of it had happened. It was a figment of the author's imagination.

I

The first date that the court had available to try my case, which was expected to last two weeks, was 17 November. It was typical. We were making the final arrangements for the trial, due to start the following week, when disaster struck. My sister Four Eyes had gone missing. She was not to be found. She disappeared shortly after sending a text message in which she expressed support and said that she would always be there for me and would give evidence on my behalf. Without her I was in trouble. She was the only one who could say what had really happened in the room when my mother came in. Precious Puss had made it clear in her various statements that she supported my mother and Beauty was sitting on the fence. Tony, my partner, had sent her a letter asking whether she was prepared to honour her pledge to support me but we had heard nothing. All my solicitor's letters had gone unanswered and those that were sent recorded had been returned. On the few occasions that Four Eyes answered the phone she promised to return the call but she never did. We were resigned to the fact that there would be no one from my side of the family giving evidence supporting me.

I was removing her statement from the file when I took a call from my solicitor, Sarah Webb. She had just received the Social Services file that we had requested over nine months previously. Two large files were now at the office. Copies had been served on the court and my mother's solicitors at the same time. It was now Wednesday afternoon and we had less than two working days to go through the files and extract from them anything relevant. I was absolutely certain that the files would contain some of the dark secrets of my family. I would go through the files as quickly as possible and highlight anything of relevance for my lawyers. I agreed to drive to the office and pick up my files. They were waiting for me in reception. Returning to my car, I opened the blue file first. I was very disappointed: there was nothing in it that assisted my case. Next I started to read the red file. The manuscript and copy notes were all in order. When I got to notes about my brother Carl I started to laugh and by the time I had finished the notes in relation to Norma I was beside myself with joy. If my mother had read the documents as I had she would know that the storm clouds were gathering. My mother did not just abuse me and I had the evidence to prove it. I went through the entire file again and marked all the relevant pages in yellow marker. When I was finished it was getting dark. I returned my marked pages to reception with a note marked urgent for the attention of Sarah Webb. I was in a relaxed mood. My mother was in for a surprise and as for Precious Puss, there was no way that her interventions could help my mother this time.

2

Monday 17 November 2008

Day 1

The trial started on November 17 2008. On the first day I
made my way to my lawyer's office and at nine forty-five we
all went over to the High Court. It is an imposing Victorian
Gothic building at the junction of the Strand and Fleet Street
in London. I was used to entering as counsel; it felt strange to
be doing so as a litigant. As we negotiated the pedestrian
crossing to the front entrance, I could see a group of
photographers. I had been advised by my friend Richard
Willmott-Smith not to try to avoid them. If I did they would
only pursue me. They took their photographs. The next
morning many of them appeared on the front pages of the
newspapers. We were definitely going to be trying this case in
the full glare of publicity.

As we went through security I set off the alarm system – a
bad omen? I spotted my mother over on the right sitting on a
low plinth. She was surrounded by several members of my
immediate and extended family. I recognised Precious Puss,
Martin, Cynthia, Norma, Winston, Gina, Denise and her
child, Ianna, Pauline's eldest child. Jean Bignall, the daughter
of Josephine and Peanut Nose, was a distant relative on my
father's side. I counted eighteen of them as we walked past. I
was mortified. It was just I and my solicitor. In court I sat
with Sarah on the front row closest to the jury box. There
was space for family members if they wished to join us but I

knew that was not going to happen. It was another fifteen minutes before my mother and her witnesses and supporters came into court. They occupied the back four rows and their lawyers, Mr Panton and Mr Rene, sat immediately in front of them. They seemed to fill the court. I was on my own. I had asked my partner and children not to come. I had always fought my way in the world alone. It had been my decision to publish and I would see it through myself.

At ten thirty the lawyers were ready. My Queen's Counsel, Andrew Caldecott, smiled encouragement at me as he sat in the row behind. The usher by the judge's door called on everybody to stand as the judge entered court. Mr Justice Tugendhat was quite majestic. The dais where he sat was well above the level of the rest of the court and in any event he was over six feet tall. As he took his seat both lawyers remained on their feet while the rest of us rested our bottoms on the lightly varnished oak.

'Are we ready for the jury?'

'Yes,' replied both counsel.

The usher disappeared and we all waited for her to return.

'My lord,' said Mr Caldecott. 'We have prepared jury bundles for the jury. We have decided that since our bundles are chronologically paginated, the bundles should be put before the jury rather than those of the claimant, Mrs Carmen Briscoe. If the jury require additional documents then they can be inserted into the bundles at a later stage.'

My mother had some surprise documents she wanted to show the jury. We had no idea what they were but we would find out eventually.

'Do you agree, Mr Panton?'

'I do, my lord.'

The usher returned followed by a line-up of fifteen potential jurors. I tried my best not to look at them. In my experience it was never wise to stare at the people who would have the responsibility of deciding issues during the trial.

The clerk of the court stood up, shuffled her cards and said to the waiting jurors: 'Members of the jury, when I call out your name will you please say yes and walk over to the jury panel.'

I sat with Sarah, my solicitor. Andrew Caldecott was sitting behind us and his junior, Kate Wilson, was sitting behind him. The jury were sworn in and as number twelve was sworn in, I looked discreetly over in their direction. Seven men and five women. One juror of mixed parentage.

'Members of the jury, this trial is set to last at least two weeks but both counsel have said that it may go into a third week, so could you please just check your diaries and make sure you are available. This is a case that is likely to attract a fair amount of publicity, so please make sure that you do not discuss the case in public; you should only discuss the case when you are in your room together. If anyone tries to talk to you about this case please let the usher or a member of the staff know and I will deal with the matter. From time to time, matters of law will arise; when they do I will rise and invite you to retire in order to deal with the matters. The reason for that is that matters of law are a matter for me and matters of fact are for you. Finally, you are about to be handed copies of the book called *Ugly*. You will see immediately that certain passages are marked in yellow with a blue sticker on the relevant pages. We have all agreed that you will be invited to take the book home with you overnight and you should read as much of the book as possible, so that you are able to place the marked passages in context. But it will be the marked passages that you will be invited to decide on in due course and I will direct you later at the end of the trial. The trial will start tomorrow, that is to say that counsel will open the case then, but in the meantime Mr Panton would like to say a few words to you.'

'Yes, my lord,' said Mr Panton. 'Perhaps the jury could be handed a copy of the book *Ugly*.'

The court usher approached Sarah and she was at the ready. Twelve copies of my book were handed up.

Mr Panton cleared his throat. 'Members of the jury. You

have now all been handed a copy of *Ugly*. I have just a few words to say. Firstly my name is Mr Panton and sitting beside me is Mr Rene. We act on behalf of the claimant, Mrs Carmen Briscoe. The defendant, Constance Briscoe and Hodders Publishing House, are represented by Mr Caldecott QC and Miss Wilson. On behalf of Mrs Briscoe it is not our case that Constance Briscoe has exaggerated events that she has chosen to include in her book. It is our case that from start to finish she has invented events that did not happen. She has included serious allegations of assaults, not just occasional but repeated assaults, persistent neglect and criminal acts. She has chosen to say these things in her book. She chose to put them in her book; it is our case that they are pure fiction.

'These things did not happen. She claims that she was punched by her stepfather and that on one occasion he stubbed out a cigarette on her hand and that there was an occasion when she needed surgery on her breasts because of traumas caused by her mother's assaults. These are very serious allegations and you would expect cogent evidence from Miss Constance Briscoe and Hodders to establish the truth of these matters. You must ask yourself, can you rely on the memory of Constance Briscoe? When I read the book, I kept looking back and asking myself, how old was the author when these events happened? You have to decide whether the direct dialogue between Miss Constance Briscoe and the others is real. And whether someone can remember that far back? Mrs Briscoe's evidence will be that these incidents never happened. Mrs Carmen Briscoe is seeking damages for the libel in relation to the defamation action especially the parts that have been highlighted for you.

'You will have to decide whether these incidents did happen or whether they are a piece of fiction as Mrs Carmen Briscoe suggests. Members of the jury, I will continue with my opening address tomorrow.'

As Mr Panton sat down the judge turned towards the

jury. 'Members of the jury, that is all for today. Please take a copy of the book *Ugly* with you and we will meet again tomorrow.'

'All rise,' said the usher, as the court stood to attention.

'All persons having anything to do with the Queen's Peace will meet again here tomorrow at ten thirty.'

The judge walked out of court, followed by his clerk. My legal team gathered their documents together to walk back to Mr Caldecott's chambers for a conference.

It was a very odd experience for me to be a defendant. I was being sued by my mother because she claimed I had told a pack of lies. She had been sitting to my left about five or six rows behind and she was in her element. I was astonished that she was supported by so many of my siblings. What on earth could they say? Norma was there. Norma! She had such a poor relationship with my mother that I was surprised that she would sit on the same bench with her, let alone give evidence supporting my mother's account that she was not an abusive mother.

I avoided eye contact with my mother; she was the last person I wanted to see. I had dismissed her from my life many years ago and I saw no reason to change that decision. She did not exist as far as I was concerned and her defamation action was as hilarious as it was ridiculous. I only hoped that the jury would look at the evidence with care and not be persuaded by the numbers. My mother was calling six witnesses on her behalf to say the abuse never happened, that she was a good mother and that she never hit one of her children. I was apparently the only liar in the family. I only had a witness statement from Angela Fuentes, the Spanish lady who gave me my first cleaning job when I was fourteen. She was now aged seventy-four and suffering from lymphatic leukemia, bronchitis and other ailments. She wanted to give evidence on my behalf but her son Terry had refused to allow her to travel back to London. Under no circumstances would he allow her to travel. He argued that she was too ill to travel back to London. As Angela's health deteriorated we were advised to take a sworn statement. If she died before the trial we would need to persuade the judge that the jury should be allowed to hear what she would have said.

3

Day 2

The court stood to attention as the judge entered.

'Are you ready, Mr Panton?'

'My lord, yes, I believe we are ready.'

The jury returned. Mr Panton resumed his opening.

'My lord. Ladies and gentlemen, I am sure you have all had an opportunity to read the relevant sections of the book. I am not sure if you have actually read the whole thing, but during the next nine days you will take the opportunity to do so. At some stage today, or later in the trial, you will be told that in terms of the dates – well, the years mentioned in the index of the book – it is not 1968 for example that the particular incident occurred, but it is some time in the late 1960s or early 1970s, and the focus of what you will be told is that the dates do not matter. The allegations of child abuse are certainly matters that you should concentrate on. Constance Briscoe chose to write the book and it is for her to prove its truth. Having written this book, having put a year against each chapter, you will now be told, "Well, forget about whether or not it is 1965, 1966, 1971, 1972, that does not matter." If you simply concentrate on child abuse in one sense it does not matter, but it is important, in my submission to you, to the credibility of Constance Briscoe because if a book is published with those dates set out and you are then told, "Forget about years, concentrate on decades, the 1960s and the 1970s," you may begin to wonder. This book deals with a period of thirty to forty years ago. If we go to 1965, according to the book, by that stage Mrs Briscoe had six children of her own and adopted a seventh. Therefore, she was looking after seven children under ten. The book tells you that her husband, Mr George Briscoe, was hardly ever to be seen.

'The picture painted by Miss Constance Briscoe is that every opportunity that her mother had she was being punched, kicked and beaten with a stick. You will see from documents and evidence that will be produced that Constance visited Dr McManus on a number of occasions, but she was never treated for any of those injuries she claimed were inflicted by her mother. There is a suggestion that after a fight with Mr Eastman she had seen a doctor, but in terms of the other allegations it is not said that she was seen by a doctor.

'For example, she mentions that she drank Domestos, in order to try and kill herself. Remember her saying, "Domestos kills all known germs" because she was called "a germ". She refused medical help.

'You will also see in the book that on two occasions she mentioned going to the police station. So there were opportunities to complain about ill treatment, if that ill treatment had in fact taken place.

'There is also the incident where she talks about the split-split stick. You get the impression, members of the jury, that this twelve-year-old child was beaten with a plank, or was it a stick, constantly. She said that she went to her room. Her stomach was hurting from her mother's kick. She lay on the floor with her hands under her chin. She then describes – I am sure you read that last night or yesterday – that she did not feel like doing her homework or organising her schoolbag for the following day. She remained on the floor and at some point fell asleep. "Someone covered me with a blanket in the middle of the night. Someone also woke me and reminded me to go to school." As she came through the school gate she was feeling quite ill. Her head still hurt although it had stopped bleeding long ago; her lip was still swollen, her eye partially closed. Then she describes her schoolmaster, Mr Timmons calling her. "Clare Briscoe," he said, "Clare Briscoe, come here immediately." He saw her with these injuries and all he did was send her to go to the first-aid room; he later called Mrs Briscoe and it was decided that Miss Constance could go and live with a teacher, Miss K.

'A child turning up at school in the condition she has described, her head in the condition she described, an eye closed, as she described, and all the head teacher did was agree that she could go and live with one of the teachers; did not call Social Services; did not call the police! And Miss Briscoe, ladies and gentlemen, who, you have heard, went down to the Magistrates Court at twelve to complain about Mr Eastman, did not complain to her teacher on this occasion? And the story about Miss K, ladies and gentlemen, describes many happy weeks living with her. Then it is said Miss K had her leg amputated and would require constant prayers for her recovery. No one ever spoke about her again except at Friday prayers. It is fiction, ladies and gentlemen. The suggestion in the book that Mrs Briscoe gave her consent to Constance Briscoe living with Mrs Korchinskye never happened.

'It is extremely sad that a family should find itself in court in these circumstances. Mrs Carmen Briscoe provided for her children, all of them equally, to the best of her ability. It is interesting, ladies and gentlemen, that in the book it is said that, in relation to the other sisters, none of them were treated the same; the other children were not touched. That is the story of the book. Is it true? Is it substantially true or is it a story made up by Miss Constance Briscoe? Because, at the end of the day, that is something you will have to decide. You will also hear from other siblings of Miss Constance Briscoe and they will tell you about their experience of their mother. There is a suggestion in the book that Miss Constance Briscoe always had her own room. She says, because of her bed-wetting, she was given her own space. Not true. She says she was abandoned by her mother at

Sutherland Square. There was no question of Miss Constance Briscoe being abandoned. A large number of matters that this book touches on are disputed.'

As Mr Panton sat down, I wondered if the jury would appreciate that abused children usually did not complain or report their abuse. I had seen it often enough myself in court cases. They kept quiet, sometimes through fear or simply because they thought the way they were treated was the norm. Why would I make all this up? If I lost this case my whole career in the law would be over. You cannot practise as a lawyer if you are a proven liar. Why would I risk everything I had worked so hard to achieve?

4

Day 3

The next morning the papers were full of what a liar I was. No doubt there were those who would be happy to believe that I'd written an untruthful misery memoir. In any event, my book was much more than a misery memoir. It showed what could be achieved if you tried hard enough.

In court the jury would hear Andrew Caldecott's opening for the defence. He is a wiry man with a gentle, rather academic manner. I knew he was concerned about how to cross examine an elderly lady without losing sympathy. I also knew how persuasive his powers of analysis could be. He rose and faced the jury.

'Ladies and gentlemen of the jury,' he said, 'I am going to start, if I may, with an unpopular move, by crowding your jury box with six files of documents, a set between each two of you. You will also be given highlighters for your own assistance. The only document that Mr Panton has referred you to in his opening is the book. You will see that there are a number of other documents in this case and we shall submit at the end of the case that these documents are very important. Can I just give you one example? Mr Panton told you that Carmen Briscoe's case is that Constance Briscoe never had her own bedroom. There is an article which you will find, an article published in the *Mail on Sunday* on the 22nd January 2006, not long after this book was published. This is Mrs Carmen Briscoe and some of the family giving their response to the book, saying in summary, "It's a pack of lies." Patsy, the closest sister in age to Constance, gave an interview. Constance was known then and still is to the family as Clare. Look at what was said to the *Mail on Sunday*:

' "But Patsy remembers it very differently. She says Mum tried everything to help Clare. She took her to lots of doctors. Clare was given a room by herself to give her some privacy." We will have to wait and see what she says now. The importance of this little issue is obvious, if Clare was sharing a bedroom with her sisters, any assault on her in her bedroom would have been in their presence. If she was not sharing a bedroom with them, they obviously were not there.

'Of course, mothers are older than their daughters and in this case Carmen Briscoe is now in her mid-seventies; her daughter is twenty-four years younger. But what you must remember throughout this case is that we are dealing with events when Mrs Briscoe was in her prime and when Constance Briscoe was a child. The most important years in this case run from 1964, when Constance Briscoe was seven and her mother was thirty-one, to 1975 when Constance Briscoe was eighteen and her mother was forty-two.

'You will find in your files a list of the children and when they were born. When you turn to the step-family, the Eastman children – Cynthia, Norma, Winston and Georgina – you will see that the gap between Constance and Cynthia is already eight years. So there is quite a gap between Constance and the Eastman children. During the key events, they would either not be around or very young.

'Now, Constance Briscoe's case can be summed up, really, in a few words. She says that she was the victim of sustained cruelty and serious neglect while she was a child. She chose to say it; she has to prove it. Proving it means proving it by evidence. The book itself is not evidence. Please bear in mind this is not a trial of the accuracy of every word and paragraph in this book. If it were, we would probably be here until next Christmas and not merely this Christmas. It is for you to determine whether it is true or not that Constance Briscoe was physically and emotionally abused and neglected by her mother over a lengthy period in circumstances which were cruel and demeaning.

'Nobody's memory is perfect and there are a number of mistakes in the book. One area where Constance Briscoe accepts that she is in error is in relation to some of the dates, but you will see in the third sentence of the book, Chapter One, "My Family", there is this sentence, "It's difficult to remember the order of things."

'One of the important issues in this case is how memory works. With the most painful things we have experienced in our childhood, we tend to remember the events themselves. We also, perhaps, tend to remember the most satisfying or pleasant experiences, but what we do not necessarily remember is the exact year in which they happened. Where you have sustained abuse over a long period of time it is likely that some events will stick in the mind more than others and that the timing will be less clear than if those instances of abuse had stood alone. Another point, about conversations – nobody in their right mind would think that Miss Constance Briscoe has a tape recorder in her head and that every conversation in here is verbatim accurate. It obviously is not. It is her attempt to re-create what she remembers, how she remembers the exchanges with the characters. This is not the Old Bailey and you are not sitting in a criminal case. You do not have to be satisfied that the book is true beyond reasonable doubt, you merely have to be satisfied that Constance Briscoe's account is, in substance, more likely than not. It is what lawyers call "the balance of probabilities".

'This is a case about reputation. That is what a libel case is about. Parents who regularly inflict cruelty on their children and neglect them have no reputation left to protect. You may think at the end of this case that there is not actually much room for shades of grey. Indeed, Mr Panton says it is either fiction or it is not. You may think that whatever errors of detail there are, the core question here is: is Constance Briscoe a fantasist, a malicious inventor, or has she done her best to tell the truth of what was a very unhappy childhood?

'Members of the jury, I want to take you on four very short tours down memory lane using some of the key documents as signposts as to what was happening in the case of Constance Briscoe.

'You will remember in the book that Constance Briscoe's bed-wetting is a source of many of the assaults on her account. The first document I want to show you is dated 3rd April 1964, so Constance is about six weeks away from her seventh birthday. She is six years old when this document comes into existence. The letter is addressed to Dr McManus, who is now dead. It reads: "I understand that you are this child's family doctor. She was seen by one of the council's medical officers at St Joseph's Roman Catholic School and was found to be suffering from enuresis." That is the doctor's Latin word for bed-wetting. Now, just using a little common sense about this document, six year olds are not commonly examined by council medical officers at school. What provoked this examination? Constance Briscoe will say it was because she smelt of urine and that is how this problem came to the attention of the school. So this is one small document on the trail.

'The second journey I want to take you on starts with a rather intimate medical problem but it is important to deal with it because of the context of what follows. These are Dr McManus' manuscript notes. Like many doctor's notes they are not the easiest to read unless you are Dr McManus. The date is 10th September 1971. It reads: "Hard mobile lump breast" then there is a diagram with the mark as to where the hard lump is and then the word "ref", which is a referral to hospital.

'We now turn to the next month and 21st October 1971. This is a letter from St Thomas's Hospital to Dr McManus: "I have recently seen your patient in Mr Pullam's Outpatients complaining of lumps in both breasts for two and a half years." The next letter in January 1972 reads: "This girl was admitted on 12th January complaining of lumps in both breasts, that in the right breast had been present for two years and that in the left for two months. They were removed on 13th January under general anaesthesia. There was no evidence of malignancy. She made a normal post-operative recovery and was discharged home on 15th January. She will be seen again in Outpatients later this month."

'You will next see a reference to a visit to Outpatients on 9th February, recorded on 10th February: "This young lady attended Outpatients yesterday following a recent excision of fibroadenomata at puberty. There is no sign of recurrence and she has been discharged back to your care."

'Carmen Briscoe's case throughout this action has been that there was only ever one lump on one breast. This operation left scars. There are, in fact, three lumps that were removed, two on one breast and one on the other. The scars are still there and have been photographed. It is curious that a mother does not seem to remember how many scars there were on her daughter's breast, how many lumps were removed. It is a small matter but it is a matter that I shall explore in due course with Carmen Briscoe.

'What then happened on 9th February is important. Constance was not aware of the next two letters when she wrote the book. This is a letter dated 11th February and it starts off: "This young girl attended Outpatients two days ago. She told a nurse that her mother had hurt her breasts because she wet the bed. When questioned she was tearful and upset. She said her mother and stepfather had hit, kicked, punched and pinched her. She was made to sleep in a wet bed and was beaten with a stick. She claimed that she had previously tried to get in a home but had been unsuccessful. She expressed a wish to die and go to heaven. As she has now been discharged back to your care you may wish to investigate the matter with some urgency."

'This letter is written some thirty-three years before the book is published. Constance is talking to a nurse in a hospital. She is not talking to the headmaster at her school. She is not talking to a policeman. She is talking to a nurse at a hospital. You may be able to think of reasons why she might have made that choice. The impression you have is that she is not talking about a chapter which is closed. She refers to wishing to go to a home and she refers to a wish to die and go to heaven. So she is in a state of some distress.

'The next letter is dated 17th February and it reads, "This young girl attended Outpatients yesterday . . ." so that is a visit on 16th February. It is exactly a week after the first visit to Outpatients on the 9th. "This young girl attended Outpatients yesterday and spoke to a nurse with whom she had previously spoken [that is reference back to the other letter] and requested information about homes for unwanted children and hostels in the area. She was anxious, tearful and unwilling to go home. She told nurses her mother had crashed a plane into her face and cut her hand with a knife because she upset a chicken. She claimed that her stepfather had burned her hand with a cigarette butt and touched her privates. She is not suicidal but admitted a prior failed attempt at taking her life to go to heaven. As she was discharged back into your care on 10th February you may wish to add this information to the investigation in progress." 10th February is, of course, the day after the first visit to Outpatients. The reference to the aeroplane is on page 86 of the book; that is just three lines from the end of the first paragraph. The reference to the chicken incident is on pages 70 to 73 of the book. The cigarette butt is pages 131 to 132 of the book. The reference to Mr Eastman touching her privates is at pages 39 to 40 of the book and the unsuccessful suicide attempt at pages 2 to 5.

'The third trip down memory lane relates to a social work assessment in relation to Norma Eastman. She is almost ten years younger than Constance. It is written by a social worker called Michael Owen and it is dated 5th October 1998. Again, several years before the book *Ugly* was written. Mr Owen starts off by giving a short summary of Norma Eastman's life. "Miss Eastman describes her experience of being a child as difficult. Her mother Carmen Briscoe used physical methods to discipline her and her siblings and some of these chastisements were severe. Her mother would use implements to discipline them. Miss Eastman left home when she was fourteen years of age."

'One of the matters I shall be probing with Mrs Briscoe is her picture of a happy family. I will suggest this family was very far from happy under the surface. Look at what Norma had to say about her own upbringing: "Miss Eastman's own childhood was troubled. There was, by her opinion, severe physical abuse inflicted on her by her mother."

'Next there are a number of magistrate court documents about an assault. You will see that the name of the informant is Constance Briscoe and the defendant Mr Garfield Eastman. You will see at the very top of the page, date of entry, 27th August 1975. Just note she is eighteen by this time, so she is really more a young woman than a girl by this stage. This is a memorandum of an entry and the register of Camberwell Green Magistrates Court. That court had to be satisfied that the incident referred to here happened before ordering what we see in the penultimate box, that Mr Eastman be "bound over for twelve months in the sum of £10". That is to keep the peace; to behave yourself. If you breach a "bind over" you can go to prison. So it is more serious than may at first appear. The assault, you will see in the fourth box down, takes place at 19 Sutherland Square where Constance Briscoe is living, and the date of the assault is 13th July 1975.

'Mr Eastman, you will hear, was a powerfully built man; Constance Briscoe was a girl of eighteen. The matter did not end here on 13th July, because look what happened on 27th August. This is nearly two weeks after that fight took place. Bear in mind, please, Mr Eastman does not live at 19 Sutherland Square. He has had a fight with Constance Briscoe, putting it neutrally, on 13th July, but for some reason he goes back and this records what happened when he went back: "He did unlawfully use certain threats towards the said complainant whereby she apprehends she was in danger of her life or some bodily harm that he will do or cause to be done unto her against the peace."

'Even that was not an end of it, Mr Eastman goes back, again to Sutherland Square, where he does not live, and he gives her another dose of threats on the following day.

'The last chapter is moving away from the question of cruelty, to the question of neglect. This requires me to give you a little background as to where the family were living at important points in the story. Now, Mrs Briscoe's case is that when she bought 5 Vaughan Road the three Briscoe daughters moved there, while the rest of the family stayed in Sutherland Square. She then says that after a few weeks the daughters thought that 5 Vaughan Road was haunted, and so she decided to reverse the roles and the three Briscoe daughters came to Sutherland Square and the rest of the family went to 5 Vaughan Road. So there is a change around after a few weeks. But the most important part of her case is this: Mrs Briscoe says she continued every evening to come to Vaughan Road with the entire family to make the evening meal.

'Constance Briscoe says that is completely wrong. She never went to Vaughan Road and she was not welcome there. When in early 1973 the other eight children and Mrs Briscoe and Mr Eastman went to 5 Vaughan Road, she and her two sisters were left to fend for themselves at Sutherland Square. Constance Briscoe's case is that Mrs Briscoe would turn up and make demands for money from Constance to pay for the utility bills at the house. She would cut off the electricity if she was not paid and Constance had to use candles when that happened.

'But what is extraordinary about this is the idea that Mrs Briscoe, with eight young children, I think the youngest at this time are one and three, would travel every night all the way to Sutherland Square and all the way back. Why on earth, one asks oneself, did the Briscoe daughters, Pauline, Patsy and Constance, not simply go from Sacred Heart School to Vaughan Road to eat, if this was to be the arrangement, and then go back to Sutherland Square?

'There is here another question, which you might ask yourself. If Mrs Briscoe was going to Sutherland Square every evening, surely she would know a fair amount about what her daughter was up to. She would know if she was working early in the morning every day before she went to school. This was in fact the case. Constance used to work from six a.m. to eight a.m. and then she would change into her school uniform in an alleyway and go to school. She did this to meet the bills her mother was demanding to be paid.

'In sad stories, nearly always, thank God, whether it is Dickens or real life, there is a rescuer or two, and you will hear at least from one of the rescuers. She is a very ill lady now, rather old, who is in Spain. You will hear evidence about how she helped Constance Briscoe out at this difficult time. Girls aged fourteen or fifteen would not normally be very enthusiastic about working from six to eight in the morning before going to school, because obviously, to start work at six a.m. you have to get up a fair deal earlier, and the details of this will be dealt with by Miss Briscoe in evidence. This is just to give you a glimpse of what is going on with Constance Briscoe's working life, as well as her studying life, as a relatively young girl.

'The last boring file relates to Constance Briscoe's national insurance records. Constance Briscoe's date of entry into the national insurance scheme was 22nd July 1972 and the address on the record at the time was 19 Sutherland Square. Look at 1972 to 1973, September to September, thirty-six contribution weeks, and you will see that there are sixteen weeks credited for full-time education, making up the full fifty-two. She is fifteen in September 1972, sixteen in May 1973. She is still at school. Look at September 1973 to September 1974 when Constance was sixteen to seventeen, every single week, she worked. She is still at school, every single week she is working, paying her contributions. A full fifty-two. In September 1974 to April 1975 there are thirty-one weeks. You may think it is a pretty young age and pretty demanding to have to be working like that while you are also trying to pass your exams.

'I end only by standing back once again, as I did at the beginning. There is obviously a very big question in this case as to why Constance Briscoe wrote this book. I think it is one of those questions where it is best that I do not try to give the answer for her. She is an articulate lady and I think she should tell you why she wrote the book. But I only say that if this book is from pillar to post a work of fiction, it is an extraordinarily wicked thing to do or a mad thing to do. But we say this book was properly put in the Biography section of a bookshop, not in the fiction section. That, members of the jury, at the end of this case, is ultimately the issue, which you are going to have to try.'

Mr Justice Tugendhat turned to the jury: 'Members of the jury, it is time to take a short break in any event.

'It is unlikely that there will be anything useful you can do before two p.m. in this court, so I will invite you to retire now and to be back in the jury box at that time.'

I felt a lot better now the jury had heard the defence opening. Surely the documentary evidence would give the lie to my mother?

5

Thursday 20 November 2008

Day 4

The next morning, I was not feeling very well. As I looked at myself in the bathroom mirror, it was obvious that I had had a bad night. For the first time in my life I appeared to have bags under my eyes. Today was an important day for me. My mother would give her evidence. Maybe I would get some answers. I wanted to know 'why me?' Why not Four Eyes or Precious Puss? What was it about me that made my mother decide that I was the chosen one? How does she feel about it now?

When I arrived at court I again followed the advice of my friend Richard Willmott-Smith and slowed down for the photographers. I hoped the bags under my eyes would not show. Inside the High Court my mother was sitting in the same location as the previous day. The number of her groupies had grown overnight.

Mr Justice Tugendhat was a stickler for punctuality and entered precisely at ten thirty.

'Yes, Mr Panton?'

But it was not Mr Panton who stood up. Mr Rene stood up. This was very unusual in a case like this, which had attracted so much publicity and would be reported. The person who should have stood up and asked questions was the leading lawyer. Mr Rene was the junior lawyer and he was only allowed to speak with the agreement of Mr Panton. He was of slim build. His long plaited hair descended below his wig to his shoulders.

'We call our first witness, Mrs Briscoe.'

My mother got up from her seat at the back of the court and walked towards the witness stand. She was in a felt hat and a black and red coat. She looked quite smart. She had aged quite well, but I could still see in my mind's eye the abusive streaks when she burst into my bedroom on her nightly visits. She was exactly as I remembered her as a child: tough, uncaring, I felt complete revulsion as she looked around the court.

'Mrs Briscoe,' said the judge, 'you are welcome to stay seated if you wish, but it is more difficult to speak loudly when you are seated.'

'Can you give the court your full name?' Mr Rene said.

'My name is Carmen May Briscoe-Mitchell.'

'And your address?'

'Nineteen Sutherland Square, London, SE17.'

'How many children do you have?'

'I have got eleven children. Six Briscoes and one adopted. Pauline, Patsy, Constance, Carlton, Martin and Christine and Denise was adopted, but she is a Briscoe. The next four children: Cynthia, Norma, Winston and Georgina have the surname Eastman.'

'Your relationship with George Briscoe: what part did he play in the children's lives?'

'My husband was not there to help me along with these children. He would not maintain his children. George Briscoe was in and out of my life. He would just come and make a baby and go to his girlfriend and that was my life. He did not make any contribution. My husband refused to pay.'

'Had he ever made any voluntary payments to you in respect of the children?'

'No, not at all, but the children they would have gone to him and his mistress's house in Peckham to see him there.'

'What about in relation to food parcels?'

'No. He did not want to know about his children; got no interest them at all.'

I knew that wasn't true. At one stage my father had tried to get custody of us. He failed because he could not look after us, but he did care. He would be turning in his grave to hear all this.

'What about visits made to see the children?'

'He never made visit to see the children.'

'Can you explain to the court the sleeping arrangements in relation to the whole family. Can we start with the ground floor?'

'I was the one that slept on the ground floor with two small children. On the first floor is a kitchen at the back and Mr Bem in the other room in the middle there, and Denise and Christine Briscoe at the front. On the second floor Pauline and Patsy and a folding bed the other side for Constance. And Martin and Carlton, the two boys were in the back. While the whole family were living at 19 Sutherland Square no child occupied their own bedroom. We were a very happy family.'

'Did you ever have any problems at all with the children?'

'I never had any problem with my children. The boys they could be a little bit mischievous, but my girls they were excellent and my children were my pride and joy.'

'In relation to Constance Briscoe, what name did you call her by?'

'I call her Clare. Clare was the fairest one, very fair. She was a pretty girl. Beautiful. Constance did wet the bed and I had to take her to Dr McManus for help.'

I could not believe my ears. She said I was beautiful. What a joke. Oh how it must have pained my mother to describe me as beautiful, fair and pretty. I thought she had got the wrong child. She was really describing Precious Puss.

'Do you remember how old she was when you first took her to Dr McManus about bed-wetting?'

'About say, three, four. She was continuing to wet the bed and the rest stopped and she did not stop. But I could cope with it until when Dr McManus send me to get this beep, beep alarm.'

'Tell us how this alarm worked.'

'Well, this alarm, I remember taking her to Stockwell and we got a sheet. It plug into the electric and as soon as the urine hit that sheet it would make a beep, beep noise and she would wake up or I would go up and make sure, if she completely empty her bladder I would empty, clear – change the bed sheet. Or if she wakes up I would assist her.'

'From the age of four, up to what age was Constance Briscoe still wetting the bed?'

'Well, the beep, beep alarm did help at an early stage. So when she was going to St Joseph's she was not wetting the bed.'

'From what age are we saying that she stopped wetting the bed?'

'Well, if she start to wet the bed at four, about five. Five when she start infant school, she was not a wet bed girl any more.'

'You are sure that it was at the age of five?'

'Yes because she did not even have to use the beep, beep alarm any more because she was not wetting the bed.'

'What triggers your memory about the age of five?'

'Because I would have to wash the wet bed sheets, but she was not wetting the bed then.'

So, I thought, what about the letter from St Joseph's when I was six? What about making me sleep in wet bed sheets from the night before?

Mr Rene paused and picked up a copy of the book.

'Mrs Briscoe, I will now be dealing with the contents of the book, so I will be referring you to different sections of the book. I would first of all like to refer you to page eighteen of the book. This deals with an incident in 1962 when Constance Briscoe says you stabbed your husband with a pair of scissors over a chicken. Mrs Briscoe, do you remember this incident ever happening?'

'My husband never bring chicken to my house at all. I remember the incident with the scissors. My husband, he was a gambler and he came to take half my children family allowance money off me, and I refused to give it to him. When my husband was fighting me I have got the scissors in my hand, right, and accidentally he got stabbed with the scissors. I can tell you at that time Constance was not born. I was pregnant with Patsy, and Pauline was just a little tot at my side. Constance was not born.'

'Right. You are saying that the incident with the scissors had nothing to do with chickens?'

'No, not at all.'

I knew my mother was confusing two incidents. The one I described and another my father had told me about another earlier attack before I was born.

Mr Rene moved on to page 24.

'This refers to Georgie Porgie. What was his real name?'

'George Harris. He was very nice, loving.'

'What was his relationship like with the children?'

'Very good. Very good. He and his wife cared for them.'

'The book talks about Georgie Porgie tickling Constance Briscoe and sitting her on his knee. You understand the sugges-tion that is being made in the book about Georgie Porgie. What do you say about this suggestion?'

'Georgie Porgie was a second father for my – first father for my children. He – they cared for my children. They look after my children and Georgie Porgie is not that type of a man. Not at all.'

'During the period that you knew he had spent time with the children, had there been any complaints at all from the children to you in relation to his conduct?'

'No. No, and it was not Mr Harris on his own, it was Mr and Mrs Harris. Mr Harris was a dustman. He emptied bins. He and Rose would look after my children. So they were well cared for.'

'Next can you tell us about the time when you were giving birth to Christine and what happened around that time and in relation to Denise as well?'

'Well, Denise and Beauty my youngest Briscoe were born the same day. I and Denise's mother met up in the same ward and she explained to me that she had a problem with her schooldays' boyfriend. She get pregnant and the father did not want to have anything to do with the baby. She was living in Manchester and she came down to London to have the baby. And she explained to me her problem and she said she was going to leave the baby in the hospital. I told her that I would look after the baby until she go back to Manchester and sort herself out. And she leave that child on me. Well, I decide I would adopt Denise because I have got a place in my heart for Denise and I would not let Denise go away from me.'

'In relation to the Social Services visits, did you ever receive a letter from Social Services expressing concern at the way that Denise was being treated?'

'No. No.'

'Did you ever receive a letter from Social Services at that time highlighting any concerns about any of your other children?'

'No. No.'

'Chapter Three of the book, which is titled "A New Father", that is in relation to Mr Eastman. Can you describe Mr Eastman's character? What kind of a person was he at that time?'

'Mr Eastman? He was a better father than Mr Briscoe, my husband, anyway. He was loving, he was caring and he was helpful.'

'By the time you then had children with him, how did he treat the Briscoe children in relation to his own children?'

'He treat the Briscoe children well. I was the one in control of my children. I was the mother and I was everything, and he – he was there for the children. Oh, God, do I have to go through this?'

My mother was shaking her head from side to side as she patted her large brimmed hat down on her head. As I looked at her I could see that she was not crying at all. There were no tears. No weepy eyes. Her head was slightly down and she had a very pained expression on her face. When she looked across the court I knew she was looking at Precious Puss.

The judge intervened.

'Would you like us to take a short pause, Mrs Briscoe?'

'Yes. I could continue, sir, but my heart is breaking.'

The jury followed the usher out of court as my mother sat with her head in her hand. She gave the appearance to everyone in court that she was distressed. I am sure she was, but I was interested in the cause of her discomfiture. Her barrister had not asked her any difficult questions. There was nothing that was outside the remit of her knowledge. If she was going to get distressed so readily I wondered how she might cope when my barrister asked questions of her. After a few minutes the case resumed.

'Mrs Briscoe,' said Mr Rene, 'I am going to read you a passage from the book about Clare and Mr Eastman, when he comes to speak to her in her bedroom. "I listened and then decided that I really did not want to listen any more, so I stretched past him and reached for my black doll. I pulled Dolly in with my right hand, but lost my balance and I tried to scoop her off the floor. The covers fell away from me, half exposing my bottom. I did not have any clothes on. As I tried to regain my balance, I was partly on the floor on my hands and knees and partly on the bed with my feet in it and my bottom halfway out. I crawled backwards on my hands and ended up on my back in the bed, revealing my minnie. As I reached to cover myself up, Eastman grabbed my minnie and said, 'What a nice little mit'."'

'What do you say in relation to what has been said in the book about Mr Eastman's conduct there?'

'This is a disgrace to me and my family. It is a disgrace. Mr Eastman is not that type of man. No way. I do not even know what "minnie" is anyway. I have got no idea. And Mr Eastman . . . no, no, no. No. Oh, my God . . . Mr Eastman is a gentleman and he will always be a gentleman in my sight.'

'Have there ever been any complaints from any of the Briscoe girls in relation to Mr Eastman's conduct towards them?'

'No. No, never.'

'Has there ever been any complaint of sexual impropriety towards them?'

'Oh, for God's sake, do not even mention that. No. No.'

'Next, Mrs Briscoe, we are now looking at chapter four of the book. The heading is "Christmas Cheer" and the year is 1965. It describes a tussle between Mr Briscoe and Mr Eastman on Christmas Day. What do you have to say about this?'

'This sort of incident did not take place.'

It was obvious by now that if my mother was right, I had the most incredible imagination. Perhaps I should turn to writing fiction.

'I am now looking at chapter five,' said Mr Rene. 'The heading is "Ugly", and the year is 1966 according to the book. This is in relation to school photographs and it says that you would not buy the photograph of Constance Briscoe because she was too ugly. I just want to read a paragraph to you. "Jesus Christ, me gave birth to that?" She stared from the photograph to me. "Lord, sweet Lord, how come she is so ugly? Ugly, ugly. If I had not given birth to her, sweet Lord, I would have sworn she was a fraud. Heavenly Jesus, sweet and kind, why have you given me a swine? Look at that nose. Where did you get it from? Not from me." What do you say about those words?'

'No one could use this sort of language, no way. And Constance is not ugly.'

Her words were burnt into my memory. I remembered exactly the way my mother talked, calling on our Lord, but would the jury believe this?

'Could you turn to page seventy-two at the bottom of the page. It says that you were complaining that Constance who was plucking a chicken has missed some hairs and that you cut her arm with a knife. Can you tell the court did this incident ever happen?'

'This incident never happened and I do not think a mad person would have done this. No way. And I am not a mad person. I am not a mad woman.'

'Would you allow your children into the kitchen to do any form of cooking at that age?'

'No. No. My children do not even want to go and wash the dishes when I cook. They leave them there for Mummy to wash and I have to do it.'

That, I thought was over-egging the pud. Anyway I still had the scar on my arm.

'I will read a further passage to you and I would like your comment on that. "When the blood mixed with the water, it was a very pretty pink colour in the sink, swirling around with the hairs pulled from the chicken. I went down and got some toilet roll, wrapped it round my arm and went back to the kitchen."'

'Given the extent of what is said to have happened, would you expect that a child of nine years of age would have been able to go back and continue attending to the chicken in the kitchen, as is stated there?'

'Constance never go in the kitchen to do any cooking at nine years old, no.'

Mr Rene suggested to the judge that was an appropriate moment to adjourn to the next day. The judge agreed and warned the jury not to discuss the case with anyone. I did not look at them as they filed out, but could not help wondering if they found my mother plausible. I thought that she was doing well. I knew that she was telling a pack of lies but her soft sing-song voice could not hide a heart of solid steel. She was giving a very good impression of being a caring and loving mother but we had a few surprises for her when it was our turn to cross examine her.

Thursday 20 November 2008

Day 4 (continued)

Someone was laughing at the back of the court. My mother was holding court among her followers in the back rows of the public sitting area. Precious Puss was staring at me and I stared back. She had pure hatred in her eyes. She looked more like a skinny mouse than a precious puss. Her short haircut accentuated her sharp edges which she had sharpened for me. She had earlier sent me a letter in which she made it clear that she was looking forward to giving evidence against me. She had also sent me a card which had a message. She told me to repent because the Devil was looking for me. We had not got on well for very many years. Of all my sisters she was the one I liked the least.

'Mrs Carmen Briscoe, will you please come back to the witness box.'

As my mother walked across the court Mr Rene rose to his feet. 'Did Clare ever have new shoes which were in fact old shoes that you stretched?'

'I don't know anything about that, it is all lies.'

'Constance Briscoe's friend Mary visited the house. You apparently showed her the bed-wet alarm.'

'No, I did not.'

'What about the Holy Communion dress? She says that you gave her a yellow second-hand hand-me-down dress?'

'I did not. She had a pretty Holy Communion dress with lace. I remember it well.'

Mr Caldecott rose to his feet. 'My lord, I am getting very concerned. Mrs Carmen Briscoe has said that the New Shoes, the Mary incident and the Holy Communion dress were lies. She has never said that before today. We have come to court ready to deal with all the matters that Carmen Briscoe has identified as lies. It really is a little late in the day to raise other matters now. She has had well over a year to tell us what she accepts and what she does not.'

'Mr Rene,' said the judge, 'you have never previously said that the issues that you now raise are lies.'

'That is correct, my lord, but we would like to do so now. It would not be fair if you prevented us from dealing with these matters.'

Mr Rene had the audacity to talk about fairness. He knew perfectly well that he was out of order. Trying it on. It was Day Four and for the first time they were saying that there were other passages in the book which were apparently lies. Mr Panton knew perfectly well that he was under a duty to tell my solicitors well in advance of the trial what statements he would challenge so we could get our evidence to show the opposite. I strongly suspected that the reason it was not mentioned in the past two years was because they wanted to take us by surprise in court. The judge was not happy. He was not amused by this particular ploy.

'But your client is the claimant. She could have said that the whole book was a pack of lies. She chose not to do that. She made her choice and Constance Briscoe has come to court ready to deal with the matters that you have claimed were lies. She could not have anticipated that Carmen Briscoe would come with the suggestion of more lies in the middle of her evidence. If she had, she would have come armed with even more evidence and I intend to tell the jury at the end of the trial that the only matters that they should concern themselves with are the passages of the book which you have pleaded as untrue.'

'My lord, it is not in the interests of justice to stop me,' said Mr Rene.

'Well, if you continue I will direct the jury to ignore it.'

Mr Panton considered his options as the jury waited for his next question.

'Mrs Briscoe, the next incident is the aeroplane incident. Your daughter says that you flew it deliberately into her face as she entered the room. What is your recollection of the incident with the aeroplane?'

'Carlton, my son, did have a remote-control aeroplane. Georgie Porgie bought it for him and he was playing with it. I wasn't there. I hear screaming and Patsy called for me, that's all I know, and I went into the room and dressed it and that's it. It was a little scratch.'

'And what did you do when you heard the screaming?'

'I went down to find out what was going on and Patsy explained to me that Carlton accidentally fly the remote control aeroplane and she – she had a small scratch on her cheek. I just washed it, cleaned it. I did not fly the plane into her face.'

'Now to Notre Dame School. Did you stop your daughter from applying to that school?'

'First I've heard about that.'

'There is also the suggestion in the book that Constance Briscoe was given hand-me-down clothes?'

'That is not true, my daughter is a liar and before you ask me, I don't know about a split-split stick. There wasn't one in the house.'

'She said that you beat her with it. You grabbed her by the nipple then you let go, doubled your fist and punched her in the breast. The force caused her to fall backwards and then you raised the stick over her.'

'I wouldn't have done that. Where are these sticks? Not even a mad person would do these sort of things, even if you're completely mad, and I wasn't mad and I'm not mad now. I was there to look after my children, which I do. All of them.'

'Now, Mrs Briscoe, you said that you wouldn't have to hit Clare. So how would you basically discipline her?'

'Well, as I said yesterday, my children didn't give me any problems. The boys may be a little mischievous but Blackie, the dog, would sort them out until Mummy arrived. He wouldn't bite them but he would keep them quiet. Blackie, that was my dog. So, I wasn't mad, and I'm still not mad and I didn't hit Clare with no split-split stick. So, I don't even know what it look like.'

'If for instance, the children didn't do something you wanted them to do, how would you go about getting them to do what you wanted?'

'Constance was Clare, my favourite daughter, good daughter. She was a classic girl. I was the slave in the house and I love it. If I ask the girls to wash the dishes after supper they would hide them underneath the sink. I did all the work but those children were my pride and joy and they still are.'

This was all news to me. I am sure that my mother must have spent a great deal of time practising those words; she looked almost as sick as I felt. She kept looking over at her supporters. I glanced over my shoulder. Precious Puss was staring at me and I stared back and half laughed. My mother's evidence was comical.

'Now, Mrs Briscoe, the date in the book is 1969 and Constance Briscoe would have been twelve years of age at that time. She says that her boobs were of different sizes and shapes and when she examined them after "one of Mother's nipple-squeezing sessions", that she realised both were lumpy and deformed.'

'I did not squeeze Clare nipples. I took her to the doctor when she had a problem. I would not allow her to go and see the doctor on her own any time under the age of eighteen. Away from the letter that Dr McManus give her to go to the hospital there was no need for her to go back.'

'What happened when you went to the hospital?'

'The doctor examined her and said she had a minor cyst and they have to remove it. She spent about three, four days in hospital and I went to the hospital to visit her.'

'In the trial documents there is a letter from Saint Thomas' Hospital, dated 21st October 1971, and it is addressed to Dr McManus and the gist of the letter is that Clare Briscoe had recently been seen in Outpatients complaining of lumps in both breasts for two and a half years. Now, did you attend with Clare for that hospital appointment?'

'Yes, I attended with Clare for the appointment but I have never seen this letter sent to Dr McManus.'

'And, after the lumps had been removed, was there any follow-up surgery, as you remember?'

'I've never seen this letter before. Where did it come from?'

Mr Rene tried his best to move on as my mother looked at the letter, shaking her head and pointing her finger at me.

'Mrs Briscoe, in Chapter Sixteen of the book, which is called, "Good Morning, Heartache", and the year, according to the book, is 1971. Constance Briscoe would've been fourteen at the time.'

'She never had good morning heartache.'

'Did you mock her by telling her that she had no tits? Did you tell her that you were the only woman in the house because you had your tits and she had had hers removed?'

'No. I did not.'

'Did you shove her backwards by her tits, Mrs Briscoe?'

'No.'

'Did you call her a dirty, dirty little whore?'

'No, never.'

'Did you bang her head into a door or say that as long as she had a split up her crack, she could sell it.'

'Where did she get the disgusting language from? Clare wouldn't use that language and I wouldn't use that language and this is not even a fairy story and it's not even a mad person's story. It is just a mad story. It's just rubbish so I don't know where Clare get this language from.'

'Mrs Briscoe, do you ever remember Constance Briscoe going into school with injuries to her face caused by you?'

'Never, they were very good teachers, and they would have done something about it. I should think they should call in the Social Services if the parents had been beating up the children.'

'Well, according to the book, Constance Briscoe was very fond of Miss Korchinskye. When she was at home, did she ever mention Miss Korchinskye?'

'No. This is the first I have heard that she was fond of her. I did not know the names of her teachers, anyway there were so many of them but I never heard this one.'

'She also mentions that you gave permission for her to go and stay with Miss Korchinskye. Did that ever happen?'

'Lies. It didn't happen.'

'Did you leave Constance Briscoe on her own at Sutherland Square?'

'I did not leave Constance on her own. I bought the house at Vaughan Road for my children to do their study because our house was overcrowded with all the children and they couldn't do their studies. When I moved out I made arrangements for the three girls they would have their main meal at Sutherland Square with me but they did not stay in the house on their own for long because there was a ghost in the house and the ghost would play the piano. Constance was the one find out it was the cat walking on the piano keys, but they actually went back to live at Sutherland Square and I and the rest of the family went to Vaughan Road.'

'How did the three girls then occupy Sutherland Square?'

'It was three floors, Constance was in the middle, Pauline was on the ground and Patsy on the top.'

'How old were they at the time? Do you remember?'

'Well, old enough.'

'Constance Briscoe says that she needed your permission in

order to make an application for a grant application for a place at university and that you discouraged her and refused to sign the application form?'

'I don't think any mother or any parents would discourage their children to get a university grant or whatever to go to university, so that was not true at all.'

'So did you sign the form?'

'She never asked me.'

'What about when she was applying to university?'

'I did not know that she was applying, she did not tell me.'

'Did Clare have a cleaning job in the early mornings?'

'No. She definitely did not.'

'Mrs Briscoe, this is a document from what was then called the Department of Health and Social Security and it is dated 7th September 1973, addressed to Ms C. B. Briscoe. What can you tell us about the national insurance number?'

'Oh, that number. Constance was not actually working as a cleaner. She would have been about fifteen at the time. I was the one working on her insurance number, not Constance.'

My entire legal team looked over at my mother who was peering through an enormous magnifying glass which hung around her neck. I thought for a second that I had not heard my mother aright. I was looking over my shoulder at my barrister. He was looking at my mother and she was still shaking her head.

'That's right. It was me. I was working on her national insurance number. Constance never had no cleaning job. That girl is a liar.'

My mother was claiming that she was me. I was astonished. She was admitting an offence. She really had no choice. My National Insurance record was clear evidence that I had worked since fourteen and luckily for me they had kept a record of all the jobs I did. So I could prove that I did have all my jobs when I was at school. She had to explain my work record in order to discredit me. My barrister was writing furiously. This was an unexpected turn of events but I had warned him that my mother was not a normal seventy-four year old.

'Let's just stop there,' said Mr Rene. 'Mrs Briscoe, what do you mean, you were working on her cards?' .

'I used her cards and national insurance number. Those documents are referring to my work record not hers. She is just such a liar.'

'What contact did you have with her after 1979 when she went to university?'

'A lot of contact, actually she was my favourite daughter.'

'Mrs Briscoe, it is lunch time, you can step down from the witness box until five to two,' Mr Justice Tugendhat said.

My mother stepped down from the witness box as the jury filed out of court and once again my barrister was on his feet.

'My lord, we disclosed the exchanges between HM Revenue and Customs and ourselves to Mrs Carmen Briscoe in our list of documents on 4th September 2008. She knew that we were relying on a national insurance work record for Constance Briscoe. It came as a complete surprise to us that she is claiming that she worked on Constance's insurance document. She has never suggested that these records were used by her until today and only after I explained the importance of them to the jury. If Carmen Briscoe is serious about this, we would like her full employment records. It really is extremely unsatisfactory that we are confronted with this completely new case in the middle of examination-in-chief on what is a very important issue on neglect, which is central to our case.'

'Mr Panton, Mr Rene, who is dealing with this?' said the judge.

They remained seated on their bottoms for a moment and then both stood up in unison.

'Mr Panton, Mr Rene, when did Mrs Briscoe claim for the first time that she was in fact working on Constance's national insurance number?' said the judge.

'Instructions to me and Mr Rene are extremely recent, less than twenty-four hours old.'

'You have not answered the question. When did she tell you?'
'This morning.'
You mean less than three hours ago?'
'Yes.'
Mr Justice Tugendhat was not at all happy with the situation. My mother's solicitors knew perfectly well that if they were going to suggest that my work records were not mine they had to give us prior notice, but my mother had only just come up with the idea. It would be interesting to see what else they came up with. My mother had problems with my work record. Her real problems would begin when my lawyer asked questions of her. I was actually looking forward to that.

'What was your relationship with Angela Fuentes back in the early seventies?' asked Mr Panton.
'I know her for quite a long time. When she went back to Spain she would give me a ring now and then and she would return and bring a little present for me and things like that and we are still friends.'
I knew that my mother and Angela were not on speaking terms and Angela had refused to have any contact with her. She was just making up the evidence as she went along. Angela would have to be asked about their continuing friendship.
'Now the book also states that Angela Fuentes actually employed Constance Briscoe as a cleaner. What do you say about that?'
'I can't remember Angela employ Constance as a cleaner, and to be quite honest, Constance would never do cleaning jobs like that. She's not a cleaning girl. She would not want to get her hands dirty. This is another story that she has invented.'
'Finally, when you read the book *Ugly* how did you feel?'
'When I heard about the book *Ugly* I was shocked, devastated. I cried, and I actually phoned the publisher to tell the publisher it wasn't true. It's all lies. When Constance was growing up she was never ill treated. She was brought up in a very happy household. A very, very happy household.'

*   *   *

Mr Panton had finished his questions and it was our turn. As he sat down, my barrister stood up and there was a mutter from my mother's supporters. They all knew what was coming. The chatter hushed to a whisper and then it was still. Things were about to get a little uncomfortable for my mother.

7

Thursday 20 November 2008

Day 4 (continued)

'Mrs Briscoe, I ask questions on behalf of Constance Briscoe. If you don't understand any question I ask, please say so,' said Mr Caldecott.

'Okay,' said my mother.

'If at any time you need a break, please say so.

'This morning you told the jury that you used your daughter's national insurance card. When did you first come up with that idea?'

'Today. I came up with the idea today. I was the one that was doing all those work. She is too posh for that. She would never dirty her hands. Not Constance. Okay?'

She was raising her voice and getting quite agitated. Her large Sunday school hat was perched precariously on her head, its brim well below her hairline. She peered at Mr Caldecott as she waited for the next question.

'So you came up with that idea after I had finished telling the jury about how hard you daughter had worked when she was a child?'

'Yes, I went home last night and thought about it and then I remembered it was me, not Constance. I worked hard day and night. Did Constance tell you that she worked as a cleaner? She is such a liar.

'Liar,' she shouted as she wagged her finger at me. 'Constance is a liar. Have you got that?'

My mother pulled the brim down on her kiss-me-quick hat as she glared at my barrister. Her oversized spectacles were hovering on the brink of her nose. Using her left hand she pushed her glasses up and on her left wrist I spotted the bangle. Every third bead was a cat's eye. The beads were blue and white and my father had long ago told me about the power of the cat's eye. I knew that my barrister was in trouble. If my mother did not get him the duppies would sort him out.

'You told the jury that you raised your children with love and understanding?'

'That's right.'

'And I think you said that the girls were excellent and sometimes the boys behaved mischievously?'

'Yes. That is right. The boys were not naughty but my girls were marvellous. They were no trouble to me at all. We were just a happy family. One big happy family really.'

'I suggest that it was not a happy household; it was a very unhappy household.'

'That is not true. I am not sure where that suggestion came from. Lies. Lies and more lies by that one over there.' My mother was pointing at me again. She started off with a baby voice. A voice that I had not recognised previously but now Mother was aggressive and a touch disrespectful.

'I want to start, please, with your son Carlton Briscoe. He was born on 31st January 1959?'

'Yes.'

'He's therefore less than two years younger than Constance Briscoe?'

'Yes.'

'There is a reference to him in the Social Services file disclosed to the court. It deals with a visit made by you to the Social Services when he was fourteen years of age. It reads at the very beginning: "Mrs Briscoe in the office." Do you see that? You are visiting the Social Services. You were there at a time when Carlton was fourteen and you were demanding that he be removed from home because of various difficulties of behaviour involving Carlton, both at home and at school. Now, firstly, is it right that when he was fourteen you demanded that he be removed from the home?'

'You want me to answer that?' said my mother aggressively.

'Yes please.'

'Well I'm not the type of woman – mother – to remove any of my children from home and I don't know about this letter.'

'So you say you did not make the demand?' asked the judge.

'No, sir. I did not.'

'I'll just read from the second paragraph. "He finds it difficult [this is Carlton] to read and write. Mrs Briscoe takes this as being a disgrace on the whole family."

'Now, that must have been the view you expressed to the social workers, Mrs Briscoe, or they wouldn't have written it down, would they?' Mr Caldecott said.

'Well, whoever is the social worker that wrote this down, it was my instruction, and I wouldn't want my child to leave home. Not at all. Not me. I would never request my child to be removed from home to go to any Social Services. Who is the social worker, it must be that one over there?'

My mother was pointing at me again. The jury listened without a flicker of emotion as my mother blessed herself and pulled her hat down just above her eyebrow into a confrontational posture. She looked idiotic.

'I'll read to you the next words: "She has had him locked in a room at home." Now, is it true that you locked Carlton in a room at home? How old was Carlton?'

'Fourteen.'

'How long had you kept him in a locked room for?'

'You think I could lock a fourteen-year-old boy in a room?'

'I'm asking you if you—'

'No I did not. I did not. I don't know where this come from. Lock him in a room.'

My mother looked shocked. She clearly was surprised that we had the documents. Mr Caldecott carried on reading from the report.

' "Said she would keep him at home, off school, until something was done. She did not seem to have a good one-to-one relationship with Carlton in the way she was describing their home life. She threatened to strip him naked and beat him for what he had done."

'Now you did say that, didn't you, Mrs Briscoe?'

'No I did not. I did not say that.'

'Why on earth would a social worker write it down if you didn't say it?'

'Well, I do not know who the social worker is. Maybe the social worker was Constance. Maybe she wrote the report.'

My barrister was surprised at her suggestion but he pressed on. My mother was in combative mood and she was more than willing to take the lawyer on.

'This, Mrs Briscoe, is the original manuscript produced by the London Borough of Southwark Social Services Department under a witness summons last week. Are you suggesting that Constance Briscoe wrote this?'

'Constance Briscoe have wrote quite a few letters, I'm telling you. Well she could have done. I don't know. She could have done. And after all this time, it's only last week this been released? It is a bit fishy?'

'I've already told you, Mrs Briscoe, these documents were produced by the Social Services department under a witness summons to us last week and shared with your lawyers at the same time. Can I just read on, please, what is written here?'

'I don't think you need to read it again because I do understand it. Get on with it. Ask your questions.'

Mother was nodding her head again and she looked distressed. She understood perfectly what my lawyer was suggesting.

'It's my duty to ask you the questions, I'm afraid, whether you want me to or not, because these are quite serious issues.'

'Okay, carry on. Yeah sure. I'm listening.'

'This is after you've made this threat: "I said I didn't feel this would solve anything." "I" is the social worker speaking . . .

"nor keeping him off school, and would only result in a fine for cruelty to children and not sending them to school." Then you are recorded as saying: "Mrs Briscoe blamed much of the problems on the English leniency towards children compared with the West Indies."

'Now, is it your view, Mrs Briscoe, that the English are too lenient to their children?'

I was curious to hear her reply but she did not have a sensible answer.

'Who said that? I never said that. Who wrote that report?'

She was looking around the court again and as she looked in my direction I ducked behind Sarah who sat impassively looking at my mother.

'This is Clare again. I brought my children up English style not West Indian style.'

'Is it right that Carlton Briscoe did in fact leave home when he was fourteen years old and went to live in a property at 215 Camberwell New Road?'

'He went to live with his dad. If you say he was fourteen he was fourteen. But I can't remember. But he wasn't abandoned,' my mother said desperately.

'I suggest that he *was* abandoned.'

'I suggest that he was not,' my mother insisted.

'Let us examine what happened to the next son down, Martin Briscoe.'

'Yeah. What about him?'

'His date of birth is 22nd September 1961. He's four and a half years younger than Constance Briscoe. Now it's also true, isn't it, that Martin left home at the age of fourteen?'

'Well, he wanted his freedom, that's their problem.'

'Was it anything to do with your discipline that Martin left home at fourteen?'

'No.'

'I just want to show you this witness statement made by you in some Chancery proceedings which have nothing to do with this case; as we can see the date is 29th May 2001. Martin Briscoe is the claimant and you are the defendant. The first paragraph of this witness statement reads, "I am the mother of the claimant in these proceedings. He is one of my eleven children. He was born in 1961 and he lived with the family at 19 Sutherland Square until he was about fourteen years of age. Martin, at the time, was becoming a problem at home, and as he was not prepared to accept my discipline, he had to move out to live with his father, from whom I had separated." '

'I didn't – I don't know about this one,' my mother said.

'Well, Mrs Briscoe, it's a witness statement made and signed by you in legal proceedings. And I don't suggest that anything in that paragraph is untrue. I suggest that Martin was a problem and you threw him out.'

'Martin wasn't becoming any problem. I remember now. Oh yeah, Martin did not leave home until he was older. That is right, he was older.'

'Mrs Briscoe, what was it about your discipline which Martin was not prepared to accept?'

'I didn't have any strict discipline that Martin would not accept. He just wanted to go and live with his dad.'

'But I thought you told the jury yesterday that Mr Briscoe contributed nothing to helping the family.'

'Course Mr Briscoe contributed nothing to helping the family.'

'So far, we know that from when they were fourteen he appears to have been having at least some custodial role in relation to both Carlton and Martin, both of whom had been thrown out of your home. You told the jury this morning that your way of disciplining the boys was not to let them take the dog Blackie out. Taking the dog out or not taking the dog out is not a reason to leave home is it?'

'They are my children, and if I speak to my children, I think they should take their orders.'

'Did you ever use physical methods on Martin, Mrs Briscoe?'

'No, no, no.'

'The next daughter is Cynthia Eastman.'

'Yes.'

'You said of your daughters yesterday, "They were all excellent and they never gave me any trouble."'

'That is right.'

'Cynthia Eastman was born on 9th September 1965, and she therefore is some eight and a half years younger than Constance Briscoe, and she is the eldest of the Eastman children.'

'That's right. My daughters were perfect.'

'This is 12th June 1980. Cynthia is now fourteen. This document opens: "Mrs Briscoe feels that her daughter Cynthia's behaviour has become unbearable, and as a punishment she would like her to be RIC." RIC is social work speak. It means reception into care. "She has apparently threatened her with this option before, but has given her several chances. I explained to Mrs Briscoe that if her daughter is bad now, reception into care would make her worse. She understood and agreed that we would try an alternative course of action, perhaps to instil some kind of fear into her daughter in order that she considers her present behaviour. The fear is Mrs Briscoe's idea. I went along with it."

'Now, Mrs Briscoe, firstly, so it's not true that your daughters were, in your memory, always excellent and you never had problems with them?'

'The only problem that I had with Cynthia was when she became pregnant at a young age. And it wasn't fourteen, anyway, I'm sure it wasn't fourteen. And my house was overcrowded. So I don't know where these photocopy letters come from. You can send these letters back where they came from.'

'We will come to what happened to Cynthia when she got pregnant. This is before she got pregnant, that you are complaining about her behaviour as unbearable.'

'Cynthia's behaviour wasn't unbearable until when I find out she was pregnant from her school friend, or something like that. And that was it. So do you know – have you got any idea who wrote the copy letter? Had somebody else written it up or whatever? I suspect that it is Constance? That one over there,' said my mother pointing at me again. 'Please take them away from me because they are stressing me out. For God sake take them away from me.'

My mother tossed the letters to one side and held her head as her hat fell backwards.

'We do have the original files here, if your lawyers wish to look at them at any time. You'll see the signature, although it's not very easy to read, is of the relevant social worker at the bottom of the page. The first squiggle looks like "Roy Griffith" or "Griffiths".

'Mrs Briscoe, is it right that fear is, in your view, one of the appropriate ways to ensure that children behave themselves?'

'What do you mean, fear? What do you mean by fear?'

'Well, you frighten them into good behaviour presumably by threatening them?'

'No, I don't frighten my children into good behaviour.'

'Can we go to the 13th August 1980? All I want to read to you is what you say at the beginning of this report when Cynthia is nearly fifteen. This is in the second line: "She stated that Cynthia is beyond her control. She complained that Cynthia is simply bad, and for fear of killing her, she would rather we received her into care." Then you refer to her being out without your consent, being brought home by the police.'

'So what do you want me to answer about this?'

'Why did you say to Social Services that she's simply bad and they should take her into care for fear of you killing her?'

'How do you know I said that? I never said that! I didn't say I would kill her. I didn't say I was in fear of killing her, because it's not my nature to kill anybody. It is not in my nature to kill my children. I gave birth to them, struggle with them and do everything I could for my children. So if I kill them, I wouldn't have them any more, would I?'

My mother's voice had been very soft, almost polite, with a touch of steel at the start but she was now shouting. Her tone was pure aggression. I had witnessed that many times as a child. She had not changed at all. She wiped her eyes and dried her invisible tears. I was certain the jury could see what I did, a tearless woman crying. It was comical.

'They are my children, not yours. Mine.' My barrister was momentarily stunned into silence, as was the rest of the court. My mother was in her aggressive frame of mind.

'By now Cynthia is fifteen. Social Services are coming to see you at home on 10th December 1980: It reads as follows: "Mrs Briscoe was in the office this time but no sign of Cynthia. She claimed she had no idea where she was. Mrs Briscoe started off as very aggressive and unhelpful, saying that she passed responsibility over to us and wanted no more to do with Cynthia. I asked her to tell me exactly how she saw the problem, and she told me that Cynthia was rude, stayed out without saying where, and would not go to school."

'Then three paragraphs from the end: "I've found Mrs Briscoe a very difficult and rigid character to deal with and had the feeling that she'd resigned herself to putting up with Cynthia. She said that if Cynthia was a dog, she'd take her to Battersea Dogs Home and leave her there."

'Now, Mrs Briscoe, that is not the remark of a caring and loving mother, is it?'

The whole court was looking at my mother in silence. I turned slightly to my left and saw Cynthia out of the corner of my eye. By the look on her face she had obviously not been warned as to my mother's views and the threat of the dogs' home.

My mother was cornered and struggling to find an appropriate answer.

'What do you want me to say? That I wanted to book my child into Battersea Dogs Home? At the present moment I love dogs and I've got three at home now, two Staff and one Springer spaniel. So don't you dare suggest that I class my child as a dog.'

'The message was that you'd take her to the dogs' home and abandon her as a stray. She was a bitch in your eyes. That's effectively what you're saying, Mrs Briscoe?'

'No, no, no. Who is the author of the report? Was it Constance Briscoe? Cynthia is over there,' said my mother, pointing in the general direction of her supporters. 'If she was a dog she'd still be in Battersea Dogs Home or somebody adopting her as a stray but she is over there, she is in court, how do you explain that?'

Mr Caldecott ignored her question.

'Now it is May 1981, Mrs Briscoe, but before 18th May, which is the second entry in the social service file: "Mrs Briscoe to the office and asked to see me regarding correspondence from the Education and Welfare Service, of Cynthia's non-attendance. Told her I wasn't her social worker therefore not at liberty to do anything. She wants her daughter taken into care as her behaviour has got worse. Then on 18th May Mrs Briscoe rang. I explained that she was not allocated to me. She got quite angry and said that she chucked Cynthia out of the house yesterday because her behaviour is so bad, and because she'd heard that Cynthia was pregnant. She didn't know where Cynthia was and she said that she'd washed her hands of her. She said she wouldn't notify the police that Cynthia was a missing person."

'Now, Mrs Briscoe, it's true, isn't it, that you threw Cynthia out of the house when you heard that she had got herself pregnant aged fifteen?'

'No, I did not throw Cynthia out the house. I make arrangement with the Social Services department and they find a young mother and baby home. She wasn't on her own there; other young mothers and baby was there. I did not throw my daughter out the house.'

'If there is any time at which a young daughter of this age needs help and affection, it would be if she found herself pregnant at this sort of age, at fifteen, wouldn't it?'

'And I did help my daughter.'

'Why wouldn't you notify the police when she was missing and you had no idea where she was?'

My mother started to laugh. It was a belly laugh and my mother thought it was hilarious. Cynthia the dog was missing.

'Cynthia was missing! She was not missing.'

'If she had gone missing it was very urgent that she should be found, Mrs Briscoe. Is that right?'

'Do I look like a mother that if one of my child was missing I would not report it to the police station, and the police is two minutes round the corner at Carter Street? I could stay in Sutherland Square and call the police.'

'The baby was due in November 1981, so it is extraordinary that on 3rd June 1981 there is this entry: "Mrs Briscoe came to the office requesting RIC for Cynthia and Norma. Cynthia was with her mother. Mrs Briscoe said that she'd been asking for RIC for Cynthia since last year. Cynthia had been coming and going over this time and is now pregnant, and she doesn't want her any longer. Cynthia said her mother had told her often to go, which she does. She then asked to come back, which her mother agrees to for a while. But although she wants to be at home, mum now refused to have her. Mrs Briscoe also informed me that she had told Norma to leave. She was homeless and if we found her, she didn't want her back as she is following in Cynthia's footsteps."

'Now, Mrs Briscoe, all these reports speak with one voice. You did not want Cynthia at home despite the fact she was pregnant, and despite the fact that she said in your presence that she wanted to be at home. I suggest to you this indicates not only a lack of loving affection and care for Cynthia, but also a household which is deeply unhappy, and not the happy household you sought to persuade the jury of yesterday.'

'Cynthia is here in court. She will talk for herself. She's alive, she's not dead, so she can explain all that to you,' shouted my mother. 'But some of these allegations that you are bringing forward to me here I just can't understand them, and I won't accept them. I'm sorry, I won't.'

My mother made crying sounds but from where I was sitting I could see no tears. She turned her face away from the court to hide her invisible tears.

'If you want a break, Mrs Briscoe, just say so. We've been going for some time.'

'I'm fine,' she said.

'I just want to read the second half of the first paragraph headed "Present situation".

' "I [the social worker] did have one long interview with her in the office, which was a very one-sided affair and was chiefly limited to Mrs Briscoe denouncing Cynthia as bad, evil, worthless, et cetera."

'Now, Mrs Briscoe, this is very strong language to use of your daughter to a social worker, isn't it? "Bad, evil, worthless?" '

'I didn't use that language to any social worker.'

'You see, if that's how you speak about your children to a social worker, you probably speak to them to their face, on occasion, in even stronger and more unpleasant terms.'

'No, I did not, and I don't. And I would never do. And I'm not the type of woman to use that sort of language. My children, they are my pride and joy until when I go in the box down there. So I don't want you to press me with all these things. They are my children, my children! They are my children! They are my children!'

My delightful mother had begun to show her true colours and it was not a pleasant sight. Shouting at the barrister she was aggressive, confrontational and rude. Oh what joy!

'We'll take a short break,' said Mr Justice Tugendhat. As he spoke my mother started to thump the witness stand. She shouted across at the jury.

'I was the only child from my parents, and I'm proud of having eleven of them, and if you have a child you don't want, bring it to Mrs Briscoe, and she will take it from you. Please leave me alone. For God's sake, leave me alone. If you have a child you don't want, bring it to me and I'll take it. I love my children, and I love everybody's children. How much more of this can I take?'

The judge stared judiciously and then rose. The jury sat unmoved until they were ushered out of court and Cynthia rushed to my mother's aid. I sat in court and waited. After fifteen minutes the lawyers carried on.

*   *   *

'Mrs Briscoe, I want to move on to Constance Briscoe's bed-wetting problems which Mr Panton asked you about yesterday; do you remember?'

'She wants to say something,' said the usher as my mother whispered in her ear.

'Can I help, Mrs Briscoe?' Mr Justice Tugendhat said.

'I'd like to say to the jury I'm sorry about my behaviour, but the counsel is attacking my children and I don't allow anyone to attack my children and I'm very, very sorry about that, because they are my children and they're my pride and joy. And I'm very, very sorry about my behaviour. I ask you forgive me, please.'

My mother was now adopting a voice that I had not heard before. A soft baby-doll-type voice. She must be regretting showing the court her aggressive streak, which was quite unusual in someone of her age. She would not let her mask drop again so readily and I was sure that she had been advised in the short break.

'Mrs Briscoe, yesterday you told the jury that Constance Briscoe's bed-wetting problems stopped at about the age of five; do you remember that?'

'Yes.'

'Are you sure about that?'

'I am sure about that.'

'You probably would agree with me that it is a very distressing condition, particularly if it happens regularly, wetting the bed at night?'

'It wasn't distressing to me.'

'It's distressing to the child. Now, is it right that you have no recollection of helping Constance Briscoe with this particular problem after the age of five or so?'

'No, it was under control. There was no need to help any more because the alarm that the doctor gave her done a great job.'

'This is a letter dated 3rd April 1964, and we're now six weeks from Constance Briscoe's seventh birthday. Obviously, the older you get, the more unpleasant and the less usual bed-wetting becomes.'

'Yeah.'

'It's normally a problem for fairly young children?'

'Yes. From birth, children wet the bed.'

'This letter refers to this being an ongoing problem when Constance is nearly seven, because that Latin word, enuresis, means bed-wetting. The reason why she was examined about this is that there was a distinctive smell about her at school when she was seven which led to this examination being done.'

'I don't know about this letter. I definitely don't know about this letter.'

'Can I just ask you a little about the bed-wet alarm. Constance Briscoe was the only child in the family to have an alarm, wasn't she?'

'Yes.'

'She was the only one to have an alarm because her problem was far worse than anybody else's, if anybody else had a problem.'

'The other children, if they want to go to the toilet, they would wake up. Constance wouldn't wake up, so she need an alarm. She would never wake up and go to the toilet and go back to the bed like the other children.'

'I assume, from that, that it follows that Constance Briscoe's problem was much worse?'

'She just wouldn't wake up.'

'The alarm made quite a loud noise, didn't it?'

'Definitely.'

'I think in the book, Constance Briscoe describes it like the fire brigade or a fire alarm. It was quite loud because the purpose is to be loud enough to wake a child from a deep sleep?'

'It's not that loud. It's just loud enough to wake her, and sometimes she wouldn't even wake up.'

'Mrs Briscoe, do you remember giving an interview to the *Daily Mail* in January 2006, very shortly after the book came out? This long article is, broadly speaking, putting your side of the story. The lady journalist, Fiona Barton, had come to see you at your house for an interview. The article begins effectively by saying that you don't look like the monster which appears in the book. So this is an interview giving your side of the story.'

'I can remember I gave an interview when my solicitor was present at their office. That's the only one.'

'Can you read the passage, I loved all my children dearly.'

'Yes. I have got that.'

'Can I just read on a little bit what you say here: "It is not true. Nothing like that happened. Clare wasn't singled out. I loved all my children dearly. She did wet the bed but she wasn't the only one. I had a lot of children and children wet the bed. It was no big thing. We went to a clinic and they gave us an alarm that will wake her up if she wet. It helped a lot until she was about eleven." Do you see those words; "It helped a lot until she was about eleven," Mrs Briscoe?'

'I know what you are getting at. Constance did not carry on wetting the bed until she was eleven.'

'Well, she will tell the jury that this was a problem that went on and on and on. And that after a time, the alarm didn't always wake her, did it?'

'Well sometimes the alarm does not wake her. Depends how you plug it in, and it might not have been set up properly.'

'You see, Mrs Briscoe, what I'm puzzled by is why you told the jury yesterday that it was all under control at the age of five, and yet here you appear to be telling the *Daily Mail* that it was still a problem when she was eleven.'

'Constance did not carry on wetting the bed until she was eleven, as far as I can remember.'

'If you please look at those words, "When the alarm went off I would wake her and change the bed." Now the alarm would go off often in the early hours of the morning, wouldn't it, Mrs Briscoe?'

'It depends when she wet the bed.'

'I agree. And it varied from time to time. Sometimes it was late at night but sometimes it was early in the morning. There was no set pattern, was there?'

'I can't remember if it was a set pattern.'

'But if you came and woke her up, it follows that you also must have heard the alarm?'

'It's just a simple alarm. It make not a loud noise, just beep, beep, beep, and that's good enough to wake anyone.'

'Your evidence about where the bedrooms were puts yourself on the ground floor and Constance on the top floor with her sisters?'

'That's right.'

'If she was that far away from you, you would never have heard the alarm, would you?'

'Yes, I would hear it. I'm on the ground floor and I've left my bedroom door open so I could hear.'

'Yes. Now, Constance's bedroom in fact was on the first floor immediately above yours. And she was there on her own, which is why you were able to hear the alarm.'

'What do you mean, on her own? I don't understand that. And I never slept with my door closed, she was with her three – two – older sisters.'

'Her evidence will be that she was on her own in that room, and her two sisters, Four Eyes and Precious Puss, were on the top floor sharing a room.'

'Not true. No, not at all. Not until when they become a certain age and returned from Vaughan Road, and I went up there. That's the time they had their own floor. And she wasn't wetting the bed at that time.'

'Now, Mrs Briscoe, the reason why you won't face up in court to how she was wetting the bed is because you know perfectly well that it was commonly the reason for physical punishment inflicted by you on Constance Briscoe long after the age of five. That is why you told the *Daily Mail* what you did and why you won't come out with the true story in court.'

'I can face up to whatever I know, and I think Constance should face up to it as well, because she knows she's telling lies. And you know it, Constance, so will you please tell the court the truth. And nothing but the truth. We are here for the truth, Constance – or Clare. Please do that.'

My mother was pointing her finger at me again. Jabbing out manically as though I was still a child and she was disciplining me in a way that only she knew how. The jury sat in silence. The judge waited for my mother to stop.

Setting her hat back on her head my mother steadied her glasses and looked towards the barrister.

'You often put her damp sheets in a plastic bag to keep them damp, didn't you?'

'Oh, please, no. What? No, and I've got two washing machine? No. No, Clare. Please admit, please do that. Don't sit there staring like that. Please, Clare, just explain to the court the truth and nothing but the truth. This is nothing but the truth, Clare. I've sent you to a good Roman Catholic school.' She was glaring at me in a threatening way.

'Mrs Briscoe, which is true: what you told the *Daily Mail* or what you told the court yesterday about the age when this problem stopped?'

'That does not make any difference. Constance wasn't wetting the bed at that age. Okay? She wasn't. And in her book, if you read her book, she said she had boyfriend and she wouldn't want to wet – to pee on her boyfriend, that's what she said. And she did stop wet the bed.'

'Do you at least agree with me that in the book this is a common theme, that she was beaten for wetting the bed?'

'No, no, no.'

'You see, for this case you produced a very long witness statement, running to forty-seven pages, but nowhere in it do you tell us when this problem started and when the problem finished. And the reason why you won't face up to this issue is that it was the cause of a lot of cruelty inflicted on Constance by you.'

'I can't face up to what is not true. Constance is trying to make it sound like truth. Constance,' my mother shrieked. 'Constance, please tell members of the jury it's not true. God will bless you, God will take care of you, Constance. I've teach you to be honest, but you weren't an honest girl, Constance. So tell the jury, Constance. For once, make a change in your life, girl. Please do it. It would save you a lot, Constance. This won't help, Clare. Families are supposed to take care of family, and if you can do this to your mother, your own mother, Clare, please. Tell the members of the jury, Clare. Tell them. Tell them now. Clare, please. I'm asking you. You know it's not true, Clare. You know it's not true, Clare. You know it's not true, Clare. And Clare, you know how hard I had it to grow you children to the best I could. Please, Clare, just explain to the members of the jury and say it wasn't true. You won't get punished for that, Constance, but if you continue like that, Constance, God is going to punish you. You hear me, girl. God is going to punish you.'

My lawyer interrupted this tirade as some of the jury averted their eyes.

'You see, Mrs Briscoe, you threatened to beat your son Carlton in a conversation with the social workers and that's what you did to Constance when she slipped below your high standards.'

'Constance,' said my mother shouting at me. She did not get far. She was abruptly interrupted.

'You regarded bed-wetting as a disgrace as it went on later and later.'

'So why couldn't I cope with Constance bed-wetting? Clare, tell the truth, please. You tell the truth, Clare. It's not a disgrace to speak the truth, Constance. It's not a disgrace, girl. Don't sit there. God will punish you, I can tell you that. I'm only asking you to tell the truth. It will go a long way, girl. A long way.'

'You commonly beat her with a stick, didn't you?'

'No. If I was beating Clare with a stick she would be dead by now. Why would I want to beat her with a stick? A stick! Do you know what a stick is? She said in her book a rail from the stairs. Do you think she would be alive if I was hitting her with a rail, a plank of wood from the stairs?'

'Members of the jury, we'll stop for today now, and please leave the building in good time so we can start tomorrow,' the

judge said. My mother was still ranting and raving when Mr
Justice Tugendhat interrupted her.

'Mrs Briscoe, you're giving evidence at the moment,' said the
judge. 'Your evidence hasn't finished.'

'Okay.'

'There's a rule that while you're giving evidence you mustn't
talk to anyone about the case. Do you understand?'

'Yes, I do.'

'So overnight you mustn't talk to anyone about the case, do
you understand?'

'I do. I won't. Okay.'

8

Friday 21 November 2008

Day 5

I spotted her as I crossed the road to enter the High Court. Every day since the start of the trial my mother had worn a fashionable velvet hat. She was wearing a light brown coat with a white scarf, a black and dark brown bible hat pulled low down on her wig and black knee-length shorts.

My mother was half way through her evidence and still I had no idea why she had singled me out all those years ago. Not once had she even conceded that she'd hit me, never mind about admitting abuse. She was defiant. My barrister had made some headway but my mother was having none of it. She even suggested that I had impersonated the social worker and doctored the reports that had been sent directly to the court. The jury sat stony faced and even my barrister was taken aback as her legal team tried to look righteous. My mother was no ordinary little old lady: even when she was on the ropes she was giving Mr Caldecott a run for his money. Today there would be more questions about various documents and I could not wait. Maybe now I would have the answers to questions that had for so long remained unanswered.

'Back in the witness box,' said the judge as my mother walked towards the front of the court. Mr Caldecott got to his feet as my mother was adjusting her glasses.

'The chicken incident, Mrs Briscoe. When Constance failed to remove seven hairs from a chicken properly you hit her over the knuckles with a milk bottle and then you ran a knife up her arm. Her left forearm.'

'That did not happen,' said my mother looking directly at me. 'She was never allowed into the kitchen. Has she got a scar as a result of this particular abuse? Go on, tell me, has she got a scar after this so-called-imaginary incident?'

'Well as a matter of fact she has. Did you ever notice a long scar running down her forearm about ten centimetres long?'

'Scar, scar. She never had a scar when she was a child.'

'But you have told the jury that your children were not allowed to go into the kitchen so she could not have been helping out with the preparations of a chicken.'

'That is correct.'

'Did you ever kick and punch her and knock her out?'

'No.'

'Have a look at the document at the front of the file. You will see that when Constance was twelve you were asked by a social worker how you managed in the kitchen and she recorded the reply. It says: "Mrs Briscoe said the older children helped out in the kitchen. The elder children at the time were Four Eyes, Precious Puss and Clare." '

'Just hold it right there. What are you trying to say? I never said that and they did not help out. I did it all. Me and do you know what? I loved it.'

Mr Caldecott was wearing his glasses as he kept an eye on my mother. I had told him what to expect and now I was sure that he had got the measure of her.

'I never said that my children help out. I never said it. That Constance Briscoe she thinks that she is so much better than the rest of us.'

'Mrs Briscoe, you were visited by a social worker when Constance was twelve. You were asked how you managed in the house and your reply was recorded. You said that the three eldest girls helped out with the housework. I can point you to the entry in the records.'

'Lies, lies, I never said that. I did it all on my own. I was the slave. Me.'

'Mrs Briscoe, I would like to move to another topic. The aeroplane incident on the 31st January 1973, which is the birthday of your son Carlton.'

'Before you start, I know all about this incident. I was not in the room at the time. Pasty, Clare, Carl were in the room when the accident happened. I was called to the room after I hear Clare screaming.'

'It was you, Mrs Briscoe, who flew the aeroplane into your daughter's face not once but twice.'

'I did not! She is such a liar and anyway she had only got a little scar on her face. It was not serious. It was a tiny little graze.'

'It was a lot more serious than a little graze, Mrs Briscoe, in fact her face was sliced open twice.'

'She is a liar, aren't you, Clare? A little liar. It is not too late. You can always tell the truth. God will punish you if you continue to tell lies.'

My mother was looking directly at me as I was wondering what God had to do with it.

'So she never had two cuts on her cheek, is that what you are saying?'

'That is right. She never had any scars on her face. So I don't know where you are coming from. Have you seen a scar on her face? She hasn't got one.'

'Have a look at this photograph, Mrs Briscoe. It is a photo of your daughter when she was at university. Can you see that she had two long scars running down the side of her cheek?'

My mother took the photograph and stared at it. Two scars stood out like skid marks. It was a while before she responded.

'That,' said my mother, 'is not my daughter.'

'Sorry?' said my lawyer.

'This is not my daughter, don't forget that. She is my daughter, not yours.'

'Mrs Briscoe, I am a little confused. Can you help? Is that a photograph of your daughter?'

'No it is not. I know my daughter and this is not my daughter. That is not the face of my daughter.'

'Did you ever call your daughter Scarface after you sliced her cheek open?'

'No and she does not have a scar on her face, she is telling the most serious and wicked lies.'

'Mrs Briscoe, your daughter ended up in hospital when she was very young to have lumps removed from her breasts. Three lumps. How is it that you do not know to this day that she had three lumps removed?'

My mother was looking directly at the barrister with pure hatred in her eyes as she spat out her reply, 'I know how many lumps she had removed. She only ever had one lump, not two not three. She has made it all up.'

My mother was shaking her head furiously at the jury. 'She has told lies. Lies. All not true.' She was becoming distressed again.

'Have a look at these photographs. The usher will hand to you a set of three.'

My mother was still shaking her head as the usher handed her the photographs. My mother looked at the first and then the second and finally she turned the last photograph over and started to shake her head again.

'Can you please tell us how your daughter got those scars on her breasts? You will see that she has two scars on the right breast and one on the left.'

'These are not the breasts of Constance Briscoe. I do not accept that this is her. All lies. You don't know that girl.'

'She will say that you pinched and punched her breasts as part of the punishment.'

'I have given you my answer.'

'Tell us about Eastman. He is Clare's stepfather. How would you describe him?'

'He is a perfect gentleman, a perfect stepfather. He is perfect in every way.'

'Did he ever hit any of the children?'

'No, he never laid a hand on any of the children.'

'Would you like to think about that answer or are you sure?'

'I am one hundred percent sure,' said my mother.

'I have three documents that I would like you to look at,' said Mr Caldecott. 'The first is a conviction dated 13th July 1975 from the Camberwell Green Magistrates Court and then two weeks later two more dated 26th and 27th July. On these occasions Mr Eastman turned up at the house where Constance was living and he threatened to kill her. That is what these convictions are for.'

'These documents are all forgeries. They have been forged by that one over there. Constance Briscoe or whatever she calls herself.'

'You are making very serious allegations. Are you saying that your daughter forged all these documents?'

'I am, yes.'

'Well, if you look in her medical notes you will see that she went to the doctor on 14th July with a wound. She told the doctor that it was a laceration caused by her stepfather and the doctor made a note of what she said.'

'Are you listening to me? My daughter Constance Briscoe or whatever she calls herself was never assaulted by the perfect Mr Eastman. These events did not happen. These documents are a forgery as well. She is quite capable of getting someone to write the entry into her medical records. This is just another one of her tricks.'

She looked over to where her supporters were sitting, arms folded and nodding in approval. When she looked at the jury they were impassive. The judge continued to make a note of the evidence she was giving. My barrister was polite at all times but he was becoming slightly exasperated by the slippery old lady.

'You may be elderly, Mrs Briscoe, but are you just saying the first thing that comes into your head? Are you making these allegations because the incident portrayed you in a poor light?'

'Allegations! Allegations! You have heard nothing yet. Just wait until I get started. Go on. Carry on. Ask your next question.

I am ready for you. I am not stupid,' shouted my mother. 'I am the mother of eleven children. Do not try and make out that I am stupid. Do I look mad to you? Do I look like I have just escaped from the Maudsley Psychiatric Hospital, that well-known mad house. Sorry, judge, sorry, members of the jury, but I am not mad.'

'You are making false allegations against your daughter because you will not face up to what happened between Eastman and Constance. What happened, which ended up in court, is to your disgrace.' Mr Caldecott waited for an answer as the silence swirled around the court.

'Do I look like I am a disgrace to you? Get on with your questions,' she said.

'Eastman put a cigarette out on the back of Constance's hand and when she reported it to you, you did nothing about it. What do you say about that?'

'Have a good look at me, Mr Man, and when you have finished let me tell you something. This is yet another one of her tricks. She is a liar and a thief. She is Fagin. That is what she is. Fagin. Oh God, please help me. I hate to think that I have a liar and a thief in the family. Oh God, help me.'

'Mrs Briscoe, it is important to listen to the questions and to answer them. If you can it will save a lot of time. When you moved out of Sutherland Square leaving Constance and her two sisters, you rarely visited the house except to demand money and to assault her. You had no idea that Constance had an early morning cleaning job and a cleaning job in the evening after school, did you?'

'I visited my daughter every day. I would cook and clean for her. Constance did not have a cleaning job. I can absolutely tell you one hundred percent that she did not have a cleaning job. She was not the type to get her hands dirty doing office cleaning.'

'She was paying you rent. That is why she had the cleaning jobs.'

'That girl is a liar.'

'You tore up her grant application form when she applied to go to university.'

'I never did. I encouraged her to go.'

'Can you explain how she ended up going to university with an independent grant that she worked for? You did not fill in the grant form.'

'No I did not, but that was because she did not tell me that she was going to university. If she had mentioned it I would have given my support.'

'Did Constance ever visit you after she went to Newcastle University?'

'Yes,' said my mother. 'She would quite often visit me. She would often come down when she wanted to go shoplifting.'

'She came down to work in a hospice at weekends, looking after the very ill.'

'I don't know who told you that. She came down to steal from them. And she brought her stolen goodies round to my place for me to get rid of.'

'You have never mentioned that before, Mrs Briscoe. During all the time that you have been preparing for this case you never mentioned a word. In all the three statements you have served as your witness statement, you have never mentioned it. Are you just giving the first answer that comes into your head?'

'I know what my daughter is guilty of and she is a lying, thieving crook. Fagin. Have you heard of Fagin? That is who she is.'

'When Constance graduated from university did you attend the ceremony?'

'Yes definitely. I was there. She looked wonderful in her robes. I did enjoy that.'

'Are you sure that you attended the ceremony, Mrs Briscoe? Are you confusing this ceremony with one of the other children?'

'No absolutely, not. I went to the ceremony. I have a photograph of the ceremony. We had a wonderful day.'

'Mrs Briscoe, Constance did not go to her graduation ceremony. She graduated in her absence. There are no photographs of her graduation in existence. That photo that you say you have of her, may we see it?'

'No, you cannot see it. I have left it in my trunk in Jamaica when I was last there.'

'Are you sure that you have the photograph of an event that did not take place?'

'Well, I could be confused.'

'Have you got any photographs of your daughter when she was at school that you can produce to this court? Because Constance will say that you never bought any photographs of her at all and returned them all to the school because she was too ugly to be photographed.'

'I have lots of pictures of her. I cannot produce them to the court because I have left them in my trunk which is not in this country.'

'The plain fact of the matter is that this child of yours, that you tell us was your favourite, you are quite unable to produce a single photograph of her as a child except for a few photographs when she attended family weddings and events.'

Mr Caldecott sat down as my mother looked around the court and started to smile her sickly sweet smile at the jury. She had failed to capitalise on any natural sympathy that she might have secured because of her age and she had lost a lot of good will by her confrontational and aggressive performance. I sat there waiting. It was over and I still had no answers as to why she chose me for such cruelty. There would be no answers because as far as my mother was concerned the whole event never happened. It was a figment of my imagination.

9

Day 5 (continued)

Precious Puss was up and out of her seat before Mr Panton called her name. As she walked to the front of the court I glanced sideways towards her as she was looking in my direction. The sheer hostility in the air should have warned me about what was to come. As she took the oath she stared at me and then she smiled. I smiled back. It was mutual disrespect. She started to speak before Mr Panton asked the first question.

'My name is Patsy,' said Precious Puss. 'I am the second eldest sister and I am older than Clare by fourteen months. I have read the book *Ugly*. Well, when I say that I read it, not all of it. I found it to be a very difficult book to read because it is totally untrue and I could not believe what I was reading.'

She had started to raise her voice and she was almost shouting at her own counsel.

Mr Panton was acutely aware, as was I, that Patsy was my mother's star witness. She had come to court to support my mother come what may and it was important that she made a good impression on the jury.

Mr Panton threw my sister a soft ball and all she had to do was to catch it.

'How did you get on as sisters?'

'We got on very well. My sister was always assertive, always having a laugh, always funny.'

'When did you hear about the book?'

'I first heard about the book from my sister or my brother. They said that Clare was saying terrible things about the family. When I heard that the book was on the way we tried to stop it but her publishers told us to go away.'

'And what happened?'

'Well we then went to the Bar Council to get her struck off the register but they told us to go away.'

'Were you at the same school as Clare?'

'Yes, I was at the Sacred Heart School when she was there and we used to travel to school together. She wrote in the book *Ugly* that she once travelled to school with a swollen eye and a cut lip. I read that and laughed.'

'Was there a reason why you laughed?'

'Invention. That is what made me laugh. Invention.'

'Did she ever try to commit suicide to your knowledge?'

'My sister Clare would not know what suicide was. The suggestion that she tried to commit suicide is absolutely ridiculous. She also says that from time to time she was covered in an assortment of bruises and marks. As far as I am concerned she has made it all up and she knows it, don't you, Clare?' she said, looking at me. 'My sister says that she was sexually abused by Mr Eastman when she was a child.'

'What do you say to that?'

Precious Puss started to laugh. It was a low belly laugh that echoed around the court. I sat with Sarah, waiting for her to stop.

'My sister knows that she was never sexually abused. Deep down she knows that it never happened and that it is a wicked lie.'

'Do you know anything about an incident with an aeroplane?' Mr Panton asked.

'Yes I do. My brother Carl had it and he was playing with it when Constance tried to stop him and he stabbed her in the face with it once. My mother was not in the room at the time. When Clare started to scream I called for my mother and she came into the room. It really was no big deal. It was a tiny little scratch and my mother cleaned it herself and the incident left no scar.'

'What sort of a man was Eastman?'

'He was a gentle giant. Never harmed a fly. He did not assault Clare. He did not sexually assault her and by the way my sister never had a cleaning job when she was fourteen. There is no way that she would get up out of bed at five thirty in the morning without me knowing about it. She could hardly get up in the middle of the night, never mind getting up to go to work. She is a liar.'

'What do you know about the parts of the book that you have read?'

'Constance said that she was cut with a knife when she was preparing a chicken. That is an invention on her part. She said that she was abused – these stories are a malicious invention.'

'Are you aware of any previous convictions relating to Eastman?'

'No. I do not know about them. They are a forgery.'

'Was Constance beaten for wetting the bed?'

'No.'

'Just wait there, will you, there may be some more questions.'

Andrew got to his feet and settled his gaze on Precious Puss.

'Miss Patsy Briscoe. I want to make it clear to you what we say about your evidence.'

'Go on.'

'I am suggesting that you knew perfectly well what was going on and you chose to turn a blind eye.'

'That is not true.'

'You were called Precious Puss because you liked your home comforts.'

'First I heard about that.'

'You told a reporter from the *Daily Mail* that your sister had her own room.'

'I did but I made a mistake. She never had her own room.'

'Has your mother got any photographs of you as a child?'

'She has loads.'

'Do you know why she doesn't have any of Constance?'

'She does but she left them in Jamaica.'

'Eastman assaulted Clare when you were all living together at Sutherland Square.'

'He never did.'

'How do you know?'

'Because I was in the house at the time and it never happened.'

'Oh, I see. You can remember where you were over thirty years ago, can you?'

For the first time Precious Puss looked embarrassed. She was having an awkward moment in the witness box.

'Well, can you remember what you were doing on that occasion?'

'I cannot remember where I was but I am sure he would not have done that.'

'You said that he was a gentleman and would not harm a fly.'

'That is correct.'

'He did assault Constance, didn't he?'

'He did not.'

'He has a number of convictions in relation to Clare.'

'I did not know about them until we started investigating this matter. I was in the house with Clare. If he had assaulted her I would know all about it and these conviction records are not genuine.'

'The records were obtained from the Records department.

'Are you close to your mother?' Mr Caldecott tried another tack.

'I have always been close to my mother. Even as a child I was always around my mother. I have never fallen out with her. I was known as my mother's little helper.'

'That is all very interesting. Tell me, did you both make your statements at the same time?'

'No, we did not.'

'Did you ever discuss the evidence that you put into your statement and have a joint recollection, or is this your completely independent work?'

'I did not discuss it with anyone.'

'Do you know why some of the paragraphs in your statement

are exactly the same, word for word identical with the paragraphs in your mother's statement?'

'No, I do not.'

'Well, did you include passages in your statement because your mother told you to?'

'No.'

Precious Puss was handed a set of identical passages that had been extracted from my mother's statement and hers. As she looked over them, copies were handed to the jury. The similarities of the passages could not be explained by sheer coincidence. My mother and Precious Puss had put their heads together. This fact had not escaped the judge and jury.

'Can we agree that some eighteen to twenty paragraphs are identical, word for word, to your mother's statement?'

There was no escape for Precious Puss. She had been caught out and she knew it.

'Yes, I would agree that some of the passages are identical.'

'And you have no idea how that happened?'

'No,' she said.

'And it would be quite wrong to suggest that both you and your mother prepared a joint statement in order to come to court and tell lies jointly. Thank you, Miss Patsy Briscoe, I have no further questions for you.'

10

Friday 21 November 2008

Day 5 (continued)

Norma Eastman was the next to take the oath. Although she was nearly ten years younger than me she had put on a great deal of weight and was easily three times my size. She was generously built. I had last seen her many years ago and she was on a diet then.

'Have you read the book *Ugly*?'

'Yes, I have read little bits of the book. I refused to read it all because it is full of filth. The bits that I have read made me feel hurt and disgusted.'

'When you were growing up, how were you treated?'

'I was treated good, I was never abused. My mother was strict but fair. She would never abuse us and we were never abused. And we were never neglected. I had a really really lovely childhood and if I could I would quite like to go back to my happy childhood and live it all over again.'

Mr Panton sat down, satisfied that he had done a good job.

'Oh really,' said my barrister. 'You would like to go back would you?'

'Yes.'

'Can you just help the court, please? Were you not thrown out of the house when you were fourteen?'

'No,' came the reply. 'I was not thrown out of the house. I chose to leave home.'

'I suggest that you were thrown out onto the streets.'

'Well I suggest that you are wrong.'

'Did your mother not tell you that you were following in the footsteps of your eldest sister Cynthia and threw you out?'

'I've told you before no.'

'I have a note here from Social Services. The social worker who was involved with the family made a record at the time.'

'I don't remember a social worker,' said Norma.

'Well, there is another record of a conversation with your mother where your mother tells the police that if they should ever find you on their travels, she did not want you back. Can we assume, from that, your mother did not want you and had in fact abandoned you at that time?'

'I don't know about that,' said Norma, deflated.

'You will appreciate that by this time you are living on the streets.'

'I was not.'

'There is a record here that says that you were homeless, having been thrown out earlier. Can we assume that from the age of fourteen you have lived independently?'

'Yes.'

'Do you remember, Norma Eastman, that your eldest child Bianca was thirteen approaching fourteen when you had a problem with her?'

'That is correct.'

'Did you assault her and cause her to end up in King's College Hospital where she had a broken arm and she complained that you had attempted to strangle her?'

'No, I did not. She fell down the stairs, that is how she got her injuries.'

'Well, she ended up in care, didn't she, from the age of fourteen to eighteen?'

'Yes she did.'

'And is it your claim that she ended up in care for four years because she accidentally fell down the stairs?'

Norma thought about this and the sheer stupidity of her own

suggestion was obvious to her in the full glare of the jury. It was not even worthy of consideration.

'I don't know. All I can tell you is that I did not assault her.'

Mr Caldecott was not giving up. After all, Norma was another star witness for my mother. Little did she know that she was also my star witness. I was getting nervous, hopping from cheek to cheek waiting for my barrister to get to the crucial point and then to nail Norma very firmly with her own lies.

'Were Social Services involved with this incident of your daughter falling down the stairs according to you?'

'Yes they were.'

'And did they tell you that Bianca was claiming that you had assaulted her?'

'Yes, I was told that but it was not true.'

'When Bianca was released from hospital did you have several visits from a social worker who was called Mr Owen?'

'Yes, that is correct.'

'Do you remember telling him that you had been the victim of severe physical punishment with implements, inflicted on you by your mother?'

'I never told him that. I don't know where he got that from. Not me.'

'Do you remember telling him that your mother had beaten you with implements and that some of the beatings were severe?'

'I never told him that, never.'

'Well, we have got a copy of the report here that he prepared. The original document is here, if you want to examine that.'

Norma was handed several documents which she read while the court read their copies. When she was finished she started to shake her head and as I turned to my left I saw my mother was also shaking her head in unison with Precious Puss.

'This is another one of Constance's fakes,' I heard my mother say as Precious Puss nodded in agreement.

'I have never seen this document before. I believe that the information in this document is made up.'

'Miss Eastman,' said my barrister, 'social workers are normally accused of missing abuse; they are rarely accused of inventing abuse. The reason he wrote it down was because you told him that.'

'I disagree,' said Norma.

Norma was followed into the witness box by Cynthia. She had not aged as well as she could and although she was only five foot tall, she must have weighed at least fifteen stones. I thought she looked like a sumo wrestler in her track suit. As she took the oath she looked across the court. The jury had heard much about her from the Social Services reports but once again they were in for a surprise.

'My name is Cynthia Eastman and I just want to say that my mother was brilliant. She was a brilliant mother. She was never cruel. She never abused me or anything like that. I am very lucky to have had such a wonderful childhood. As for my father, he was better than my mother in my eyes. My sister Constance has made it all up in her book.'

'What was your relationship like with your mother?'

'It was really good.'

'What about your father, Mr Eastman?'

'It was even better.'

'Were you ever physically abused by your parents?'

'Never.'

'Your sister Constance is eight years older than you, isn't she?'

'Yes she is but when she was small my mother treated us all the same. She never abused any of us. My sister has just invented her story to make money.'

Mr Panton sat down and it was the turn of my barrister.

'Do you remember your mother telling the social worker that if you were a dog she would book you into Battersea Dogs Home?'

'No,' said Cynthia. 'I do not believe she said that.'

'Well we have a record of the conversation and you are quite welcome to examine the original records.

'Do you know why your mother told the social worker that she had washed her hands of you and your sister Norma and had thrown the pair of you out onto the streets?'

'No, I don't.'

'It does not sound like the brilliant childhood that you have described. I have no further questions.'

Martin George Briscoe was a dapper dresser. He made his way to the witness box and took the oath in a strong and confident voice.

Mr Panton rose to his feet.

'Tell us about your childhood.'

'I had a brilliant childhood. My mum was one of the best. She looked after me so she was my saviour. She did not have to beat me. I was brought up with all my brothers and sisters and I never saw any abuse. My mother had eleven of us and if she spent all of her time beating us she would burn herself out basically. It was better to use psychology, it would be less energy draining.'

'Can you tell the court about a split-split stick?'

'I have never heard of it or seen one.'

'Did your mother use bad language and beat Clare?'

'My mother is a Christian. I don't think she would know what bad language was, and as for Eastman, he was a gentle giant. He was six foot four. He was a very powerful man. If he'd slapped you he would have taken your head off.'

'Were you thrown out of the house when you were fourteen?'

'No, I was having a gap year when I went to live at my dad's.'

'How old were you?'

'I was fourteen.'

'So your mother did not throw you out, you were having a gap year from home and school, is that right?'

Martin thought about it and to Mr Caldecott he said: 'You have been confusing my sisters a moment ago and you are not going to do it with me. I've told you I was having a gap year.'

Mr Panton closed his case. The jury were sent home until Monday when we hoped to call our surprise witness. Norma had called Mr Owen a liar and claimed he had made up his report in which she stated that she had been abused by my mother. We had taken a decision to find Mr Owen. We had no knowledge whether he was dead or alive or even if he still worked in social care. Time was not on our side. The hunt was on for Mr Owen and we had just forty-eight hours in which to find him.

Monday, 24 November 2008

Day 6

It was now my turn and I was ready to give my evidence. I'd
spent the weekend arranging the clothes I would wear on the first
day. I knew exactly what evidence I would give to the court. I
was feeling confident. All I had to do was tell the truth. The court
was full. My mother's supporters seemed to have doubled in
number. They took up the majority of the four rows and there
was a buzzing sound at the back of the court. I knew why they
were there: to see me give my evidence in court.

My mother, Precious Puss and the Eastmans were in discussion.

'Mr Panton,' said the judge, 'how are you putting the case in
relation to Miss Briscoe?'

'It is our case that the allegations have been published mal-
iciously by Constance Briscoe. She knew that the allegations
complained of are false but nevertheless published them following the breakdown of her relationship with her mother.'

'Are we ready for the jury?' the judge asked. As counsel
nodded, the usher disappeared and returned with the jury. As
they took their regular seats my barrister stood up.

'Your Honour, I call Miss Constance Briscoe.'

I walked to the witness box and to a hushed court I took the
oath. Precious Puss was staring at me.

'What is your full name, please?'

'My full name is Constance Beverley Briscoe and my home

address is known to the court. My date of birth is 18th May 1957.'

'Have you always been called Constance?'

'No. People really started calling me Constance when I went to university in 1979. My name prior to going to university was Clare.'

'Where did you live in 1964?'

'I lived at 6 Burnett Street and we moved to 19 Sutherland Square, which is SE17. I was seven at the time.'

'Did you have your own bedroom or share a bedroom in Burnett Street?'

'My own.'

'Did you have your own bedroom or share a bedroom in Sutherland Square?'

'I have never shared a bedroom because I had a dirty little habit. I did wet the bed and my mother said that no one should ever have to put up with my habits.'

'Are the events in the book *Ugly* true?'

'Yes.'

'How did you get to university?'

'I was offered an unconditional place, but I did not take it up because I needed to get a grant; and I had to get my parents – it was my mother, at the time – to fill the grant form out. And when I asked her to do that she tore the form up and so I couldn't get a grant. The certificate from the records of Newcastle University shows that I completed my course in June 1982. I became a member of Inner Temple on 20th August 1981; and I was called to the Bar on 22nd November of 1983.'

'Did you ever suffer from hair loss?'

'Yes. It started quite young. I was definitely in a wig by the age of thirteen or fourteen and I wore them in bed.'

'When you were a child, did anyone comment on your appearance?'

'Yes. My mother, in particular; Eastman; and sometimes some of my sisters and brothers, when we were in an argument. My mother would call me ugly. She'd call me a dirty little whore.

She'd call me potato head. She'd call me Miss Piss-a-bed, but that was a name that was often used by Eastman. And after I had my incident with the aeroplane, I was called Scarface.'

'Did your appearance change in any way when you were at university?'

'I started at Newcastle University, I got my grant and I was able to have surgery. I had surgery on my nose, to start off with. If you look at the first photograph you will see that I had surgery to the bridge of my nose. I had surgery across the bottom of my nose. I had surgery on my upper lip; and I had surgery on my lower lip. And I had my eyes done eventually.'

'Why did you have that treatment at university?'

'I had it because my mother had, for a very long time, called me ugly; and I was conscious of my looks and I wanted to get rid of the ugliness.'

'My next heading is bed-wetting. When did this problem begin?'

'Ever since I knew myself really. I was finally cured when I was about fourteen and my mother left me in the house on my own. Most nights I would wet the bed, I would have a double accident.'

'There is a letter to Dr McManus from the London County Council. It says: "I understand that you are this child's family doctor. She was seen by one of the council's medical officers at St Joseph's Roman Catholic School and was found to be suffering from enuresis." The date is 3rd April 1964 when you are nearly seven. Do you remember at all how that examination at school came about?'

'I don't actually remember this examination at all. So I don't have a recollection of this. But I was examined at the school. I'm just not quite sure when that was in relation to this document. I think I was examined because of the smell. I was provided with a superdeluxe alarm at Sutherland Square. My mother tried to get me to stop drinking in good time. So if I was going to bed at nine o'clock she would get me to stop drinking at seven o'clock, or something like that. And she was trying to help me at that point, really. Once my mother had started to help me stop wetting the bed, the next thing that happened was that she would come and beat me when I did wet the bed. That progressed, really, because the problem was not solved. Oh, I was beaten quite often by my mother, quite often. She would come in; and if she was pulling me out of the bed by my knickers she would hold on to the side of my knickers with one hand and she would be removing her shoe with the other. That's how it started. I was beaten with a belt; and I was beaten with a stick, a sort of cane stick. That moved on to other things – the split-split stick.'

'Did you and the Briscoe sisters help your mother in the kitchen?'

'Yes.'

'Miss Briscoe, we were talking about work in the house and work in the kitchen. Is there any particular incident in the kitchen involving your mother that you recall?'

'Yes.'

'Could you, please, tell the jury about it?'

'I was preparing the chicken and I was in the kitchen and I had to get all the little hairs off the chicken. My mother came in and stood behind me and said, "Have you finished? Have you finished seasoning the chicken?"'

'I said, "Yes."'

'She said, "Look good. Have you finished?" And I noticed that there were three white hairs that I hadn't pulled off the chicken. I started saying, "Oh, I didn't see those hairs," and I started to try to pull them off using the flat side of a knife. She grabbed me by my right ear, pushed the knife here on my wrist and she pulled the knife across towards her. And she said, "What have you done? You've got blood all over my tablecloth."'

'Did the incident leave any scar?'

'Yes.'

'How long did the scar remain?'

'I still have it.'

'Miss Briscoe, there are some photos. When was this photograph taken?'

'The photograph was taken last Friday or Thursday, I think, by a professional medical photographer.'

'What does the photograph represent?'

'This photograph shows my arm; and it shows my scar which starts at about one centimetre and finishes at fourteen point five centimetres.'

'In what year do you place this incident in the book?'

'I place this incident in the book when I'm about eight or nine.'

'That brings me to the next heading which is the aeroplane incident. It is agreed that there was an incident involving an aeroplane. Can you help us as to the date on which you think the incident happened?'

'Thirty-first of January because that's my brother Carl's birthday.'

'Can you describe the aeroplane as you remember it?'

'Yes. It was a remote-control aeroplane. My mother had the controls in her hand and it flew around the room.'

'Was it fixed to a base or did it fly free?'

'It was never fixed to a base. It flew freely.'

'Who was there when this incident happened?'

'Me, Carl and my mother.'

'And please tell us exactly what did happen.'

'I think my mother was showing my brother how to fly the aeroplane. I opened the door and came into the room. When I opened the door, my mother flew the plane into my face, across the left side of my face. Then the plane flew up again and when it came down it cut the same side of my face.'

Mr Justice Tugendhat remarked, 'You're showing your left cheek.'

'My brother, Carl, thought it was funny and my mother said, "Get out, you're not welcome in here", so I did. That's what happened.'

Mr Caldecott said, 'Your sister, Patsy, said that Carl hit you with the aeroplane in his hand. Might that have happened?'

'No.'

'Did this incident leave any scars?'

'Yes.'

'And how long have those scars remained?'

'I still have them.'

Mr Caldecott showed me two photographs and asked me about the scars they revealed.

'This was described, I think, by your mother and your sister Patsy as a minor or little graze. Is that your recollection of the injury?'

'No. It's not. In fact, the one area of cosmetic surgery I still have to have done is to get this scar removed. But the technology in this country is not advanced enough yet to erase these scars, which is why I still have them.'

'How deep were the wounds?'

'They opened up pink flesh.'

'Just tell us where that runs from and to by reference to the numbers on the tape measure?'

'It runs from just above – just below ten point five and it runs to just below seven point five.'

'Can we move on to the next heading, which is the operation on your breasts.'

'Well, when I wrote my book I wrote the book from memory. I didn't have my medical notes at the time. And I only got my medical notes after my mother brought an action against me – this action. So when I was writing the book, I didn't know that there were any records dealing with the operation or that time of my life. And I got them in September 2006.'

'Before you saw the doctor, what did you think the cause of these lumps was?'

'My mother poking me all the time; poking me when she was talking to me; twisting my nipples; punching me in the breast whenever she asked me why I was wetting the bed; and twisting– twisting my breasts when she was making a point and she thought that I wasn't listening, she would just twist them.'

'How many lumps did you, in fact, have removed and from which breast?'

'Two from the right, one from the left.'

'Are the scars still visible?'

'Yes.'

'Again, please, could you now look at three further photographs, F, G and H. With your lordship's permission, if they could go to the jury too.'

'Did you ever complain to the police or Social Services about the matters you've referred to?'

'No.'

'Did you take any action to escape this treatment prior to 1973 and the Vaughan Road changeover?'

'Yes. I had decided that I didn't particularly want to stay with my mother; and I had gone to Social Services. I'd gone to try to get myself booked into a home.

'And when I turned up and asked if they could book me in, they said they needed my mother's consent, which was ridiculous. And the woman said that she couldn't just book me into the home when I felt like it, lovey. That's what she said, "We can't book you in here, lovey, just because you feel like it," and asked if I had any problems at home. And I said that I would deal with it myself. And then she wanted to contact my mother, but I wasn't having any of that. And I – I then went back home and—'

Mr Justice Tugendhat asked, 'Would you like a short adjournment?'

Without realising it I had become seriously distressed. I was crying and short of breath, but there was no way I was going to agree to an adjournment. That would make me look like a victim.

'No, I don't. Thank you.

'I went back home and I decided the best way to deal with it was to drink some Domestos because my mother had spent a lot of time telling me that I was a germ; and I thought that if I drank it then that would be okay.'

'Did you drink it neat or dilute it?'

'I diluted it.'

'And what were the effects?'

'I diluted it and I drank it. And it just made your tongue feel like a sort of velvet cloth, if you know what I mean. It just made it quite smooth. But when I diluted it and drank it, I had to work out what was going to happen to me afterwards because I thought that – I thought, as a Catholic, if I died, which I was quite happy to do, that I wasn't going to get to heaven because, as a Catholic, you can't take your own life. So I decided that I was quite prepared to go to halfway house for small-time sinners which is where we Catholics go.

'I knew that I'd go to purgatory but before I did that I decided that I was going to – while I was doing my time, because I'd taken my life – was going to spend my time on the stairs in Sutherland Square, because my mother had to go up the stairs every day. So I thought I'd just wait on the stairs while I'm doing my time before I go to heaven; and every time she went past me on the stairs I was going to give her the treatment she gave me. I was going to punch her on the head and trip her up and pull the blankets off her when she was in bed because I thought that was about fair, really. So I drank the bleach and it wasn't strong enough because the next day my mother came in to the room, told me to get up and I couldn't get up, so I flopped on the bed. Then she realised that there was something wrong, so she shouted for Four Eyes Pauline. Pauline shouted for Precious Puss Patsy and they came into the room. Eastman came into the room. And my mother was saying something about I was going to get her into trouble, you know, "Look what she's done this time. She's going to get me into trouble."

'When that was going on, Eastman was saying something like, "Lord, God, Carmen, call a doctor. Call a doctor." And my mother was saying, "No, wait. Just wait. Let's see." When they were all in the room, my mother told Pauline to change my nightdress and to put me in another bed. And I had my nightdress changed. I remember that Pauline fed me water and oxtail soup. Both my mother and Eastman disappeared out of the room.'

'Did you go to the doctor's?'

'No.'

'Moving to another topic, did you ever stay the night at 5 Vaughan Road?'

'No.'

'Were any other arrangements made by your mother for feeding you after the 1973 changeover?'

'Do you mean when my mother moved out?'

'Yes.'

'No.'

'How did you eat?'

'Well, to start off with, I had to get myself a job; but I was very, very friendly with Angela Fuentes because she is Spanish and I taught her eldest, Luis Fuentes, English when I was very young – not fluent English, but just to help him out. And Angela lived at 173 Lorrimore Road. And so –'

'You've told us that you helped teach her eldest English. How did your relationship with the Fuentes family proceed?'

'I had a very good relationship with her; and when my mother moved out there were times when I really didn't have any food – well, I did have food because I had my free school dinners; and I was working at Rose's.'

'Can we just pause a minute? People always use this word "dinner" interchangeably; is this lunchtime dinner or evening dinner?'

'It's sort of secondary-school dinner that you have at one o'clock.'

'Thank you.'

'So I had my free school dinner there. And I didn't tell Angela to start off with that my mother had moved out because I didn't really want my mother to come back. If people thought I was on my own they might try and get her to come back. So I decided to look after myself. My priority was to get another job.'

'How was Sutherland Square provided for in terms of hot water and lighting?'

'Right. Well, in terms of the hot water, we had – just between the living room, and the bedroom, where my mother kept her split-split stick, there was a meter on the wall.'

'Who paid the bills for the lighting?'

'Well, we didn't always have lighting at Sutherland Square because once my mother had left us in the house, she would come back and ask for a contribution for the bills. That's how it started. And I didn't have any money, at that time, because I'd only just got my first job. When I didn't give her any money my mother would pull the fuses out and take them with her. And we didn't get the electricity back until a contribution was made for the electricity and she'd come back and plug the fuse in.

'Angela Fuentes had got my job for me because she was supervisor at a cleaning company and I'd go with her in the morning to Trafalgar Square to clean offices. Then I had to get another job, which Angela got me as well.'

'Did you ever work at a hospice at Lyndhurst Gardens?'

'Yes, I did.'

'What sort of place was it?'

'Lyndhurst Gardens is just off Belsize Park and it is a hospice for respite care and for the terminally ill. And when I started to work there I would just make people comfortable, because they were very, very ill; and just make sure, for example, that they had their teeth quite close to them, or whatever. And if they were in pain, I'd have to tell a nurse; and when they died I would have to, with the trained staff, just give them a bed bath and make them look – make the person look quite attractive because when – when their family came it would be distressing if they didn't look nice. So I would just, you know, put a bit of make up on or tidy their hair, or change their bed sheets so that they looked quite nice for when their relatives came. That was my job. Just to make people feel okay about themselves and take their mind off their illness really.'

'What period were you working at Lyndhurst Gardens?'

'Before I went to university – way before I went to university. Also I started working for them with an agency; I always did the night duty, always. And that was because if you do the night duty, if you start at nine you finish at seven, you can always do another job during the day. You know if you do another job between, say, nine and six, then you could get a couple of hours sleep and then go and do another job at Lyndhurst. Then you could rest when you had a moment.

'When I was at university, because I had worked there for quite a time and everyone knew me, if the agency needed a bit of cover, say an auxiliary for the weekend, I would come down and help out. At Lyndhurst Gardens there are wards on the first floor, wards on the second floor and, on the third, is accommodation. So I could sleep on the third floor. And I always worked there at Christmas and New Year for a number of reasons. Firstly, you got double time if you worked on Bank Holidays; and, secondly, because nobody else wanted to work at Christmas because they wanted to be with their family and I really didn't have anywhere to go at Christmas. So I was much better off making the patients feel a bit happier about themselves. And I got Christmas dinner as well when I was there.'

'Did you ever steal any property from Lyndhurst Gardens?'

'No, that's a comment that only my mother could make.'

'Prior to her making that comment in the witness box, had you had any notice of that allegation?'

'No, absolutely not. Not even a whiff of it. Not even a whiff.'

'Were you ever questioned by your employers at Lyndhurst Gardens about any suspected theft?'

'No.'

'After you wrote the book, did you receive any letter from anyone at Lyndhurst Gardens?'

'Yes, I did.'

'I just want to show you a copy document, which is not a very good copy, unfortunately. I just want you, please, to tell us whether you recognise it and, if you do, who it is from.'

'Yes. I do. I know who this is.'

'Can you just, please, read for us the slightly cut-off name at the end?'

'Yes. It's – she was Sister Hazzard when I was there. She was Night Duty Sister Hazzard. It's now Gloria Henry.'

'She says: "Dear Constance, I was given a copy of your book *Ugly* as a gift and it wasn't until I got to page 303 regarding

Lyndhurst Gardens that the penny dropped. Do you remember the night sister you worked with? Yes, that's me. Do you remember one night I asked you to review a book about the National Health Service and make notes in the column. Well, using your notes and some of my own I was able to do a critique of the book which was accepted by Coventry Polytechnic where I was offered a place to do a health visiting course. I have never forgotten this beautiful, intelligent, keen and professional young woman who I felt I was privileged to know. Never for a moment did I have an inkling as to the abuse that you had suffered."

'Now I'd like to move on to Mr Eastman. Can you describe him physically?'

'Mr Eastman was about six foot three and he was large and fit.'

'What was his job?'

'He did work in a place called Advance Laundry but he was a labourer. He could lift things. He was quite strong.'

'After the changeover, did he ever come to Sutherland Square?'

'Yes, he did.'

'And for what purpose did he come to Sutherland Square, generally speaking?'

'He came with my mother to collect rent; and he stubbed a cigarette out on my hand.'

'Tell us about that incident.'

'Yes. It was a Sunday and we had just come back from church and we were in our Sunday best at Sutherland Square: me, Precious Puss and Four Eyes. And we'd changed our clothes to get into our ordinary gear to start helping out in the house. And I had gone into the kitchen and he was outside the kitchen spying on me. And so I called him a stupid fool because he was always spying on me and he hit me. And I hit him back. He punched me and I hit him back.

'And he called my mother then he went past me and I called him a stupid fool again and he said, "You call me a fool, call me a fool." I said, "I didn't call you a fool, I called you a stupid fool."

And he took the cigarette out of his mouth and he stubbed it out on the back of my hand.'

'Did that incident leave a scar, Miss Briscoe?'

'Yes.'

'What do you recall of the incident on 13th July 1975?'

'Eastman and my mother had come to the house because my mother wanted to collect money for the bills. My rent. They had come up the stairs into my bedroom and I was making it clear that I needed my money to look after myself. Both of them were in my room. And there was a fight and Eastman punched me, I punched him. My mother held me while Eastman punched me and it ended up with blows being exchanged. Eventually, they left the house.'

'Can you, please, deal with the two later incidents.'

'After that first incident, Mr Eastman and my mother came back again. But I heard them; I heard the door go downstairs. And when I heard the door go, I locked myself in my bedroom and quickly pushed the bed up against the door. So when they came on this occasion, which was a Saturday, they couldn't get into my bedroom and I was refusing to open the door.

'So Mr Eastman was outside threatening me; telling me he was going to kill me, he was going to beat me up, banging on the door. My mother was saying, "Open the door. Open the door." I just remained inside. I did not open the door. Eventually, they went away.'

'And on another occasion, do you remember going to the doctor about an injury?'

'Yes. I had – I was wearing my Michael Jackson wig when we had this fight; and he had cut the back of my head because when I was fighting my mother held me and he hit me from behind and cut my head. And I had to go to see the doctor because I was concerned that I'd get some sort of infection because I always had my wig on, so it needed to be looked at.

'When I told my dad, my dad, who was at 215 then, he went into the cellar and he picked up his axe and he put it in the back of his Capri and told me to come with him. And he was going to go back to see Mr Eastman. And I said to him that I would deal with it myself because my father was very cross and, clearly, was going to use his axe on Mr Eastman.

'So I went to the Camberwell Green Magistrates' Court with my dad and I told them that I wanted to bring a charge against Eastman. I was assisted to fill out the forms, and I did. And Eastman and I eventually went to that court and he was bound over.'

'Just dealing with Martin and Carl. Did you ever see them after the age of fourteen when you say they left home?'

'Yes.'

'Where did you see them?'

'I saw Carl at 215 Camberwell New Road, which is where he lived when my mother threw him out of the house. And I saw Martin at the same address because when he was thrown out he had a room as well at 215 Camberwell New Road. So when I went there, my dad would be there sometimes collecting rent, and if you caught him when he was collecting rent he would give you some money. So I would go there to see my brothers and I saw them quite often.'

'What about your relationship with Norma, as a relatively young lady?'

'Norma and I had a really good relationship, better than any of my sisters – better than any of the Briscoe sisters and better than any of the Eastman sisters. And that is because Norma had a really, really hard life. She had been thrown out by my mother. She was pregnant with no one to help her. She's actually really clever and she could have done just about anything she wanted if she'd had support. And she understood me because she knew my difficulties with my mother; and I understood her because she really, really did struggle. Then, when she had her own daughter, Bianca, she had a few problems and Bianca ended up in King's College Hospital with an injury to her neck and a broken arm and she accused Norma of abusing her. Norma was questioned by the police and Social Services became involved. There were a number of meetings with Norma.'

'And what happened?'

'My recollection of that meeting was that Norma was asked a number of questions and she told the social worker, Mr Owen, that she, herself, had had a bad childhood; and she had had severe physical discipline by my mother and that implements had been used.'

'Miss Briscoe, you have been assisted by a document that you've seen; did you remember the name Michael Owen before you saw that document?'

'No.'

'Lastly, just some general questions about the book. When did you start writing it?'

'Two thousand and three.'

'Did you have a ghost writer for the book?'

'No, absolutely not. No.'

'Apart from your memory, did you have any other aids to recollection?'

'I talked to my dad, who was alive at that time. And I didn't have anything else.'

'Did you ever keep a diary when you were young?'

'Yes.'

'Did you have it when you wrote the book?'

'No. My mother took my diaries just before I went to university.'

'And, lastly, Miss Briscoe, why did you write the book?'

'Well, I wrote the book for a number of reasons. The first reason is I do not believe, for a split second, that I owe my mother a bond of silence. I don't. I had a story to tell and that story really is that I, someone from dirt poverty, from absolutely nowhere, with absolutely no assistance whatsoever, having faced adversity at every turn, could come through. And I wanted to say to whoever read the book, you know: yes, you can. You can be whatever you want to be, you just have to believe in yourself. And it's often said that, you know, people at the Bar are posh; that they're privileged. Well, actually you don't have to be posh or privileged to be at the Bar, you just need to believe in yourself.

And I truly, truly believe that my book has done an enormous amount of good. That's why I wrote the book. It's a journey. And my – the abuse of me, which involves my mother, is just one tiny part of the book. It's about looking forward, never making excuses for yourself and having the confidence, no matter what, to succeed. And I think I've done a great deal of good for a lot of people.'

'My lord, that is Miss Briscoe's evidence-in-chief.'

Tuesday 25 November 2008

Day 7

'Good news,' my lawyer Sarah said.

'What is that?' asked Mr Rene.

'We have found Mr Owen, the social worker and he is here to give evidence today.'

My lawyers had done a very good job tracking down Mr Owen.

'He can't possibly give evidence today. We are not ready to cross examine him.'

'Well, he can come back tomorrow. Will you be ready by then?'

Mr Rene did not answer. He would have to suggest to Mr Owen that he was a liar, a fantasist and that his record of his meetings with Norma was just a lie. He had good reason to appear preoccupied.

Mr Panton pulled in his belly as he stood up to cross examine me and demonstrate that I was a liar and a fantasist. He locked eyes with me as I waited for his first question.

'It is our case, Miss Briscoe, that the events that you recount in your book did not happen. In the words of your teacher, you are away with the fairies.'

'The events in the book did happen. The events in my book are true.'

'Would you like the jury to believe that throughout your

childhood and teenage years there weren't any happy moments?'

'There were a number of happy moments that I specifically remember.'

'But are they in the book?'

'Yes.'

'Which ones in particular?'

'The first happy moment is when my mother gave me a fairy cake which had hundreds and thousands on the top, when we were in Burnett Street. That was a very happy moment because it was the last occasion that I can remember when she was nice to me. The second happy moment, I suppose, is when my mother gave me Dolly back, because I quite liked my doll, and Dolly had been recycled for four years, so when I got Dolly – my mother took Dolly after Christmas, and then I got her back again the next Christmas, so that was a happy moment. And when my mother moved out.'

'Miss Briscoe, why did you not obtain your medical records before you wrote the book?'

'Because I did not believe that there would be records of the abuse going back all those years.'

'You didn't seek any medical attention for the cut to your arm?'

'No.'

'The toy plane, you say that your mother was showing your brother how to fly it?'

'My mother was behind the controls, yes.'

'How long had your brother had this plane?'

'I thought it was his birthday present, so this happened on his birthday on 31st January.'

'Your evidence is that your mother flew it at you. Using the controls, directing it at you, yes?'

'She flew it into my face, using the controls she hit me in the face. The plane came round again slicing down the cheek again and then it was buzzing around.'

'So it went up and came back at you?'

'Yes.'

'And you think that your mother had that kind of expertise on a plane that had just been handed to your brother?'

'I don't know what expertise my mother had. My mother flew the plane into my face, and it caused this scar.'

'Miss Briscoe, what happened was you interfered with your brother's plane, you broke it off its base, and he hit out at you with the plane. That's what happened.'

'That's complete rubbish.'

'This was another incident that you used in your book to say things about your mother that's not true.

'Now Miss K.'

'Yes.'

'You went to stay with her for a few weeks?'

'My mother agreed that I could go and stay with her for a few days and it lasted for quite a few weeks. And then she went to Poland.'

'How many weeks?'

'I'm not quite sure how many weeks. Maybe six or seven, maybe a bit more.'

'You said your mother agreed?'

'She did. She absolutely agreed for me to go and stay for a few days.'

'Can I suggest this to you: that your mother didn't agree that you should go and live with anyone?'

'My mother did agree and quite frankly my mother didn't really care where I was. She really didn't care.'

'Where did Miss Korchinskye live?'

'Streatham.'

'You said you went to live with her at the time you were still bed-wetting, if you were to be believed?'

'Yes.'

'Did you take the alarm with you?'

'No.'

'Why not?'

'I went straight from school and I did not take the alarm.

When I went to Miss K's, I didn't wet the bed and that is what I've said in the book. But when I went back to my mother, I started wetting the bed again.'

'You say one of the problems associated with bed-wetting is you being nervous or anxious?'

'Yes.'

'And going to stay at a teacher's house for the first time, surely you would be somewhat anxious?'

'I was.'

'So you spent up to six weeks there and bed-wetting was cured?'

'My bed-wetting was not cured, because when I went back, my lord, to my mother's house, I was wetting the bed on the first night back.'

'You never went to stay with Miss K and you were never abused by your mother. It is all lies, Miss Briscoe, told by you to sell your book.'

'That is incorrect.'

'Do you have any idea why Mrs Briscoe would have children sitting with her in court and giving evidence in support of her case that she did not abuse you?'

'They are all in collective denial. They want to pretend that it did not happen and also this is about money. My mother sued me and hoped that I would offer her money to go away but not one penny piece was offered.'

'Are you seriously suggesting that this is all about money?'

'Yes I am.'

Wednesday 26 November 2008

Day 8

In a break from the High Court, we all went along to the Law Society to receive the evidence of Angela Fuentes. She would give her evidence via a video link from Madrid. My mother's lawyers had objected to her giving evidence in that way, and wanted her to get on a plane and come over to London. It was only at the last minute that their objections were satisfied. My legal team got there at 9.15 in the morning to establish a video link. As I sat in the link room the operator called Madrid. After three attempts the Madrid conference suite accepted the call and Angela beamed on to screen.

She was with her son and her official interpreter, but had expressed a preference to give evidence in English. Angela looked tired. Her skin was yellow and her hair the same colour. Her hair had been black but now it was the colour of time; she was very ill and her appearance shocked me to tears. I was certain that if she had to she would have travelled back to London to give evidence but looking at her now I am sure that the journey would probably have killed her.

'Can you please tell us your full name,' said Mr Caldecott.

'My name is Angela Fuentes Izquierdo.'

'You live in Spain?'

'I do.'

'And we know that you are not well at the moment. Can you tell the court what the problems are?'

'I have too many illnesses to mention but the main illness that I am suffering from is leukaemia and I have a cyst on my left kidney, also I have some problems with my lungs.'

'Did you know the Briscoe children?'

'I did.'

'Did you know any child better than the other?'

'I knew Clare. She was often crying and looking for comfort. I knew her from the age of six or seven.'

'Did she ever come to your house?'

'Yes she did when she was hungry or when she did not have any money. She taught my eldest son English one or two hours a week and I paid her. After that I found her a cleaning job with me in the morning cleaning offices in Trafalgar Square. I would collect her at five thirty because we had to be there by six.'

'When did she work?'

'She worked during term time and also during the holidays. She was always dressed in her school uniform and when she finished she would go straight to school.'

'How old was she when she started working with you?'

'Fourteen.'

'How did Clare get on with her mother?'

'She was not close to her mother. She was always arguing with her stepfather. Clare was always very reserved because she did not want anyone to know what was going on but I knew what was going on.'

'Can you tell the court what you knew was going on?'

'Well they used to hit her but they would never do it in front of me.'

'That is all the questions I have to ask.'

Mr Rene stood up and introduced himself. His questions were conversational, friendly.

'How old was Clare when she started to work for you?'

'She was fourteen or thirteen.'

'Was she old enough to work?'

'No she was not but I would take her like a member of my own family just to give a hand.'

'Did she have a national insurance number?'

'No. She was too young to have one and besides you could not employ someone at that age. I paid her in cash. I gave her the job because she needed money. She had to eat.'

That was it. Angela was a credible witness. She was not the type to lie and that was why Mr Rene did not cross examine her extensively. To my utter astonishment he did not challenge the fact that I worked with her as a cleaner or that I was fourteen when I did. He did not even suggest to her that she and I did not have a cleaning job. She was my star witness to Mother's disgrace. Mr Rene did not suggest to her that she was wrong and confused about my age or my jobs.

Both my mother and Precious Puss had said in evidence that I did not have a cleaning job in the morning at the age of fourteen. Angela's evidence had shown that they were telling lies and that if they were lying, they had put their collective heads together.

The court adjourned for lunch to give us enough time to go back to the High Court. Precious Puss was not looking her usual confident self.

14

Wednesday 26 November 2008

Day 8 (continued)

Mr Owen arrived in a fluffy jumper and a woollen hat. It was the second day that he had attended court to give his evidence and on both occasions my mother's lawyers were not ready to cross examine him. This time he walked to the witness box and took the oath.

'My name is Michael Owen and I am a social worker in charge of a team of sixteen.'

Andrew asked, 'Can you tell us whether you have ever worked with Norma Eastman and if so in what circumstances?'

'I worked with Norma as a result of a referral when her daughter made an allegation of inappropriate discipline. I went to see her and she said that her daughter should not complain because in her day, when Norma was a child, she was abused by her mother and her abuse was much worse than what had happened to her child so she had nothing to complain about.'

'The court has a document signed by you and the last three lines read as follows: "Miss Norma Eastman describes her experience of being a child as difficult. Her mother used physical methods to discipline her and her siblings and some of these chastisements were severe. Her mother would use implements to discipline them."'

'Norma has told the court that she never said that or anything like that to you. Have you any comment to make about that?'

'I would have to say that that is grossly incorrect. I stand by the

statement. A lot of our conversations were about the inappropriate discipline and how her experience as a child might have
affected the way she dealt with her own children. There were
many meetings with Norma, not just one, and the report was
read back to her. This is a legal document and at any time we can
be called upon to produce our documents in court.'

'Did you come to any conclusions about Norma's behaviour
in relation to the discipline she carried out?'

'Yes, we both concluded that this was history repeating itself.
She used inappropriate methods of discipline because her
mother had used similar methods which were more severe.'

Mr Rene patted his wig down on top of his head as he stood
up. He asked questions on behalf of my mother and ascertained
that Mr Owen had never met her before. He could not suggest
that Mr Owen was a liar. He had no reason to lie. He was a
professional and social workers do not as a general rule make up
allegations of abuse.

'Did Norma ever talk about her mother Carmen Briscoe?' he
asked.

'Yes she did but she did not paint a positive picture of her
mother and at the time none of her children had direct contact
her mother so we were not concerned about her. She was not
deemed to be a risk factor because she did not have access to any
of Norma's children.'

'Did you ever interview Mrs Briscoe?'

'No. I did not feel the need to do that because Norma showed
enough insight for me not to question the information that she
was actually providing.'

'How long were you involved with Norma?'

'We visited the house once a fortnight and I continued to work
with Norma for up to a year; after that I visited her daughter
Bianca once a month when she was placed in care.'

'Did Norma ever see your notes in which you state her mother
had abused her?'

'Yes. I would normally summarise what we had discussed.
Norma would be given an opportunity to make corrections and

the notes would not be placed in the file until they were signed off, until Norma agreed them.'

'Did she actually get a copy of the notes?'

'Yes. It was the practice at the time in Lambeth to meet with the parent before the report was presented to the case conference. Norma would have seen the report before the case conference and she would have been presented with a copy at the conference. It was normal practice at the time.'

Mr Owen was followed into the witness box by Mr Jeffrey Rosenbaum. He told the court that in 1974, when I was still at school and working weekends at Kings College Hospital, I had often asked him if I could stay at his flat. The reason I had given was that I was studying for my exams and needed peace and quiet. He had visited me at Sutherland Square but had never met my mother.

The final witness was Mrs Barbara Snaith. She lived in America. She had known me since the age of fifteen and we had met at the Peckham Odeon. I was still at school. Although I worked weekends at the Odeon she knew that I had two other jobs. She was aware of the fact that I had a very poor relationship with my mother. Her statement was read to the court.

'Members of the jury that is it for today. We will resume tomorrow.'

I sat and waited for the jury to leave court. It had been a terrible day for my mother. Angela and Mr Owen had painted a picture that was inconsistent with the evidence of my mother and Precious Puss. They both were independent and they had no reason to lie. I looked over at my mother and then to Precious Puss and in that moment I knew that however long it took the jury to return a verdict my journey was over. I had been saved once again by Angela. Thank you, God.

15

Thursday 27 November 2008

Day 9

The jury returned and Mr Caldecott was ready to address them one final time. It was an important speech, and it was our final opportunity to persuade the jury that they should find in favour of us rather than my mother.

'Members of the jury, I'm going to start with a little digression. Last year, a number of literary critics and writers got together to choose the most famous novel of all time. Their choice of book doesn't really matter, but the first sentence of the book, you may think, has some relevance to this case, and also has a ring of truth about it. The first sentence of the book started as follows: "All happy families are alike. Each unhappy family is unhappy in its own way."

'The claimant's case in her evidence, and the oral evidence of the other members of the family from whom you have heard, is that their family was happy, like other happy families. The two Briscoes – Patsy and Martin – the Eastmans – Cynthia and Norma – all came along to paint this happy picture. And you will remember how Mrs Briscoe put it to her own counsel early in her evidence: "You say that it was a happy family [she was asked]?"

' "A very happy family," [she said].

' "From about 1964 to, say, the late 1960s, to about 1969, did you ever have any problems at all with the children?"

'Just note that the question was limited in time. But Mrs

Briscoe chose to take her happy paintbox and go much wider. The answer she gave was this: "I never had any problem with my children. The boys, they could be a little mischievous, but my girls they were excellent. My girls, they were excellent, and my children were my pride, pride and joy."

'Martin describes his mother as brilliant and there was more evidence from the others to like effect. And during this trial, as you look round the courtroom, you will have seen at one side of the court, the rest of the family or many of them, and at the front, Constance Briscoe on her own. A picture of a united happy family, against the one lone voice said to be either wicked or away with the fairies in painting this very different picture of what was actually going on. Now, members of the jury, it's very important to get to grips with the truth of that general picture before you come to consider the particular matters you have to decide. That's partly because abuse does not happen without a context and a background, and we don't shrink from saying that this picture of a harmonious family and a caring mother at its head is a fake. Frankly, it's a fake which doesn't stand up to a moment's scrutiny.

'Some of the most reliable voices in the past in this case are those in the Social Services reports. They are reliable, I suggest, because they are not records made from memory; they are records made at the time by professional people concerned with the welfare of children, concerned with where they are to live, concerned with what their parents may do or may threaten to do.

'You heard a number of suggestions in this case that documents were not genuine and I'm going to ask you to look quickly, so that we understand the position about this, at a new document which you won't have seen before. It admits the following: "The Social Services documents included in the bundle are authentic and are true copies of the records held by the London Borough of Southwark Social Services department. It is not admitted that they are an accurate record of the conversations to which they refer."

'Then a reference, you may remember, to the bind-over

documents, admitted to be authentic and accurate; the same for the medical records with the exception of the two February letters which I will come back to; and then again it's accepted that the national insurance records are an accurate account of the work done on that card.

'So you needn't worry. I will come back to you later, about any question about authenticity at all. The Social Services files are there in front of you in those blue files, that's what Southwark Social Services produced, and that's what I'm going to be referring you to in a minute. Now, Social Services have had a rather bad press in recent months, or at least some of them have. But of course, it is inevitable that in the press you read about the failures. What we do not read about are the successes. We don't read about invisible people like Mr Owen: you may think a thoroughly charming man who was not only charming but committed and humane. He has progressed since those years in 1998 to now running a team of sixteen all in charge of the welfare of children facing hard times.

'One of the most striking aspects of the Social Services documents is that they speak with one voice. It's a consistent picture that emerges, although they relate to different children at different times, often many years apart. They portray, I'm afraid, a picture of Mrs Briscoe as having a cruel attitude to children, which is more suitable to Dickens than to the 1970s and the 1980s. What we say the family have been doing is airbrushing out the darker corners of this story, in the interests of family solidarity. It is understandable that in some circumstances families close ranks and stand together. But it is not an excuse for painting a false picture from the witness box in the hope that you will swallow it.

'The reports record both Mrs Briscoe's acts and her words. It is often said that acts speak louder than words, but in this case, they again both speak, we say, in the same voice. Can I just remind you, first two weeks before Christmas, 10th December 1980, what the social worker records Mrs Briscoe as saying: "She has resigned herself to putting up with Cynthia despite saying that if Cynthia was a dog, she would take her to Battersea Dogs' Home and leave her there."

'Now, she didn't put up with Cynthia, in fact, for very long. This is two weeks before Christmas 1980. The 18th May entry: "She then got quite angry, and said that she had chucked Cynthia out of the house yesterday because her behaviour is so bad and because she had heard that Cynthia was pregnant. She didn't know where Cynthia was, and she said she had washed her hands of her."

'But then this, which really is quite extraordinary: "She said she wouldn't notify the police that Cynthia was a missing person."

'This is a fifteen year old, pregnant, out on the streets and missing. Her mother does not know where she is and she cannot even be bothered to tell the police. But perhaps the saddest document of the whole sad collection is a month on. The baby, we know, is due in November, and was in fact born in October 1981. Mrs Briscoe goes to the office with Cynthia; for the first part of the meeting they are there together. Look at what Mrs Briscoe says in front of her own pregnant fifteen-year-old daughter: "Mrs Briscoe came to the office requesting reception into care for Cynthia and Norma. Cynthia was with her mother. Mrs Briscoe said she had been asking for reception into care for Cynthia since last year. Cynthia had been coming and going over this time and is now pregnant, and she doesn't want her any longer. Cynthia said her mother had told her often to go, which she does. She then asks to go back, which her mother agrees to for a while. But although she, Cynthia, wants to be at home, mum now refused to have her. Mrs Briscoe also informed me that she had told Norma to leave and if we found her [so she is now missing as well] she didn't want her back as she is following in Cynthia's footsteps."

'Washing her hands of her children. Our case is that is what she did with Constance when she was fourteen. Mrs Briscoe washed her hands of her as well. Now, another recurring theme in these documents is the question of punishment, fear and

threats. Mrs Briscoe wanted Cynthia put into a children's home
as a punishment. This is why I say these voices come in
choruses, the document reads Mrs Briscoe feels her daughter's
behaviour has become unbearable, and as a punishment, she
would like her to be received into care. The first paragraph,
under the heading "Present situation": "I did have one long
interview with her in the office which was a very one-sided affair
and was chiefly limited to Mrs Briscoe denouncing Cynthia as
bad, evil, worthless."

'Now, we suggest to you these are the true colours, not the
fake ones that you were asked to accept. Norma, we know, got
the same treatment as Cynthia did. You have Mrs Briscoe's own
words in relation to Martin which reads: "As he was not
prepared to accept my discipline, he had to move out to live
with his father." You may remember Carlton also had to leave
home at fourteen. Now look at physical violence: you will find an
important document which moves further away from mere
mental cruelty towards at least discussing physical violence.

' "She didn't seem to have a good one-to-one relationship with
Carlton in the way she was describing her home life, and had not
even at fourteen years of age explained to him the facts of life.
She has threatened to strip him naked and beat him for what he
had done. This is a boy past the age of puberty, a boy of
fourteen. She is talking about stripping him naked and beating
him.

'The social worker took her threat seriously; the passage reads:
"I did not feel that this would solve anything, nor keeping him
off school, and would only result in a fine for cruelty to
children . . ."

'Does Mrs Briscoe come back and say: Oh, you misunder-
stood me, it was a joke in bad taste, I didn't really mean it? Not at
all. She stands her ground: "Mrs Briscoe blames much of the
problem on the English leniency towards children." What is the
English leniency she is talking about? Not beating them, it would
appear.

'Now, if you accept, members of the jury, this consistent

picture of unhappiness, cruelty, a family which is riven, you must treat with great caution the evidence from the witness box from those witnesses who have sought to give the opposite rosy picture. Nowhere in their witness statements did any of these witnesses refer to leaving home at all. These documents emerged on the Tuesday before this trial began, under a witness summons served by us on the Social Services. They revealed the detailed truth, and it's only on account of the production of those documents that you have been spared, we suggest, buying the fake happy family that they were trying to sell you. Now, at the beginning of this case, I accepted that memory is an imperfect instrument. It isn't perfect and it would be highly suspicious if Constance Briscoe's account fitted all the evidence that has emerged since like a glove.

'These are the two copy letters from Dr Hadley to Dr McManus, the family doctor. The first one written two days after an Outpatients' appointment on 9th February; the second, it appears, written after a follow-up Outpatients' appointment a week later.

'They relate to a conversation with a nurse which Ms Briscoe does not now recall. They refer in outline to several of the main events in the book. We know that the originals are missing. Constance Briscoe collected the copies of her medical records in September 2006. Now, it's entirely a matter for you as to whether you accept, on the balance of probabilities, the burden being on us, that those two copy letters are genuine. If you do accept them as genuine, they tell you one thing which is important, which is that these allegations cannot have been recently invented or fantasised, because here they are, being mentioned by her to a nurse when she was fourteen. If you are not satisfied, on the balance of probabilities, that they are genuine, then you simply ignore them and confine yourself to the other evidence.

'If this book is a pack of lies from start to finish as the claimant says it is, there is no doubt that you should award the claimant a substantial sum by way of damages.

'But if we are right, and she has inflicted abuse and neglect on Constance Briscoe year in, year out, she does not, members of the jury, deserve a penny piece. The assessment of the evidence of what was done to Constance Briscoe turns partly on your common sense, partly on what you make of the witnesses, and partly on the background about how the characters are and were as revealed in the documents.

'Just one or two things about families. It has been said that no two siblings have the same parents.

'And you may have formed a view: to take an example, Patsy Briscoe and Constance Briscoe are very different personalities. This is Patsy's evidence to you, and we don't have any quarrel with it: "Constance never spent a lot of time with her mother." Now, if you have a mother who has a capacity to be vicious with those who fall short of her standards, there is nothing surprising or unsual about one child being picked on by her and the rest. Siblings do sometimes join in bullying and we invite you to accept, and the documents again are important, that Mrs Briscoe is certainly capable of being a bully.

'You may remember that rather vivid little piece of evidence when Constance Briscoe is sent to test the water with her mother, and the other two children were looking down the stairwell to see how she gets on. Testing the water because it can be scalding with Mrs Briscoe. This is what Constance Briscoe said to you about this: "Four Eyes would always ask me to go and do something and I would get into trouble and she wasn't around. Or, for example, when we were going to Cobblestone Road, the event at the church, I had to go and ask my mother. I went downstairs to ask my mother and I knew that Four Eyes and Precious Puss were on the top landing waiting to hear what my mother had to say, and I knew that because when my mother started to shout at me, the door went, so I knew they were upstairs and they had gone back inside and closed the door."

'Why was Constance Briscoe picked on, members of the jury? There's one obvious and dominant reason, and it's a single word: bed-wetting. The bed-wetting lies at the heart of this case. She was the only child who had an alarm in that family, and she had an alarm for years. In fact, she went through several models.

'Carmen Briscoe's case features two big lies, because they are not matters which you could readily forget or muddle up. The first lie was told both by Mrs Briscoe and by Patsy. And it is that Pauline, Patsy and Constance shared a bedroom at Sutherland Square all the way through from 1964 when the house was bought, to 1973 in the spring when the move to Vaughan Road took place. The importance of this lie is obvious. If Constance Briscoe shared a bedroom with her sisters, there would be eyewitnesses to the frequent beatings that she suffered, other than her and her mother, and of course, you might think it's inherently less likely that in the middle of the night she would be beaten in front of other young children who were trying to sleep. This is as stark a conflict of evidence as you could get.

'Constance Briscoe says: "I had my own bedroom from 1964 to 1973." Children don't forget their bedrooms. It's not just a matter of geography. It's the whole going-to-bed business, whether there's someone, a sibling, next door to talk to after the lights have gone out. Children don't forget their bedrooms, and mothers don't forget where their children sleep and slept.

'There are three critical points which resolve this central issue in Constance Briscoe's favour. The first is the interview with the *Mail on Sunday*. There is a paragraph starting: "But Patsy remembers it very differently. She says, actually, Mum tried everything to help her. She took her to lots of doctors. Clare was given a room to herself to give her some privacy." This makes complete sense. Mrs Briscoe was sympathetic about the problem at the beginning before the beatings started. Constance was going to wake the other occupants of the room every time the alarm goes off, every time sheets have to be dealt with. Now, Patsy Briscoe's attempt to get out of this in the witness box made absolutely no sense. The next point is Patsy Briscoe's. She slipped. On the first, she said: "Constance mainly kept to her room anyway." On another occasion she said: "She would take off to her room."

'The second big lie is the duration of the bed-wetting problem. Constance Briscoe's evidence is that it was only when her mother moved out with the rest of the family apart from her two elder sisters that the problem ceased. In a sense she was saying – to use a long word – that the problem was psychosomatic: once the person who was beating her left, the problem stopped. But Mrs Briscoe's evidence to her own counsel, and he manfully tried on several occasions to get her to change it, was that the problem stopped at the age of five.

'Now, Patsy Briscoe, in the *Mail* article, said: "She did wet the bed and it did go on into secondary school." It goes on into secondary school, which is where you go when you are eleven. Patsy Briscoe tried to rescue her mother. No one asked her a question on the matter, she just came out with it.

'She suggested that Mrs Briscoe had suffered strokes in consequence of this book. You may remember that. That has never been suggested in any letter or in any witness statement, or in any claim for damages. We asked for the medical documents to establish that that was so. People do not have strokes without seeing the doctor. Not a single document has been produced. There were no such strokes. There was not a shred of evidence at all to support it. Mrs Briscoe is an elderly lady, and she is deserving of the respect that age brings, but on this issue she was not telling you the truth.

'There is a curious thing about lies. They do sometimes illuminate the truth. This is one of those lies that do. Mrs Briscoe cannot face up to how long this problem went on, how shameful it was, year in, year out. It's perfectly normal to have bed-wetting at the age of five. The longer it goes on, the less normal it becomes and the more unpleasant it is to deal with.

'We invite you to accept that this untruth reveals a deep unease in Mrs Briscoe about this whole question. That unease is borne out by the fact that the problem did go on and on and on, and Constance Briscoe was frequently beaten for it. That is the reason why she will not face up to this question. Now, we would suggest to you, that if you were to find that this young girl was beaten night in, night out, for wetting her bed, that she was made to sleep in wet sheets, that in any moral universe this mother, Mrs Briscoe, doesn't deserve a penny. But I'm afraid it doesn't end there, because there were other matters which are part of this bullying.

'You may remember the insult which gives the book its title, "Ugly". Remember the acne, the references in the medical notes. Patsy Briscoe trying to explain this away on the basis that Dr McManus was free and easy with his acne diagnosis? That may or may not be so in relation to her. But Constance Briscoe's evidence is that she had acne bad enough to go to the doctor on several occasions. We've seen the prescription for penicillin, and that of course is only consistent with it being a medical condition.

'I now come to what is perhaps the most unpleasant form of assault in this case, and those are the assaults on Constance Briscoe's breasts. The critical question here is: is Constance Briscoe telling a gross and wicked lie when she says her breasts were interfered with by her mother in the way she described, or is she telling the truth? Mrs Briscoe has always said there was only one small cyst removed. It's a small point but it's also a big one, because if she wasn't interested in the scars, the question is why? It may be that she had a sense of shame about what had happened. One would like to think so.

'Constance Briscoe says she has two scars on her face from that aeroplane because it was flown into her face twice: you have the photographs. If it has been flown, one collision in the face is explicable as an accident, but it's very hard to see how two could be. The chicken incident. Mrs Briscoe says this couldn't have happened because the Briscoe sisters were never allowed into the kitchen. They appear to have been rather like the ugly sisters in Cinderella; they never helped. The only difference with Cinderella is that Mrs Briscoe does all the work and none of the daughters do any. But does this have the ring of truth? This is a family which had ten children by 1968 and eleven children by 1971. Constance Briscoe's evidence is exactly what you would expect: there was a rota and the three elder daughters helped out equally. What is Mrs Briscoe's explanation for the mysterious absence of the three eldest daughters from helping in the kitchen?

'Again, you have the scar on Constance Briscoe's forearm. Now, there are no two ways about this. Either she is right and the scar was caused by that kitchen knife being drawn by Mrs Briscoe down the forearm; or Constance Briscoe has done something very wicked indeed. She has a scar for some other completely different reason that we do not know about, and she has invented this incident to fit it.

'Which is the more likely? You have to decide.

'Mrs Briscoe has chosen four specific incidents to complain of as the worst examples. They are the chicken incident, the aeroplane incident, the assaults on Constance Briscoe's breasts, and that further kitchen incident which I've just referred to. We say all those incidents happened and the evidence that they happened is compelling.

'It is our case that Mrs Briscoe emotionally and psychologically abused Constance Briscoe throughout her childhood by taunting her about bed-wetting, telling her she was ugly, calling her various derogatory names and saying she wasn't bright enough to go to university. We say that that is true too, and you will remember the university form, particularly that last sentence: "The student had a grant as an independent student from ILEA and was offered a deferred place in 1978 to start in 1979."

'And you will remember Constance Briscoe's explanation, that she had to work the extra year because she didn't get a grant of the conventional kind because her mother wouldn't fill in the form which would require her to set out her means and so forth, and it was torn up when she went round to Vaughan Road.

'Now, the last meaning that is complained of is a meaning which can be simply summarised as neglect. Going back to those words she used about Cynthia: "I wash my hands of her." She did exactly the same thing to Constance Briscoe in a different way, and you have Constance Briscoe's evidence, you have Angela Fuentes's evidence. There is one sentence in her evidence which you may think rings a chord. She talked about this young girl coming round and she said she was looking for comfort and hugs. Why did she think that, members of the jury? Remember her evidence, meeting Constance Briscoe from the age of about fourteen, sometimes going to the house, sometimes meeting her outside the house at half past five in the morning on school days, going to Trafalgar Square, letting her help out with the cleaning and giving her some money from her pay. She is a rescuer in this story, that's what Mrs Fuentes is, and she deserves the greatest credit for it.

'Now, consider the scenario that you are invited to accept by Mrs Briscoe. We start off with a ghost playing the piano, and then we have a wagon train of eight children and two adults – I think one of the children is one and one of the children is three – heading south every evening, you are told, from Vaughan Road to Sutherland Square for a family get-together, and then heading all the way back to Vaughan Road.

'It is all nonsense. We invite you to reject that evidence out of hand. The true picture is early-morning jobs, lonely meals at the Wimpy, and help and support from Mrs Fuentes. There are demands for rent. There are fuses removed.

'And that brings me to the 1975 episode. You may think if ever there was a mismatch, it's between the lightweight Constance Briscoe and the heavyweight Mr Eastman on 13 July. But whatever happened then, what sheds real light on this case is what happens about a fortnight later. You know that Constance Briscoe went to the doctor on 14th July, and said she had had a blow from her stepfather. Mr Eastman goes back to Sutherland Square where he does not live and where his daughters do not live, only Briscoe children live, and he threatens her twice, if you accept that formal memorandum of entry as we invite you to do. Mr Eastman has not come here to give you any evidence to the contrary.

'Now, there is one last voice in this sad story. This is a case about abuse and neglect of children and that's why I'm going to end with another voice from another child, Norma Eastman, a lady of potential and talent, according to Constance Briscoe, her half-sister, someone whom she was fond of, and someone she helped. You will remember from yesterday the document that read: "She [Norma] is close to her side of the family and only speaks to the Eastmans." Then we have an exception: "She does, however, speak to her half-sibling Clare [that's Constance] on the other side. Clare has been a source of support for Ms Eastman in helping her deal with Bianca's difficult behaviour. Ms Eastman describes her experience of being a child as difficult. Her mother used physical methods to discipline her and her siblings, and some of those chastisements were severe. Her mother would use implements to discipline them. Ms Eastman has learnt to survive at a young age and speaks passionately of how she has had to fend for herself."

'What is the message of this book? We say the message is that from abuse and neglect can come determination, and with determination you can rise from poverty to a decent living. It's a reminder to the privileged, and I mean those privileged to have a happy childhood, of how some have a very different life on the other side of the tracks. Ask yourself if Constance Briscoe would jeopardise all she has achieved by telling a mountain of lies in this book. The message of this book is worthless if it's based on lies from beginning to end. If the core of her story is true, it's a comfort and encouragement to anyone whose start in life can, in a word, be called "ugly".'

Andrew sat down. He was done. The jury had listened to him and most of them had made notes. I thought that he had made a good speech.

16

Thursday 27 November 2008

Day 9 (continued)

Mr Panton stood up to sum up on behalf of my mother.

'My lord, ladies and gentlemen of the jury,' said Mr Panton, 'it's now my turn to address you on behalf of the claimant. It's not my case that this was the perfect family; far from it. There is a suggestion I mentioned Dickensian conditions but let us look at the reality.

'This wasn't a poverty-stricken family. You also heard that the father was nowhere to be seen. He won the pools so he didn't have to work. Ladies and gentlemen, the book. You look at the book and it gives you various years when it's said that these things happened. We now know that, as far as this book is concerned, we need to insert circa early sixties, late sixties, early seventies. She is in the newspapers. She is in magazine articles, judge barrister, et cetera, et cetera, it's painted all over. It's written about Constance Briscoe, the abuse that she suffered; and look how well she has done. Is that the truth, ladies and gentlemen, that Constance Briscoe was abused in the way she described? Can you place reliance on what she says in the book and in her evidence? Because, at the end of the day, your decision may turn on to what extent you believe she has told the truth.

'There is no dispute that there was bed-wetting. There is a problem, ladies and gentlemen, about this routine beating. There were siblings living in the same household. Which one has come forward to say: "Yes, I recall Constance or Clare being beaten by my mother for bed-wetting?" None, ladies and gentlemen. What Ms Briscoe says is she was treated differently to the other girls in the family. Her mother didn't abuse the other girls in the family; that's what the book says. So, ladies and gentlemen, you have heard my learned friend say shortly before the start of this trial Social Services were asked to produce whatever records they had. Now, here is a book written completely independent of research, from memory, making these allegations, not a single sibling willing to come and support her, so we look at Social Services' records. What Constance Briscoe is asking you to do is to return a verdict in her favour on the basis of Social Services records. She did not see any abuse inflicted on them. She didn't see Norma or Cynthia being abused by their mother but she is inviting you to decide whether or not she is telling the truth by inviting you to look at Social Services' records.

'Mrs Briscoe took home another lady's child and she went through an adoption process.

'She was assaulted or abused by Mr Eastman. My learned friend referred to the uneven fight; Mr Eastman six-foot plus, Ms Briscoe probably less than five foot then. As a twelve year old, if the book is right, she got her dad to drop her down to Camberwell Green Magistrates' Court. That's what the book tells you.

'Ladies and gentlemen, Constance Briscoe fabricated the story of abuse as a child. She makes up stories. Will she make up stories about abuse? There are two letters apparently from Dr RM Hadley to Dr McManus. The first one tells you about a conversation that Ms Briscoe had with a nurse. Do you remember her evidence from the witness box about this? She has no recollection of any conversation with a nurse, on the first day or subsequently. She cannot recall having that conversation. "Anxious, tearful, unwilling to go home. Mother had crashed a plane into her face, cut her hand with a knife because she upset a chicken. Her stepfather had burnt her hand with a butt and touched her privates. She is not suicidal but admitted a prior failed attempt at taking her life to go to Heaven. As she was discharged back into your care on 10th February, you may wish to add this information to the investigation in progress."

'Ladies and gentlemen, for the first time, in 1972, Ms Briscoe is telling somebody about her problems at home, and that, ladies and gentlemen, was soon after she told one of the doctors who was going to conduct the operation, when he asked her if she had suffered any trauma, she said, "No. As if I was about to tell him about my home life."

'So she wasn't prepared to tell the doctor, but some nurse she cannot assist you with her name, she cannot remember having the conversation; in any event, you are being asked to believe her when she says: I was abused by my mother, I was beaten with these implements by my mother.

'The evidence you heard was that there were sleeping arrangements for Patsy and Pauline on one side and Constance had a bed on another side; that's what the family says. Ladies and gentlemen, when Patsy Briscoe says that Constance was always in her room or she would often be found in her room, does that suggest that she had a room to herself? Should she have said, well, Constance was always in "our" room? Because, ladies and gentlemen, it's important. If her sisters were sharing with her, they would have witnessed the beatings that she talks about. But, ladies and gentlemen, it's more than that. The sisters live in the house with her and they say there were no beatings. If you want to tell a tale, why trouble yourself with the facts?

'Photographs, ladies and gentlemen. Mrs Briscoe, I think confirmed by Patsy Briscoe, confirmed that there were family photographs. You have seen the one in the bundle produced where you have the three sisters, teenagers, but the others are missing.

'You have heard from Patsy Briscoe, her mother, Martin, Cynthia, Norma. Do you think that the family are outraged by what happened, or have they come to court to try and get some money off Constance Briscoe?

'Mrs Fuentes. You recall her giving her evidence yesterday. She said she had not seen Mrs Briscoe for three years plus. She also told you that she never witnessed any physical abuse of Miss Constance Briscoe, and she said that she took Miss Briscoe to go cleaning. She gave her some money. And I don't know if it was your understanding that this was an informal arrangement between them, whereby she would pay her out of whatever she earned, rather than a formal matter with Miss Fuentes' employer. What is significant, I would say to you is this; it was not a matter whether Miss Briscoe was paying a national insurance contribution because as Miss Fuentes said it was an informal situation where she gave her some money. Balanced against what Miss Fuentes says is the evidence from Patsy. Constance never went to work at five thirty in the morning.

'You have got to decide whether or not there were these three teenagers living at 19 Sutherland Square, and if Constance could have got up at five thirty in the morning, to go to work and her sisters would not have found out. Those are matters for you.

'Again, ladies and gentlemen, you have heard the evidence and you have to decide who you believe. Mr Owen, the social worker, now a team leader in Bromley. He interviewed Norma Eastman in 1998. There is a suggestion that Norma said she was beaten with an implement by Mrs Briscoe, but that is not part of the case, because the book says something different in terms of Miss Constance Briscoe's experience of her mother's treatment of her siblings.

'The book contains very serious allegations of assault by Mrs Briscoe on her daughter, allegations which she says are completely untrue. Allegations which a number of her children have said are untrue and they have come here to say so. You will have to decide that these very serious allegations of the assault and abuse would not have been noticed by Constance Briscoe's siblings because you will recall that it was very rarely that either of her sisters would not be around. They would be somewhere keeping an eye, but keeping their distance when all this is going on.

'You will have to decide whether or not you can believe Ms Constance Briscoe in what she says in her book; or is this book the latest in the grief memoirs, someone writing about things that did not happen in order to make money. Because if there was abuse on the scale that has been described in this book, you would think that someone, somewhere, would have noticed. I do not think any of Mrs Briscoe's children have said she was not a strict mother. She was. But she never used implements to chastise her children and that is why she is here, ladies and gentlemen. I hope, ladies and gentlemen, that when you have considered these allegations of serious child abuse, you will come to the conclusion that the evidence simply does not stack up. They are grave allegations and if you did conclude that they did not happen, they are not true, then you will consider the extent of any damages to Mrs Briscoe arising from the publication of this book. I hope that you will consider them to be so serious, that the damages would reflect that degree of seriousness.

'I close by drawing your attention to one matter. You will recall that I asked her about happy memories in childhood and she said a fairy cake my mother gave me just before my fifth birthday. Ladies and gentlemen, on behalf of Mrs Briscoe we invite you to say that having seen Constance Briscoe in the witness box, having looked at the evidence in this case, you find that she is a fantasist and a liar. She was never abused as a child. Mrs Briscoe is entitled to substantial damages for the very serious and wicked allegations made against her by Constance Briscoe.'

'Members of the jury,' said the judge, 'that is the end for today. The next stage of the proceedings is for me to sum up the case following which you will retire to consider your verdict. Please be here for a prompt start at ten o'clock.'

17

Friday 28 November 2008

Day 10

As I walked over to the court my mind was on other things. What if the jury returned a verdict in favour of my mother? What if they were unable to come to a verdict at all? My mind was in a daze as I sat in court. When the judge began his address to the jury I had some trouble concentrating.

The judge spent the whole day summing the case up to the jury. He made very complex law sound easy. He summed up the case fairly and persuasively. My mother's case had changed radically since the start of the trial but the judge reminded them of what I had to prove and I was happy with his approach.

'Now, members of the jury, Mrs Carmen Briscoe has brought this action. She claims that the words complained of in the book that are highlighted in yellow defame her. She is asking you to vindicate her reputation by your verdict in her favour. She also asks you to make an award of damages to compensate her for the injury which she claims has been done to her reputation and her personal feelings.

'Constance Briscoe's defence is that the words complained of are substantially true. She says that she was justified in writing what she did. Her defence is justification. She must prove that what she wrote was true. If she can do so then she is entitled to your verdict. If she cannot then Carmen Briscoe is entitled to your verdict and damages. This is a sad case. A mother is suing her daughter.

'Constance Briscoe must prove that she was physically and emotionally abused repeatedly. You the jury are representatives of society, it is for you to decide what happened. Mrs Briscoe did not complain about the whole book. She could have done so if she wanted to. She chose the worst examples of what she says defames her. If Constance can only show a specific act of abuse that would not be good enough. She must prove persistent physical abuse, abandonment and neglect. Both Carmen and Patsy said that Constance did not have a cleaning job in the early morning. Angela Fuentes gave evidence that she gave her a cleaning job. No one suggested that she was telling lies. The question you will have to decide is whether Carmen and Patsy had forgotten that she had a cleaning job or whether they were not telling you the truth. Remember, as far as Constance is concerned, she is not saying to you that her sisters were unaware of what she suffered at the hands of her mother. She says that Patsy and Pauline knew what was going on and chose to keep out of harm's way. She told you that she blames Patsy for keeping out of the way when she was getting her beatings, pretending that she, Patsy, had not seen what was going on.

'Constance had a number of scars. The one to her face both Carmen and Patsy say that she did not have when she was a child. The scar to her wrist was not caused by a knife drawn by her mother.

'Please remember that the burden of proving justification is on Constance Briscoe. Please retire now and consider your verdict. When you return you will be asked whether you find in favour of Constance Briscoe, the defendant, or Carmen Briscoe, the claimant.'

The jury bailiff led the jury out of court as we collected our files. The long wait was about to begin. Turning round to leave court I saw that my mother was again surrounded by her supporters. I walked out of the rear exit and walked to Middle Temple. Four fifteen arrived swiftly and we returned to court. No decision. The jury were told to go home and return on Monday.

Over the weekend I made arrangements with Tony. If the verdict went in favour of my mother we would leave the Bar and retrain as gardeners.

On Monday we returned to court. The judge directed the jury to continue with their deliberations. The verdict came at fourteen minutes past three. As the foreman rose the court clerk asked, 'Mr Foreman, have you reached a verdict upon which you are all agreed?'

'Yes.'

'Do you find in favour of the claimant or the defendant?'

'We find in favour of the defendant, Constance Briscoe.'

'And are you all agreed on your verdict?'

'We are.'

'Thank you, Mr Foreman, you may sit down.'

There was no response from my mother or Precious Puss. Her supporters had been silenced by the verdict of the jury. Never again would she be able to say that Clare Constance Briscoe was a liar and a fantasist and as a child was away with the fairies.

The jury filed out of court for the last time. I waited with Francesca my daughter and my legal team. As I gathered my belongings I thanked my lawyers and then I walked to the front of the court. The press were waiting. As they took photographs I read from a prepared statement.

'I would like to thank all my readers who have sent me messages of support, including the very many children who provided helpful advice. I can quite understand why my family went into collective denial but while child abuse may be committed behind closed doors it should never be swept under the carpet.'

As I walked down the steps of the Royal Court of Justice I started to laugh. There was an echo in my right ear and I knew instantly what it was.

'That's right, my girl. I told you years ago that you could be anything you wanted to be. Now look at you.'

It was Miss K. She was back and I knew that we were both at the end of a journey that we had started when I was twelve. My bones still ache, my head is heavy and I am tired but I will only ever look forward to the happy times that await me.

If you have been affected by any of the issues in UGLY, *you may find the following helpful. However, the Publisher is not responsible for the contents of these websites.*

• Barnardo's
Website: www.barnados.org.uk

• BAWSO (Black Association of Women Step Out)
24 hour helpline : 0800 731 8147
Website: www.bawso.org.uk

• Black Women's Mental Health Project
Tel: 020 8961 6324
Website: www.bwmhp.org.uk

• Childline
24 hour helpline: 0800 1111
Website: www.childline.org.uk

• ERIC
(Education and Resources for Improving Childhood Continence) is a UK charity that provides information and resources for children, parents and professionals on bedwetting and other childhood continence problems.
Helpline: 0845 370 8008
(weekdays 10–14)
Website: www.eric.org.uk

• The Hideout
Website: www.thehide out.org.uk

• Kidscape
24 hour helpline: 08451 205 204.
This is for the use of parents, guardians or concerned relatives and friends of bullied children. Children experiencing bullying problems should ring Childline (see above).
Website: www.kidscape.org.uk

• NSPCC
(National Society for the Prevention of Cruelty to Children)
24 hour helpline: 0808 800 5000.
Textphone: 0800 056 0566
Website: www.nspcc.org.uk

• Refuge
24 hour helpline: 0808 2000 247
Website: refuge.org.uk

• Shakti Women's Aid
Tel: 0131 475 2399 (weekdays 9–5. Answering machine service.)
Website: www.shaktiedinburgh.co.uk

• Southall Black Sisters
Tel: 020 8571 9595 (weekdays 10–5. Answering machine service.)
Website: www.southallblacksisters.org.uk